SHAKESPEARE AND LAW

THE ARDEN SHAKESPEARE

THE ARDEN CRITICAL COMPANIONS

GENERAL EDITORS
Andrew Hadfield and Paul Hammond

ADVISORY BOARD
*MacDonald P. Jackson   Katherine Duncan-Jones   David Scott Kastan
Patricia Parker   Lois Potter   Phyllis Packin   Bruce R. Smith
Brian Vickers   Blair Worden*

Shakespeare and Renaissance Europe
ed. Andrew Hadfield and Paul Hammond
Shakespeare and Renaissance Politics   *Andrew Hadfield*
Shakespeare and the Victorians   *Adrian Poole*
Shakespeare and Comedy   *Robert Maslen*
Shakespeare and Music   *David Lindley*
Shakespeare and Elizabethan Popular Culture
ed. Stuart Gillespie and Neill Rhodes
Shakespeare and Law   *Andrew Zurcher*
Shakespeare and Religion   *Alison Shell*
Shakespeare and the Medieval World   *Helen Cooper*

Forthcoming
Shakespeare and his Texts   *Tom Lockwood*

THE ARDEN CRITICAL COMPANIONS

SHAKESPEARE
AND LAW

ANDREW ZURCHER

Arden Shakespeare

1 3 5 7 9 10 8 6 4 2

First published in 2010 by Methuen Drama

Copyright © Andrew Zurcher 2010

Arden Shakespeare is an imprint of Methuen Drama

Methuen Drama
A & C Black Publishers Limited
36 Soho Square
London W1D 3QY
www.methuendrama.com
www.ardenshakespeare.com

A CIP catalogue record for this book is available from the British Library

ISBN 978 1 904 271727

Typeset by Mark Heslington Limited, Scarborough, North Yorkshire
Printed in Great Britain by the MPG Books Group

... euery word almost being operatiue, and materiall.

Sir Edward Coke, *The First Part of the Institutes of the Lawes of England* (1628), f. 15^v

The Common-Laws of England are more particular than other laws, and this, though it render them more numerous, less methodical, and takes up longer time for their study, yet it recompenceth with great advantages, namely it prevents arbitrariness in the Judge, and makes the law more certain and better applicable to the business that comes to be judged by it. Generall laws are indeed very comprehensive, soon learned, and easily digested into method; but when they come to particular application, they are of little service, and leave a great latitude to partiality, interest, and variety of apprehensions to misapply them; not unlike the common notions in the Moralist, which when both the contesting Grecial Captains most perfectly agreed, yet from them each deduced conclusions in the particular case in Controversie, suitable to their several desires and ends, though extremely contradictory each to other. It hath therefore always been the wisdome and happiness of the English Government, not to rest in Generals, but to prevent arbitrariness and uncertainty by particular Laws, fitted almost to all particular occasions.

Sir Matthew Hale, 'Preface' to Henry Rolle, *Un Abridgement des Plusieurs Cases et Resolutions del Common Ley* (London: 1688), sig. a3

Whichever device, precedent or legislation, is chosen for the communication of standards of behaviour, these, however smoothly they work over the great mass of ordinary cases, will, at some point where their application is in question, prove indeterminate; they will have what has been termed an *open texture*. So far we have presented this, in the case of legislation, as a general feature of human language; uncertainty at the borderline is the price to be paid for the use of general classifying terms in any form of communication concerning matters of fact. It is, however, important to appreciate why, apart from this dependence on language as it actually is, with its characteristics of open texture, we should not cherish, even as an ideal, the conception of a rule so detailed that the question whether it applied or not to a particular case was always settled in advance, and never involved, at the point of actual application, a fresh choice between open alternatives. Put shortly, the reason is that the necessity for such choice is thrust upon us because we are men, not gods.

H. L. A. Hart, *The Concept of Law* (Oxford: Oxford University Press, 1961), pp. 124–25

CONTENTS

ABBREVIATIONS AND CONVENTIONS

Certain primary and secondary works often recurring in the notes are cited throughout in abbreviated forms. These are:

Baker, *IELH*	Sir John Baker, *An Introduction to English Legal History*, 4th edn (London: Butterworths, 2002)
Baker, *LPCL*	Sir John Baker, *The Legal Profession and the Common Law: Historical Essays* (London: Hambledon, 1986)
Baker, *OHLE 6*	Sir John Baker, *The Oxford History of the Laws of England, volume 6: 1483–1558* (Oxford: Oxford University Press, 2003)
Bracton, *De legibus*	(?) Henry de Bracton, *De legibus et consuetudinibus Angliae* [*On the Laws and Customs of England*], ed. George W. Woodbine and transl. Samuel E. Thorne, 4 vols (Cambridge, Mass.: Harvard University Press, 1968)
Coke, *Institutes 1*	Sir Edward Coke, *The First Part of the Institutes of the Lawes of England* (London: Adam Islip for the Society of Stationers, 1628)
Coke, *Institutes 2*	Sir Edward Coke, *The Second Part of the Institutes of the Lawes of England, Containing the Exposition of many ancient, and other Statutes* (London: M. Flesher and R. Young, 1642)
Coke, *Institutes 3*	Sir Edward Coke, *The Third Part of the Institutes of the Laws of England, Concerning High Treason, and other Pleas of the Crown* (London: M. Flesher for W. Lee and D. Pakeman, 1644)
Cowell, *Interpreter*	John Cowell, *The Interpreter: Or Booke Containing the Signification of Words* (Cambridge: John Legate, 1607)
d'Ewes, *Journal*	Sir Simonds D'Ewes, *A Compleat Journal of the Votes, Speeches and Debates, Both of the House of Lords and House of Commons Throughout the whole Reign of Queen Elizabeth* (London: Paul Bowes, 1693)
Hughes and Larkin, *Tudor Royal Proclamations*	Paul L. Hughes and James F. Larkin, *Tudor Royal Proclamations*, 3 vols (New Haven: Yale University Press, 1964–69)
Les Termes de la Ley	*Les Termes de la Ley: Or Certaine difficult and obscure Words and Termes of the Common Lawes and Statutes of this Realme now in use expounded*

	and explained (London: Miles Flesher and Robert Young, 1642)
OED	*Oxford English Dictionary*, 3rd edn (Oxford: Oxford University Press, 1993–)
Plowden, *Commentaries*	Edmund Plowden, *The Commentaries, Or Reports* (London: Catharine Lintot and Samuel Richardson, 1761) [first English edition]
Proclamations of Elizabeth	*A Booke Containing All Such Proclamations, as were Published During the Raigne of the late Queene Elizabeth* (London: Bonham Norton and John Bill, 1618)
Rastell, *Statutes*	*A Collection in English of the Statutes* (London: Deputies of Christopher Barker, 1597)
Statutes	*The Statutes at Large*, 2 vols (London: Bonham Norton and John Bill, 1618)

Postpositives

J	Justice
JJ	Justices
CJ	Chief Justice
LCJ	Lord Chief Justice
LC	Lord Chancellor

Languages

L	Latin
Gr	Greek
OE	Old English

Statutes and cases

25 Eliz. I cap. 5	The fifth chapter of the statute passed in the twenty-fifth year of the reign of Elizabeth I (i.e. 1582)
3 Jac. I cap. 3	The third chapter of the statute passed in the third year of James (VI and) I (i.e. 1605)

Editions

All quotations from the works of William Shakespeare are, unless otherwise noted, from *The Arden Shakespeare: Complete Works*, ed. Richard Proudfoot, Ann Thompson and David Scott Kastan (London: Arden Shakespeare, 2001). Individual works are cited parenthetically in the text by act, scene, and line number (plays), or by line number (poems).

All quotations from the Bible are from the Geneva translation, and are cited by book, chapter, and verse: *The Bible, translated according to the Ebrew and Greeke, and conferred with the best translations in diuers Languages* (London: Deputies of Christopher Barker, 1599).

ACKNOWLEDGEMENTS

I hold euery man a debtor to his profession, from the which, as
men of course doe seeke to receiue countenance & profit, so ought
they of duty to endeauour themselues by way of amends to bee a
helpe and ornament thereunto; this is performed in some degree,
by the honest and liberall practice of a profession, when men shall
carry a respect not to descend into any course that is corrupt, and
vnworthy thereof, and preserue themselues free from the abuses
wherewith the same profession is noted to bee infected; but much
more is this performed, if a man bee able to visite and strengthen
the roots and foundation of the science it selfe; thereby not onely
gracing it in reputation and dignity, but also amplifying it in
perfection and substance.

Francis Bacon, 'Preface' to *The elements of the common lawes of
England* (London: Assigns of John More, 1630), sig. B1^r

So Francis Bacon. In the history of corrupt unworthiness, abuse, and
infection that chronicles my work on this book, I can claim this one
certain virtue, that I have been the cause of honesty and liberality in
many others. And while I remain very much in arrears to my profession,
the kindness and sharpness of friends, colleagues, and family have made
the debt a dignity. I am sincerely grateful to several people who read and
commented on portions of this book, at various points during its
composition, or who offered advice, discussion, or encouragement at
timely moments, and especially to Colin Burrow, Robin Kirkpatrick, John
Kerrigan, Jon Stainsby, Christopher Burlinson, Michael Hetherington,
and Jason Scott-Warren. For help with matters Greek and Latin, I
resorted to that device of mine – constant badgering – and must warmly
honour the patience of James Diggle, Jo Willmott, and Johanna Hanink.
Ian Patterson has, as ever, discharged the part of a generous ear and a
keen eye, and fed me with his brainy enthusiasms. I have been fortunate
to retain the counsel, at several times, of Amanda Perreau-Saussine (and
the whole firm of wise-headed Queens' lawyers), whose wide learning,

judicious insight, and intellectual rigour have both inspired and schooled me. Karen Begg has tirelessly suffered my regular resort to the Queens' Old Library to read, take pictures, and despair. To the President and Fellows of Queens' College, generally, I go on owing debts material and substantial; without the College's unwavering support I could neither have begun nor concluded this work.

From Methuen Drama I received more of Margaret Bartley's patience than I deserved. My thanks go to her, and to Charlotte Loveridge and Anna Brewer for their regular kindnesses. The anonymous reader of the manuscript offered important encouragement and very helpful criticism, to most of which I hope I was able to answer. I have much and vigorously abused the forbearance of the series editors, Andrew Hadfield and Paul Hammond, but they weathered it stoically, for which I will remain grateful.

By her labour and learning my sister Amelia Zurcher has continued to underwrite all my work of any credit. I cannot thank her enough for the hours and powers she has unstintingly expended on my thoughts, doubts, and drafts. My children Aoife, Una, and Eamon may justly charge me with distraction, short temper, self-involvement, and a docket of other less mentionable crimes. How remarkable, then, that they have thrown their hearts into this book, and cheered me at every stage of its composition! But to my wife, Fionnuala, last and best of all abettors and accomplices, I render up her right and interest in anything this work accomplishes; kind, steady, patient, without grudge or grief she's listened, judged, and given me direction; a kick to start, but in the end relief; a hand to right; an eye for circumspection. Some gifts are made in trust, that though a thing once aliened be lost, that loss renews it; albeit the loss be suffered, time will bring the sufferance of the loss to loss, and lose it. Her years, her love, she did by pains reduce into this title. Let hers be the use.

ILLUSTRATIONS

Chapter One

PREAMBLE: 'HOW SHALL I UNDERSTAND YOU?'

No man can be a compleat Lawyer by vniuersalitie of knowledge without experience in particular cases, nor by bare experience without vniuersalitie of knowledge; he must be both speculatiue & actiue, for the science of the laws, I assure you, must joyne hands with experience. *Experientia* (saith the great Philosopher) *est cognitio singularium, ars vero vniuersalium.* [Experience (according to Aristotle) is the understanding of particulars, art truly of universals.]

Sir Edward Coke, 'Preface' to *A Booke of Entries*
(London: Societie of Stationers, 1614), sig. $\pi 2^r$

The dramatic and poetic works of William Shakespeare, as has long been recognized, are marked by an intense but often inscrutable engagement with the language and concepts of the early-modern English common law. From justices and officers, lord mayors and constables, sheriffs, aldermen, heralds, and senators, to tribunes, emperors, princes, dukes, and kings, the executors, agents, and instruments of legal power populate Shakespeare's plays and poetry. These characters administer oaths, serve writs, judge trials, perform sentences, and arrest malefactors (and sometimes benefactors). They engage in legal parody, recite legal maxims, argue legal positions, and even cite early-modern legal writings. The presence of a wide-ranging and sometimes very precise understanding of legal diction, legal process, legal theory, and legal texts (classical, medieval, and contemporary) has led some readers of Shakespeare's work to make incredible claims about the authorship of his plays, or no less audacious pronouncements about their audiences or their significance.[1] Many readers – among them most forcefully legal historians themselves – have rightly resisted these attempts,[2] and it is only in recent years that, following on advances in historical and legal historical studies of the sixteenth century, Shakespeare critics have returned profitably to this material. Recent studies in both shorter and longer formats have achieved fresh insights into poetic and dramatic texts that, increasingly, had seemed to resist innovative but still plausible thinking.[3] The quality and diversity of these distinguished critical studies demonstrate how pervasively significant legal language and thought must be to any balanced understanding of Shakespeare's works.

As an introduction to this field of study, this book addresses many of the legal topics that, as recent criticism has shown, play such conspicuous and important parts in Shakespeare's writing. But this book also goes, if not beyond, then behind its distinguished predecessors in seeking to understand a more fundamental critical problem. What was it that so attracted Shakespeare to legal ideas, generally? It is here that an introduction must begin, because any inquiry into Shakespeare's particular legal interests must of necessity be framed by more general hypotheses about his attitudes to, and assumptions about, law. The Greek verb *krinein* means 'to judge', and a *kritēs* is a judge. Hence criticism is called criticism, and a critic a critic – that is, a critic's criticism is a kind of judgment, and the action of criticizing is judging. It was the analogy between assessing lawsuits and assessing literary works that prompted Aristotle (in the *Poetics*, at 1449a) to adapt the Greek verb to this usage, but the analogy runs deep, probably deeper than even Aristotle supposed. The judge in judgment faces a set of interpretative problems very similar to those that confront a literary critic. Perhaps most importantly, judges, like the political powers who create them, have interests, and these interests sometimes affect the execution of the law. Critical readers of literary works, too, have interests, interests which influence their understanding of their material. In what follows, I look briefly at three moments of judgment in three of Shakespeare's plays – the first an instance of legal judgment in *King Henry VIII*, the second an instance of literary judgment in *Hamlet*, and the third an instance of legal and literary judgment in *Timon of Athens*. These three particular moments share an interest in interest, they interpret interpretation, and they offer means of judging judgments. Taken together, they offer a first glimpse of the thesis that shapes this book: that the law offered Shakespeare not just an analogy for the interpretative opportunities and perils facing his own literary art, but a rich and apt language in which to posit and test these insights.

Shakespeare's part in the collaborative play *King Henry VIII* (or *All is True*) stresses the complex interactions between personal interests and legal processes. Katherine of Aragon knows that, in his sham legal suit to divorce her, Henry is cynically manipulating the law to realize both his lust and his political ambition for a male heir. When Cardinal Wolsey and the papal legate Campeius come to visit her in Act 3, Scene 1, they try to dissuade her from continuing the legal contest over the divorce, insisting that she would find better favour from Henry, and risk less disgrace, if she were to 'put [her] main cause into the King's protection'. Katherine responds with angry desperation:

> Ye tell me what ye wish for both – my ruin.
> Is this your Christian counsel? Out upon ye!
> Heaven is above all yet: there sits a judge
> That no king can corrupt.
>
> (3.1.98–101)

Wolsey and Campeius urge Katherine to desist in her legal suit, but even as she condemns the corrupt judges who will preside at her public trial, Katherine prefers this trial to a more private settlement made directly with the king her husband. Although she knows she will lose, Katherine preserves her dignity by submitting not to Henry's power, but to his abuse of power. The king may have the judges in his pocket, but Katherine prefers the judgment of law to the judgment of the king

because she knows that, for Henry to get his verdict, he must acknowledge himself bound *to* the law, even as he openly manipulates its
process. Her position is best expressed by the Duke of Buckingham in
an earlier scene, when he has just learned of his politically motivated
treason conviction:

> I have this day received a traitor's judgement,
> And by that name must die; yet heaven bear witness,
> And if I have a conscience, let it sink me,
> Even as the axe falls, if I be not faithful.
> The law I bear no malice for my death –
> 'T has done upon the premises but justice –
> But those that sought it I could wish more Christians.
>
> (2.1.58–64)

The final scene of *King Henry VIII* culminates in the paeanic prophecies
told of Queen Elizabeth, and of King James – reigning at the play's first
production in 1613. Henry's pretence of joy at Elizabeth's birth and
baptism marks his conversion to a performative kingship required, even
of the king, by law: a sovereign who goes through the motions of suing
for divorce is one who can, equally, go through the motions of pride in
another unwanted daughter. Elizabeth's forcedly auspicious baptism
thus makes her the play's emblem for the rule of law, even over kings.
But this golden age of Elizabethan and Jacobean Britain, conjured with
such servility by Cranmer in his final speech, is beset by the play's
repeated, harrowing question: how can the law be good, if the suitors
and judges who use it can so easily turn it to their bad ends?

Critical readers, like the authors who write for them, also have interests. Shakespeare (following Aristotle) recognized how the competing
interests of authors and critical readers presented an interpretative
structure analogous to that presented by law. In a famous scene in
Hamlet, the prince instructs the player in the performance of *The
Murder of Gonzago*, a play that contains at least half a dozen lines by
Hamlet himself. 'Speak the speech, I pray you,' he tells him, 'as I
pronounced it to you, trippingly on the tongue; but if you mouth it as
many of your players do, I had as lief the town-crier spoke my lines'

(3.2.1–4). An actor who wags his arms in the air and hollers his agonies, Hamlet tells the player, 'out-Herods Herod. Pray you avoid it' (3.2.14–15). Hamlet here may take the part of the author ('my lines'), heavy-handedly insisting on his authority over one of his interpreters, or he may simply be asserting his own pre-eminence as a critical reader of the play's text. In any case, his own account of his lines has a judicial authority because he has 'pronounced' it, as a judge might a judgment (see *OED*, 'pronounce', *v.* 1) – a sense of the verb reinforced when Hamlet reflects that the town-crier might make a better mouthpiece for his ruling. But as the discussion goes on, it becomes less and less clear on what Hamlet bases the authority of his interpretation, or of any interpretation of literary art:

> Be not too tame neither, but let your own discretion be your tutor. Suit the action to the word, the word to the action, with this special observance, that you o'erstep not the modesty of nature. For anything so o'erdone is from the purpose of playing, whose end, both at the first and now, was and is to hold as 'twere the mirror up to nature.
>
> (3.2.17–23)

The legal diction that punctuates this passage ('discretion', 'suit', 'action', 'observance') spins out the semantic emphasis of the conversation so far. At first Hamlet tells the player to use his judicial 'discretion' in interpreting the lines of the play. Here the authority of interpretation is thrown wholly on the reader's judgment. But it is in the technical significance (the 'special observance') of 'special observance' that we see Hamlet's critical insecurity surface, and that suddenly. 'Observance' could mean, simply, 'care', but in this collocation it had a more technical usage, closer to 'the fulfilling of a law or custom' (see *OED*, 'observance', *n.* 1, 2, 4a) – the sense in which Hamlet uses the word earlier in the play (1.4.16). The player must imitate humanity and hold the mirror up to nature because this is a 'special observance' – a custom or law to be honoured – in playing. In this subordination of discretion to mimesis, the authority of interpretation is thrown back on the author: the text says what it wants, and the player might as well be a town-crier. To speak what is not 'set down', as Hamlet concludes, is 'villainous, and shows a most pitiful ambition in the fool that uses it' (3.2.44–46). As Hamlet concludes his lesson, the player must be speechless, mainly because Hamlet's configuration of the competing claims of author, reader, and nature (or reason) in the construal of a literary text remains so confused, so undecided. Perhaps the only thing of which we can be sure, after his speech, is that critical readers, like corrupt kings, had better beware their own interpretative ambitions. To out-Herod Herod is to bully the role of a bully; but it is also to impose one's own interests on the representation of a tyrant, himself famous for making his will his law.

The analogy between legal and literary interpretation is just one of the points of contact in Shakespeare's work between what his plays do, and say, and what early-modern lawyers said, and did. But it is a fundamental and originary point of contact, because the legal analogy both helps Shakespeare to pose a question about the interpretation of his own works, and it also suggests an answer – an answer with which this book will repeatedly engage. *King Henry VIII* made a grand play on legal interpretation in 1613 in a particular political-historical moment: James VI and I was fighting with his judges, and with Sir Edward Coke above all, over the relative capacities of kings and their judges to authorize law. But Shakespeare's interest in the topic stretches back far beyond the composition of *Hamlet* over ten years earlier, because legal interpretation (or hermeneutics) provides a model for how literary authors might be thought not to authorize, but to collaborate in the authorization of their own pronouncements. At the end of Francis Bacon's essay 'Of Judicature', published in the 1625 *Essayes or Counsels, Civill and Morall,* he writes, '*Nos scimus quia lex bona est, modò quid eâ utatur legitimè*' ['And we know that the Law is good, if a man vse it lawfully'].[4] Bacon's point in adducing this proverbial maxim at the end of an essay on justice and judgment is ostensibly to insist on the fundamental position of the judge in interpreting, administering, and thus in a sense animating the good law. Should a judge fail in the responsibility to interpret and apply the law 'lawfully' (*legitimè*), the worth of the whole system of laws might be compromised, even vitiated. But on closer reading, the maxim seems to present a circular paradox: how is it possible to know whether or not a law be used lawfully, except by recourse to the law which one is using? A lawyer, like any moralist, must make appeal to some external authority in order to confer legitimacy on the interpretation or application of a law, for the warrant for the interpretation cannot be drawn from the exercise or construal of the law itself. If we locate legitimacy in 'the law' more broadly conceived (as the etymology of *legitimè*, from Latin *lex*, *legis*, 'the law' would suggest), we may suppose that 'lawfully' refers to the natural law of reason, and we have merely asserted that we know a law to be good, when it is good. If we locate the legitimacy of the law in 'the law' narrowly conceived, we suppose that 'lawfully' refers to a, even the, particular set of laws of which this law is one; and we have asserted, tautologously and dangerously, that we know a law to be good when it is used in a way consistent with itself. If we leave open the question of legitimacy, we find ourselves pausing upon another dangerously doubtful conclusion: something, or someone (a king? a judge?), is going to confer legitimacy on a law, and that someone may constitute legitimacy at best by mere authority, and at worst, by naked power. Bacon directs his parting maxim in 'Of Judicature' to the judges of the English common law, in order that 'they may remember what the apostle saith of a greater law than theirs';[5] and by this means he may seem to draw human law into the incontestable warrant of a divine dispensation. But when we turn back to 1 Timothy, we find that Paul's injunction to Timothy forms part of a polemical argument against co-religionists who do not share his construction of the Christian message. If Bacon seems to close down the ambiguity of the maxim's appeal to authority, his source (like Hamlet) throws it wide open.

Bacon almost certainly anticipated this kind of questioning. For his essay begins with a lengthy meditation on the exactly opposite argument, that 'judges ought to remember, that their Office is *Ius dicere*, and not *Ius dare*; To *Interpret Law*, and not to *Make Law*, or *Giue Law*'. 'The Mislaier of a *Meere Stone*', or boundary marker, 'is to blame'.[6] The essay as a whole apparently takes a very conservative stance on interpretation and on epistemology – that is, the study and enquiry into whether things can be known, what may be known, and how those things may be known. Bacon exhorts the judges of the common law, the whole of whose profession can be reduced to an act of interpretative application, to avoid engaging in any kind of creative activity, and rather to limit themselves to the sanctioned exposition of a law which, like a mere-stone, binds and contains them surely within a known range. The epistemological assuredness of the opening of the essay thus stands as a foil to the blatant tautology of the essay's conclusion, only indicating and heightening, rather than resolving, the paradoxical lack of confidence in *scimus* ('we know'). The incompatibility of the essay's end with its beginning is, furthermore, shadowed by Bacon's essay's relation to its own source in 1 Timothy. There, the word *legitimè* refers back to the articulation, a few lines earlier, of the nature of Paul's Christian law: 'For the ende of the commandement is loue out of a pure heart, and of a good conscience, and of faith vnfained.'[7] Paul appeals to a law in verse 8, but only after he has made it clear in verse 5 that that law is something known in the heart and by means of the conscience. By detaching the quotation from its context, and applying it to human rather than divine law, Bacon appears to close the circuit of *lex* and *legitimè*, but cannot (and surely does not intend to) erase the sense that an appeal to some higher, warranting authority must – despite all his warnings – be made. The incorruptible judge to whom Katherine appeals will not judge us in this life; meanwhile, how to interpret law without in some sense giving it remains the fraught challenge of Bacon's essay. As the player reassures the author Hamlet, 'I warrant your honour' (3.2.16).

Bacon's merestone suggests that Shakespeare's obsessive interest in law is of fundamental importance not only to many particular places in his works, but to our critical approach to his works in general. Do we know that our criticism is good, if it is performed critically? To what extent do we act as authors of Shakespeare's works, rather than merely as interpreters of them, when we criticize them? How can we know the limits of our critical legitimacy? The law and the legal in Shakespeare's works appear to be tied intimately to the interpretative problems and parameters by which they may be understood. What is more, Shakespeare anticipated the critical collocation of interpretative and legal ideas in our reception of his writing. In the final scenes of *Timon of Athens*, the misanthropic Timon erects the only merestone in Shakespeare's work, at the boundary of the sea where Timon intends to make 'his everlasting mansion' (5.1.215). That Shakespeare intends Timon's tombstone, or gravestone, to be taken also as a merestone is obvious from the repeated emphasis on the stone's position: Timon tells the senators that they will find his stone 'upon the beached verge of the salt flood' (5.1.216), while the soldier reports to Alcibiades that it is located 'upon the very hem o' th' sea' (5.4.66); here Shakespeare suggests a play on 'mere' as both 'boundary' ('verge', 'hem') and 'ocean' ('salt flood', 'sea'), even as he figures the stone (and grave) as a mark that will divide the earth from the water.[8] But if this stone physically marks the perimeter between land and sea, like Bacon's merestone it also presents an interpretative problem. The soldier who discovers this stone in 5.2 cannot read the inscription, and so devises a plan to find its meaning:

> The character I'll take with wax;
> Our captain hath in every figure skill,
> An ag'd interpreter, though young in days.
> (5.3.6–8)

When the soldier finds his interpreter in the following scene, the general Alcibiades has just sworn to keep 'the stream / Of regular justice' in Athens. (5.4.60–61) He reads the inscription easily enough, but discovers from it only that it wishes not to have been read, and that it gives Timon's name along with a simple injunction to '*seek not my name*' (5.4.71). Shakespeare's merestone, like Bacon's, succeeds in delimiting interpretation and making it possible, only to occasion its failure. Alcibiades' promise to observe the law of Athens within its 'stream' makes him the stone to the law's good course, for his word is the only power constraining the unruly behaviour of his riotous army. As the soldier had said of Alcibiades in the preceding scene, 'Before proud Athens he's set down by this. / Whose fall the mark of his ambition is' (5.3.9–10). Here 'the mark' of Athens' defeat, another merestone, shows the limit of Alcibiades' power, just as Alcibiades' power offers, in the closing lines of the play, the limit of Athenian law.[9]

Shakespeare's words and characters, his plays, like Bacon's laws, may interpret themselves – they 'make each / Prescribe to other, as each other's leech', as Alcibiades comments (5.4.83–84). But who will judge whether or not the interpretations be good?

Timon's merestone, then, functions as a physical symbol of the play's arbitrary, mutually constitutive but also deconstructing dyadic pairs: land and sea, power and law, gift and friendship. Timon's emphatically histrionic exposure of this arbitrariness, in the placing of a 'graven' stone 'embossed' by the action upon it of sea and sand, at once both 'insculpt[ed]' and 'impress[ed]' and 'brought away' with wax, leaves Alcibiades to enter Athens in a spirit of unresolved, and insoluble, tension between the olive and the sword (5.1.217, 5.4.67–69, 82). The failure of interpretation that Timon's merestone confers on Alcibiades, though, reaches past the relation of power to law, and into the fabric and tissue of the play itself. *Timon of Athens* is distinctive among Shakespeare's works for providing us with two characters – the Poet and the Painter – whose generic identities point reflexively to some sort of argument about the nature of the play's own art. These two characters open the play with an object lesson in literary-critical inter-pretation. The Painter to the Poet shows his piece: a portrait of a noble man 'to th' dumbness of [whose] gesture / One might interpret' (1.1.33–34). In response, the Poet expounds to the Painter the allegor-ical work he himself has in hand, in which the Poet's 'free drift / Halts not particularly, but moves itself / In a wide sea of wax', flying 'an eagle flight, bold, and forth on, / Leaving no tract behind' (1.1.45–50). The painter, understandably confounded by this plain declaration of obscu-rity, remonstrates, 'How shall I understand you?' In reply, the Poet 'unbolts' his representation of the goddess Fortune throned on a hill, whose capricious favours first beckon, then spurn a man of Timon's frame, the index of whose both greatness and abjection can be found in the troops of dependants who first follow, then abandon him. The Painter, now making sense of the Poet's more particular explanation (and application) of his work, more or less dismisses it:

PAINTER 'Tis common.
            A thousand moral paintings I can show

That shall demonstrate these quick blows of Fortune's
More pregnantly than words. Yet you do well
To show Lord Timon that mean eyes have seen
The foot above the head.

(1.1.91–96)

Here the process of understanding a work's meaning results in an assimilation of the particular work to the general (or generic) type; the painter sees the Poet's 'drift' because it is common. But in his final words, he also recognizes the importance of this model of interpretation to one particular reader, who will see that 'understanding' (or 'under-standing') literally means seeing 'the foot above the head'. The course of this conversation reveals the way in which the nobility of an uninterpreted aspect – the Painter's piece – gives way, through understanding, to the abjection of the Poet's application. The promise of understanding is what confers value on an art work, ennobling us as interpreters, but the experience of that understanding always devalues both it and us. It sets us down.

The Poet and the Painter are still expounding this mystery at the end of the play. Just as Timon is writing his epitaph (see 5.1.185), the two artists approach his cave, speaking of the 'promise' and 'intent' with which they will, in place of finished work, present him:

PAINTER   Promising is the very air o' th' time; it opens the eyes
           of expectation. Performance is ever the duller for his
           act; and, but in the plainer and simpler kind of people,
           the deed of saying is quite out of use. To promise is
           most courtly and fashionable; performance is a kind
           of will or testament which argues a great sickness in
           his judgment that makes it.

(5.1.23–29)

The relations that the Painter here implies between promise, performance, a testament, and death, prefigure the operation of Timon's merestone in the final scene of the play. To Alcibiades' act of exposition, which recognizes the merestone as the symbol of the arbitrary frontier between power and law, Shakespeare conjoins another kind of interpretation, that of the literary or artistic work. The Painter and the Poet make us ready to see that, in the mutually constitutive and deconstructing relation of power to law, we are also to find the mutually constitutive and deconstructing symbiosis of intention (promise) and performance, of meaning and interpretation. But this model of the dynamics of artistic creation and construal only obtains *if* we insist (with the Poet and the Painter, and with Timon) on seeing the literary text in the same way that we see the law; ultimately Shakespeare seems to be asking us not merely to grieve for art, but to question ourselves: how good is this metaphor? How sure are we of the interpretative skills that see Alcibiades – that most beautiful, powerful, and seductive of men – as the necessary arbiter of our critical and interpretative experience? Everything depends, finally, on what we make of the merestone.

This book is an attempt to dig out, to examine, and to evaluate – but not to mislay – the merestone. It takes as its subjects some of Shakespeare's poetic and dramatic works, and addresses the kinds of ethical and political, as well as epistemological problems relating to law and interpretation that these works pose – problems also thrown up by Bacon's citation of 1 Timothy: What would it mean for us to know something? What makes something good? By what standard can a method or act of interpretation itself be judged? In this sense, *Shakespeare and Law* provides an exploratory account of the importance of the law to the interpretation of Shakespeare's works, but one that attempts to join our understanding of legal language and thought to the larger human and intellectual problems that were the usual subject of early-modern literary writing. As Bacon's humanist compositional habits also demonstrate (not least in his citation of 1 Timothy), early-modern literary writing tended compulsively towards allusion and intertextual indication; and this study attempts to be faithful to the intertextual situation of Shakespeare's works within a larger English and classical literary and philosophical community. Like other kinds of thinking and meaning, legal arguments and ideas in Shakespeare's writing can no more be understood in isolation than a law can be authorized by itself.

If this book explores the importance of the law to our interpretations of Shakespeare's works, it also thinks methodologically about the importance of law to the process of interpreting Shakespeare's works. In particular, I will take a strongly historical and linguistic approach to reading the poems and plays. There is no readier way to justify these interpretative positions than by appeal to English common legal practices in the sixteenth century, which similarly stressed an almost hairsplittingly humanist commitment to the twin common legal sources of historical precedent and the language of written statutes and deeds. The humanist grammar-school curriculum, in which Shakespeare and many of his readers were trained, foregrounded – in its attitude to classical authority, its emphasis on *imitatio*, and its preoccupation with language – exactly those intellectual habits upon which contemporary legal learning and practice were also based. The account given in the first chapter, of Shakespeare's humanist education and firm situation in a world richly soaked in legal practice and theory, should go some way to demonstrating why my adherence to these interpretative principles makes sense. Shakespeare was a playwright, and it may be true, as some critics have argued, that as a playwright he produced plays much larger and more richly significant than in their language merely. But Shakespeare was also a poet, and my approach to the words of his works, as I think my readings will justify, is that of a reader of poetry. More, Shakespeare's plays, like his poems, were not written in a vacuum, but in a culture of imitation, translation, and adaptation; even those who encountered his play-texts only in performance would have known the stories well enough, and perhaps even the plays themselves well enough – either in different versions, or by repeated viewings – to desire, and to achieve, a meticulous 'reading' of his language. Neither we nor Shakespeare gains much from supposing him less precise in his words than in any other aspect of his composition. Giving space to Shakespeare's early-modern language sometimes means painstaking (even painful) parsing of phrases, long-winded expeditions into etymology, or copious adduction of examples showing the history of a word's usage, its regular collocations, its legal valencies, and so on. Very often it requires, less painfully, long quotation from Shakespeare's writing. For these excrescences I ask the reader's patience.

The historical attitude I take to Shakespeare's language – and thus to the ideas and narratives that it transmits – develops from the kinds of questions that, as users of the *Oxford English Dictionary*, we have come to consider standard: What could the words that Shakespeare used have meant to his audience, and why? In what texts were they used in these ways, and by what rhetorical communities? In a similar way, I try to honour early-modern habits of thought by construing 'law' and 'the legal' in this book not only as a system of political administration, but as a breed of philosophical concepts, as well as a linguistic register, a demographic grouping, and even a metaphysical stance. For example, the questions to which Shakespeare's use of law continue to return often seem to foreground the relationship of an individual to a universal, of a person (agent, subject) to a type (kind, category) or to a code (rule, law). The tendency to propose analogies is one Shakespeare hardly ever resists, so that such analyses of individuals and universals might well encompass not only political, but ethical, epistemological, and metaphysical meanings: a subject living under an ordinance, an agent endeavouring to express or achieve a virtue, a mind striving to possess a truth, a soul hoping to comprehend the divine. One of the purposes of this book will be to test the degree to which law functions in Shakespeare's work as a bridging discourse that joins one kind of philosophical representation, or reasoning, to another. The impulse to such connectivity, for us, arises from a historically informed recognition of the way in which the term 'law' was construed by a society and readership to whom the semantic associations of natural law, civic law, moral law, and divine law still enjoyed more than a shadow of substantive interdependence. As a (or perhaps the) meta-discourse that, as Bacon saw, must enfold its own authorization, law would seem to be a useful tool for any literary writer's attempt to understand his or her own works' ability to signify. My emphasis on law and the legal as a conceptual language for formulating and exploring philosophical problems is based on the way in which law, like language itself, sits near the boundaries or origins of thoughts. It is an emphasis that leads, throughout the book, to attempts to understand Shakespeare's legal language and thought in the broadest possible philosophical terms: as they did in the education and professional lives of English humanist writers, Plato, Aristotle, and Seneca rub shoulders here with St German, Plowden, and Coke.

Rigid adherence throughout the book to my two pole stars,

language and historical context, has left me little latitude to visit some of the literary-critical monograph's usual ports of call. In particular, I have almost wholly avoided reference to other critics' readings of Shakespeare, even within the sub-field of law and drama. That this is no mark of disrespect, nor of careless inattention, I remit to the reader's generous trust, and urge careful use of the carefully constructed bibliography. In a similar way, I have avoided discussion of some of the conventional characters, scenes, and concepts that have become staples of legal studies of Shakespeare in recent decades – simply because they *are* well known, and have been amply, sometimes over-amply, documented elsewhere. A comprehensive survey of legal ideas and language in Shakespeare's plays, for example, would include some discussion of spousal contracts in *Measure for Measure, All's Well That Ends Well,* and *The Taming of the Shrew*;[10] some analysis of the great 'trial scenes' of *King Lear* and *The Merchant of Venice*; or an assessment of the importance of natural-law theory to plays from *Hamlet* to *The Tempest.*[11] In this respect, *Shakespeare and Law* offers an introduction not to the full range of legal thinking operative in Shakespeare's writings, but to how to think about Shakespeare and law. There will be many more cases; I can only hope to show a precedent.

Bacon's injunction to the judges in 'Of Judicature' takes its conservative, but ultimately paradoxical, line on interpretation as a direct response to more than a century of legal innovation and upheaval, which had culminated, during the reign of James VI and I, in legal and intellectual crises of considerable importance. In the chapters that follow, I will turn repeatedly to the history and legal history of the Tudor and Stuart period, describing the changes in legal thinking and practice against which Shakespeare constructed the legal allusions and arguments of his poems and plays. The rise of *assumpsit* and of new evidentiary practices, for example, allowed litigants and judges new scope in using material and verbal evidence to construct or 'import' the existence and significance of interior states like intention or malice. Or again, the tensions between the monarchy and common lawyers, as they were played out in treatises on the Chancery, or judicial decisions in cases of error, created opportunities for argument about the nature of individual rights in the face of common goods. If an interpretative narrative emerges from the present study, it is characterized not by concrete arguments ('Shakespeare was a republican'; 'Shakespeare thought legal fictions were poppycock'), but by Shakespeare's exploitative tendency to think-through. The law and its problems, like other discourses and their texts and traditions, provided Shakespeare with a language of forms and ideas – readily accessible to his audience and readership – by means of which and through which he could frame moral issues, political arguments, epistemological cruxes, metaphysical paradoxes. Bacon's citation of 1 Timothy leaves the validity of law to depend adverbially on itself. For Shakespeare, too, the enquiry into interpretation made possible by law – interpretation's limits, its warrants, its value – was not conclusive, but modal.

This kind of provisionality extends, I think, to all instances of Shakespeare's conflation of legal ideas with literary expression; one of the primary reasons for judging Shakespeare's legal thinking to be philosophically deliberative, rather than (say) practically polemical, is its pervasively modal character. The celebrated jurist Sir Frederick Pollock composed in 1914 a genially savage attack on 'law and literature' studies of Shakespeare, in which he ridiculed 'the law of Shakespeare commentators', who are possessed by a 'determination to take Shakespeare seriously at all costs, even when he is most comic'.[12] In a summary deconstruction of critical attempts to 'take . . . seriously' the Doge's trial of Shylock, Pollock imagines Shakespeare quipping to a detractor from Lincoln's Inn: '"My dear man, I am a maker of plays, not of law-books; I wanted a good scene, not justice."' We must remember, Pollock insists, that 'Shakespeare wrote his dialogue not to be refined upon in learned leisure, but to be heard and understood on the stage'.[13] At a moment in the critical history of Shakespeare's plays when legal-historical readings are becoming ever more technical and ingenious, Pollock's dismissive treatment of legally informed readings of Shakespeare's plays may seem attractive. He rightly condemns critics who would see in Shakespeare's attention to law a professional, rather than a conceptual, precision. But a brief look at the opening of *King Lear*, which itself turns on the idea of modality in interpretation, will suggest why I think Pollock is as hasty as some of his more inept stooges.

At the moment *King Lear* begins, the court is assembling to hear

Lear 'express [his] darker purpose'. Nearly the entire cast of the drama is on stage to witness this act of self-disclosure, and Lear makes it clear in his opening speech that he has something to communicate to them: he will 'express' and 'publish' his 'purpose', 'will', and 'intent', and while he's at it, he will 'answer' the suit of France and Burgundy, long since depending. Shakespeare makes it very clear that we are to see this scene as a watershed epistemic experience, summed up in Lear's forceful imperative 'Know ...' (1.1.35–48) It is not a surprise, then, to find that many critical readings of the play as a whole consider this scene the key to understanding the rest: Lear's confidence in his ability to get something across, here, has naturally made an impression on all of us. But what is it that he communicates? What do we know, after watching or reading this scene? Very many silly things have been said about the opening of *King Lear*, many of them by critics interested in the legal language and thought of the play. It is very clearly a play that deals with primogeniture and gavelkind, two customary forms by which heirs succeeded to estates in the early-modern period: either the eldest son takes all (by primogeniture, the more general custom), or the estate is divided up between co-heirs (by gavelkind, common in Wales before Henry VIII's reign, and in Kent). By the use of words like 'dowers' and 'divest', Shakespeare patently means us to see that Lear is undertaking some sort of legal partition of his royal estate; and indeed the phrases he uses to confer portions on Goneril and Regan echo early modern legal formulae for the entailing of estates.[14] This has led some critics to make very specific claims about the nature of the play and its meaning. One critic has argued that Lear's grant of his estates, with the reservation of 'the name and all th' addition of a king', amounts to the creation of a trust in the kingdom, whereby his daughters become (fictional) trustees of the estate – its legal owners – while Lear remains the practical beneficiary, known to the medieval common law as the *cestuy que use*.[15] In this reading, *King Lear* as a whole functions as an indictment of the legal fictions by which early-modern culture organized its social and political life. Another recent critic has gone so far as contending the play is 'an intervention into contemporary debates about inheritance practices, a defense of early modern England's particularly strict system of primogeniture'.[16] I feel confident that Pollock would laugh: *King Lear* is a tragedy, not an indictment of legal fictions or a defence of primogeniture. In any case, an enfeoffment of the kingdom to Lear's use would make him the beneficiary of the estate, whereas (as he says) the 'revenue' along with the 'execution' of his royal office is to be conferred upon his daughters (and their husbands). And if *King Lear* is a defence of primogeniture, then why are Lear's oldest daughters so odious?

But if critics sometimes rush to excess, we should all the same not be too hasty in sweeping away, with Pollock, the potentially significant specificity of Shakespeare's legal allusiveness. For all that Lear refers in his opening speech to his 'will', the nature of his act is not testamentary but donative. He makes a gift – a fact that Shakespeare insists upon in the play's folio text, when Kent urges Lear to 'revoke thy gift' (1.1.165). The law of gifts was, by Shakespeare's days, long established. Its complexity derives from the conditions a donor can attach to the gift, binding the donee to certain kinds of performance or non-performance, to the donee's either benefit or cost. As the subject is treated by its most famous medieval exponent, Henry de Bracton, a gift can be of three kinds: simple and absolute, conditional, or subject to a *modus* (*simplex et pura, condicionalis*, or *sub modo*).[17] A simple gift is outright and secure: the donor transfers the property to the donee absolutely, and both donor and donee are thereafter free of any obligations to one another. Less straightforward are situations where the donor wishes to limit the gift in some way, either by attaching special provisions to its reception (an entail), or by requiring some reciprocation, in property or service, in return for the gift. Having explained how the gift of an estate may be restricted, in succession, to a certain class of heirs (to heirs male, issue of a particular woman, etc.) Bracton writes:

> A donor may always make any provision he wishes with respect to the thing given, since it is his completely . . . Just as the class 'heirs' may be enlarged, as was said above, so it may be restricted by the *modus* of the gift, so that all heirs generally are not called to the succession. For the *modus* imposes a law on a gift; the *modus* must be observed even if contrary to common right and to what the law would provide, for *modus* and agreement defeat law.[18]

But in framing this limitation on the gift the donor has an option. He can stipulate the limitation on the gift either by a condition (using *si*, 'if'), or by a *modus* (using *ut*, 'that'), a difference which will, in turn, lead to a distinction between his available remedies, should the limitation not be observed by the donee. If the donee fails to observe a conditional limitation, the donor can be restored to the possession of the thing given; but if the donee fails to observe a limitation made *sub modo*, the donor can only legally compel the donee to *perform the terms of the limitation*, and has no right to the restitution of the thing given:

> A gift may be made completely subject to a *modus*, as where the four innominate contracts enter into a gift, namely, I give that you do, I do that you give, I do that you do, I give that you give. I give that you give, as 'I give you a Digest that you give me a Code,' so that if I deliver a Digest, you are bound to deliver me a Code. Or if I say, 'I give that you do,' that is, 'I give you a Code that you cause a Digest to be written for me.' Or 'I do that you give,' that is, 'I build you a house that you give me a Code.' Or 'I do that you do,' that is, 'I build you a hall that you build me a chamber.' These gifts subsist under a *modus* and bind the contracting parties, so that if I give or do, you are bound to give or do as you agreed. But they do not enable me to recall what I have given if you are unwilling to do what you promised. I can only sue to compel you to do, unless it is otherwise agreed at the beginning. For to this gift subject to a *modus* a condition may be added at the outset, as if I say, 'And if you do not give or do what you agreed that I may recall what I gave, or recover the charges incurred in connexion with what I did.' If no condition is added, however, I cannot.[19]

With Bracton's explanation of donation in hand, we may return to the opening scene of *King Lear* with a fresh sensitivity to the pitfalls surrounding Lear in his attempt to divest himself of rule. What is conspicuously missing from Lear's gift – to Goneril, to Regan, and even (in prospect) to Cordelia – is a condition. Lear makes his gift *sub modo*, stipulating the 'reservation of an hundred knights', along with the retention of 'the name and all th' addition to a king', as a limitation, but not one that can, or will defeat the grant of the estate. Lear's readiness to 'give them all', without retaining any power to compel performance of the limitation, is of course his point – he desires to trust his daughters. When Kent accuses him of 'hideous rashness' and counsels him to 'reserve [his] state', Lear sees immediately that Kent's advice tends toward a suspicion – of non-performance – that would break Lear's fantasy of obligation:

> Hear me, recreant, on thine allegiance, hear me,
> That thou hast sought to make us break our vows,
> Which we durst never yet, and with strained pride
> To come betwixt our sentences and our power,
> Which nor our nature, nor our place can bear,
> Our potency made good, take thy reward.
>
> (1.1.168–73)

Lear's rejoinder consists of a simple stress on the actionability of his words: I mean what I say, he tells Kent, and don't you forget it. But in a cruel parody of the course Kent had urged on him, Lear now *does* make a gift, and this time, the 'provision' is conspicuously conditional:

> Five days we do *allot thee for provision,*
> To shield thee from disasters of the world,
> And on the sixth to turn thy hated back
> Upon our kingdom. *If* on the next day following
> Thy banished trunk be found in our dominions,
> The moment is thy death. Away! By Jupiter,
> *This* shall not be revoked.
>
> (1.1.174–80; italics mine)

Lear remits Kent his life, on condition that he leave the kingdom; if he does not, the gift, he informs him, will be void. In his repetition of Kent's word 'revoked', Lear spits, 'take that'.

That Shakespeare was fully aware of the importance of legal donation *sub modo* to the ethics of his play is clear from two details. Indeed, these details show that he had been reading about the philosophy of gift in Bracton's text. The Latin verb that Bracton uses to describe the imposition of limitations on a gift (whether *condicionalis* or *sub modo*) is *onerare*; to remove the limitation from a gift, *exonerare*. These verbs are derived from the Latin noun *onus, oneris*, meaning 'burden', and they were always translated into early-modern English as 'to burden', and 'to unburden'. When Lear says in the opening scene that he plans 'unburdened' to 'crawl towards death' (1.1.40), he is announcing his intention to make a free gift. From Bracton, too, Shakespeare takes his cue for that curious collocation, 'constant will': 'We have this hour a constant will to publish / Our daughters' several dowers, that future strife / May be prevented now' (1.1.41–43). As Bracton writes:

At the outset, at the inception of his gift, the donor may well impose a law upon it and by his will disburden [*exonerare*] the thing given to the advantage of the donee and to the contrary of what the law of the land would ordinarily require ... He may disburden [*exonerare*] the land given to his own prejudice and that of his heirs and remit for himself and his heirs what is his, either service or customs, of whatever kind. This remission suffices because he once willed it, for nothing is more in accord with natural equity than to make effective the will of a lord wishing to transfer his property to another. [*Et sufficit quia hoc semel voluit, quia nihil tam conveniens est naturali æquitati quam voluntatem domini volentis rem suam in alium transferre ratam haberi.*][20]

Bracton's phrase '*voluntatem ... ratam*' literally means in English 'constant will': that than which no thing can be more convenient to natural equity, is to enable the 'constant will' of a lord who wishes to give away his *rem suam*. The force of these borrowings from Bracton's Latin – 'unburdened' for *exonerare*, immediately followed by 'have a constant will' for *voluntatem ... ratam haberi* – is clear. Their importance cannot, I think, be overstated: Shakespeare composed this scene from *King Lear* with a copy of Bracton's Latin text sitting before him.

The second link between the two texts is more complicated, but also cuts deeper toward the significance of the common law of gifts for Shakespeare's play. Shakespeare never uses the word 'mode', in any of his works, but there is one play – *King Lear* – in which he uses a name that sounds much like it. 'The prince of darkness is a gentleman,' Edgar announces in Act Three, Scene One, 'Modo he's called, and Mahu'. The names Modo and Mahu Shakespeare is generally reckoned to have lifted from the Samuel Harsnett's 1603 *A declaration of egregious Popish impostures*, and there is no doubt that, when Edgar recites the names, he means nothing other than the mock-folk incantation he appears to mean.[21] But Lear hears something else, because (as Edmond Blunden was the first to point out[22]) he has been reading Horace's second book of *Epistles*:

> ac ne forte putes me, quae facere ipse recusem,
> cum recte tractent alii, laudare maligne,
> ille per extentum funem mihi posse videtur
> ire poeta, meum qui pectus inaniter angit,
> irritat, mulcet, falsis terroribus implet,
> ut magus, et modo me Thebis, modo ponit Athensis.[23]

> [Lest thou should thinke that I disprayse
>   the thing which I do make
> Because it is a kynde of charge
>   which other vndertake:
> That poet on a stretched rope
>   may walke and neuer fall,
> That can stere vp my passions,
>   or quicke my sprytes at all.
> Stere me, chere me, or with false feares
>   of bugges fill vp my breast,
> At *Athens* now, and now at *Thebes*,
>   by charminge make me rest.[24]]

When poor Tom says, 'Modo he's called, and Mahu', the addled King Lear hears a philosopher – Horace – saying '*ut magus, et modo*'. This is why he subsequently insists on calling Edgar a philosopher, and then refers to him as 'this same learned Theban' (3.4.153) and 'good Athenian' (3.4.176). The shift from Harsnett's *Modu* to Lear's 'Modo' is crucial, because it allows him to confuse 'the prince of darkness' with a word that was on his mind when he 'express[ed his] darker purpose', a word that is on his mind when he pulls poor Tom aside and demands, 'Let me ask you one word in private': *modo*.[25] The ablative of *modus* – which means 'limit, constraint' – is used adverbially in Latin, in this coordinated construction, to mean 'now ... and now ...' Lear's confusion of the two moments links what a tragic poet, as enchanter, can do *sub modo*, and what Lear tried to do, *sub modo*, at the inception of his gift. Lear gave his daughters all, expressing himself so plainly that he reserved no vantage by which to claim back his dignity no power to compel his daughters' love; Horace's tragic poet, by contrast, is a lord of limit – his ability to coordinate *modo* makes him nothing less than a *magus*.

What I am suggesting is nothing so evolved as a reading of *King Lear*. I will not presume to say here what I think Shakespeare meant by this concatenation of texts, and slippages between words. Indeed, Shakespeare himself seems to warn me from the attempt: if Lear emerges from this play of intertextuality as a poet figure, and his gift is an attempt to express himself clearly – remember that epistemic watershed? – then the danger of interpretation, and its tragic sadness, is that whatever we venture to understand, Shakespeare has no recourse to reclaim his words. All the future strife of interpretation has been (for him) unhappily prevented. The ethical burden that this places on me, as a construing reader working through this particular scene, may be intolerable. Instead, I want to insist on the way in which Shakespeare's engagement with the words, the texts, and the ideas of the law can be meticulously exact, so exact that we ignore it at our peril; to insist on the way that these linguistic and conceptual allusions, as here, are seamlessly joined to contemporary and classical texts very much outside the ambit of 'conventional' legal thought; and, finally, to insist on the provisional, modal character of interpretation that Shakespeare's legal allusiveness occasions. If Shakespeare has left us a legacy, it is one beset (like Timon's merestone) not by a condition – for he can never reclaim it – but by a terrible *modus*: he simply isn't here to tell us what it means.

Chapter Two

SHAKESPEARE'S LEGAL LIFE

To whom therefore is the Law profitable? Marie, to them that be best learned, that haue readie wittes, and will take paines. When is the law profitable? Assuredly, both now and euermore, but especially in this age, where all men goe together by the eares, for this matter, and that matter. Such alteration hath been heretofore, and hereafter needes must ensue much alteration. And where is al this a doe? Euen in little England, or in Westminster hall, where neuer yet wanted businesse, nor yet euer shal.

Thomas Wilson, *The Arte of Rhetorique* (1553)

THE TUDOR LEGAL CRISIS:
EXPANSION AND INNOVATION

'I suppose', wrote William Caxton in *Game and Play of the Chesse* in 1474, 'that in alle Cristendom ar not so many pletars attorneys and men of the lawe as ben in englond onely':

For yf they were nombrid all that lange to the courtes of the channcery kinges benche. comyn place. cheker. ressayt and helle And the bagge berars of the same / hit shold amounte to a grete multitude And how alle thyse lyue & of whome. yf hit shold be vttrid & told / hit shold not be byleuyd.[1]

Caxton's is a conventional complaint about civil, and particularly legal, bureaucracy, one that might have been made (and often has been) in any age; but there are a number of elements to the passage that might profitably give a historian pause. First of all, Caxton makes the comment in the middle of an otherwise faithful translation of an Italian work, composed originally in Latin and concerning the state not of Yorkist England but of fourteenth-century Rome, and the candid and slightly jarring suspension of the translator's usual pretension of fidelity seems to confer on this passage a particular sincerity.[2] Along the same lines, Caxton's enumeration of some central Westminster courts – Chancery, King's Bench, Common Pleas (or Place), the Exchequer, the Court of Receipt, and Hell – draws further attention to the idiosyncrasies of English common-law traditions and institutions in contrast to the Continental legal structure discussed in the main body of the original work. England's fiercely independent common-law tradition, rooted in Magna Carta, propagated case by case, and carefully trained up by reason, custom, maxim, and statute, seems in Caxton's formulation to have become unruly and oppressive precisely for its otherwise celebrated heterogeneity. If courts and polities on the continent find themselves oppressed by a legal system as simple and streamlined as that of the *corpus juris civilis*, reasons Caxton, how much more should England suffer, weighted by the yoke of so many distinct jurisdictions, each with its own forms, processes, judges and other functionaries, not to mention charges? Finally, Caxton distinctly imagines the weight of England's legal millstone as a London problem: all of the courts he mentions, with the extortionate bad practices of the lawyers he associates with them, are located in the capital. Poised (unwittingly) on the brink of a coming century of geographical consolidation and administrative expansion in the princely government of England, Caxton's characterization of England's legal crisis would only become more, rather than less, apt.

When legal historians afford time to Caxton's complaint at all, they tend to focus, as I have, on his evidence of the profusion of courts and pleaders.[3] But Caxton has much more to say. 'What hurte doon the aduocats. men of lawe. And attorneyes of court to the comyn peple of the royame as well in the spirituell lawe as in the temporall / How torne they the lawe and statutes at their pleasir / How ete they the peple / How enpouere the comynte'? And later in the same passage he returns to this failure of the legal profession to defend the commonweal: 'For

FIGURE 1 A trial in King's Bench, c. 1450–1460. Inner Temple, MS Add. 188. The bureaucratic bustle of the court is evident – a court in which the judges, clerks and other officers substantially outnumber the defendants and other onlookers.

they entende to theyr synguler wele and proufytt and not to the comyn / How well they ought to be of good wyll to gyder, and admoneste and warne the cytes eche in his right in suche wise that they myght haue pees and loue one with an other'? Not only by its sheer size, nor merely in its heterogeneity, but in the agonistic and self-serving behaviour of its practitioners, the English common-law system has, for Caxton, already betrayed its responsibility to the commonweal, to the civic health of the nation. For the humanist Caxton, who goes on to cite the opinion of Cicero on friendship as a corrective to this abuse of good government, England's longstanding civil wars are the direct result of a legal system in which lawyers and judges attempt to deliver common justice while simultaneously pursuing their own preferment and financial gain. The opposition that Caxton draws here between the interests of the individual and the interest of the commonweal – whether that individual be the lawyer who pleads or the client who hires him to do so – foreshadows a century of procedural innovation, theoretical discussion, and highly public dissension over the rights and prosperity of persons (and particularly of the sovereign) measured against the common benefit of the institutions and supposedly disinterested judgments of the law.

The common law that was received, practised, and discussed in sixteenth-century England comprised a motley accretion of courts and educational institutions; judges, clerks and officials, attorneys and solicitors, and apprentices and students; written texts (including statutes and both manuscript and printed reports of landmark cases) and longstanding customs; and administrative procedures. The common law was often said to be a rule of law unwritten (or *jus non scriptum*), the life of which subsisted in the practice of the judges; and in this sense it was utterly distinct from the Roman (or civil) law that dominated the states and principalities of continental Europe, which had been revived upon the rediscovery of Justinian's *Digest* in the twelfth century and had quickly taken hold (in Oxford and Cambridge, as well as at Paris and Padua) as a prescriptive, textually based code. Sir John Fortescue, Chancellor to the exiled Henry VI, wrote in the *De laudibus legum Angliae* (c. 1470) that '*omnia iura humana aut sunt lex nature, consuetudines, vel statuta que et constituciones appellantur*' ['all human laws are either law of nature, customs, or statutes, which are also called constitutions']; England's common-law tradition, based flexibly on these three *fontes* or sources, excelled even the civil law of the 'Roman princes' in its particular suitability ['*ad eiusdem regni utilitatem ... accommodam*'] to the English nation.[4] Sir Thomas Smith, similarly, celebrated the English common law in his *De Republica Anglorum* ('On the Commonwealth of England', written 1562–5) by recording its origins in ancient customs and forms, and stressing the sacred legitimacy of those forms: 'Certaine it is that it is always a doubtfull and hasardous matter to meddle with the chaunging of the lawes and governement, or to disobey the orders of the rule or government, which a man doth finde already established.'[5] Where Caxton had seen an oppressive weight of overlapping jurisidictions and competing interests, common lawyers like Fortescue and Smith saw an organic tradition, and a supple fabric of interlocking bases and functions.

The *republica Anglorum* described by Smith in his treatise of the 1560s, though, was already very much on the move. A boom in legal

FIGURE 2 The Court of King's Bench and Chancery in Westminster Hall, c. 1620. British Museum, British Roy PI. The hall was also home to the court of Common Pleas and to the Exchequer Chamber.

business under the Tudors, alongside the advent of new conciliar, or ministerial, jurisdictions in the late fifteenth century – and particularly the courts of Chancery and Star Chamber – had pressed the royal common-law courts into innovation and expansion. At the same time, the consolidation of executive functions in the hands of the prince and privy council had made Westminster both more powerful and more bureaucratic than ever before. Henry VIII's break with Rome enriched the crown, and increased not only its authority in ecclesiastical affairs, but its power over secular suits and matters once controlled by the bishops and church. The rapid flourishing of the printing press in London over the sixteenth century, too, changed the face of legal education and administration: under great legal-humanist printers like John Rastell (1475–1536), William Rastell (1508–1565), and Richard Tottel (1528–1593), legal encyclopedias, collections of statutes, reports of cases, and other legal literature circulated in extensive runs never before possible. The four superior Inns of Court – the Middle and Inner Temples, Lincoln's Inn, and Gray's Inn – trained students and apprentices in ever expanding cohorts, and by the end of the sixteenth century were universally reckoned, alongside Oxford and Cambridge, the third university of the realm.[6]

By the time James VI and I succeeded to the throne of England, the Tudor legal expansion had hit its peak. The profusion of pleaders, attorneys, and men of the law that had so offended Caxton in 1474 had, by the early years of the seventeenth century, become an intractable and entrenched problem, and James's early parliaments took up the reformation of legal business in the courts at Westminster as a matter of the first priority. In 1605, in the second parliament of James's reign, the commons and lords passed 'an Act to reforme the multitudes and misdemeanours of Atturneys and Sollicitors at Law, and to auoyde sundry and vnnecessarie Suites, and charges in Law'. The act rehearses in its preamble 'the abuse of sundry Atturneys and Sollicitors by charging their Clients with excessiue Fees and other vnnecessary demaunds . . . whereby . . . the practise of the iust and honest Sergeant and Counsellour at Law, greatly slandered' – an abuse of legal process that the authors of the act attribute to ambition for 'the priuate gaine of such Atturneys and Sollicitors'. The act also makes particular provision for the sheer number of attorneys and solicitors, giving the judges the authority to admit only those 'as haue beene brought vp in the same Courts, or otherwise well practized in Solliciting of cawses, and haue beene found by their dealings to be skilfull of honest disposition'.[7] On the face of it, this statute clearly seems to take in hand the general abuses attending the huge Tudor legal expansion; but the eagerness of James's first parliament to enact such legislation was probably not only motivated by a desire for the reform of solicitors and attorneys, but directed at another target entirely: the King's Bench. The two traditional courts of common law situated in Westerminster Hall, the courts of Common Pleas and King's Bench, had for centuries shared the business of royal justice, according to the jurisdictional divisions established by Magna Carta. The King's Bench originally sat before the king (*in coram rege*) and held jurisdiction over all criminal suits in England, as well as, on the 'plea' side, private suits for trespass, felony, and error; the Common Pleas, by contrast, enjoyed the substantially bulkier jurisdiction over all suits in which the king had no interest – 'civil' suits including actions for debt, contract, and the recovery of property.[8] At the beginning of the Tudor period, the Common Pleas was by far the busier of the two courts, and generated substantial income for its judges, clerks, pleaders, and other functionaries, through lucrative fees and fines for civil actions. The King's Bench, by contrast, languished in comparative neglect, especially when, during the late fifteenth century, both courts came under increasing pressure from newer, conciliar courts presided over by the king's ministers ruling by prerogative dispensation. In an attempt to halt the decline of business in the court, over the course of the sixteenth century the King's Bench judges encouraged lawyers to develop new strategies that would allow them to expand the court's jurisdiction into civil cases. These innovations had to exploit fictions or ambiguities either in process or in law. A successful challenge to conventional process was the new 'bill of Middlesex', often paired with a new use of the *latitat*; by a pretence that the defendant was resident in the country of Middlesex (in which case the court was allowed to proceed by bill rather than by expensive Chancery writ), the court could order his appearance to answer a criminal charge and then, once he was in custody, quietly drop that charge

in favour of a civil suit.[9] The King's Bench similarly stretched its jurisdiction by ambiguities in law. The venerable exceptional remedy of the
'action on the case', or *assumpsit*, allowed the court to hear contractual
cases when the contract in question had certain unusual features;
when litigants began to allege these features, and the court began to
accept their allegements, plaintiffs in debt in the Common Pleas
migrated *en masse* to the King's Bench *assumpsit*.[10]

Attorneys devised this system of fudges to provide their clients with
more efficient and more flexible legal remedies in civil cases. The judges
of the King's Bench, for their own part, allowed the procedural innovations probably because they recognized that an expansion in the
court's jurisdiction was not only good for the administration of justice
in the realm generally, but good for themselves. The effect was
dramatic; as J. H. Baker notes, 'From a trickle of latitats at the end of
the fifteenth century, and a few hundred rolls a year, within a century
the court was issuing – according to a contemporary estimate –
20,000 latitats a year and filling 6,000 rolls. Between 1560 and 1640
the increase in King's Bench suits was particularly dramatic, perhaps
as much as tenfold.'[11] The expansion of the civil jurisdiction in the
King's Bench did not go unchallenged: in 1585 Parliament passed an
act 'for redresse of erronious Iudgements in the Court commonly
called, The Kings Bench', which created a new court, called the
Exchequer Chamber, to hear suits of error brought against judgments
in the King's Bench. The provision of the statute for redress in 'sute or
action of debt, detinue, couenant, account, action vpon the case, eiec-
tion firme, or trepasse, first commenced or to bee first commenced
there', makes it clear that the judicial review intended by the statute
was directed at the expanding civil practice and ambit of a court once
confined to pleas of the crown and criminal cases.[12] That the new
review court of Exchequer Chamber was to be made up of the Common
Pleas judges sitting with the barons of Exchequer makes it only clearer
that the statute was directed at bringing the procedure, and volume of
business, of the two common-law courts more evenly into line. The
sixteenth-century expansion in the jurisdiction of the King's Bench,
along with the efforts taken by the crown and the judges to control it,
reveals in miniature a more general transformation taking place in

public life in this period, and a new set of tensions arising from that transformation. More and more people were turning to the central courts to try to resolve their relations with their neighbours, their families, and their business associates; more and more, not only in the suits themselves, but in the practices of lawyers and judges in the processing of those suits, the interests of individuals were being pitted against one another, and against the common interest. The rapid and seemingly unstoppable growth in Westminster legal activity helped to transform London during this period, and made the seasons of the courts' sittings – known as 'term' or 'term time' – densely populated festivals of legal, economic, and social activity not only in Westminster, but in the city lying to the east, on both banks of the river.

The main effect on litigants of these King's Bench innovations and Common Pleas reactions – through statutory legislation, review decisions in courts of error, and so forth – must have been to render ever more ambiguous and fluid what to Caxton was already a confusing network of overlapping jurisdictions and competing standards and processes. Lawyers took advantage of this confusion to enrich themselves at the expense of their gullible or at least optimistic clients; as the 1605 statute restraining solicitors and attorneys makes clear, the public perception of Westminster at the end of Elizabeth's reign had shifted to one of guarded suspicion. Thomas Wilson writes of Tudor lawyers in *The Arte of Rhetorique*:

> Sometymes a doubt is made vpon some worde or sentence, when it signifieth diuers things, or may diuersly bee taken, whereupon full oft ariseth much contention. The Lawiers lacke no cases, to fill this part full of examples. For rather then faile, they will make doubtes oftentimes, where no doubt should be at all. Is his Lease long enough (quoth one:) yea sir, it is very long said a poore Husbandman. Then (quoth he) let me alone with it, I will finde a hole in it I warrant thee. In all this talke I except alwaies the good Lawiers, and I may wel spare them, for they are but a fewe.[13]

Directly because of this fluidity and uncertainty in the expanding legal society of sixteenth-century England, it became increasingly important for litigants, and for potential litigants – a class that included the entire landed and monied population of the realm – to know as much as possible about the law, in as much detail as possible. A careless promise or an imperfectly effected loan might land an unfortunate plaintiff in court, or a series of courts, for years; and even if a wronged plaintiff were to succeed in a common-law action to recover lost property or money, the ambiguity of civil jurisdictions, combined with the preposterous mutual review of the King's Bench and Common Pleas, meant that just remedies might be overturned in subsequent actions. As we will shortly see, the culture of complicated and seemingly interminable legal disputes touched Shakespeare and his family both obliquely and very directly; for an Elizabethan with any kind of property at all, the law – with its language and process, and the various cultural forms that sprang up around it – was an inescapable landscape, and even language, of civil life.

Unfortunately, even the tangled and enfolded cloth of the common-law jurisdictions, as briefly described above, did not cover the whole frame of legal life in which an Elizabethan had to move, and might hope to prosper. Twice a year outside of term, royal justices serving as commissioners of assize brought common-law justice to the country, two judges or serjeants being assigned to each of the six circuits. Local courts – manorial feudal courts, Leet courts, piepowder courts, and so on – survived and in some boroughs and market towns performed very active roles in the day-to-day lives of early-modern men and women. Ecclesiastical courts in England, dating from a period of intensive legal centralization on papal authority in the twelfth century, persisted after Henry VIII's break with Rome in January 1534. While these courts had always been subject to jurisdictional control exercised through prohibitions issued by the common-law courts at Westminster, during the Elizabethan period they were still trying cases relating to defamation, fornication, and marriage, and probate courts were long to retain their authority over last wills and testaments.[14] The ecclesiastical courts seem to have enjoyed an expansion in business over the sixteenth century comparable to that in the Westminster courts, and in the 1580s the ecclesiastical jurisdiction of the Queen acting through her archbishops was consolidated in a new High Commission. Similar prerogative powers were conferred by the Tudor sovereigns on their ministers, for exercise in conciliar courts: the Chancellor judged by his conscience in the Chancery, the Lord High Admiral by civil process in the High Court of Admiralty, the Earl Marshal in the Court of Chivalry, and other ministers and appointed officials in the Court of Requests, the Court of Wards and Liveries, and the Court of Receipt.[15] The most famous of the conciliar courts in this period was, of course, the Star Chamber, which was essentially a judicial sitting of the king's privy councillors in the *camera stellata* in the palace of Westminster (for Star Chamber meetings, the councillors were joined by the two chief justices of the King's Bench and Common Pleas). The Star Chamber developed an extraordinary and appeal jurisdiction, mostly in criminal suits, during the sixteenth century, and gave the government an ideal forum for developing remedies, and reaching summary prosecutions for libel, sedition, forgery, perjury, conspiracy, and other attempts or even intentions to commit crimes. While many of these courts – the High Commission and Star Chamber, in particular – would occasion popular grievances in the 1630s and so come to their final (and permanent) dissolution in the Interregnum, they were under the Tudors and early Stuarts an active and very visible part of the confusing array of legal sites, processes, and outcomes. Royal justice, then, as confusing and contested as it became under the Tudors, was only part of the puzzle, and Shakespeare's contemporaries increasingly felt the regulating hand of legal process governing their lives at even the most local, intimate levels: in matters from fornication to legitimacy, from market transactions to personal promises, from land tenure to purchase, from nuisances to felonies and family quarrels to treason, the courts and its officers conspicuously permeated early-modern English society.

The impact of legal business and thought peaked at the turn of the seventeenth century in England, too, for another reason. In 1616 two of the most able lawyers of their generation – Sir Edward Coke, Lord Chief Justice of the Common Pleas, and Sir Thomas Egerton, Baron Ellesmere and Lord Chancellor – collided over the longstanding ambiguity of the relation between the common-law courts in Westminster (the cradle of the English legal constitution as set out in Magna Carta) and the prerogative court of Chancery (because of its plenipotentiary status the symbol of an increasingly absolutist royal authority). In an ill-tempered exchange, fought over several years through antagonistic judgments and writs of prohibition, Coke and Ellesmere so much disgraced the courts that the king himself intervened in 1616, depriving Coke of his place. That the simmering confrontation between Ellesmere and Coke should have boiled over in 1616, the year of Shakespeare's death, brings us full circle to the moral of this long and unavoidably breathless overview of the Tudor legal crisis. The profound religious, social, economic, and political changes that swept England during the reigns of Henry VIII, Edward VI, Mary I, and Elizabeth I encouraged a period of legal and political development unparalleled for its vigour and creativity until the explosion of industrialization in the nineteenth century. Probably the most important element of this rapid legal development for the study and interpretation of Shakespeare's art lies in the ambiguity it created in the fundamental questions of right and wrong, redress and punishment that a legal system exists to address and administer. In both practical and intellectual terms, the law represented for the nobility and rising gentry of Shakespeare's generation one of the most dynamic and important fields of endeavour open to a creative and ambitious mind; like the atomic physics of the 1930s or the media and information technology of the 1990s, the common law of Plowden, Coke, Bacon, and Selden was the fashionable, dominant discourse of the day. As we will see, it brought John Shakespeare to civic authority, and to London; his son William, though he probably went to London to write and to act, could not help but be caught up in the Inns and in the courts. The forms of the law, its language, its students and officials, and its regulatory presence everywhere apparent in the actions of men and women had helped to transform London into the congested, dynamic metropolis it had, by Shakespeare's day, become; and, probably more so than any other institution or activity, the law and legal life provided the plasma in which that congested dynamism could quicken, and flourish.

SHAKESPEARE AT LAW

The long arm of Tudor legal expansion and innovation reached well into Warwickshire, where as a boy Shakespeare certainly witnessed the suits and actions, contracts, bargains, conveyances and mortgages, sureties, and writs prosecuted, sued, and supplied by his father, John Shakespeare – not to mention the not infrequent debts for which his father was himself sued. The standard biographies of Shakespeare's early life are united, as in little else, in their presentation of John Shakespeare's rapid rise to municipal authority in the Stratford-upon-Avon of the 1560s and 1570s, and his equally meteoric fall, through unknown and perhaps multiple pressures, in the 1580s.[16] The period of Shakespeare's early boyhood also coincided with his father's civic advancement and increasingly substantial authority in the town. In 1553, just over ten years before William was born, the borough of Stratford received its charter of incorporation from the crown; the corporation would thereafter be led by a bailiff and a council of fourteen burgesses and fourteen aldermen. Having served as an ale-taster in 1556, John Shakespeare was selected as a town constable in 1558; both of these were substantial posts of some authority – regulating the quality of Stratford's main commercial product was not a light duty, and constables held significant law-enforcement, and even judicial, responsibilities in the day-to-day administration of civic life.[17] In the following year, he was promoted to the office of affeeror in the Court Leet, where he would have been responsible for impartially assessing on his peers fines and amerciaments for civic or commercial defaults.[18] Within a few years, he was serving as a burgess of the corporation, then as chamberlain (keeper of the borough's accounts), and finally, in 1565, as an alderman. In 1567 he was nominated for bailiff; in 1568 he was elected. As bailiff, John Shakespeare presided in the borough's Court of Record and served his borough as a Justice of the Peace. As the more than three hundred folios of Michael Dalton's late-seventeenth-century treatise *The Countrey Justice* make clear, the office of a Justice of the Peace was a substantial one, and John Shakespeare could by statute expect to cope with matters from buggery and fornication to usury, the spawning of salmon to itinerant soldiers, the price of wool and beer,

Catholic recusancy, or even the maintenance of sewers.[19] While the period of his office lasted only a year (unusually for Stratford, where bailiffs often served consecutive or multiple terms), John Shakespeare served as deputy bailiff to Adrian Quiney, his successor, and rode with him on borough business to London in January 1571/2.[20]

The rapidity with which John Shakespeare acquired, and then lost, his fur-trimmed gown of office recalls the sartorial instability of *Pericles* or *King Lear*, where a dog was for a time obeyed in office; and as in *King Lear*, the fall of the magistrate probably impressed itself more indelibly on the gaze of his audience than even his rise. Although the records are silent, or merely suggestive, about the cause of the decline in John Shakespeare's civic fortunes, in one way, at least, he does not seem to have retired quietly. As a young glover on the make, John had specu-lated in land and property, and in wool. Legal documents recording some of these transactions survive, as do papers recording various suits for recovery of monies lent, both by and to John Shakespeare, and are regularly recorded in Shakespeare biographies. The incorporation of Stratford in 1553, with the creation of its civic offices, represents one important element of the expansion in the Tudor state administration: the Earl of Warwick, ancient lord presiding in Stratford's baronial court, ceded his local political authority to the crown's officers – grocers, mercers, and glovers like John Shakespeare, who answered to Elizabeth's privy council. The roads continued to lead to London when John Shakespeare and Adrian Quiney journeyed south on Stratford business in 1571/2, and it was to London, again, that John Shakespeare was called to answer a debt of £30 in the court of Common Pleas in 1573 and, three times, in 1578 (he stayed at home). In the meantime he successfully sued another glover of Banbury for £50, also in Common Pleas, but resisted the order of arbitrators who directed him to repay a £7 deposit to one William Burbage, for the rental of a Stratford house.[21] In what was probably a desperate bid to raise funds in November 1578 (when John was still being sued vigor-ously for a £30 debt in Common Pleas), John and Mary mortgaged a house and fifty-six acres of land in Wilmcote to Edmund Lambert for £40; unable to repay the debt at Michaelmas 1580, they lost the land, but brought a bill of complaint against Lambert's heir, John, in the

King's Bench in 1588, and a Chancery action in 1597 in an attempt to recover it.[22] At the same time as the original Lambert mortgage, the Shakespeares conveyed another eighty-six acres in Wilmcote to one of Mary's relatives for a term of years, and sold off other estates.[23] As John's eldest son William came of age, he must have watched, and probably studied with interest, his mother's and father's desperate attempts to stay solvent, retain their standing in Stratford, and hold on to their inherited and acquired estates.

Given his parents' troubles, it is not surprising to find that William Shakespeare was shrewder, and more successful, in his legal dealings. In 1602, for example, he acted swiftly to protect his purchase of New Place in Stratford, after his title became unsafe due to the murder of William Underhill, the property's vendor in 1597.[24] In his other acquisitions, dealings, and speculations, both in Stratford and London, Shakespeare seems to have acted with the same judicious and sure-handed confidence. The Shakespeare Birthplace Trust still holds many documents recording, for example, Shakespeare's suits against partners and neighbours for the recovery of loans and payments upon contracts,[25] his acquisition of lands and houses,[26] and his investment in a half-interest in a lease of tithes.[27]

Records survive of Shakespeare's testimony, in the Court of Requests in 1612, in a case brought by a disgruntled son-in-law, Stephen Belott, against his wife Mary's mean father, Christopher Mountjoy, after he failed over many years to provide the couple with their promised wedding portion; Shakespeare, who had lodged with the Mountjoy family during the time of the betrothal in 1604 and had played Pandar to the couple, was on several occasions slated to answer interrogatories before the officers of the Requests. Here, as in his bargains and investments, Shakespeare seems to have played the matter cannily, professing to only a vague recollection, and thus avoiding the recriminations that might result, from either side, should he have weighed partially.[28] His response to Arthur Mainwaring's and William Combe's attempts to enclose tithing land in Welcombe in 1614, too, reflects the same savvy disinterest: a knowledge of his own legal limitations, combined with a determination to safeguard his investment at the expense of the Stratford corporation.[29] In all of these

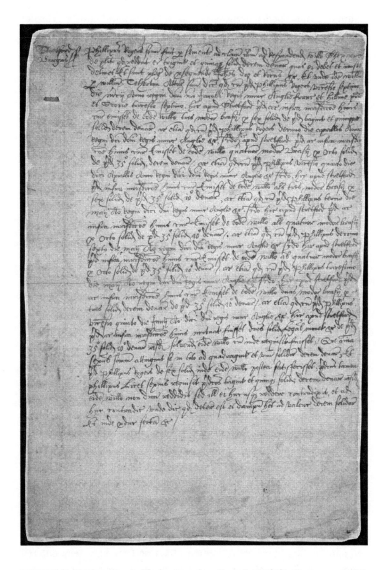

FIGURE 3 Declaration in Shakespeare's suit against Philip Rogers, c. 1604.
Shakespeare Birthplace Trust Records Office, MS ER 27/5. Shakespeare sued
Rogers, his Stratford neighbour, for a debt of thirty-five shillings and ten pence,
plus ten shillings damages, in the summer of 1604.

dealings, Shakespeare evinces the hard-headed and canny grasp of legal and financial process that secured his own interests – exactly the kind of determination that his sometimes feckless father had, even in positions of the highest civic authority, lacked. Shakespeare's associates in the quality, Cuthbert and Richard Burbage, escaped from an expiring lease on the grounds of The Theatre in December 1598 by arriving in the dead of night with a team of carpenters, dismantling the playhouse, and ferrying the pieces across the Thames to be reconstructed (as The Globe) – an action that, by a technicality, lay within their legal rights, but one that their landlord in Smithfield, Giles Allen, had not considered possible.[30] This was the kind of daring, resolute, legally informed business sense that made Shakespeare, by the end of the 1590s, a rich man. It is no surprise to find that Thomas Greene of the Middle Temple, who for years had acted as Town Clerk in Stratford, called Shakespeare his 'cousin'; or that, two years after Shakespeare's death, the trustees charged with overseeing his London house in Blackfriars conveyed it jointly to a Matthew Morris of Stratford and to John Greene of Clement's Inn – probably the brother of Thomas Greene. Shakespeare was well connected in legal circles, and knew the ropes.

The law reached into the lives of Shakespeare's acting company, too, in matters very different from his personal suits, or their commercial ventures. The printing of stage-plays, like the printing of other literary works in the period, required the Lord Chamberlain's men to negotiate a sometimes capricious licensing system – especially after the Star Chamber decree of 1586,[31] which put in place new provisions for pre-publication perusal of sensitive texts by the Bishops of Canterbury or London, or their delegates, and the Bishops' Ban of 1599,[32] which strictly curtailed the publication of literary satires. Shakespeare, either acting alone or in consultation with his company and printer, handled publication of his works very delicately: evidence exists that the company, acting in collaboration with their preferred printers, entered 'blocking entries' in the Stationers' Register as a way of preventing rivals from printing pirated copies of their own texts;[33] and Shakespeare and his associates seem to have selectively cut and rewritten the texts – as in the case of *Richard II*, where the possibly seditious 'deposition scene' (from 4. 1) was removed from all quartos of the play published during Elizabeth's reign – in order to avoid sanctions or other repercussions.[14] Ben Jonson and two fellow actors of Pembroke's Company were imprisoned for their parts in the collaborative, and now lost, play *The Isle of Dogs* in 1597, an incident that also provoked the Privy Council to close all the theatres around London; what particular offence they had given is not known, but the affair blew over without further trouble. Shakespeare's company must have recalled their experience when, in February 1601, they made a similar miscalculation in agreeing to perform *Richard II* two nights before the Earl of Essex's abortive attempt to seize Westminster; summoned for questioning before the Privy Council in the aftermath of the plot, the company protested its collective innocence, and seem not to have suffered for their involvement. Even so, such a brush with the highest tier of legal authority in the realm could hardly have failed to leave its stamp on Shakespeare, and must have influenced his representation of sedition and spectacle in works from *King Lear* to *The Tempest*.

Another kind of legal control with which Shakespeare must, like all his contemporaries, have been constantly conversant was that exercised by the church. The ascendant bishops of the second half of Elizabeth's reign, particularly under the primacy of Archbishop of Canterbury John Whitgift, began in the 1580s to enforce a strict conformity among ministers – even in the north of England, where in order to counter-balance a strong Catholic presence the Privy Council had for decades permitted nonconformist, practically presbyterian preachers and ministers considerable latitude. Conformity was exacted directly from the ministers by requiring them to subscribe to a series of articles, but also more broadly, by enforcing government of religious practice through requiring attendance at church and the publication of homilies, and by expanding and supporting the jurisdictions of the diocesan and consistory courts, which still claimed the right to adjudicate and punish in many matters of conscience. Shakespeare's father John had almost certainly fallen foul of the laws against Catholic recusants – certainly he was cited for not attending church – and Shakespeare's daughter Judith later suffered for a very public accusation of fornication. To cite such biographical details is not to say that

Shakespeare's representations of betrayal or fornication (as in, say, *Measure for Measure*) necessarily owe something to his family's own experiences, but rather that we cannot understand the significance of such episodes in the plays without understanding, as the record of Shakespeare's experience indicates he most certainly did, the legal character of these offences, with their punishments and remedies.

Shakespeare's biography has been belaboured to many purposes, many of them specious. This brief account intends merely to recognize that, like every man of even modest means in early-modern England, Shakespeare lived a life of constant engagement with the language, the limitations, the forms, and the penalties of the law. His own life record shows that he experienced legal setbacks and had personal familiarity with various kinds of legal predicament at almost every level, and in many capacities: as judge, as plaintiff, as witness, and as defendant in cases ranging from debt to contract, to land conveyancing, to sedition and treason, to recusancy and fornication. He played his part in civil suits, and watched friends tried for manslaughter, and at least one associate for parricide. Like all early-modern English subjects – and especially actors in London – he dressed with one eye on the sumptuary laws; he spoke and wrote with one eye on the Master of the Revels, the High Commission, and the Star Chamber; and he governed his personal and business affairs with the scrupulous care that would protect them from risk and predation. No Elizabethan man of means could afford to live without an attorney (Shakespeare's was a man called Thomas Lucas); but this dramatist, canny as he was, seems to have benefited from the counsel and experience of a wide network of associates in the Inns of Court and Chancery. It is highly significant that, during the dispute over tithing lands at Welcombe in 1614, Thomas Greene – a lawyer of the Middle Temple – coming to London called on his 'cousin' Shakespeare not to reassure him on the legal points of the contest, but to get *his* advice. Shakespeare was not unusual in living a life of suits, counter-suits, agreements and bargains, enrolled births and deaths and marriages and baptisms; rather, this brief account of his life reflects the very average, intensely legal experience that many people of his age had. But if it was an ineluctable mode of early-modern civil life, it was one in which William Shakespeare excelled.

LEGAL CULTURE IN ELIZABETHAN LONDON: FROM THE INN TO THE PLAYHOUSE

When Shakespeare arrived in London, probably in the mid-1580s, he moved from a world where civic administration and the law reached into his everyday family affairs, to a world where legal culture dominated the intellectual and artistic conditions of his new profession. The links between the legal and theatrical cultures of London from the 1580s straight through to the closing of the theatres in 1642 were rooted in classical rhetoric and in legal humanism; in an enduring strain of Stoicism that joined a Morean philosophical and literary legacy to a new interest in Senecan drama; in an oppositional political culture that stressed resistance to absolutism with its increasingly centralized executive council; and in the basic proximity of the Inns to the liberty of Blackfriars and, by water-skiff, to the theatres of Bankside. The domestic theatrical traditions in the four Inns of Court were legendary even in Shakespeare's day; but the Inns also provided a home to many of Shakespeare's fellow dramatists, and to lyric (even Ovidian) poets who worked, like Shakespeare, in Marlowe's wake. And it was from the Inns that students poured across the river to patronize the brothels, bear-pits, and theatres located outside the remit of the precisian City aldermen. While some of these connections between the legal and theatrical cultures of London in this period will resurface and come under closer scrutiny in later chapters – and indeed, these connections form the frame and skeleton sustaining the broader argument of this book at large – it will be useful to lay some foundations first.

The pedagogical revolution at the heart of what we now call renaissance humanism insisted upon the primacy of rhetorical education.[35] Where Aristotle and formal logic had reigned supreme at the apex of the trivium in the medieval schools, humanist challengers from Lorenzo Valla and Rudolph Agricola to Petrus Ramus offered a new emphasis on the 'likely' argument, the study of grammar and etymology, and the practice of persuasion as an art rather than a science. Conservative logicians denounced these innovations as mere

FIGURE 4   Detail from the Braun and Hogenberg map of 1572, City of London. City of London, London Metropolitan Archives. The Inns of Court were a short trip across the Thames from the bear-pits and theatres in Southwark.

rhetoric – as early as Valla's *Elegantiae* the new humanistic logic was tending towards language-based textual exegesis rather than formal syllogistical study (Valla was famous for exposing the *Donation of Constantine* as a fraud, on stylistic grounds); but in the incredibly pervasive circulation of Agricola's rhetorically minded treatise on logic, the *De inventione dialectica* (1515), and of Petrus Ramus's works on logic, the humanist educators and young scholars of the sixteenth century found themselves awash in a new learning that stressed *ad hoc* argument, persuasion, and a rhetorically pointed use of language. Moreover, the effects of this revolution in school pedagogy and, to a lesser or at least more indirect extent, university teaching, were felt most, and particularly, strongly in England during Elizabeth's long reign, for several reasons. The print circulation of Agricola's *De inventione dialectica*, which exploded across Europe from the 1530s, was in full bloom in the late 1550s and 1560s, and received added impetus by its philosophical affinity with a sceptical attitude characteristic of two other works – Cicero's *Academica Priora* and the *Hypotyposes* (*Outlines of Pyrrhonism*) of Sextus Empiricus – that enjoyed a sudden vogue in the 1560s.[36] But perhaps most importantly, Petrus Ramus, Protestant professor of logic in Paris through the middle of the sixteenth century, was martyred in the St Bartholomew's Day Massacre of 1572, while Philip Sidney took refuge with Walsingham in the English embassy nearby; Ramus's popular works on logic, which essentially disseminated in a neat and digestible form the new learning of Valla and Agricola, became radicalized and popular in England as much for their anti-Catholic pedigree as their rhetorical innovation.[37]

The ascendancy of rhetorical teaching, and a rhetorical methodology in argument, during the sixteenth century naturally displaced the primacy of Aristotle's scientific authority in favour of the rhetorical and stylistic authority of Cicero, and of that great synthesis of Ciceronian rhetorical principles, Quintilian's rhetorical handbook, the *Institutio Oratoria* (Institutes of Oratory). Desiderius Erasmus, for example, in his celebrated if breathless account of humanist teaching, the *De ratione studii* (*On the Method of Study*, 1511), combines repeated acknowledgments of the authority of Quintilian with exhortations to study and imitate Cicero, and with emphatic assertions about the centrality of linguistic and rhetorical study to the intellectual enterprise:

> In principle, knowledge as a whole seems to be of two kinds, of things and of words. Knowledge of words comes earlier, but that of things is the more important. But some, the 'uninitiated' as the saying goes, while they hurry on to learn about things, neglect a concern for language and, striving after a false economy, incur a very heavy loss. For since things are learnt only by the sounds we attach to them, a person who is not skilled in the force of language is, of necessity, short-sighted, deluded, and unbalanced in his judgment of things as well.[38]

The humanist educators, like Erasmus, who championed the shift in the school and university curricula to a more rhetorical, linguistic approach to logic and persuasion, made no secret of the fact that this shift was largely motivated by practical considerations: endless quibbling over abstruse theoretical minutiae would prove of no consequence to the public weal, while careful training in the arts of expression and persuasion would equip a young man to communicate with his peers, to offer advice to princes, to govern the people himself. In this respect, it is no accident that the classical author of the treatises and models on which humanist educators most relied, Cicero, was a lawyer, for the imagined forum where the young scholar would prove his mettle was, first and foremost, the court of law. When another humanist educator, and Middle Temple lawyer, Sir Thomas Elyot, undertook to naturalize Erasmus in English, he imagined his young scholar to be a future magistrate, and entitled his 1531 work *The Boke Named the Gouernour.*

But the aptness of the humanist emphasis on rhetoric to the particular traditions of legal education and practice in England in the sixteenth century is most strikingly evident in the work of another Protestant lawyer and Marian exile, Thomas Wilson. Wilson's 1553 treatise, *The Arte of Rhetorique,* would soon become a standard reference work for Elizabethan poets and theologians, among others, but it was always (and very explicitly) intended for Wilson's colleagues and charges studying the law, and pleading, at the universities and in the Inns of Court. Many of the elaborate examples that Wilson uses to demonstrate his lessons and precepts are taken from, or relate to, the experiences of lawyers in the English common-law tradition; while the three books of lessons and precepts themselves are taken directly from Quintilian (Books 1 and 2) and Cicero (Book 3). Wilson writes of eloquence in his 1553 dedication to John Dudley, Earl of Warwick, that 'no man ought to be without it, which either shall beare rule ouer many, or must haue to doe with matters of a Realme';[39] here we see the now familiar situation of rhetorical education in the intellectual milieu of the Inns, a situating confirmed by Gabriel Harvey, who commented of Wilson's *Arte of Rhetorique,* in a marginal note inserted in his copy of Quintilian's *Intitutio Oratoria* sometime in the 1570s, 'Wilson's Rhetorique and Logique, the dailie bread of owr common pleaders, & discoursers'.[40] But in the 'prologue to the Reader' added in the 1560 edition, Wilson goes a step further by recounting the story of his imprisonment, torture, and slightly miraculous delivery (by a frenzied crowd) from imprisonment by the Inquisition in Rome five years earlier, a spate of extreme bad fortune that Wilson assigns wholly to the explicitly Protestant and humanist project of his 1553 *Arte of Rhetorique*. By linking the project of the book, in his two prefaces of 1553 and 1560, both to the use of eloquence in legal and political affairs, and to the intellectual and political culture distinctive to the reformed courts of northern Europe, Wilson pulls off the same ideological alignment of legal humanism and rhetoric with Elizabethan Protestant nationalism that would, in the following decade, help to popularize the works of Petrus Ramus.

The profound changes to the grammar-school curriculum, and to the larger methodology of pedagogy – introduced into England first by John Colet, and afterward by Sir John Cheke, Roger Ascham, Wilson, and the likes of Richard Mulcaster, founding master of the Merchant Taylors' School in London in the 1560s – had been well entrenched by the time Shakespeare and his contemporaries picked up their first primers. These changes pushed education away from logic, and firmly away from the medieval quadrivium, towards a set of rhetorical, linguistic, imitative, and hermeneutical practices that prepared young scholars for civic office, and particularly for the sustained use of eloquence in legal pleading, in the delivery of orations and the writing of letters, and in the preparation of treatises, position papers, and tracts. Schoolboys imitated Cicero's and Demosthenes' disputations and orations, studied their arguments, and translated them back and forth from Latin and (for the more ambitious masters) Greek. A precocious student like Edmund Spenser, who enrolled in the Merchant Taylors' School under Mulcaster at about the time Shakespeare was born, naturally ended up serving as a secretary to the Queen's vice-regent in Ireland, and writing not only poetry, but a long suasory dialogue attempting to influence Elizabethan government policy in the pacification of Ireland. Masters like Mulcaster pushed their students, through an education in the rhetorical arts basic to legal humanism, towards careers and intellectual/writing preoccupations centred on law and government.

Mulcaster was also, famously, keen on acting: his boys performed plays at court on at least five occasions. The emphasis on playing in the humanist curriculum would have profound and direct consequences for the history of the English stage at about the time that Shakespeare came to write *Hamlet*, when the war of the theatres would drive innovations in genre, staging, and character, and put troupes of boys onto the stage at Blackfriars; but the use of drama in the humanist education and rhetorical training of grammar-school boys also testifies to another important and persistent element of the particularly English humanism of the sixteenth century, again linked to the lawyers of London and the Inns of Court: Stoicism. Perhaps the most famous link in English letters between Stoic moral philosophy, with its implicit politics of irony and dissimulation, and the traditions of acting in the Inns of Court appears in the first book of Sir Thomas More's *Utopia* (1516; translated 1557). The character 'More' debates with the learned traveller Hythloday throughout Book One of *Utopia* whether or not Hythloday ought to put himself into the service of some prince as a counsellor; 'More' insists, with true humanist piety, that a man of such learning and experience as Hythloday has a moral obligation to put his skills to civic use. Hythloday demurs; he is adamant that a court would find him at best irrelevant, and at worst offensive and seditious, because he is unable to speak anything but the truth, and all courts (as 'More' well knows) are corrupt. Philosophy, Hythloday argues (in open and explicit defiance of Plato's ideal in *The Republic*), has no place among kings. '"Indeed"' answers More, '"this school philosophy hath not, which thinketh all things meet for every place"':

> But ther is an other philosophye more cyuyle, whych knoweth as ye wolde saye her owne stage, and thereafter orderynge and behauynge herselfe in the playe that she hathe in hande, playethe her parte accordynglye wyth comlynes, vtterynge nothynge owte of dewe ordre and fassyon. And thys ys the phylosophye that yowe muste vse. Orels whyles a commodye of Plautus is playinge, and the vyle bondemen skoffynge and tryffelynge amonge them selfes, yf yowe shoulde sodenlye come vpon the stage in a philosophers apparrell, and reherse owte of Octauia the place wherin Seneca dysputeth with Nero: had it not bene better for yowe to haue played the domme persone, then by rehersynge that, which serued nother for the tyme nor place to haue made suche a tragycall comedye or gallymalfreye?[41]

In a bold adaptation of a dictum from Epictetus,[42] More imagines political life as a play, and the problem of humanist rhetorical and political
life – what the rhetoric books called *decorum* and the courtesy books
'discretion' – as an ability to judge genre. More, the friend of Erasmus
and biographer of Pico della Mirandola, the common lawyer from
Lincoln's Inn who, the son of a judge of King's Bench, would rise to be
invested as Henry VIII's Lord Chancellor upon the fall of Cardinal
Wolsey, the brother-in-law of the legal printer and interlude author John
Rastell, a man who would arrange for plays to be performed in his own
household at Chelsea, in which he himself often acted – this man
proposes in eloquent Ciceronian Latin, at the culminatory point of one
of the most influential European literary dialogues of the sixteenth
century, a lesson that a humanist should never forget: performing your
civic duty is like acting. For all that More was here echoing a traditional
Stoic commonplace, and probably passing on the wisdom he had
learned as a boy from another lover of plays, Archbishop and Lord
Chancellor John Morton, the influence of this passage on the resurgent
rhetorical, theatrical, and deeply politicized Stoicism of the 1590s – and
particularly on Shakespeare, Donne, and Jonson – can probably not be
overemphasized. More's *Utopia*, with its elegant, witty, and powerful
joining of theatrical representation to political life, similarly inaugurates
a peculiarly English tradition of association between the Inns of Court,
an ambivalent Stoic political engagement, and the theatre.

The Stoic emphasis on a theatrical conception of the performed self
took such sure purchase in sixteenth-century England in large part
because of the way it accorded naturally with the rhetorical concept of
decorum. This central principle of classical rhetoric, the subject of the
first half of the eleventh book of Quintilian's *Institutio Oratoria*, was
considered by the Renaissance to be the germ and kernel of all rhetorical learning, and the very principle that bound together the cultivation
of letters with the achievement of civility. The opening of Quintilian's
exposition of *decorum*, which he presents in pristine Ciceronian terms,
makes its indispensability clear:

For what profit is it that our words should be Latin, significant and
graceful, and be further embellished with elaborate figures and

rhythms, unless all these qualities are in harmony with the views to which we seek to lead the judge and mould his opinions? What use is it if we employ a lofty tone in cases of trivial import, a slight and refined style in cases of great moment, a cheerful tone when our matter calls for sadness, a gentle tone when it demands vehemence, threatening language when supplication, and submissive when energy is required, or fierceness and violence when our theme is one that asks for charm? Such incongruities are as unbecoming as it is for men to wear necklaces and pearls and flowing raiment which are the natural adornments of women, or for women to robe themselves in the garb of triumph, than which there can be conceived no more majestic raiment.[43]

Quintilian's treatment of *decorum*, which as he says 'really covers the whole subject' of rhetoric, establishes this principle of 'fittingness' as the basis of the persuasive style, that one accomplishment which, above all others, the successful lawyer could not do without. Further, in reformulating the same point, he links this rhetorical principle to the basis of moral life, saying that 'no one can be said to speak appropriately who has not considered not merely what it is expedient, but also what it is becoming [*quod deceat*] to say'. In this emphasis on speaking appropriately as a kind of duty, Quintilian suggests the connection between rhetoric and moral and political philosophy that so dominated Renaissance thinking about rhetoric: the true orator would always be a 'good man skilled in speaking' [*vir bonus peritus dicendi*] because mastery of the principles of rhetoric – and particularly this special principle of *decorum*, or fittingness – meant mastery of the moral principles, and particularly of justice. Knowing what was fitting to say could only be learned alongside knowing what was fitting to do: knowing how to speak to a given person meant knowing how to judge that person's worth, and how to treat that person justly. As a direct result of the recovery of complete manuscripts of Quintilian in the fifteenth century, humanists became infatuated with this connection between rhetorical accomplishment and moral-political perfection of the self. Crucially, the means to attaining both lay in the kind of theatricality that, as we have seen, was basic to rhetorical training. In

England, these connections between *decorum*, justice, the self, and theatricality were further intensified for writers and readers of poetry after George Puttenham, in his 1589 *The Arte of English Poesie* – apparently a bestseller – followed Quintilian in making *decorum*, in both its rhetorical and social forms, the final and culminatory goal of his aspiring poet.[44] Shakespeare would later make Puttenham's final three chapters from *The Arte of English Poesie* the basis of his analysis of artificiality, sincerity, and power in the contest between Brutus and Mark Antony in *Julius Caesar*; of course, Shakespeare stages this rhetorical contest in the forum – the cradle of Roman law and government.

Thomas More's most obvious and engaged successor in the Elizabethan period was his collateral descendant John Donne; Donne, like More, was of Lincoln's Inn, where he developed a coterie readership that consumed his literary formulations of perennial hermeneutical, ethical, political, and religious problems. Donne, like Shakespeare, often resorted to legal language for metaphor, and to make more sustained political points, and complaints, in a lyric voice that wore its oppositional attitude on its sleeve.[45] But though Donne's poetry, for his manuscript legacy and the reading practices that it discloses, sheds light on the links between the lawyers and the poets of London in this period, he was hardly the only literary man in the Inns. In fact, they were practically stuffed with poets and dramatists. Jasper Heywood, Donne's maternal uncle, translated and published three Senecan tragedies – *Troas* (1559), *Thyestes* (1560), and *Hercules Furens* (1561) – while at All Soul's, Oxford, translations that would prove important to Shakespeare's early career. Heywood's Catholicism forced him to flee to Gray's Inn in the early 1560s, there to join his uncle William Rastell, the legal printer and editor of More's complete works. From Gray's Inn he penned the famous preface to his translation of *Thyestes*, which recounts the great contribution of the common lawyers to the Elizabethan literary renaissance, and particularly to the writing of plays. Speaking to the ghost of Seneca, Heywood praises his legal fellows:

> In Lyncolnes Inne and Temples twayne,
> Grayes Inne and other mo,

> Thou shalt them fynde whose paynfull pen
> thy verse shall florishe so,
> That Melpomen thou wouldst well weene
> had taught them for to wright,
> And all their woorks with stately style,
> and goodly grace t' endight.[46]

He praises by name Sir Thomas North of Lincoln's Inn, who had translated Antonio de Guevara's *The Diall of Princes* in 1557, and would go on to produce an English edition of Plutarch's *Lives of the Noble Grecians and Romans* (via Amyot's French translation) in 1579, a translation that, probably via the hands of the Stratfordian printer Richard Field, would exert an important influence on Shakespeare's Roman plays; Thomas Sackville (later Baron Buckhurst) of the Inner Temple, who with Thomas Norton wrote the first great Elizabethan tragedy, *Gorboduc* (influenced by Seneca, and a source for Shakespeare's *King Lear*), and contributed to the 1563 *Mirror for Magistrates*; and Barnaby Googe, a kinsmen of William Cecil (later Lord Burghley) and once of Staple Inn, who in 1560 published a translation of the first three books of Marcellus Palingenius's *Zodiacus Vitae* (*The Zodyake of Lyfe*; he completed all twelve books for the 1565 edition). Heywood also names Sir Christopher Yelverton of Gray's Inn (who wrote the epilogue to George Gascoigne's *Jocasta*), William Bavande of the Middle Temple (the 1559 translator of Joannes Ferrarius Montanus's *De republica bene instituenda*), Thomas Blundeville of Gray's Inn (translator of Plutarch's *Moralia*), and Thomas Norton of the Inner Temple, Sackville's collaborator on *Gorboduc*. He concludes his catalogue suggestively:

> And yet great nombre more, whose names
> yf I woulde now resight,
> A ten tymes greater woorke then thine,
> I should be forste to wright.[47]

While the Inns of Court and Chancery had presided, with the writing and production of *Gorboduc* and Gascoigne's *Jocasta*, over the rebirth of tragic theatre in England in the 1560s, they would go on to accommodate and nurture far greater dramaturgical spirits in the coming decades. Francis Beaumont, the dramatist, was the grandson of John Beaumont, Bencher of the Inner Temple and Master of the Rolls; his uncle Henry was likewise a bencher of the Inner Temple, as was his father Francis, who was appointed Serjeant in 1589 and a Justice of the Common Pleas in 1593. In 1600 Francis (the dramatist) followed his two older brothers into the Inner Temple; and though it seems he may never have contemplated a legal career, he composed theatrical entertainments repeatedly for the Inner Temple and Gray's Inn revels, in addition to his more popular (and now better-known) work as a popular playwright, both independently and with his long-standing collaborator, John Fletcher. The dramatist John Ford was son to a Justice of the Peace, and through his mother grand-nephew to Sir John Popham, Lord Chief Justice of the King's Bench (he of *Slade's Case* fame). In November 1602 Ford was admitted alongside his cousin Thomas to the Middle Temple, where Popham served as Treasurer, presumably under Popham's charge. Ford seems never to have studied the law seriously, but that he benefited from his association with the Middle Temple is obvious: his fellow Templar (and kinsman) Sir John Stradling, translator of the works of the Dutch Stoic philosopher and political theorist Justus Lipsius, must have influenced Ford in his persistent and pervasive interest in Stoic philosophy and Lipsian politics, obvious in *The Golden Meane* (1613) and *A Line of Life* (1620), and only slightly less palpable in his tragedies. Ford continued to be styled on the title pages of his works as 'of the Middle Temple', suggesting that he continued there in residence. Also resident in the Middle Temple in this period was John Marston, who took rooms, probably with his father, by about 1595, after having been admitted in 1592; Marston certainly drafted his *Satyres* and *The Scourge of Villainie* while in the Middle Temple, and probably wrote his plays while in residence. Although not a prolific playwright – two plays (*The Wounds of Civil War* and, with Robert Greene, *A Looking Glass for London and England*) were first printed in 1594 – Thomas Lodge of Lincoln's Inn drafted in 1579 the first published reply to Stephen Gosson's anti-theatrical polemic, *The Schoole of Abuse*, defending English plays and poetry against a precise and fastidious Calvinism; later defences, including Sir Philip

Sidney's *An Apology for Poetry* (*The Defence of Poesy*), would draw on Lodge's initial riposte. Lodge was also an accomplished Ovidian poet, the author of the 1589 *Scillaes Metamorphosis*, in six-line stanzas later used by Shakespeare for *Venus and Adonis*; and a romance-writer: among other his borrowings from Lodge, Shakespeare made good use of *Rosalynde* (1590) in *As You Like It*. Judging from the evidence of dedications and title pages to Lodge's literary works in this period, he seems to have continued in residence at Lincoln's Inn until at least 1595. Some of Shakespeare's personal and professional, literary and philosophical (and possibly religious) links with many of these men are well-documented; other points of contact that may strengthen Shakespeare's association with the Inns of Court – such as the circulation of Ovidian verse in the Inns, or the prevalence of Stoic moral philosophy and a Lipsian political theory – have been less well characterized. But beyond the shared literary ambitions and the possible sympathy in ideological and intellectual orientations, Shakespeare could not have helped noticing that many of the best of his fellow dramatists and poets in London in the 1590s were tied to, or resident in, the Inns of Court, steeped in the learning, culture, language, and theatrical traditions of common lawyers.

With the Morean legacy behind them, and the associated tradition of the Rastells, and of the comic playwright and epigrammatist John Heywood, the Inns of Court enjoyed a strong theatrical tradition in their custom of holiday revels. From St Stephen's Day well into January, every year, any one of the Inns of Court or Chancery might be transformed into an encompassing stage on which the younger members of the inn could enact elaborate fictions of mock-government, and often of mock-law. Here the normal pedagogical functions of the Inn were temporarily suspended, and a Master of the Revels anointed to lead his fellows in a series of pageants and plays, some contained within the Inn, others pouring onto the streets of the City without. Attendance at the revels was obligatory, and even senior members of the Inn could be mulcted for non-attendance. These extended performances might take in banquets, embassies, declamations, and inset performances of plays and masques written for the occasion, and involve, at their heights, hundreds of participants, including on occasion distinguished guests from the Privy Council, or from other Inns. Naturally, given the environment in which such productions were devised and mounted, the matter on which they turned tended towards the intellectual, and very frequently towards the topically political. Satire and burlesque were common generic elements, and the revels, like low comedies, often parodied and deconstructed the intensively codified world in which the young students of the Inns mainly lived and worked. While our record of the origins of these entertainments is far from complete – most of the ancient historical documentation of the Inns having perished – it seems that, by the time records begin in about 1500, the annual appointment of a Master of the Revels in the Middle and Inner Temples was already customary. These holiday entertainments – which hit a peak in Elizabeth's later years, particularly with the lavish *Gesta Grayorum* of 1594[48] – would continue, sometimes sporadically and with years of greater and lesser investment, for almost a century and a half.

The extraordinarily elaborate Christmas revels at Gray's Inn in 1594 represent an example of the extents to which a revelling custom might be driven by determined students with a considerable budget; but that such a series of entertainments was possible, even thinkable, is testament to the strong tradition of theatrical, poetical, and musical activity at the Inns in the late medieval and early moderrn periods. In 1594 Gray's Inn finished off their revels with a masque, but they had already marked the season with a play: Shakespeare's *The Comedy of Errors*, performed by Shakespeare's company.[49] In 1602 the Middle Temple completed their celebrations, too, with a play: *Twelfth Night*, again performed in the hall of the Inn by Shakespeare's own company.[50] The tradition of hiring in entertainment was as old as the student-led revels, and here the Inns anticipated the practice of the royal court, which also, under James, bought in players and their plays for the holiday festivities. The major part that theatrical performance played in the festive life of the Inns – and, some have argued, in their properly educational function[51] – is crucial to understanding how the traditions of rhetorical training and mooting interacted with 'professional' drama to generate political performance of both 'theatrical' and 'courtly' kinds. The Inns were a natural place for poets and playwrights to reside, to write, and to perform because traditions of rhetoric and theatricality were basic both to the educational function of the Inns, and to their festive sporting. Law students and benchers alike were practisers of a theatrical craft, but they were also consumers of a theatrical commodity.

Audiences turning out to a performance of the Lord Chamberlain's Men in the 1590s, or the King's Men in the early years of James's reign, must have comprised men and women from many walks of life; but the energetic patronage of students and lawyers from the Inns of Court has never been in doubt, and indeed the genres, the choice of subjects and particular sources, and the language and conceptual concerns of Shakespeare's plays seem calculated, as we shall see again and again in later chapters, to appeal to an audience made up of the fashionable young lawyers of Donne's *Satires*. It is tempting to think that here, in these learned societies steeped in the legal humanism and classical rhetoric so closely tied to the craft of English poetry in this period, Shakespeare discovered an intellectual, ideological, and aesthetic sympathy to support his intense creativity. It is tempting to think that, in writing for this community, Shakespeare had the opportunity to please himself. It is one of the projects of subsequent chapters to test the likelihood of this possibility; but it is at least certain that the Inns preserved a legal and pedagogical tradition particularly suited to the new humanist learning, and it was here – rather than at Oxford or Cambridge – that this new learning most grippingly took root in sixteenth-century England. The legacy of More, Rastell, and Heywood lived on in London, at England's third university, and the men who came there to study focused on the hermeneutical, rhetorical, argument-based, and theatrical issues basic both to poetry and to the legal profession. They actively participated in dramatic production and in the patronage of dramatists, and in demographic terms they mirrored the class of players and other literary men arriving in London late in Elizabeth's reign to make good, and make history. Shakespeare's many associations with legal men, with legal traditions in rhetoric and education, with legal audiences, with legal practice on many levels, and with legal entertainments, made the Inns a central part of his experience of London theatrical life.

Chapter Three

THE LOVE OF PERSONS: COMMON LAW AND THE EPISTEMOLOGY OF CONSCIENCE IN THE *SONNETS* AND *A LOVER'S COMPLAINT*

The extent of a landowner's reach into the future was one of the more difficult legal questions of the Tudor period.

> Sir John Baker, *The Oxford History of the Laws of England*, vol. VI: 1483–1558, p. 692

In one of his most obscure and psychologically complex sonnets, number 61, Shakespeare writes of the lover's groggy mental groping through his rights and duties:

> Is it thy wil, thy Image should keepe open
> My heauy eielids to the weary night?
> Dost thou desire my slumbers should be broken,
> While shadowes like to thee do mocke my sight?
> Is it thy spirit that thou send'st from thee
> So farre from home into my deeds to prye,
> To find out shames and idle houres in me,
> The skope and tenure of thy Ielousie?
> O no, thy loue though much, is not so great,
> It is my loue that keepes mine eie awake,

> Mine owne true loue that doth my rest defeat,
> To plaie the watch-man euer for thy sake.
> For thee watch I, whilst thou dost wake elsewhere,
> From me farre of, with others all to neere.[1]

As a whole, the sonnet follows a pattern familiar from some others, in which the lover attributes some virtuous responsiveness to the beloved, but then acknowledges the imputation for a fantasy, recognizing that all virtue and care begins and ends in himself. In this sonnet the possibility of that slippage, or mistaking, between lover and beloved becomes the crux of the meditation: To what degree does a lover's love bind the beloved? To what degree can the lover's love be thought, be said, to be shared by the beloved too? In the half-light of a late-night meditation, the answers to these questions are not simple. The lover makes three demands of the beloved, asking whether the beloved's will, desire, and spirit are conspiring to bind him to his insomnia – to all three of which questions the final quatrain answers, emphatically, no; the lover has brought this on himself. But if the answer to the wishful questions is an emphatic negative, the poem nonetheless remains ambiguous. Shakespeare uses syntactical and rhetorical tricks to create what seem at first to be *tromp l'oeil* effects, to which the meditative-analytical reader of the *Sonnets* in part succumbs. For example, the poem begins, 'Is it thy wil, thy Image should keepe open / My heauy eielids to the weary night?' The first line creates two interpretive false starts for the reader, the first in the collision of 'thy wil, thy Image', which seems almost to create an identification relation between the two, as if 'thy Image' were an appositive redescription of 'thy wil'. By the end of the line, the sense of exhausted fumbling which characterizes the psychology of the sonnet has knit will and image into a different relation: the beloved's image, the lover speculates, may be keeping 'open' the beloved's will. By reading over the line break, the reader comes to see that this second reading, in turn, must be discarded, and that everything after the first four words of the first line ought to be subordinated to 'wil', as part of a dependent clause. Having assumed that the dyad of will and image could not be sundered, in a moment of astonishing subtlety the reader is forced by the syntax – restrospectively – to put them in altogether different dimensions – dimensions as different as those of a living observer, and of the imaged portraiture he watches.

The play of consciousness in the opening two lines of the poem problematizes the immediacy of the relationship between lover and beloved – 'is it thy wil' in 'thy Image' present here with me, or is this only a rhetorical question with an inevitable answer? The rhetorical plays of the sonnet, too, participate in this shadowy blending and seepage between lover and beloved. A common form of hypallage, the transferred epithet, appears at least twice in the poem, in 'weary night' and 'idle hours'. The night is not weary, but the eyes that watch it; the hours are not idle, but the man who wastes them. Transferred epithet is a common strategy in Elizabethan poetic language, often almost a reflex, and its use is rife in Shakespeare as in other contemporary poets;[2] but its precise use in this poem, by attributing qualities of weariness and idleness to the wrong subjects, helps to create the psychology of the pervasive consciousness whose meditations on will, desire, and spirit refuse to localize them. Transferred epithet is rhetorically native to a poem that sees will, desire, and spirit operating over distance ('so far from home', 'from thee far off', 'elsewhere'), and that ultimately loads the preposition 'for' (in line 13) with an equivocal, but possibly massive, weight. This permeable relation between nouns and their attributives helps, in turn, to set the stage for the most important ambiguity of the poem, the punning relationship in lines 10 and 11 inherent in 'my love' and 'mine own true love', both of which noun phrases might mean 'my (true) love for you' or, more simply, 'you'. In this final quatrain, the poem should be turning away from the fantasies of care and action-at-a-distance supposed in the opening octet ('O no . . .'); but the amphibolous quality of 'mine own true love' – a phrase that in any other context would be read as an epithet for the beloved – makes it clear that this rejection of fantasies is itself a fantasy. If the lover acts for the beloved's 'sake', it is not ridiculous to equate the poem's animating 'Will' with the beloved's 'will'.

One of the most interesting things about this sonnet is the way it flirts sleepily with legal language. Although the law of estates might not at first seem a likely bedfellow for the picture-gazing insomniac, a reader might have expected its invocation, for the poem concerns exactly the arbitration between 'mines and thines', or *meum et tuum*, that the law of property was developed to regulate. In the second quatrain of the poem this legal language comes to dominate, as it sets up the possession of the lover's self as a property the title to which is under contest:

> Is it thy spirit that thou send'st from thee
> So far from home into my deeds to pry,
> To find out shames and idle hours in me,
> The scope and tenure of thy jealousy?
>
> (ll. 4–8)

The poem imagines the beloved's spirit as the commissioned agent of an inquest, a judge or officer dispatched to determine the extent and nature of the claim 'jealousy' can make on the lover's estate. The monarch could create and authorize commissions to inquire into titles, the extent of estates, and their condition, as in the case of a 1581 act 'for the fortifying of the borders towards Scotland', by means of which Elizabeth's council sought to take a kind of census of reliable English estates in the counties of Northumberland, Cumberland, Westmoreland, and the County Palatine of Durham.[3] A more common kind of inquest, though, was that discharged by a county escheator (or, aphetically, 'cheater' as in Sonnet 151), who was empowered to inquire into the estates and tenures of anyone who had for any reason – e.g. by dying without heir, or by the commission of some substantial crime – forfeited their possessions to the crown.[4] Just like a 'cheater', here the beloved's spirit 'pries' into 'deeds' – or researches the evidence of actions here imagined, by a pun, as legal records – in order to determine the 'scope' (extent, room, application, especially in legal usage) and 'tenure' of the jealousy that has animated it, and which it serves. The evidence – 'deeds' – of jealousy's property in the lover's estate turns out, ironically, to be the 'shames and idle hours' of the lover's nightly gazing at the beloved's image, each one of which gives the beloved's jealousy title to the lover. This legal metaphor is taken further in the next quatrain, where the lover seems to argue that it is his 'own love' that does 'defeat' – or legally quash the title of – his rest. This is a carefully chosen word, for 'defeat' comes originally (through French) from the Latin *factum*; *facta* is the Latin term for the legal documents normally called 'deeds' in English.[5] To 'defeat' is literally, therefore, to 'undeed' rest.

The importance of this legal metaphor to the thought of the sonnet becomes clear in the final quatrain and couplet. Resuming the first two quatrains, the lover attributes to 'my love' the wakefulness, and to 'mine own true love' the 'defeat' of his rest, the 'keeping awake' and the 'defeating of rest' both leading him 'to play the watchman ever for thy sake'. 'To play the watchman' is literally 'to look' – here, at the 'image' of the opening poem – but because of the central quatrain this looking also gives the beloved title, and thus 'to play the watchman' also means 'to supervise, to maintain someone else's estate on their behalf'.[6] It is the metaphor of tenure that makes sense of this paradox of simultaneous self-possession and self-dispossession. The tenant 'keeps' an estate and uses it for himself, but the estate is held in the name or for the 'sake' of another, whose right and title both overlie and supersede the tenant's possession. As a caretaker, the 'watchman' of this sonnet creates a binding legal constraint on the beloved that reaches across the emphatically rehearsed distance, and separation, of the final couplet. Contemplation of his picture gives the beloved an estate in the lover's consciousness that, willy nilly, he cannot evade.

The problems faced by a reader of sonnet 61 typify those perplexing the collection as a whole; but they also suggest the rudiments of a reading of the poems that I will pursue here. The poem is both conceptually hazy – the document of a weary hour – but also linguistically precise. Its concept of person is repeatedly troubled, not only by its deconstruction into will, image, desire, and spirit, but also by the permeable way in which the lover and beloved can be present to one another, and impose obligations on one another, across distances and without consent. It echoes other sonnets in the sequence with its frustrated and self-disabusing rhetorical questions, but those echoes may turn out, on a more careful reading, to be more tensors than ligaments. Above all, in its diction it combines the psychologically authentic experience of love – with all its casualness, its urgency, its cliché, and its triviliality – with the reason and argument appropriate to a legal case and court. The problems of tone, sequence, person, and diction that this poem presents are characteristic of the collection at large, where they are, as here, often involved with the legal language that scores and notates the arguments of many of the sonnets. But if the strange and distintegrative hybridity of these sonnets intrudes on the reader, creating a sense of alienation and confusion, it is also in this hybridity that we should, and can, find the first threads of an integrated reading of the poems, as a collection. One of the most striking things about the movement of sonnet 61 is that there isn't one: a hope is raised and the promise of some sort of epistemological appetite, and breakthrough, is promised in the first eight lines, but the suggestion of discovery is quashed when the lover acknowledges, in line 9, what he has known all along – that he is isolated, unknown, unsought. The broken promise of this poem is striking because a narrative of epistemological discovery is basic to the Elizabethan sonnet, in which the lover (like the reader) moves from a position of ignorance and naivete to one of perception, experience, and often jadedness. Philip Sidney's Astrophil, for example, begins the sonnets of *Astrophil and Stella* with no understanding of the nature of love, no experience of the sincerity, the anguish, or the significance of the lover's plight, and – most importantly – without knowledge of Stella's form or virtue. The successive revelations of the sequence disclose to him, and to the reader, what love is: its conditions, its constraints, its proper object, the dangers attending it, and so on. The lover and the reader move through a graded series of revelations, both within and between sonnets, that functions like a narrative in the way it binds the sequence together and draws the reader on. Shakespeare's sonnet 61 emphatically collapses this project: the sense of epistemological frustration, of the stymying of the journey or narrative of revelation basic to the sonnet genre, leaps from the ethical dative of its final couplet.

This resistance to the narrative of epistemological discovery is a direct consequence of Shakespeare's mediation of the sonnet's philotic and erotic relationships not through the usual, politicized courtly rhetoric, but through a new discourse of right, obligation, and law: unlike in other contemporary sonnet sequences, in which poets map the ethics of erotic courtship onto the parallel politics of a narrative of courtly preferment, Shakespeare's identification of the ethical with the legal simply rejects the conventional process of desire and epiphany that may lead to resignation, contentment, or despair. The courtly lover pleads within an environment in which the object of his desire is also the source of the ethical and political power which constrains and regulates his behaviour; an approach to the beloved is therefore an epistemologically fraught project, because the game is perilous and its rules not entirely known, or perhaps knowable. But, ironically, it is the fraughtness of the epistemological journey that makes it possible in the first place: as with linguistic and metaphorical structures in general, the only thoughts worth having are the difficult ones. In Shakespeare's newly oppositional poetry, by contrast, love exists not between rulers and subjects, but between persons, thus sundering the beloved from the political and ethical power she had wielded in earlier sequences. Because the rights, duties, limits, and privileges available to Shakespeare's lover are known, or at least knowable – because, that is, they are not enshrined darkly in the breast of an unachievable mistress – his sonnets need never move through the stages of revelation, frustration, and disappointment that characterize the courtly lover. The appeal to legal language and concepts that structures so many of Shakespeare's sonnets does more than simply metaphorize enduringly ethical relationships between lover and boy, lover and friend, or lover and mistress. The rescripting of these relationships in a language of legal obligation locates the known and secure codes of right and wrong outside of the relationships themselves, leaving the lover in frustrated but full possession of the waking matter of his love.

In place of the conventional epistemological narrative, Shakespeare's assimilation of the ethical to the legal creates a new kind of narrative for his sequence, in which the lover moves not from ignorance to experience, but through the three divisions of legal thought – from possession (the kind), to right (the true), to tort (the fair) – in an allegory of self-discovery. Legal thought is both the enabler and the consequence of the paradoxical 'privacy' of these sonnets: where Sidney's Astrophil had been forced to choose between duties to family and friends, on the one hand, and on the other his love for Stella, Shakespeare's lover finds all three of his loves bound together by a pervasive language of right and wrong. His kind boy, his true friend, and his fair lady exert their influences in different sections of his sonnets, but they also interact with one another precisely because all three relationships are conducted in the same language. As an epistemologically secure standard exiguous to the relations between lover, beloved boy, and trespassing mistress, this language frees the lover from public courtship, and licenses his inward turn to more private bonds; but as a general code interiorized in the individual's psychology, in its impoverishment of the ethical it also binds the lover to, or imprisons him in, a precedential inhumanity from which, finally, he must break free. In the epigraph at the front of this book, Matthew Hale points to the English common law's peculiarly particular and knowable character: a massy and unwieldy kind of law, perhaps, but in its emphasis on precedent also a reliable and secure system. Shakespeare's carefully sequenced sonnets exploit exactly this common legal link between precedent and epistemic security in order to stage, at last, the extralegal, even refractory emergence of the passionate individual conscience from its epistemic stability.

In the larger context of the development of the sonnet sequence in English, from the publication of Sidney's *Astrophil and Stella* in 1591 forwards, many of the uncouth innovations in Shakespeare's sonnets thus make sense as a concerted, oppositional response to the increasingly centralized and absolutist literary and political tradition in which Shakespeare was working.[7] The core and structuring element of this opposition lay in Shakespeare's association with the Inns of Court, and in his concomitant interest in the forms, process, language, and philosophy of the English common law. In his bold rewriting of the usual Petrarchan and Sidneian *regulae* governing the composition and interpretation of sonnets, Shakespeare like his younger contemporary John Donne redefined the lyric mode in English as a vehicle for complaint and opposition, emphasizing the rule of law in the face of an increasingly prerogative-focused executive. But, conversely, Shakespeare also harnessed legal ideas of person, right, obligation, possession and ownership, interpretation and application, and scope or commission to interrogate the ethical and metaphysical questions customary, perhaps natural, to the lyric mode. The result is a sequence that both resists, and ultimately fulfils, the ethical and political ideologies it inherited from earlier studies in the genre.

USING AND WASTING

The Elizabethan poets who had renewed the English sonnet tradition in the 1590s had, among other things, contrived to adapt Petrarch's lyric conventions, and the philosophical, psychological, and rhetorical concerns that these conventions raised, to their social and political condition, the problem of the Queen regnant. What if the *vita activa*, to which the humanist poet would otherwise virtuously escape in order to slough off the vicious desire for his unachievably pure mistress, were dominated by another mistress? The superimposition of the political preferment suit upon the erotic suit of the sonnet tradition created an interpretative, and thus a poetic, problem for Elizabethan sonnet-writers from Sidney, Spenser, and Daniel to Donne and Shakespeare. Where Laura had represented for Petrarch an untainted ideal apart from *quanto piace al mondo*, for Sidney Stella could figure Penelope Rich, or the riches of political and financial success, or even the 'richest' prize of all, the Queen's favour and preferment; similarly for Spenser, as he explicitly acknowledges in *Amoretti* 74, the 'happy name' of Elizabeth – the name of his mother, mistress, and Queen – structures for him 'guifts of body, fortune, and of mind'. The allegorical potential in these lyric addresses made them subject to suspicion: in the hybridized terms of the Elizabethan sonnet, one man's *eros* was another man's ambition for office.[8] In this interpretatively unstable, even ironic context, legal language began to intrude forcefully, and for the first time something more than metaphorically, upon the thought of lyric poets.

The prevalence of a legal lexis in Shakespeare's lyric works has been widely discounted or misconstrued, by readers and sometimes editors, for a number of reasons.[9] Most simply, many editors and readers have failed to appreciate the legal semantic resonance of many of the words Shakespeare uses in the *Sonnets*; language change, and the profound historical ruptures in legal traditions that have rendered alien and archaic the terms of early-modern legal practice and thought, are likely to blame. It may be that editors have been reluctant to attribute careful and sustained legal word-play to Shakespeare in a context of this kind, supposing that a poet of so omnivorous appetite and so universal appeal would not, or could not, limit himself in such a way. The comparatively recent re-assimilation of *A Lover's Complaint* into the recognized Shakespearean canon, too, has left scholars and editors little time to work out its complex generic and rhetorical strategies;[10] this may explain why, in a poem where a legal imagination is funda- mental to the genre, and legal language everywhere in evidence, many readers have failed even to mention it. But probably the single most important factor occasioning our mass and selective blindness to Shakespeare's sustained legal preoccupations in the *Sonnets* has been a fundamental misapprehension about the nature and meaning of Elizabethan lyric poetry. It is curious that, where literary criticism has long recognized, and been comfortable with, the ironic posturing of the pastoral genre – in which poets feign under the 'pretty tales of wolves and sheep' a resignation from worldly affairs, all the while engaging in the most direct and critical terms the political and social subjects they affect to reject – it has notoriously failed to register a parallel ironic strategy in Elizabethan erotic lyric. The open secret of Philip Sidney's *Astrophil and Stella*, written in 1580–82 but first published in 1591, is precisely this irony: the frustration of Astrophil's suit to Stella, which should liberate the lover to return to the political duty befitting his birth and status, turns out to be the impediment to that very duty. Only in love can Astrophil pursue his political ambition, and yet love will destroy that ambition. Sidney's sonnet sequence, and the defence of poetry that he composed hard on its heels in 1581–82, inaugurated a decade and more of intensive imitation when they were finally published, posthumously, in 1591. Shakespeare, like many other poets and dramatists active in London at the time, seems to have set to work almost immediately; but the development of his own sequence was to tarry and accrete more slowly, and perhaps more sceptically, than those of his other two main influences, Edmund Spenser's *Amoretti and Epithalamion* (1595) and Samuel Daniel's *Delia*, with the *Complaint of Rosamond* (1592). Of contemporary responses to Sidney's lyric works, only Donne's *Songs and Sonets* (not published until 1635) would lurk coyly out of print for longer; but when Shakespeare's *Sonnets* and *A*

Lover's Complaint did finally see print in 1609, they advertised their relation to Sidney, Spenser, and Daniel openly. Shakespeare's lyric poetry, the composition of which probably spanned most of his active dramatic career, recruited legal diction and legal ideas as part of a response to the sonnet and complaint traditions that developed so explosively in the literary and political climate of the 1590s. His belated contribution, like Donne's, emerges as a brilliant variation on, and critique of, Sidney's original innovations.

In the context of the politicization of the Petrarchan love-suit after Sidney,[11] an increasing tendency in Spenser's and in Daniel's sequences toward absolutist, even tyrannical characterizations of the mistress,[12] the consistent tendency in all three poets to surrender self-interest even in the struggle for self-realization, and the shift of a lyric culture during the 1590s from court, to the Inns of Court, Shakespeare's own sonnet sequence begins to look decidedly oppositional, and in political terms even, perhaps, seditious. Instead of a politicization of the love-suit that celebrates in Platonic terms the virtue and chastity of the mistress, Shakespeare's is a sequence that alternately chastises and celebrates a mistress, and a friend, for their tremendous and undisciplined sexual energies. In place of a submission to the absolute 'sovereignty' of the mistress in erotic and political terms, Shakespeare presents a lyric world populated with more men (or male personae) than women (or female personae), a lyric world where the mistress is in competition with the friend, the lover with a rival. In one of the earliest poems in the sequence, the lover urges the 'tender churl' (1.12) to let himself be refigured 'ten times' in his posterity, and by those 'ten of thine ten times' (6.8–10) refigured again, in an exponential multiplication of self; this proliferation of person in Shakespeare's sonnets represents a potent political challenge, in itself, to the rhetoric of unity and constancy that had characterized the English sonnet tradition under Elizabeth. Sidney, Spenser, and Daniel had all disavowed 'ambition' – Astrophil repeatedly argues that his only 'ambition' is to surrender his ambition, Spenser's lover can capture his fleeing deer only after he has given up the chase, and Daniel's lover concludes both his sequence, and its companion complaint, in self-effacing despair. Shakespeare's lover, by contrast, refuses to relinquish his self-interest, and fights, pleads, scorns, suffers, and pardons.

Structuring all of these divergences from the English sonnet tradition of the 1580s and early 1590s is Shakespeare's repeated resort to a lexis and, equally importantly, to a conceptual tradition based on *meum* and *tuum*, on the law of property, on the law of right, on the law of tort – on the common law. Debt, contract, bail, use and usury, trespass, title, account: these are the recurrent heads of Shakespeare's 'deep-brain'd' argument in his sonnets; and it is in the exposition of the legal relations and obligations that Shakespeare figures by these topics, that we may most exactly source and chart the flow of an unpublishable, oppositional innovation.

The emphasis in the opening sonnets upon the obligations of 'succession' must have teetered, no less dangerously, on sedition: Elizabeth's privy council adopted a policy throughout the 1580s and 1590s of suppressing public discussion (and private, manuscript circulation, where it could be located) relating to the succession to the crown.[13] While this policy had first arisen as a direct response to the threat posed by Mary Queen of Scots, it remained useful for Elizabeth and her government to keep tight control over the succession question after the failure of the Armada (1588), and in the ticklish times of bad harvests, renewed threat of Spanish invasion, and fierce factional positioning in the early 1590s. A royal proclamation of October 1584 set the terms of this control for the last two decades of her reign, linking debate over the succession ('pretended titles . . . most dangerous and prejudicial to the safety of her highness' person and state') to religious sedition and innovation ('the defacing of true religion now established'), and to 'slander' of the administration of justice ('reproach, dishonor . . . and . . . abominable lies' about 'her highness' judges and ministers of the law').[14] In the first instance, proclamations and statutes of this kind were directed towards circulating manuscript books such as the anonymous *Leicester's Commonwealth*, a scurrilous *ad hominem* attack on Leicester and his influence over the queen, which advanced the supposed right of Mary Queen of Scots to depose the 'bastard' Elizabeth and return the realm to Catholicism.[15] The deaths of Leicester and Sidney coincided with the advent of a new threat of religious innovation in the form of dissenting Puritan preachers, who in the Martin Marprelate tracts of the late 1580s attempted to polarize public opinion against the episcopate and bring in a Presbyterian purgation; this outbreak of virulent Puritanism must in some sense be regarded as a result of the power vacuum in court patronage, which some hoped would be supplied by Walter Ralegh and the Earl of Essex, young and ambitious favourites who courted Elizabeth in the erotic terms inherited from Sidney (Essex, of course, went so far as to marry Sidney's widow). While Essex recruited with a Machiavellian grasp of the politic from both the Catholic and hot Protestant disaffected, Ralegh was soon perceived to acting as a partisan of the Martinists, partly through his association, by marriage to Bess Throckmorton, with the Martinist conspirators Job Throckmorton, Thomas Cartwright, John Penry, and John Udall. Thomas Nashe meddled in the succession in 1592 with his sensational *Pierce Penilesse His Supplication to the Diuell*, a pamphlet loaded with allusions to the now-banned *Leicester's Commonwealth*, which managed in one brilliant display to satirize the recent 'glorianification' of Elizabeth in *The Faerie Queene*, attack Ralegh (and his precisian connections), and advance the cause of a new 'English hero', Ferdinando Stanley, Lord Strange.[16] While Nashe just managed to escape the censors (though only for a time) his very public, if satirically oblique, intervention in the succession question signals, like the tip of an iceberg, a great mass of much more private conversation, taking place at the same time, in the circulation of manuscript debates, discourses, dialogues, and other materials concerning the succession and related, banned, political questions. The writers and readers of many of these seditious texts were part-time poets, and full-time lawyers, who lived in the Inns of Court.

The initial wave of intense political debate over the succession question occurred in the 1560s, in the months leading up to, and in the years following, the parliament of 1563.[17] The most debated question was the legitimacy of Mary Queen of Scots, whose claim to the throne turned upon her alien status:[18] the statute *De natis ultra mare* (25 Edward III), which established the legal position of Englishmen born overseas – and thus out of the allegiance of the crown of England – might seem to have barred Mary's claim. Although the question was officially silenced by the 1566 parliament, at least one important legal treatise, a manuscript dialogue on the statute *De natis ultra mare* probably written by William Fletewoode, was composed sometime in the 1570s, and continued to circulate in the Inns of Court during Elizabeth's reign, and long after Mary's death; one contemporary copy is dated 1601, and many of the prominent lawyers of the period, including Sir Edward Coke and Matthew Hale, had copies.[19] The continuing interest in the question of Mary's alien birth was motivated, of course, by the claim of her son James, whose right of accession depended on the same point. The Inns of Court circulation of manuscripts of this kind – beyond the specific and often highly dangerous arguments that they contain – provides an important context for the opening sonnets of Shakespeare's sequence. 'Succession' was a topic that could be discussed, even had to be discussed, within the closet- and chamber-spaces of the closed confraternities of lawyers in London; debate on this topic had to and could be tolerated within such communities because, as Elizabeth's privy council tacitly recognized, any change in monarch had to be carefully managed and prepared, possibly even with legal polemics at the ready – if the accessions of Mary Tudor and Elizabeth had been anything to go by, recent experience, ever where heirs of the blood were available, required careful legal finessing. Shakespeare's address to a male beloved, encouraging him to breed sons who will inherit and maintain unbroken the supply of his beauty to an external, obliging, and 'common' world, participates in this tension. It answers Elizabeth's chastity by refusing to praise it, and answers the public gag order on royal succession by focusing, instead, on personal succession.

The 'private' status of these opening sonnets further insists on the closed, coterie community in which both lover and beloved – in clear distinction to the actors of earlier sequences – move. Shakespeare follows the first nineteen sonnets on the male succession with a short group of five poems that emphasize the inwardness of the 'heart' in contrast to the words, shows, acted parts, and other outward forms associated with political ambition and civic life. In three of these poems, Shakespeare's lover makes statements that seem to oppose a private, manuscript-based coterie environment to the court-centred lyric context of Sidney, Spenser, and Daniel. 'So is it not with me as with that Muse', the lover asserts in 21, 'stirred by a painted beauty to his verse':

> Who heaven itself for ornament doth use,
> And every fair with his fair doth rehearse,
> Making a couplement of proud compare
> With sun and moon, with earth, and sea's rich gems,
> With April's first-born flowers and all things rare
> That heaven's air in this huge rondure hems.
>
>   (21.1–8)

Shakespeare's lover explicitly rejects, with an almost agoraphobic piety, the hyperbolic ornamentation of the outer world, preferring a 'fair' of truth, a 'bright' not of suns and moons, but of terrestrial candles, a report not of 'hearsay', (13) but one that he can 'write'. (9) The final line of the sonnet makes complete Shakespeare's dissociation from the erotic praise of the sonnet writers following Sidney: 'I will not praise, that purpose not to sell' (14). Shakespeare's sonnets will continue to resist the Petrarchan convention of *blason*, concentrating not on the conventional catalogues of beauty, but on the negotiations of relation and obligation subsisting between lover and beloved. 25 shows the lover making a similar kind of claim for the inward, refusing 'public honour and proud titles' (2) from which fortune 'bars' (3) him, and preferring to spread in those 'leaves' (5) and that 'book'(12) 'where I may not remove, nor be removed'. (14) The choice of and insistence on the verb 'remove' here are important: this word straddles the political (where 'remove' in both its verb and noun usages was semantically connected to the stripping of public office, like the more modern 'deprive' and 'transfer') and the legal (where the verb 'remove' meant to transfer a case from one court or jurisdiction to another).[20] Further, the emphasis in these two sonnets on writing – like the eloquence of 'my books' in 23 (l. 9) – goes hand in hand with their turn inward into the candle-lit chamber; it also takes in its train an unassuming litany of nearly subaudible legalisms: 'plead', 'recompense', 'writ', 'hear', 'bars', 'remove' (23.11–14; 25.3, 14). If the opening group of sonnets has implicitly turned away from the court and the celebration of its chaste beauty, Shakespeare's lover clearly positions himself, in the next handful, within an architectural and coterie space defined not by self-interested public transaction, but by private, sincere reading and writing. It is an environment not characterized by the liberty of the hyperbolic skies, but by the regulated relations of constraint, argument, and judgment. It is, in short, a judgment chamber.

If the space in which these sonnets take place is therefore to be construed as oppositionally private, the actions taking place in that space are even more so. The moral and political obligation of the beloved to perpetuate beauty by succession unfolds, after the explosive exposition of sonnet 1, as the legal and financial duty sustained by an heir, legatee, or debtor. It is typical of Shakespeare to recruit, as the two main metaphors of this part of the sequence, two parallel ideas, structurally congruent but ethically in tension: tenure and usury. Though both the landholder in a tenurial relationship and the usurer in a financial transaction are charged with, or charge themselves with, husbanding, maintaining, and developing their assets, these two custodians of property work within diametrically opposed systems of interest: the landholder seeks to preserve his estate and to develop it to the benefit of his heir or reversioner, while the usurer seeks to maximize the return on a loan for his own enrichment. One system was theorized in the Renaissance as conspicuously disinterested in the self, and the other as conspicuously defined by its self-interest; though of course the investment in and cultivation of an estate to be passed on to one's heirs, though a translation of interest from one's self to one's succeeding heirs, was not far from a straightforward self-interest. The quickening equivocation of Shakespeare's emphasis in these sonnets on a turning away from one kind of self-interest to the cultivation of another kind, of course, exactly mirrors this conflation in the metaphorical currents of landholding and loansharking.

The first of two keystones arching these currents is the word 'use'. 'Use' no longer carries today the extensive legal associations basic to the sixteenth-century understanding of the word. As a legal term, its origin lies in the medieval legal traditions of manorial tenure, largely derelict by the sixteenth century, but nonetheless preserved – in form and language if not in chivalric spirit. Because the forms of the English common law were so resistant to innovation and change – and at no time more so than the sixteenth century – language and even legal processes no longer consistent with real practice tended to survive long past the scope or period of their original devising or enactment. As John Cowell simply defines it in his 1607 dictionary of legal terms, *The Interpreter*, 'Vse (*vsus*) is in the originall signification, plaine enough: but it hath a proper application in our common lawe, and that is the profit or benefit of lands or tenements.'[21] Cowell's recording of the simplicity of the word is important, both because it was, in its 'originall signification', a simple concept, and because, even in its legal construction, the term was so well and widely known that it hardly required definition. To a modern eye, though, the 'profit or benefit of lands or tenements' might seem to be, when placed next to outright ownership, a superfluous distinction: if one owns land, one is entitled to the profits and benefits deriving from that land – that is, in a sense, what title means. But for the sixteenth-century lawyer's understanding of title to land in a tenurial context (rather than a context of outright ownership), the 'beneficial ownership' and the 'legal ownership' of land were two very different things.

The distinction between legal and beneficial ownership of land had arisen in the fourteenth century after a statute of 18 Edward I (1290), usually known as *Quia emptores terrarum*, made it possible to purchase lands freely, without payment of the customary fine to a feudal superior.[22] The statute was designed to prevent widespread defrauding of feudal lords through 'subinfeudation', a form of conveyancing by which a seller converted lands to the use of a purchasor by making him his feudal inferior – the lands would thereafter be held from the seller, now an intermediary between the purchasor and the chief lord of the seignory, for a nominal (i.e. worthless) service. The chief lord of the land would be defrauded by such arrangements, as the usual feudal services due on the land so conveyed, once owed by the seller, had now been converted into a nominal service (now owed by the purchasor). *Quia emptores terrarum* made it illegal to transfer lands through subinfeudation, and stipulated that all future conveyancing must be by process of 'substitution', whereby the purchasor took the place of the seller in the original tenurial hierarchy; as a concession to landholders, the act also removed the requirements that sellers obtain the consent of the chief lord to any bargain, and pay that lord a substantial fine for the privilege – effectively placing substitution outside the lord's control. In their eagerness to prevent abuse of their feudal prerogatives, the landed heavyweights who pushed *Quia emptores terrarum* through parliament failed to notice that, in surrendering their control over substitution, they had freed their feudal inferiors to devise ever more ingenious and satisfactory ways to evade the payment of their feudal incidents, and the performance of their feudal services.

It was very quickly recognized – in the early fourteenth century – that by a fictional conveyance of land to the custody of a group of trustees, a feudal inferior and his heirs might continue to live upon his land without owing any further financial obligations to the lord. Feudal incidents on an estate were due upon inheritance: the heir taking up his title to an estate owed a fine known as primer seisin and, if under age, would become the ward of his lord until his maturity, during which time the land could be managed to the lord's benefit. By interposing between himself and the chief lord a new group of trustees, who as a corporate body would never die and thus never be succeeded, a tenant managed to preserve his 'beneficial ownership' of the land without having to pay the feudal incidents, or suffer the feudal constraints (such as the inability to dispose lands in a will), on the tenure of his estate. Instead, he might trust in the guardianship of his nominated trustees, whose own actions in respect of his land would be constrained by equitable courts such as the Chancery, which enforced as legal instruments any orders directed from the real owner to his trustees. The interest held by the real owner in the land was known as the 'use', and he thereafter as the '*cestuy que use*'. The beneficial ownership of the land had been sundered, apparently permanently, from the legal ownership of the same land; given that tenants could now, simply by a direction to their trustees, devise their land by will and thus sidestep primogeniture, it seemed unlikely that landholders would ever consent to a renegotiation of their privileged position.

Chief lords, however, lost out; and the chiefest of them, the king, chiefly lost out. In the effort to increase crown revenue, Henry VII had instituted some minor reforms to the system of uses,[23] but it was left to his son to prosecute a wholesale reform, in what turned out to be a revivification of the whole feudal system, including its extensive legal literature and terminology. In 1536, after a landmark review case had thrown the fundamental legality of the use into doubt (thereby raising the spectre of tenurial chaos),[24] Henry VIII persuaded (or, more accurately, compelled) parliament to pass the Statute of Uses, a reformation of the law utterly doing away with the practical distinction between beneficial and legal ownership of land.[25] By a celebrated legal fiction, the statute 'executed the use', transforming all the beneficial owners in England into outright owners, and lopping away the now redundant 'real' owners – most of whom were lawyers living in the Inns of Court. Landholders found themselves immediately subject to the traditional feudal incidents (fines) and constraints on their tenure – most importantly, primogeniture, which foreclosed the option of devising land by will. The use, which from the time of *Quia emptores terrarum* to the accession of the Tudors had expanded to become by far the most common way of holding land throughout the realm, disappeared; but the idea of the use, of the 'beneficial ownership' of land, survived, not only to describe genuine trusts in land (such as that of a lord for his ward), but also to describe the relationship between owners and lessors in a lease arrangement, and even to describe the relationship between individual landholders and the heirs or reversioners who would enter into the estate upon their death or forfeiture.[26]

The beauty of the youth has, by sonnet 13, become just such a use:

> O that you were yourself! But, love, you are
> No longer yours, than you yourself here live.
> Against this coming end you should prepare,
> And your sweet semblance to some other give:
> So should that beauty which you hold in lease
> Find no determination; then you were
> Yourself again after your self's decease,
> When your sweet issue your sweet form should bear.
>
> (13.1–8)

The string of legal terms in the second part of this octet – 'lease', 'determination', 'decease', and 'issue' – retrospectively figures the 'give' of line 4 as a legal endowment, a 'frank gift' or free donation to another of title to lands. Because the youth's beauty is not his own, but a 'lease'

given him by nature, his obligation is to 'use' the lease in such a way
that he can pass it on in the same, or better condition than that in
which he received it – a 'use' of beauty that is in his own interest, as
well as his potential heir's. The 'house' of line 9 thus becomes not only
a physical house, or estate, but a 'line' of progenitors and descendants:

> Who lets so fair a house fall to decay,
> Which husbandry in honour might uphold
> Against the stormy gusts of winter's day
> And barren rage of death's eternal cold?
>
> (13.9–12)

The responsibility to preserve and maintain beauty's estate against the
ravages of both winter and the eternal winter – a connection between
estate management and seasonal hardship that will recur in the
famously short date of 'summer's lease' at 18.4 – figures the youth's
reproduction as an obligation to nature, the chief lord who has enfe-
offed him in beauty. The 'sweet semblance' that the beloved will give to
'some other' (4) is here a frank gift (of love) from the beloved to his
lover, and a more conservative, self-interested gift (his likeness) from
the beloved to his heir, born of that lover.

The term of the beloved's estate in beauty – 'so long as you here live'
(13.2) – is carefully spelled out as an estate lasting the period of the
beloved's life. Sir Thomas Littleton, author of the handbook on tenures
generally known to sixteenth-century lawyers as *Littletons Tenures*, and
of whom Coke famously remarked, 'not the name of a lawyer onely, but
of the law it selfe', defined the understanding and negotiation of
English tenures for the entire Tudor period: the *Tenures* went through
more than forty Latin editions in the sixteenth century, and more than
twenty editions in English, making it one of the most popular legal
handbooks of the age. In the typical English edition published by
Richard Tottel in 1576, Littleton's text provides this account of an
estate 'for terme of lyfe':

Tenaunt for terme of life is, where a manne letteth landes or
tenementes to a man for terme of life of the lessee, or for terme of

life of another man. In suche case the lessee is tenaunte for terme
of life. But by common language, he that holdeth for terme of his
owne lyfe, is called tenante for terme of life, and hee that holdeth
for terme of an other mans life, is called tenaunt for terme of an
other mans life. And it is to be vnderstande, that there is feoffour
and feoffee, donour and donee, lessour & lessee. The feoffour is
properly where a man enfeoffethe an other in anye landes or
tenementes in fee simple, he that maketh the feoffement is called
feoffour, & hee vnto whom the feoffement is made, is called feoffee,
and the donoure is properly where a manne geeuethe certaine
landes or tenementes to an other in the taile, he that maketh the
gifte is called donour, and he to whom the gift is made is called
donee. And lessoure is proprely, where a man letteth to an other
certayne landes or tenementes for terme of lyfe, for terme of yeres,
or to holde at will, he that maketh the lease is called lessour, & hee
to whom the lease is made is called lessee, and euery one that
hathe estate in landes or tenements for terme of his owne life, or
for terme of another mans life, is called tenaunt of free holde. And
none of lesse estate maye haue free holde, but theye of greater
estate may haue free holde, for tenant in fee simple hath free holde,
and tenant in the taile hath also free holde.[27]

It is worth considering Littleton's exposition of tenancy 'for terme of
lyfe' in full because he raises a number of important issues for
Shakespeare's use of the legal metaphor. Shakespeare is clear in the
fifth line that the beloved's tenure of his 'sweet semblaunce' is to be
thought of as a 'lease'; but he also suggests that the beloved should
'give' this form to his 'sweet issue', converting a lease into a fee simple.
In strict terms, this is obviously legal nonsense: though a lessee for term
of life was considered a 'freeholder' (*franktenant*), he could not alien (or
transfer tenancy of) his estate in such a way as to prejudice his lord – a
hereditary estate was not in his power to grant. But from another way
of looking at the relation between the fee simple and the lease for term
of life, what Shakespeare writes in this sonnet is eminently reasonable.
If nature acting as a feudal lord has given to the beloved a hereditable
estate, his failure to produce an heir converts that estate, effectively,

into a tenancy for term of life only; the only way to escape this fate is to produce the heir, and realize the full scope of the grant – that is, the fee simple. This relationship between 'fee tail' (a hereditable estate in freehold) and 'tenant in tail after possibility of issue extinct' (an estate for term of life only) can be clearly seen in Sir Edward Coke's 'figure of the diuision of Possessions'. Though Shakespeare confounds the terms 'lease' and 'give' in his sonnet, the confusion only persists so long as we think of Nature's estate in beauty as a prefixed, rather than a retrospectively determined, grant.

The logic of retrospective conversion outlined in sonnet 13 makes sense of a similar argument in sonnet 4, which also confounds ideas of leasing and giving. Here Nature is imagined not as an enfeoffing lord, but as a dying legator, whose legacy to the beloved is encumbered by conditions:

> Unthrifty loveliness, why dost thou spend
> Upon thyself thy beauty's legacy?
> Nature's bequest gives nothing, but doth lend,
> And being frank, she lends to those are free:
> Then, beauteous niggard, why dost thou abuse
> The bounteous largesse given thee to give?
>
> (4.1–6)

This sonnet brazenly disclaims Nature's gift, insisting that the legacy of beauty is a lease only ('gives nothing, but doth lend'); but then goes on, in line 6, to talk about that legacy again as something 'given'. The equation of lease and frank gift makes no sense without the interpretive guide of sonnet 13, from which we have learned that the lease, passed on, will come to seem a gift so long as it is, in turn, given. Here the logic of the poem turns on the puns on 'frank' and 'free', which mean both 'of free, not villain status', and 'bounteous'; so long as the beloved is bounteous with his estate, his estate will not be bound. Nature's loan to the beloved is conditional on its being loaned on; the lease, when 'by succession made perpetual', becomes a fee simple, and again we can make the otherwise nonsensical leap from a lease to a freehold.

These opening sonnets use a technical understanding of the law of

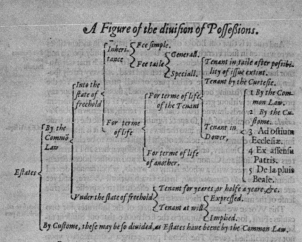

A Figure of the diuision of Possessions.

Our Author dealt onely with the Estates and termes abouesayd, Somewhat Wee shall speake of Estates by force of certaine Statutes, as of Statute Merchant, Statute Staple, and *Elogit*, (whereof our Authour intended to haue written) and likewise to Executors to whom lands are deuised for payment of debts, and the like.

I shall desire, That the learned Reader will not conceiue any opinion against any part of this painfull and large Volume, vntill hee shall haue aduisedly read ouer the whole, and diligently searched out and well considered of the seuerall Authorities, Proofes, and Reasons which we haue cited and set downe for warrant and confirmation of our opinions throughout this whole worke.

Mine aduice to the Student is, That before he reade any part of our Commentaries vpon any Section, that first he reade againe and againe our Author himselfe in that Section, and doe his best endeauours, first of himselfe, and then by conference with others, (which is the life of Study) to vnderstand it, and then to reade our Commentary thereupon, and no more at any one time, than he is able with delight to beare away, and after to meditate thereon, which is the life of reading. But of this Argument we haue for the better direction of our Student in his Study, spoken in our Epistle to our first Booke of *Reports*.

And albeit the Reader shall not at any one day (do what he can) reach to the meaning of our Author, or of our Commentaries, yet let him no way discourage himselfe, but proceed; for on some other day, in some other place, that doubt will be cleared. Our Labors herein are drawn out to this great Volume, for that our Authour is twice repeated; once in French, and againe in E N G L I S H.

FIGURE 5 Diagram showing the division of estates, from Edward Coke, *The first part of the Institutes of the Lawes of England* (London: Assigns of John More, 1629), sig. 6v. British Library 508.g.16. Coke's diagram clearly shows the relation between a heritable estate (fee tail) and an estate for term of life (tenant in tail after possibility of issue extinct).

real property to create and to resolve an ethical paradox. The beloved is at first admonished for his niggardliness, but then encouraged to act in his own self-interest, precisely by being generous. The legal analogue of estates law models the way in which, retrospectively, the generous husbanding and transmission of an estate in beauty can transform that beauty from a temporally limited to an eternal estate. Essential to this model is the idea of 'use' as practically indistinguishable from possession, in such a way that Nature's enduring lordship over beauty comes to serve not as the perplexing determination of the beloved's beauty, but rather as the means of its endurance. Because the beloved enjoys the 'use' only of beauty, his generous resolution to pass it on will allow him to participate in something eternal even though his own custody, the 'lease', is bounded. Furthermore, this generosity will make him *generosus* – it will enoble and dignify him – because the proleptic conversion of the beloved's estate in beauty, from a lease to a freehold, imports the degree of the *franktenant*. But the legal model is important for Shakespeare's development of the ethical status of beauty not only because it mediates this ennobling paradox, but also because it under-mines it. In sonnet 4, for example, the opening six lines quickly give way to another concept of use entirely, and one that continues to haunt the succeeding poem:

> Profitless usurer, why dost thou use
> So great a sum of sums, yet canst not live?
> For having traffic with thyself alone,
> Thou of thyself thy sweet self dost deceive;
> Then how, when nature calls thee to be gone,
> What acceptable audit canst thou leave?
>
> (4.7–12)

Here Shakespeare pivots on the meaning of the word 'use', which, by the attraction of 'usurer' at the opening of the line, comes to mean 'the fact of using money borrowed or lent at a premium', or even the interest on this loan.[28] Unlike the temporary 'use' of an estate, which the beloved might husband to the benefit of the heir or reversioner following him, here the beloved is imagined as a 'usurer' who invests his loaned beauty for his own profit – a strategy that, paradoxically, leaves him 'profitless'. Indispensable to a reading of these lines is a basic understanding of the general Elizabethan repugnance for usury on ethical grounds, and the ways in which this attitude was expressed in contemporary polemics and legal instruments.[29] In these tracts and proclamations, the usurer was imagined as a self-interested agent who, in refusing to extend trust and credit to his associates, barred himself from Christian charity. The 'profit', 'traffic', and 'audit' that this poem imagines for the beloved are thus not financial, but ethical, and the life of which he deceives himself by his actions is not his worldly, but his eternal, life. The combination in a single sonnet of these two opposed legal conceptions of 'use' foregrounds the paradoxes of self-interest that the beloved faces in husbanding his beauty, and pits a self-negating common interest (which results in the self's enfranchisement) against a self-seeking personal interest (which results in the self's disenfranchisement). As the succeeding sonnet argues, 'that use' will not be 'forbidden usury' if the beloved resists the temptation to be 'self-willed'.

The ethical obligation of the beloved in these opening sonnets is in no word so neatly summed as it is in 'waste' – the second of the two terms mediating the divide between the old ethics of tenured 'use' and the new ethics of the market's 'usance'. Indeed, it is the dangerous possibility of 'waste' that colours the (ethically) proper interpretation of 'use' in these poems. The paradox of the opening sonnet – that the 'tender churl' makes 'waste in niggarding' – is resolved by the continuing focus of these opening sonnets on the law of estates, in which the concept of 'waste' had an important, narrow application. As the 1642 dictionary of legal terms, *Les Termes de la Ley*, has it:

Wast, is where tenant for terme of yeares, tenant for terme of life, or tenaunt for terme of anothers life, tenant in dower, or tenant by the curtesie, or gardian in Chiualry doth make waste or destruction vpon the Land, that is to say, pulleth downe the house, or cutteth downe timber, or suffereth the house willingly to fall, or diggeth the ground, then he in the reuersion shall haue one Writ for that waste, and shall recouer the place where the waste is done, and treble dammages.[30]

The crime of waste is basically one committed by the temporary custodian of an estate against its future possessor(s), and amounts to the stripping of that estate of its capital assets – timber, soil, mineral or metal deposits, and any buildings. Laws passed against waste attempted to prevent the temporary tenant of the estate from making short-term profits to the prejudice of the future owners, who might be reversioners (those to whom the property in the state would 'revert' upon the death or term of the current tenant) or heirs in the broad sense. As the *Termes de la Ley* makes clear, 'waste' was a crime of which tenants for term of years or life were particularly to be suspected, as their limited interest in the estate – not bound to a natural interest in, for example, an heir of their body – reduced their ethical obligation. In the context of Shakespeare's insistence on the danger of 'waste' (the word reappears in sonnet 9, and the concept in the first two quatrains of 10, and in the final sestet of 13), the correct 'use' to which he exhorts the beloved is clearly imagined as the selfless custody of beauty for the benefit of the heir.[31]

A technical understanding of tenurial law thus comes to structure the ethical logic of succession in the opening group of sonnets. Shakespeare moves in these poems from a tradition whereby – for Sidney, Spenser, and Daniel – the self was effaced or subsumed into the single person of the monarch, perhaps hoping (as in Spenser) for a re-grant of personal subjectivity or authority, to a self that turns away from that absolute prerogative, preferring rather a model where authority is vested in an extraneous ('strange') obligation or system of duties and responsibilities, much like the duty to the common weal – to the heir or reversioner, in the legal philosophy of primogeniture and tenure. It is important to recognize that this is not a departure from absolutism to self-interest, but rather from self-interest (where that interest is the sovereign's, where the sovereign's body contains in microcosm the whole estate of the weal public), to common interest, to the rule of law. Both structures might be said to be unself-interested, and yet the common-law system pushing out from the first 14 sonnets of Shakespeare's sequence dispenses even with the necessary evil of the transition, in Spenser, through the self of the monarch to the commonweal. Thus there is an emphasis within this opening group on the idea that the beloved 'is not himself', that the aspects of selfhood of which he enjoys tenure are not his in outright ownership, but only in use. Where Elizabeth had failed to provide for the succession, and sought to concentrate lyric, erotic, and political power into her body (howsoever plausibly to the benefit of the realm), Shakespeare's opening sonnets by contrast urge the succession, dispossess the beloved of consistent self-hood, and appeal to a system of rules, duties, and obligations that exist beyond person, regulating the possession and the beneficial use of self-tenure. In preferring to vest ethical authority not in a central icon – a virtuous Stella, a 'triumphing' Elizabeth – but in an ethical system modelled on a customary form of English common law, Shakespeare's opening sonnets broke, in the most oppositional way possible, with the usual subject and ideology of the English sonnet genre.

In its focus on legal ideas about possession – and specifically the self-possession of the 'tender churl' – this opening section of the sonnets establishes the sequence's inward-looking and private tone. The high political considerations shadowing early sequences have here given way to an intimate and personal series of arguments. Furthermore, the way these arguments are, in turn, joined to ethical ideas about interest and self-interest creates a new kind of operation for the legal within the lyric in this period. Shakespeare here maps the ethical upon the legal, not simply appealing to legal arguments as analogues or metaphors for the ethical considerations truly under focus, but rather imagining those ethical problems as decidable on legal grounds. As a result of its density, repetition, and vantageous positioning, so operative does Shakespeare's diction of 'use' and 'usury' become that the structures and traditions of the law are interiorized as ethical and psychological phenomena. These opening sonnets thus join a politically oppositional stance – male succession, primogeniture, personal property – linked to the socially oppositional coterie literary culture of the Inns of Court, to a new mode for the weighing of the ethical problems native to the sonnet genre. This transition is effectively also an epistemological shift, because (again, in a way linked to the politically oppositional nature of these poems' preoccupation with succession) the grounds and codes governing the relation between the lover and his beloved now subsist in an authority exiguous to their relationship – a fixed, secure, and knowable authority, universal in its reach and permanent. What the opening sonnets of Shakespeare's sequence achieve most persuasively is a new localization for lyric thought: as readers of ourselves, we are no longer dependent on a perilous and inscrutable courtly suit, but may secure self-realization (like self-possession) through that most customary of English common-law practices – the gift.[32]

'THE SESSIONS OF SWEET SILENT THOUGHT': THE RIGHTS OF LOVE

Following the startling repositioning of lyric focus and ideology in the opening sonnets, Shakespeare's collection hardly abandons its legal positioning. If the language and argument of the law, there, attracted the oppositional social and political positioning of the Inns of Court, the middle sonnets of the collection take the relationship between lover and beloved more firmly into the spaces and forms of the law. These middle sonnets also, in their focus on the true friend, give up the earlier preoccupation with possession for a new focus on the lover's rights and obligations in love. In sonnet 30, for example, the lover imagines his thought about the beloved as a judicial sitting, in which he has been charged with hearing the 'account' of his loves:

> When to the sessions of sweet silent thought
> I summon up remembrance of things past,
> I sigh the lack of many a thing I sought,
> And with old woes new wail my dear time's waste:
> Then can I drown an eye (unused to flow)
> For precious friends hid in death's dateless night,
> And weep afresh love's long since cancelled woe,
> And moan th' expense of many a vanished sight.
> Then can I grieve at grievances foregone,
> And heavily from woe to woe tell o'er
> The sad account of fore-bemoaned moan,
> Which I new pay, as if not paid before;
> But if the while I think on thee, dear friend,
> All losses are restored, and sorrows end.

The judicial 'sessions' to which remembrance, for evidence, is 'summon[ed]' reveals the 'waste' the lover has committed of the many things he has sought.[33] It becomes clear, in line 11, that these sessions have been called on a writ of 'account', in which a bailiff or other receiver could by contemporary law be ordered to deliver a reckoning of monies received and due to the receiver's lord. By the second statute of Westminster, the action of account had been further strengthened to allow for imprisonment of the defaulting receiver:

Concerning Seruants, Bailiffes, Chamberlaines, and all manner of Receiuers, the which are accountable: It is agreed and ordained, that when the Maisters of such Receiuers doe assigne Auditours to take their account, and they be found in Arrerages vpon their account (all things alowed which ought to bee alowed) their bodies shall be Arested, and by the Testimony of the Auditours of the same account, shall bee sent vnto the next Gaole of the Kings in those Partes, and shall bee receiued of the Sheriffe or Gailer, and Imprisoned in yron and vnder safe Custodie, and there shall remaine at their owne cost, vntill they haue satisfied their Maisters cleareley of Arrerages. Neuerthelesse, if any Person being so Committed to Prison, do complaine, that the Auditours of his account haue grieued him vniustly, charging him with Receits that he hath not receiued, or not allowing him expences, and Liberties reasonable, and can finde friends that will vndertake to bring him before the Barons of the Eschequer, the Partie shall be bailed vnto them. And the Sheriffe (in whose Prison he is kept) shall giue knowledge vnto his Maister, that hee appeare before the Barons of the Exchequer at a certaine day, with the Roles and Talies, by which he made his account, and in the presence of the Barons or the Auditours, that they shall assigne him, the account shall be rehearsed, and Iustice shall be done to the parties ...[34]

Shakespeare's lover, called to account, finds himself unable to satisfy (the implied lord) for loves past and lost, regardless of the fact that he has already moaned, grieved, and paid for them, 'long since cancelled'

(7). The tallies, now lost ('hid in death's dateless night' – 6), he must 'tell o'er' (10), and repay the 'expense' (8) on his 'account', 'as if not paid before' (11–12). As in the statutory provision for account, it is the intercession of the 'dear friend' that offers some relief, as the remembrance of present love 'restore[s]' (14) the loss of past love, and the account is satisfied. The conspicuous difference between this sonnet and those of the first section is that, here, the lover himself is at law, measuring his rights and his obligations against both those of the friend, and those of time and nature. Where the earliest part of the sequence had concerned itself explicitly with self-knowledge and self-possession, this part of the sequence introduces the lover into the social and emotional – though not yet erotic – world of duties and obligations, rights and privileges. Here the lover can ransom himself from debt, but only by means of the friend's intercession.

This is only the first of many sonnets in the central part of Shakespeare's collection where the relationship between lover and beloved is structured by legal forms and processes. These sonnets recruit an almost dramatic legal imagination in their construction of the duties and obligations, rights and privileges obtaining between the lover and beloved. As in sonnet 30, these sonnets are conspicuous, within the context of the larger sonnet tradition in English, for their imagination of the bond between lover and beloved as one between two agents mutually regulated by a shared code or law; never does the lover appeal to the beloved's innate or absolute power, or to any privilege beyond the reach of regulation. Again as in sonnet 30, the judge to whom or code to which both parties appeal remains a fixed and inexorable, but inhuman presence. So in sonnet 35 the lover conspicuously does not pardon the beloved for his 'trespass' (6), but, despite being the 'adverse party' (10), acts as his 'advocate' (10) and 'accessory' (13) in a 'lawful plea' (11) to excuse him of his theft. Similarly, the beloved is imagined in sonnet 46 as a kind of property the right to which the lover's heart and eye are contesting. The eye seeks to 'bar' (3) the heart the sight of the beloved, but the heart counters by denying the eye 'the freedom of that right' (4); when the heart 'plead[s]' (5) that it contains the true image of the beloved, the 'defendant' eye 'doth that plea deny' (7):

> To 'cide this title is empanelled
> A quest of thoughts, all tenants to the heart,
> And by their verdict is determined
> The clear eyes' moiety, and the dear heart's part:
>> As thus, mine eyes' due is thy outward part,
>> And my heart's right, thy inward love of heart.
>
>   (46.9–14)

Again, by invoking the jury (or 'quest' or 'inquest'), Shakespeare displaces the traditional political rhetoric of courtship into a different kind of court altogether. Here the reader is brought by a dramatic encounter face to face with one of the oldest and most celebrated elements of the English legal constitution, guaranteed by Magna Carta as a defence against the vagaries of a centralized, codified justice. The presiding figure of some political or ethical authority is completely effaced in the mutual submission of lover and beloved to a customary law.

The legalization of the love bond runs very visibly through many of the sonnets in this central section, and particularly sonnets 41, 42, 48, 49, 58, 65, 92, 116, and 117. But two others, 87 and 88, have a particular claim on our attention not only for their rich and exact legal texture, nor for the continuing way in which the two parties to the relationship submit themselves to the impersonal arbitration of a system regulating rights and duties, but for their flirtation with the rhetoric of disparagement that had featured so unremittingly in the lyric poetry of Sidney, Spenser, and Daniel. In these two poems the lover admits the superiority of the beloved, acknowledging in 87 that:

> ... thou art too dear for my possessing,
> And like enough thou knowst thy estimate.
>
>   (87.1–2)

It almost seems as if Shakespeare is ready to throw in his lot with the courtly sonneteers, admitting an impediment to the mutual arbitration of love that has so far characterized the relationship of the collection. But the rest of this sonnet, like the next, goes on to undermine this brief suggestion of privilege. It is not merely the beloved's 'worth' that liberates him, but 'the charter of [his] worth gives [him] releasing' (3); similarly, while the lover acknowledges that his estate in the beloved originated in a 'fair gift' of the beloved's 'granting', yet this gift was occasioned by the 'cause' of the lover's supposed desert, and led to a 'patent' in which the gift was enrolled (7–8). In both 'charter' and 'patent', we witness Shakespeare's recourse to the evidentiary forms of common-law process, the 'specialty' required for the social and legal arbitration of rights. Again, in the following companion sonnet, the lover imagines the time when the beloved will have cast him off, and subjected his 'merit' to public 'scorn' (2), but instead of simply allowing the beloved the right to this contempt, the lover vows to 'prove' the beloved's virtue by 'set[ting] down a story' (where 'story' is the English translation of the Law French *count*, or declaration beginning a legal suit) 'of faults concealed, where I am attainted' (4–7). In both sonnets, the brief suggestion that the beloved has escaped from the code and process binding him to the lover is immediately undercut and clawed back, as the lover reaffirms the importance not only of material evidence and written legal instruments, but of declarations and causes. The result is not to destabilize the by now well-developed sense of this love relationship as a legally arbitrated bond, but to confirm it resoundingly at its point of imagined weakness.

The middle sonnets of the sequence thus push the lover out beyond the conditions and problems of self-possession to the social experience of contract and fidelity. Here the lover can begin to see himself not only in relation to himself, but to others, as he negotiates standard common law processes of account, arbitration, and right. But in the transition to the more public and social aspects of person, Shakespeare's lover continues to be regulated not by the will or the power of the beloved, but rather by the impersonal and abstract system of rights and duties imposed upon both parties by the customary law. Once again Shakespeare assimilates the ethical and the legal, construing interpersonal debts and privileges not only as analogous to, but fully interpreted by the universal code of legal practice governing English civil life. The focus of these middle poems on the 'truth' of the friend to his constant lover returns again and again not to some personal, human standard of ethical fidelity, but to the rights and obligations conferred and imposed by charters, juries, verdicts, and accounts.

PAYING THE WHOLE: THE BODY OF THE LAW IN THE *SONNETS* AND *A LOVER'S COMPLAINT*

If, generally speaking, the sonnets to the 'lovely boy' (126.1) treat love as an ethical discourse of interest assimilated to a legal discourse of kindly self-possession; if in the middle sonnets dealing with the friend 'truth' is represented recurrently as as a system of legal rights and obligations; the transition (after 127) to sonnets addressing the 'fair' mistress allows Shakespeare to turn from possession (self-love) and right (friend-love, the philotic) to tort (mistress love, the erotic), the appropriate legal prism through which to view a love grounded not upon rights, but wrongs.[35] Here the law becomes a tool to be exploited in power negotiations between not two but three agents, in an environment much more explicitly concerned with the body, physical desire, and sex. The opening of 133 seems in some ways to stick to traditional lyric convention:

> Beshrew that heart that makes my heart to groan
> For that deep wound it gives my friend and me;
> Is 't not enough to torture me alone,
> But slave to slavery my sweet'st friend must be?
>
> (133.1–4)

The idea of the tyrant mistress, who deals pain, even torture, is familiar enough, and both Sidney and Spenser had spoken of love for the mistress as slavery.[36] But two elements, even in this first quatrain, raise considerable problems, social problems so difficult to resolve that this particular sonnet has rarely been anthologized. The 'wound' of which Shakespeare writes here is Elizabethan slang for 'vagina',[37] a pun that immediately signals a traverse of the usual escape-clause for eroticism, the neo-Platonic allegory. The force of 'for' – which can here mean 'on account of', but can also mean 'in desire of, longing after' – leaves the first two lines shimmering between courtly complaint and sex-starved vindictiveness, but the possibility of a body–spirit allegory seems foreclosed by the more obvious ambiguity, and anyway 'groan . . . wound' is far too visceral and physiological to be credibly sublimated. Where a neo-Platonic interpretation of erotic desire in the sonnets of Michelangelo, or of Spenser, might construe such longings as prefigurings of spiritual ambition (and both Michelangelo and Spenser generously encouraged such interpretations), Shakespeare might even be said to offer the reverse: the primary meaning of 'wound' here is the metaphorical love wound of Cupid's arrow, and the secondary ('higher') meaning the hard fact of the hot bed. The second problem with this quatrain is more obvious: the lover is not alone in his longing, but shares his use of the beloved, and his desire for her, with his friend. Shakespeare here figures not a dyadic approach of lover to beloved, on the Petrarchan model, but a triadic relationship, a triangulation of co-partners. The combination of Shakespeare's valorisation of physical love, on the one hand, with the triangulation of that love, results in a decidedly seedy picture of an apparently biographical or historical narrative lying behind the poetry.

The next quatrain creates another kind of problem, one that takes us out into the critical bibliography that has accreted around Shakespeare's sonnets over the last twenty years. On the face of it, apart from the ongoingly curious interposition of the friend into the usual dyadic structure of lover and beloved, we seem to see a conventional rehearsal of the idea of erotic rapture, in which the sight of the beloved transports the lover, in an ecstasy, outside his own self-possession:

> Me from myself thy cruel eye hath taken,
> And my next self thou harder hast engrossed:
> Of him, myself and thee I am forsaken,
> A torment thrice threefold thus to be crossed.
>
> (133.5–8)

The sexual references become firmer: 'engross' can mean 'to make (the body) gross or fat; to fatten', or more generally 'to make thick or bulky';[38] in combination here with 'harder', it produces a distinctively sexual overtone. But now another semantic plane unfolds upon the sexual, originating in the idea of 'taking'. 'To engross' also means, and was regularly used in the early-modern period to mean, 'to buy up wholesale; especially to buy up the whole stock, or as much as possible, of (a commodity) for the purpose of 'regrating' or retailing it at a monopoly price'; more generally it could mean 'to get together, collect from all quarters', or even 'to gain or keep exclusive possession of', 'to monopolize'.[39] The friend has not only been charged with desire, but his whole stock bought up, and taken away from the lover. The lover thus loses his own self-possession, his interest in his friend, and (by virtue of the friend's interposition with the beloved) the beloved herself. 'Crossed' continues the legal-financial metaphor opened in 'engrossed', as 'to cross' was regularly used in Shakespeare's English as a synonym for 'to cancel', meaning 'to render void or invalid' a legal document or deed, or (physically, as in a ledger or account-book) to cancel a debt.[40]

The 'torment thrice threefold' (8) here, however, is puzzling. The loss of self, friend, and beloved might be thought a triple torment, but Shakespeare here imagines a cancelling far more thorough (by a factor of three) than that. Colin Burrow rightly suggests that this triple triplet recalls the 'Trinitarian imagery' of 105, where Shakespeare meditates on the mystery of the 'wondrous scope' of his three themes, 'fair, kind, and true'.[41] 133 does more than merely recall this imagery: the 'fair' might be thought allegorically to figure the beauty of the beloved, the 'true' the faithful love of the friend, and the 'kind' the self-similarity of the 'lovely boy' whose initiation to love in the opening sonnets originated this odyssey of self- and social discovery; as it happens, 134 explicitly realizes at least two of these identifications in line 6: 'For thou art covetous', writes the lover to the beloved, 'and he is kind'.[42] In that sense, 133 presents a faithful allegorical staging of the tripled person of 105. But in what sense might the crossing, or cancelling, or burdening of the lover be thought not merely triple, but 'thrice threefold'? The solution is, again, in 105, where Shakespeare insists that the triplet of fair, kind, and true is 'to one, of one' and 'in one' (105.4, 12). If for a moment we take this unity of author, subject, and object seriously, even literally, and entertain the thought – which Sidney had insisted upon –

that Shakespeare was writing these sonnets to no one but himself (to, of, and in one), the meaning of the three-by-three matrix, the 'cross' or 'lattice' of self-cancelling enacted in 133, becomes clear. The author as lover has lost self, beloved, and friend; the author as beloved has lost self, lover, and lover; and the author as friend has lost self, beloved, and friend. The triangular partition of the author results in a nine-way ('thrice threefold') cancellation of identity, a cancelling 'cross' indeed.

Any interpretation of 133 that hopes to disentangle 'fair, kind, and true' and explain the force of the 'torment thrice threefold' must rely on the three-in-one philosophy of 105, which is presumably why Shakespeare ordered the sequence of sonnets so that 105 precedes 133 by exactly 27 intervening sonnets: 27, is, of course, 'thrice threefold . . . crossed', or 3^3.[43] And yet, the most recent bibliographical study of the dating (and thus implicitly of the sequencing) of Shakespeare's sonnets suggests that 133 and 134 occur in a concluding group of poems written up to ten years before the group in which we find 105, and that in all likelihood the concluding group – containing all the sonnets addressed to the 'dark lady' – ought to be considered a kind of bibliographical afterthought, a collection of early pieces that the printer of the sonnets, Thomas Thorpe, received in addition to the main sequence (and perhaps even from a different source), sonnets that he tacked on to the others to enlarge his collection.[44] A reader already struggling to cope with Shakespeare's aggressively valorized sexuality, his apparent sanctioning of the menage-à-trois, and his legal-financial diction is now asked to surmise that Shakespeare composed a pair of sonnets in the early 1590s about a trio of friends and lovers that, fortuitously, became intelligible in the early years of the seventeenth century when he wrote another sonnet about three-in-one and, sometime afterwards, accidentally reordered his sequence to give the later sonnet priority. The careful mathematical positioning of the two sonnets strenuously belies this.

The picture becomes only more complicated, because the concluding sestet of 133, like the whole of 134, is delivered in a heavily technical legal diction that continues to play in exact and complex ways with the idea of *habeas corpus*. 'Prison my heart in thy steel bosom's ward', the lover entreats the beloved in line 9 of 133:

But then my friend's heart let my poor heart bail.
Whoe'er keeps me, let my heart be his guard;
Thou canst not then use rigour in my jail.

(10–12)

These are lines that have been only partly and imperfectly explained by
even the most conscientious of Shakespeare's modern editors – which
is not surprising because they require a very precise technical knowledge of bail and mainprize. Sir Edward Coke, at the height of his career
Chief Justice of the Common Pleas under James I, compiled a short
treatise on this subject for the use of Justices of the Peace; it was eventually published, as *A Little Treatise of Baile and Maineprize*, in 1635. As
Coke writes:

Baile or Maineprize is when a man detained in Prison for any
offence, for which he is Baileable or Maineprizeable by Law, is by
a compleate Iudge or Iudges of that offence vppon sufficient surety
found for his appearance & yeelding of his body delivered out of
Prison.[45]

'Baile', for an Elizabethan like Coke or Shakespeare, concerned the
custody of the body of a prisoner, the 'yeelding of his body'. As Coke
goes on to argue, there are two important distinctions to be made
between bail and mainprize. First, anyone who 'bails' a prisoner is
responsible to return the prisoner to answer only the particular matter
for which the prisoner was bailed; someone who finds 'maineprize' for a
prisoner is responsible for seeing that the prisoner appears to answer
that charge, and any other charge arising. Bail is thus a more limited
form of substitution than mainprize, being directed specifically at the
cause for which the prisoner was originally taken into custody, and no
other. Perhaps more importantly for Shakespeare's meaning in this
sonnet, 'bail' is to be distinguished from 'maineprize' because it is itself
a form of imprisonment, and not an enlargement of the prisoner:

The Pledges and Surety of him that is deliuered to Baile, may
imprison him, whose Surety they are: for chiefe Iustice *Stuard* in

> *33. Edw. 3.* sayd that they were his gaolers or keepers, and if they suffered him to escape, they should answere for the same … the Etymology of eyther of them doth shewe and manifest the difference betwixt them, for in the one the Prisoner is deliuered by the Iudge Iudges, or Courts into the hands, and as it were, into the prison of the sureties, for the words be *Traditur in Ballium.* But in the other cases the words be, that such and such a man *Ceperat* without any such deliuery made by the Court, as in the other Case.[46]

To bail a prisoner, for Coke as for Shakespeare, was to take the prisoner into custody, and to act as his warder or even jailer. It is impossible to make sense of the conclusion of the third quatrain of Shakespeare's sonnet 133 without this emphasis, in the technical legal understanding of 'bail', on the delivery of the body of the prisoner from one keeper to another.

Exactly who is bailing whom, however, remains indeterminate, and this is surely Shakespeare's point, a point structured by the ambiguity of 'keeps' – but effaced by most modern editions of the poem, which give 'whoe'er' or even 'whoever' in line 11 for the 1609 edition's much plainer and more straightforward 'who ere'. The original edition leaves open two possible readings of this clause: either 'whoever keeps my heart (i.e. the lady), my heart will guard my friend's'; or 'I will guard the heart of that person who always ('ere') keeps my heart (i.e. the friend)'. The ambiguity of this line merely sustains the similar ambiguity in the line above, where the hortatory subjunctive 'let … bail' allows Shakespeare to leave the subject and object of 'bail' in delicious suspense: is the friend bailing the lover, or the lover the friend? Who is keeping the lover's heart: the lady, or the friend?

The final line of the quatrain, in turn, depends on both of these unresolved ambiguities, and again makes no sense without reference to Coke. Coke's main purpose in writing his 'little treatise' is to put Justices of the Peace on a surer footing in the bailing of offenders in their prisons; to this end he defines and distinguishes between his terms, considers precedents, and rehearses statutes governing the bailability of prisoners for various offences (and particularly felonies), but he is driven finally to

concede that a Justice of the Peace will have to use his own discretion in
the decision both over whether to bail a prisoner, and, if so, by what
sureties to bind him. Acknowledging that he has left the problem only
slightly clearer than when he found it, Coke concludes with a comparatively long discussion of the discretionary powers of judges in such
prerogative dispensations, and concedes that the process of determining
and setting bail and maineprize represents one of the few places in the
common law where judges are faced with an ambiguity:

> Howbeit forasmuch as all good Lawes are instituted, and made for
> the repelling of those euils that most commonly happen: For *ad ea*
> *quæ frequentius accidunt iura adaptantur*, and principally doe respect
> the generall peace and profit of the people: and therefore we vse to
> say, that a mischiefe is rather to be suffered then an
> inconuenience: That is to say, that a priuate person should be
> punished or damnified by the rigour of the Law, then a general
> rule of the law should be broken to the generall trouble and
> preiudice of many. It is therefore very necessary, that the Law and
> discretion should bee Concomitant, and the one to be an accident
> inseparable to the other, so as neither Law without discretion, least
> it should incline to rigour, nor discretion without Law, least
> confusion should follow, should bee put in vre . . .[47]

Shakespeare seizes upon bail in this sonnet, as we will witness him do
again and again throughout his career, because it is a point of interpretative weakness, or opportunity, in the otherwise solid structure of the
common law; it is a point upon which some ambiguity persists, and
which judges must handle delicately, and with discretion. When the
lover argues that the beloved cannot use 'rigour' in his jail, but must
give him the benefit of bail, his reasoning depends on the ambiguities
we have noted in the preceding lines: because the lover and the friend
exist in a state of mutual bailing, where one's heart stands surety for
the other's, the beloved must, as the judge considering bail for the lover,
offer him the same privilege she has already conceded to the friend ('let
my heart be his guard'). The legal hen comes home to roost in the final
couplet, however, where the lover has to admit that, though he and the

friend offer mutual surety for one another, they also mutually imprison one another. Thus while they all participate in a triangulated mutual emancipation, they also all three participate in a triangulated mutual confinement:

> And yet thou wilt, for I being pent in thee,
> Perforce am thine, and all that is in me.
>
> (133.13–14)

The transition in these late sonnets, primarily addressed to the lady, to a legal posture of contest over wrongs, rather than rights to possession, or arbitration and mutual submission, brings home with considerable force the oppositional character of what must be recognized, at least in its broader contours, as a sequence. While the development of a focus on sex and the body was always implicit in the poems (the verb 'to use', for example, was regularly used in the period to mean 'to use sexually, to fornicate with'), these final sonnets push well beyond the idealized courtly Platonism of earlier sequences to a privacy as tactile and intimate as that of Donne's erotic poetry. Similarly, the focus on *habeas corpus* – a right (like the jury trial) wrested from the crown by Magna Carta – deepens the sonnets' general tendency to resort to common legal topics of a constitutional and oppositional character. Sidney, Spenser, and Daniel had imagined the beloved as a powerful woman to whom their erotic advances could only ever amount to courtship; while all of these poets carve out a resistance to servility in their own ways, their sequences ultimately despair of success (Sidney, Daniel), or recognize the need for self-subjection in the achievement of desire (Spenser). Shakespeare's poems, by contrast, displace the public, female beloved with a privately solicited youth; toy with a private and customary form of tenurial succession patently offensive to the usurping Tudor line and the barren, unmarried Queen; insistently occlude political authorities and privileges in the recurrently legally focused central poems, where the philotic relationship is figured as a legal arbitration; and finally empower not the queen, nor the king, but the reader as the ultimate judge of conscience in a point of law too ambiguous to risk extension to precedent and the universal.

Shakespeare's sonnets turn away from the high politics of legal constitutionalism so evident in Sidney's and Spenser's sequences, instead
using law to focus his poems' oppositional, inter-personal, and ultimately intimate attempt to carve out a psychological, social, and sexual
enfranchisement.

While legal language obviously does not appear in every one of
Shakespeare's sonnets, the recurrence of legal diction and its structuring concepts throughout the poems pushes the usual ethical
preoccupations of lyric into something newly and decidedly social and
economic. These have been called poems of a novel psychological
subjectivity;[48] in a sense, this claim is exactly wrong, for they are, first,
poems grounded in an innovative focus on the common rights and obligations of universal human experience. The interiorization of legal
government dispossesses the human will and conscience from their
epistemologically tense joint-rule of the human subject, replacing
them with a knowable, shared code that now regulates the inward as it
must – for social peace – the outward. Shakespeare thus offers through
the *Sonnets* an epistemological challenge to the courtly lyric, in which
the codes governing the self, social relations with the friend, and erotic
relations with the beloved are rooted not in the love-objects themselves,
but in a hypostasized system, transforming the sonnet sequence from a
revelatory narrative to a much more static, argument-based explo-
ration of different facets of the known. The systematic analysis of kind
(churl), true (friend), and fair (lady) over the course of the sequence
discovers the place and nature of the lover-subject in his kin- or self-
love, his philotic or social love, and his erotic or sexual love. In ethical
terms, the effect of the legal on this sequence is to drive the subject into
a paradoxical kind of privacy and isolation: self-possession is achieved
through self-abjection, the true friend is secured only through surrendering right in him, and the erotic escape is imagined as a mutual
imprisonment. The same paradox governs the epistemology of the
poems, for the lover's appeal to the known security of a universal legal
authority perplexes the usually easy distinction between self and boy,
self and friend, and self and beloved. This epistemological aporia is
closely linked, in turn, to the metaphysical paradox of the sequence,
surely its most arcane and important: in appealing to the universal,

Shakespeare's lover is able to eschew the usual public suit of the Elizabethan sonnet sequence for the discovery, rather, of a private self; and yet this private self, in turn, must as a result of the universal conditions under which it is fashioned remain merely a type, or case. Where Sidney's, Spenser's, and Daniel's lovers might be said to portray willing and conscientious lovers unable, at least unproblematically, to access the universal, Shakespeare instead delivers us a universalized lover very nearly in peril of forfeiting his individuality.

I say very nearly because, of course, the sequence of sonnets does not, quite, conclude with the lady. Two curious things happen at the end of the *Sonnets*, which tend to be dismissed by critics because they do not seem to conform to what has come before. The first is the superficially bizarre imposition of two Spenserian sonnets dealing with Diana, Cupid, and Venus, which seem in their common preoccupation with a single narrative (about erotic love and vision) to be variations on one another. The second, of course, is the short stanzaic poem called *A Lover's Complaint*. Both of these elements contribute to the overall legally based scheme of the sequence, and help to make sense of the ethic and epistemological innovations that Shakespeare introduced into the genre. Looking back to the Elizabethan sonnet tradition, it is not so strange to think that Shakespeare might have included two transitional sonnets before the narrative poem that concludes the sequence; Spenser had bridged the *Amoretti and Epithalamion* with a short series of anacreontic poems, and the tonal debt to Spenser in Shakespeare's final sonnets is clear. But their presence is not justified merely on generic grounds, for they enact – in their mirror-like diptych, the echoic 're-word[ing]' that begins the following poem. Cupid, laying by his side his phallic brand, falls asleep beside a 'valley-fountain'; (153. 4) one of Diana's maids, finding it there, plunges it into the well, creating by an Ovidian transformation a hot spring medicinal to lovers' pains; but Shakespeare's lover, trying the virtue of the well, finds it impotent to cure his malady. The important distinction between the two rehearsals of the poem lies in their various conclusions: in the first, 153, Shakespeare's lover seeks relief in a return to the mistress's gaze, while in 154 the more overtly sexualized version of the narrative finds the lover, helpless, still bathing in the coital pool – for, here, the pool turns out to be the mistress herself. These two poems summarize in miniature the ethical and epistemological predicament in which the sonnets as a whole have left the lover, and the reader, for the lover is both renewed and abjected by the experience of love, both universalized (returned to the 'general of hot desire' – 154.7) and isolated ('touch[ed]' and 'distempered' – 153.10, 12), thrown back on the mistress herself (in 153), and on some proverbial maxim (154.14: 'Love's fire heats water, water cools not love'). The oscillation between these two forms of despair very obviously recalls Sidney's final sonnet from *Astrophil and Stella*, but in the way that it leads into the following poem, it does something very different.

Sonnets 151 and 152, just preceding, had made it obvious that conscience emerges from love. 'Conscience', to an early-modern reader, had a range of legal associations, largely bound up with the delivery of equitable judgment through the courts of Chancery and Request. These were courts in which the inflexible rigour of formal common-law process – the key to its knowable security and famed even-handedness – could (at least in theory) be redressed by the intervention of a human conscience. In Aristotle's well-known and influential formulation, these were courts in which the injustices created by a universal rule because of its universality might be redressed, with particular attention to the circumstances of an individual case.[49] The identification of 'conscience' with 'equity' was not an easy one in sixteenth-century England,[50] and there were times in Shakespeare's own career when he would seize on the important differences between them; yet at the same time there is no mistaking that, by common repute as well as in many lawyers' careful arguments, conscience and the equitable redress of Chancery were, if not identical, then at least twinned. The argument presented in 151, then, that conscience is born of love, seems to suggest the emergence of individuality and humanity from the common-law ideology of the sequence; this tendency is only taken further in the following sonnet, where the lover admits to his perjury – the kind of legal crime that might be tried in a court of error or appeal, following the supposedly secure resolution of a legal matter in some court of common resort.[51] The clear return to a legal diction shadowing conscience, equity, and appeal in the preceding two sonnets primes the reader to see something suggestive in the final sonnets of the sequence, where perhaps the fabular narratives of Cupid might seem least to allow it. The diction of these sonnets, when combined, seems to place a strong emphasis on the 'sovereign[ty]' (153.8) of the 'remedy' (154.11) afforded by the newly hybrid pool, a cure that the lover seeks in both sonnets, by 'trial', (153.10) to 'prove' (154.13). (The struggle between desire and chastity here is figured as a jurisdictional tension over sovereignty; which court, that of Diana or Venus, will bear sway?)

This case depending between desire and chastity supplies the subject of *A Lover's Complaint*, a poem as rife with framing devices and inversions as the sonnets that precede it. The narrator – who may well be the lover of the sonnets – lies down in a valley because 'accorded' to the echo it receives from a 'sist'ring vale' (2–3). Here he observes a distressed woman who, after some emblematic motions of love-jilt, tells her story to an old wise shepherd. The story itself frames the complaint of the effeminate lover who had seduced her, who in turn tells the story of a nun who seduced him. The complaint of the title thus seems to be that of the distressed woman, who (in a characteristic Shakespearean inversion) has been tempted by the youth not to surrender to his wishes, but to seek his surrender. The beauty of this youth is such that he compels his beloveds to become lovers, and is objectified by their sudden desire; his method of seduction is to incite seduction. The maid-lover, standing 'in freedom' as her own 'fee-simple' (143–44), at first resists the temptation to tempt, being by 'experience', (152) 'precedent', (155) and 'forced examples' (157) warned against the youth's perfidy; but it is precisely to the protection of 'precedent' that the youth – and the poem – direct their deflowering energies. As he urges her:

'When thou impressest, what are precepts worth
Of stale example? When thou wilt inflame,
How coldly those impediments stand forth,
Of wealth, of filial fear, law, kindred, fame?
Love's arms are peace, 'gainst rule, 'gainst sense, 'gainst shame,
And sweetens in the suff'ring pangs it bears
The aloes of all forces, shocks and fears.

'Now all these hearts that do on mine depend,
Feeling it break, with bleeding groans they pine,
And supplicant their sighs to you extend,
To leave the batt'ry that you make 'gainst mine,
Lending soft audience to my sweet design
And credent soul to that strong-bonded oath
That shall prefer and undertake my troth.'

(267–80)

The youth urges the maid-lover to lay aside the security of 'precepts'
and 'example', surrending herself, 'credent', to the impression of love
and the authority of his own 'strong-bonded oath'. The sudden equation presented here between a Stoic epistemology and a legal jargon
undoes, in a single lyrical moment, the deep-laid identification of the
Sonnets between a hypostasized legal code and the secure epistemology
it grants to subjects in their relations to themselves, their friends, and
their beloveds. Here the youth urges, instead, the surmounting epistemological power of the Stoic impression, which derives its force
precisely from its ('concave'?) opposition to all the impediments he
numbers. Then finally, in a stanza that exactly recalls the imagery of
sonnets 153 and 154, the maid-lover watches the youth drop a single
tear:

'This said, his wat'ry eyes he did dismount,
Whose sights till then were levelled on my face,
Each cheek a river running from a fount
With brinish current downward flowed apace.
O how the channel to the stream gave grace,
Who glazed with crystal gate the glowing roses
That flame through water which their hue encloses!

'O father, what a hell of witchcraft lies
In the small orb of one particular tear!
But with the inundation of the eyes
What rocky heart to water will not wear?
What breast so cold that is not warmed here?

> O cleft effect! Cold modesty, hot wrath,
> Both fire from hence and chill extincture hath.'
>
> (ll. 281–94)

The problem of the final sonnets – will fire or water, heat or chill prevail? – here resurfaces. Again, too, it is pitched as the resolution of a case 'in conscience', for the pity that the youth demands of the maid-lover is precisely the forgoing of precept, precedent, and case law that had hitherto guided her – the rectification of an epistemologically secure process of judgment, in favour of a human, a compassionate, a 'conscientious' decision. What the youth demands of her is nothing less than the suspension of the principle of common-law justice – precedential case-law itself – in favour of an *ad personam* judgment, a judgment in conscience. She falls; becoming a lover ('who, young and simple, would not be so lovered?' – 320), she proves the inverted legal maxim, 'better an inconvenience than a mischief'. Her final words ring with the total abandonment of the stable epistemology that the law had afforded the *Sonnets*, disclaiming for ever the ideology of experience, custom, and precedent upon which the common law was founded:

> 'O, all that borrowed motion, seeming owed,
> Would yet again betray the fore-betrayed,
> And new pervert a reconciled maid.'
>
> (327–9)

Chapter Four

WASTING TIME: CONDITIONALITY AND PROSPERITY IN *AS YOU LIKE IT* AND THE SECOND TETRALOGY

The conceptual movement of the *Sonnets* and *The Lover's Complaint* – from inheritance through problems of right and tort, and finally to despairing anxiety about precedence and what might be called a 'legal psychology' – is one that reappears in a number of Shakespeare's plays. Like the *Sonnets*, these plays also worry about the transition from a feudal past, for which many of the characters show a naive nostalgia, to a propertied and mercantile future where trusts have given way to debts and damages, and the traditional warrants of identity (name, title, honour) have withered under the force of new markers. Two plays in which Shakespeare takes up the concerns of the *Sonnets* are preoccupied (like the *Sonnets*) with the narrative of a boy passing into manhood. In *As You Like It*, the earlier lyric preoccupation with time and ageing forms the basis of an extended meditation on the extensibility of faith in an ethical landscape threatened by merit, reward, and profit. Prince Hal, by contrast, inherits in *1 Henry IV* the collapse of inheritance, and must chart a course between a feudal and a mercantile legal imagination in a bid for ethical and political legitimation. This chapter will look at the ways in which Shakespeare re-imagines the ontological and epistemological problems of the *Sonnets* in these two generic contexts, and will expose, again, the importance of legal language and thinking to the plays' constructions of person, time, and trust.

MUCH VIRTUE IN IF

The political and ethical condition of the opening of *As You Like It* is one of rupture to the natural order: the junior brother has usurped upon the elder, violating primogeniture in a display of power over right. Similarly, the ethical predicament of Oliver and Orlando, the eldest and youngest brothers of Rowland de Boys, is perplexed by default and disappointment.[1] Along with his father's whole estate, as eldest son Oliver has inherited an ethical obligation to his younger brothers Jaques and Orlando, a duty on which, to Orlando, he has notably defaulted. Orlando opens the play by recounting to the servant Adam the full extent of his brother's unnatural handling, which amounts to a paradoxically unkeeping keeping:

> For my part, he keeps me rustically at home, or, to speak more properly, stays me at home unkept; for call you that keeping for a gentleman of my birth, that differs not from the stalling of an ox? His horses are bred better; for besides that they are fair with their feeding, they are taught their manage, and to that end riders dearly hired: but I, his brother, gain nothing under him but growth, for the which his animals on his dunghills are as much bound to him as I. Besides this nothing that he so plentifully gives me, the something that nature gave me his countenance seems to take from me. He lets me feed with his hinds, bars me the place of a brother, and, as much as in him lies, mines my gentility with my education.

(1.1.6–20)

The result of Oliver's perversion of his duty is the breakdown in the obligation between brother and brother. Orlando considers himself not 'bound' to his brother, because his brother has failed to help him to enrich himself. The incivility between elder and younger brother is demonstrated immediately thereafter, as Oliver comes onstage to the rudest greeting from Orlando who, taking him by the throat, demands the small inheritance left him by their father. The temporal quality of Oliver's default, as described by Orlando in this passage, is striking: the virtuous 'keeping' becomes an arrestive 'stalling', and while the horses to which Orlando compares himself have achieved an 'end' purchased 'dearly', his only 'gain' is 'growth' – a state of indeterminacy and achieveless.[2] The breakdown in obligation and trust between the brothers seems, in Orlando's telling, to be a direct result of this failure of accomplishment. Orlando's language here provides the key to the relationship the play creates between time, conditionality, and the faith of human obligation. The political and ethical defaults that open the play are defined by a shared, deformed attitude to temporality: both Duke Frederick and Orlando impatiently seek to realize future promises in the present. Meantimeness, by contrast, becomes the longed-for and idealized temporal condition of *As You Like It*. In ethical and political terms, and eventually in ontological terms as well, the characters of the play seek out warrants for their actions and significance, warrants that must apply to instances of knowing or trusting as enduring or prolonged conditions.

Orlando's explanation points us back to his first line (and the first line of the play), which at first encounter is conceptually difficult – a difficulty designed to create the temporal retrospection (of disappointment) on which this passage plays. Early editors of the play often hesitated over its first line, offering to amend it because it seemed to their eyes textually corrupt.[3] It is nothing of the kind, but rather a piece of precise prose, meticulously worded to mirror syntactically what the scene will go on to represent conceptually:

ORLANDO As I remember, Adam, it was upon this fashion
bequeathed me by will but poor a thousand crowns,
and, as thou sayst, charged my brother on his blessing
to breed me well; and there begins my sadness.

(1.1.1–5)

Orlando's opening words give the legal context for the temporal conditions I have noted in his later lines. Shakespeare deliberately begins the scene *in medias res*, a trademark habit particularly important during this period of his career.[4] Adam has just been saying something; fortunately, given the verbal after-image of Orlando's demonstrative pronoun and the corroborative clause 'as thou sayst', it is just possible to reconstruct his unwritten lines. He has been reminding Orlando of the conditions set out in the written testament of his father, Rowland de Boys, concerning the upbringing of his sons; but he has also asked Orlando a question that, judging from Orlando's two replies ('and there begins my sadness'; and, further on, 'this is it, Adam, that grieves me'), must have run something like this: 'Why should you be sad, if your brother has a thousand pounds of yours, and a charge on your father's will to spend it on your breeding?' Adam touches a nerve with this question, and Orlando's exclamatory response is as much as to say, 'Why *that* is the very cause of my sadness!' The legal terms of the bequest, upon which Oliver has defaulted, were meant to provide an enduring obligation, represented financially in the capital committed to his trust; the proceeds of this trust were to be spent to Orlando's benefit in the future, an arrangement to which Oliver agreed 'on' (or at, in exchange for, by virtue of) 'his blessing' – the benediction and legitima- tion given him, as eldest son, by his dying father.[5] What began there for Orlando, however, was not benefit but disappointment; the act of entering into the obligation passed, and the money (with the blessing) committed into his hands, Oliver had no further incentive to honour the bond.[6]

The mismatch between the expectation of Orlando, on the one hand, and Oliver's lack of incentive, on the other, is one Shakespeare mirrors in our own experience of reading. What most editors fail to note about this opening passage is the way in which the word 'as' – which expresses throughout this play (from the title onwards) the temporal and ethical conditionality of actions and obligations – both binds together and rips apart what Orlando says. I have quoted above from the Arden text which, like most modern editions, obscures the instability of the original Folio text by inserting a comma before 'Adam' in the first line. What Shakespeare really (well, probably) wrote was more subtle:

ORLANDO   As I remember Adam, it was upon this fashion . . .

The force of the play's first 'as', in the earliest text, thus remains suspended between two possibilities; it is both temporal ('as I remember, Adam, it was upon this fashion') and what I will call 'conjurative' ('as I remember Adam, it was upon this fashion'). In the first reading, Orlando is pausing reflectively, and speaking vocatively to his interlocutor. In the second, he is introducing his answer with an expostulative and vehement oath – proverbial in Shakespeare's English for 'as I am a man'. The importance of this suspension lies in the way that it creates a permeability between temporal duration and ethical obligation, such that things pending come to be associated, in the thought of the play, with actions that ought to be taken. This association is immediately reinforced in the ensuing amplification, where the ethical obligation ('charged my brother on his blessing') is explicitly articulated, again in conjunction with a phrase beginning with 'as' – the 'saying' of Adam here giving corroborative testimony to Orlando's recollection of the charge imposed. The clumsy efforts of early editors to insert a subject for the verbs 'bequeathed' and 'charged', changing the verbs from impersonal passive constructions to active, only point emphatically towards Shakespeare's artful wording here: the impersonal passive verbs place absolute emphasis, for Orlando's psychology, on the temporal aspect of the verbal actions, and the zeugma ('it was bequeathed me ... and [it was] charged my brother ...') joins indisseverably the bequest by will to the charge given on blessing; the supply of a subject (e.g. 'my father bequeathed ... and [my father] charged my brother ...') would, by contrast, link the two actions by means of the (dead) father, placing them firmly in the past. The heap of prepositions in the complicated syntax provokes questions about duration: 'upon', 'by', 'on' may all imply different temporal aspects, emphasizing the disparity between the way Orlando recognizes an enduring obligation, and Oliver has concluded on a past agreement.

The narrative and conceptual structure of the play as a whole might be said to grow from the word that begins both the play and its title. 'As', like the Latin *cum* that it translated, had many grammatical functions in the common English of the period, as it does now – from temporal and correlative constructions, to conditional and conjurative uses.[7] Its particular habitat, though, was and is in legal texts, where 'as' clauses proliferate so densely that the word 'as' became, for an author like Shakespeare, practically a by-word for legal jargon. As Hamlet describes to Horatio in 5.2 of *Hamlet* the forged commission for Rosencrantz's and Guildenstern's executions, it was:

> An earnest conjuration from the King,
> As England was his faithful tributary,
> As love between them like the palm might flourish,
> As peace should still her wheaten garland wear
> And stand a comma 'tween their amities,
> And many such like 'as'es of great charge,
> That on the view and knowing of these contents,
> Without debatement further more or less,
> He should those bearers put to sudden death,
> Not shriving-time allow'd.

> (5.2.38–47)

The legal instrument that Hamlet recites to Horatio is defined by its use of the as-relation, as 'Claudius' reminds England of the conditions of the vassalage between the two nations, the endurance of which not only frames, but compels England to do Denmark's bidding. Shakespeare here associates 'as' with 'charge' in a way that was also fundamental to his conception of *As You Like It*, probably written at about the same time. The rhetoric and grammar of the 'charge' to the king of England relies on a slippage between temporal duration and conjurative force; indeed, the successive 'as' clauses enact a delay that, by that delay, conjure the charge of the charge. The commission's implication is that England, desiring to continue and perpetuate the temporal conditionality of the political structure governing Denmark's relationship to England, will need to act as commanded in this instance. It is exactly this slippage between conditional temporality and momentous conjuration that Shakespeare extends and in a sense even emblematizes in *As You Like It*, where almost all of the ethical and political relations of the play – the duties of brothers, lovers, subjects – are made conspicuously to depend on a binding force supplied by conditionality and duration, and the mere fact of extension or deferral comes to import obligation.

If duration comes in this play, as in *Hamlet*, to signify obligation, impatience and prolepsis represent the vice that threatens ethical and political bonds. The condition of Orlando's relation to Oliver must be couched in the legal terms of old Sir Rowland's bequest, in order to establish the ethical problem at the centre of the play. But equally as importantly, the nature of the bequest provokes the spectre of a charge against Oliver – as yet unexpressed, though other characters in the play will articulate and debate it soon enough. The charge is that of waste. Shakespeare uses the concept of waste in the early *Sonnets*, as we have seen, to balance with a future interest the tenant-lover's profit-driven, present cultivation of his own self.[8] Here the emphasis is similar, but the presence of real, living heirs and reversioners whose interests are being spoiled before their eyes accentuates the temporal tension between present and future interests. The waste committed by guardians on the property of their wards, or by step-parents on the property of their underage step-children – taking as much immediate profit as possible from the capital before the title reverts to its future owner – is more intimate and ethically involved a crime than the exploitation of resources which might one day revert or descend to an as yet unborn, potential heir.[9] Cowell thus stresses, in his treatment of waste, 'him in the *Reuersion* or *Remainder*', who can expect by bringing a writ of waste 'the recouerie of the things, whereupon the waste is made'.[10] In addition, Shakespeare seems to enlarge his treatment of waste in *As You Like It* by stretching it to a more political sense. Chapter 4 of Magna Carta provides for redress of an almost administrative form of abuse:

And if we commit the custody of any such land to the Shirife, or to any other which is answerable vnto vs for the issues of the same land and hee make destruction or waste of those things that he hath in custodie, we shal take of him amends and recompence therefore, the land shall be committed to two lawfull and discreete men of that see, which shall answere vnto vs for the issues of the same land, or vnto him whom wee shall assigne. And if we giue or sell to any man the custody of any such land, and he therein doe make destruction or waste, he shall lose the same custody: And it shall be assigned to two lawfull and discreete men of that see as it is aforesaide, which also in like maner shall be answerable to vs, as afore is saide.[11]

The range of possible actions that could be described under the title of 'waste' takes in a brother's intimate abuse of his brother's patrimony, at one extreme, and the very public abuse of a delegated office or custody, at the other. As You Like It gives us the ethical violation of Oliver's spoliation of Orlando's patrimony; as he remarks to himself in the first scene, 'Begin you to grow upon me? I will physic your rankness, and yet give no thousand crowns neither' (1.1.83–85). But it also gives us the public violation by Duke Frederick of the office entrusted him by his older brother, Duke Senior: while the usurpation of a younger at the expense of his elder brother might not seem, immediately, consistent with waste, Shakespeare is careful to pair it, in Charles the wrestler's report of the 'old news' from court, with waste:

> The old Duke is banished by his younger brother the new Duke, and three or four loving lords have put themselves into voluntary exile with him, whose lands and revenues enrich the new Duke, therefore he gives them good leave to wander.
>
> (1.1.97–101)

Both of these wastes insist upon the immediate enjoyment of a trust that was meant to endure, or be prolonged, over time; the ongoing obligations of Oliver to Orlando, and of Duke Senior to Frederick, have both been foreshortened, or 'cashed-in', for present profit. Frederick, heir to his son-less brother Duke Senior, takes present possession of the estate in which he had but a future right; while at the same time he also commits waste in a political sense, for he realizes the asset (political control of the country) given to him only in custody and trust. (Given the provision of Magna Carta for the 'public' form of waste, it is not surprising that the ultimate resolution of the play sees Duke Senior acquiring two 'lawful and discreet' men – Orlando and Oliver – to take custody of the two estates left vacant by Duke Frederick's sudden abdication.)

The play's other ways of thinking through the temporal predicament of waste are similarly structured by legal thinking, and involve debt and sale. A typical example appears later in the first scene, when Oliver calls on Charles the wrestler to prepare for the underhand assassination of Orlando. The exchange between Oliver and Charles is punctuated by terms that invoke the acquittance of a bill of obligation. Charles informs Oliver that he will be wrestling on the following day 'for my credit', and boasts that 'he that escapes me without some broken limb shall acquit him well' (1.1.122–24). Punning on the early-modern practice of giving a 'counterfoil' or receipt at the discharging of an obligation,[12] Charles confesses that 'I would be loath to foil him, as I must for my own honour if he come in' (1.1.125–26). Oliver then informs Charles of Orlando's alleged contrivances against him, and warns the wrestler of Orlando's murderous jealousy, certain to make Charles its target unless Orlando should win the match. To these advertisements Charles remits bluff confidence:

> CHARLES I am heartily glad I came hither to you. If he come tomorrow, I'll give him his payment. If ever he go alone again, I'll never wrestle for prize more. And so God keep your worship.
>
> (1.1.152–55)

The thousand crowns that Orlando had demanded of Oliver are promised him here, by a kind of conversion, in the form of broken limbs. The 'as' relation created by the will's 'charge' to Oliver had 'bound' the two brothers to mutual fraternal offices; in a parody of this mutuality, Charles offers a different kind of copulation (picking up another sense of the earlier 'foil'): not only will Orlando thereafter ever require assistance in walking, but his attempt to become 'independent' (by securing his inheritance and gaining honour for himself, through winning at wrestling) will result in the opposite – for ever after his value will be measured by Charles's superiority, and he will wear the sign of that debt, as it were, around his neck.

It is therefore fitting that, when Celia and Rosalind arrive at the wrestling, and receive from Le Beau a report of the sport so far, Celia's instinct is to break immediately into the same legal language that had earlier structured Charles's speech:

FIGURE 6a A bond of obligation (recto and verso) between Shakerly and Henry Marmion, on the one party, and Richard Cartwright of Aynho, Northamptonshire, on the other. Cambridge University Library, MS Doc 3710. The Marmions owed Cartwright £52 10s, to be paid by 26 June 1619; if they failed to do so, John Dillon and Gerard Coker, their associates, undertook to stand jointly bound with them to pay Cartwright 'a hundred pounds of lawfull monye'.

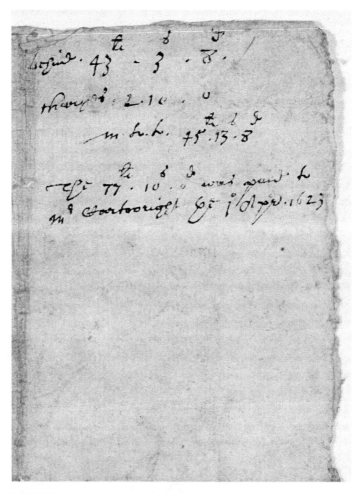

FIGURE 6b

LE BEAU   I will tell you the beginning, and if it please your
ladyships, you may see the end, for the best is yet to do,
and here where you are they are coming to perform it.

CELIA   Well, the beginning that is dead and buried.

LE BEAU   There comes an old man, and his three sons –

CELIA   I could match this beginning with an old tale.

> LE BEAU   Three proper young men, of excellent growth and
>   presence –
> CELIA   With bills on their necks: 'Be it known unto all men by
>   these presents' –
>
>   (1.2.106–16)

The formula *Noverint universi per praesenti* – 'be it known unto all men by these presents' – was the standard introduction in the early-modern period for bills of obligation (or bonds). By the usual system, a document was drawn up with an obligation to pay a fixed sum stated on one side of the paper in Latin. Upon the other side, always in English, a 'condition' was annexed, upon the fulfilment of which the obligation to which it was attached would become void. Celia fleetingly imagines that the young hopefuls coming to try a fall with Charles the wrestler will be discharged of their bills of obligation – paid, as Charles had it in the earlier scene with Oliver. Celia's joke is particularly apt because the form of the deed of obligation generally described the obligee as 'held and firmly bound' to the payment stipulated on the paper (*teneri et firmiter obligari*) – of obvious resonance when the metaphorical obligation is pictured by a wrestling. Moreover, Duke Frederick plays pointedly on the idea of Orlando's attempt to discharge his obligation when, after the fight has ended, he refers to Orlando's 'deed', before defaulting – because of Orlando's parentage – on the thanks and honour he owes him for his victory. These are instead supplied by Celia and Rosalind. As the scene ends, we learn from Le Beau, who returns to warn Orlando of Frederick's unstable and tyrannical displeasure with him, of the breakdown in the legitimate conditionality meant to govern such exchanges:

> LE BEAU   Good sir, I do in friendship counsel you
>   To leave this place. Albeit you have deserv'd
>   High commendation, true applause, and love,
>   Yet such is now the Duke's condition
>   That he misconsters all that you have done.
>   The Duke is humorous; what he is indeed
>   More suits you to conceive than I to speak of.
>
>   (1.2.251–57)

The fanciful conceit strung out by the wordplay of the scene imagines that the 'condition' of the Duke – that provision endorsed on the back of the bond, the discharge of which Orlando sought to achieve at the wrestling – leads him to reward the young man with hate, rather than with love. Orlando finds, again, that the action of an instant – the deed – fails in its relation to the supposed condition of its performance. The obligation's condition usually took a form similar to this:

> The Condicion of this obligacion is such that if the above bounden A. B. shall and will at all times hereafter well and truly hould observe performe fulfill and keepe all and singuler the Covenantes, grauntes, articles, promyses, and agreementes which on his and theire partes and behalfes are to be houlden, observed, performed, fulfilled, and kept, written declared and specified in one paire of Indentures of bargaine and sale bearing even date with theis presentes made betweene the said A. B. of the one part and the above named C. D. of the other part according to the true intent and meaneing of the said Indentures That then this present obligacion shalbe void and of none effect, or els stand and be in full force and vertue.[13]

The protasis of the conditional clause here ('if the above bounden A. B. . . . .'), when satisfied, discharges the obligation ('. . . then this present obligacion shalbe void . . .'). Orlando has been acting on the assumption that the substance of the condition would consist in doing well; instead, it appears to consist – for Duke Frederick, at least – in being anyone other than himself.[14] The conditional clause, another version of the Latin *cum* clause that also gives us the various 'as'-type constructions of the play, is one that Orlando has still not properly understood. In this scene he seeks again to become independent – in an attempt to 're-member Adam' by avoiding the fate of the broken rib, a fate met by all of Charles' other opponents – but, though initially successful, he finds himself 'bounden', both to Le Beau (1.2.276) and, more importantly, to Rosalind.

The 'waste' from which both Duke Senior and Orlando were seen to suffer at the beginning of the play appears suddenly the moment that

Celia and Rosalind gain the Forest of Arden (2.4), and again at the moment that Orlando, himself, reaches the Forest and Duke Senior (2.7). The forest is, of course, a 'waste' – communal land not owned by any man – and thus an appropriate site for the commoning, property-less antics of the dispossessed duke.[15] Charles the wrestler has already, by this point, made clear the forest's association with a 'golden' society before money and property, and linked to the pastoral; of Duke Senior, he reports to Oliver in 1.1 that:

> They say he is already in the Forest of Arden, and a many merry men with him; and there they live like the old Robin Hood of England. They say many young gentlemen flock to him every day, and fleet the time carelessly as they did in the golden world.
>
> (1.1.111–15)

But Celia's and Rosalind's arrival in this world meets with a slightly different reception from that Orlando finds. Both Rosalind and Orlando arrive in Arden bearing a starving mate, and both seek to feed them immediately; Rosalind takes a servant (Corin), who becomes her 'faithful feeder' (2.4.98), and Orlando falls into the service (becoming a 'feed[er]' – see 2.7.105 and 168) at Duke Senior's table. Rosalind's attempt to 'buy entertainment' (2.4.71) results in the opportunity to purchase a sheep-cote; apparently the vendor is not important – he remains nameless – and indeed the fact of money never soils the scene, or the hands of the parties to the exchange, for as Touchstone comments to his mistresses early in 2.4, 'I had rather bear with you than bear you; yet I should bear no cross if I did bear you, for I think you have no money in your purse' (2.4.10–12). And yet the talk between the princesses and Corin the shepherd returns again and again to 'gold', to 'sale', to 'buying', to 'pay', and to 'wages', to the extent that when Corin concludes the scene by promising to be 'your very faithful feeder', the reader cannot help but hear 'feodar', for 'feudary' – a 'retainer' or servant[16] (2.4.70–99). The Forest of Arden may be, for the exiled Duke, Robin Hood's own land, the 'golden world' of Ovid's *Metamorphoses* in which no one has property in any thing, but for Rosalind and Celia upon their arrival it is, though a 'waste' land, one that has begun to be enclosed, and by enclosure bought and sold. To be sure, the fiction of the princesses' fee-ing of their servants, and money-purchase of their new sheepcote remains a fiction, but the payment that they promise is merely deferred, not denied. Corin serves in expectation of a reward.

By contrast, when Orlando arrives in the forest, having set the faltering Adam to rest, he happens upon the cave and consort of Duke Senior, whereupon Duke Senior immediately diagnoses Orlando's disease in conspicuously feudal terms:

ORLANDO	Forbear, and eat no more.
JAQUES	Why, I have eat none yet.
ORLANDO	Nor shalt not till necessity be served.
JAQUES	Of what kind should this cock come of?
DUKE SENIOR	Art thou thus bolden'd man by thy distress?
	Or else a rude despiser of good manners,
	That in civility thou seem'st so empty?
ORLANDO	You touch'd my vein at first: the thorny point
	Of bare distress hath ta'en from me the show
	Of smooth civility. Yet am I inland bred,
	And know some nurture. But forbear, I say ...

(2.7.88–98)

While Jaques continues to play on the theme of fools and fooling which has so far preoccupied him in this scene (the answer to his question being, 'this cock's come [i.e. coxcomb] of ...'), Orlando and Duke Senior play a word game of a different kind. The allusion to the popular motto taken from Epictetus, *sustine et abstine* ('bear and forbear')[17] prompts Duke Senior to chide Orlando for his intemperate response to 'distress', and Orlando to apologize for it with another curious (and hypermetric) phrase, 'inland bred'. Duke Senior alludes to a feudal relationship when he suggests that Orlando has suffered a 'distress'; as Cowell defines it:

Distresses (*Districtio, Districtus*) commeth of the French (*Distresse, angustiae*) It signifieth most commonly in the common law, a compulsion in certaine reall actions, whereby to bring a man to appearance in courte, or to pay debt or dutie denied. The effect whereof most commonly is, to driue the party distreined to replevie the distresse, and so take his action of trespasse against the distreiner, or els to compound neighbourly with him for the debt or dutie, for the which he distreineth.[18]

Orlando has certainly by this point suffered a distress, in the appropriation and waste of his patrimony – the lands worth a thousand crowns left him in trust with his brother Oliver;[19] but Duke Senior uses the term metaphorically to refer to the 'distress' of Orlando's 'civility', pointing by a happy accident to the way in which Orlando's education and breeding have been stripped from him in order to compel a debased service. In his reply, Orlando acknowledges his gentlemanly status by reference to his 'inland' breeding; 'inland', an English synonym for the Law French *demesne*, was loosely used in feudal law to describe those parts of a lord's holding that were held to his proper use, and not leased or held by tenants.[20] In this context, the play on 'feed' that concludes this scene, mirroring the earlier exchange between Celia, Rosalind, and Corin, leads similarly to 'feodar', but in a different sense: by sitting down to Duke Senior's table, Orlando becomes one of his attendants; as Celia informs Rosalind in 3.4, Orlando's loyalties may have shifted after coming to the forest, from lover to lieger.

Both Celia and Rosalind, on the one hand, and Orlando, on the other, enter into 'feodary' relations upon gaining the forest, the former at least ostensibly in a more modern, waged sense, and the later in a more traditional, feudal sense. The division between the two is reinforced by a parallel occurrence of the word 'waste' in both scenes: the same word crops up in each of the parallel narratives, but with a decisively different temporal impact. When Celia informs Corin that 'I like this place / And willingly could waste my time in it' (2.3.93–94), she apparently means nothing more subtle than that she might discharge or spend her time in the forest to her content, without any further forward end; but given the sexual puns of the opening of the scene, in which Celia gives out that she is pregnant with Ganymede's child, her words here seem to indicate that she has chosen this place of retreat as a fit one for her 'durance' or 'bond' ('my time'[21]) – a place to 'waste', or use

EMBLEMATA.   157

Ἀνέχε καὶ ἀπέχε.

EMBLEMA XXXIIII.

ET *toleranda homini triſtis fortuna ferendo eſt,*
  Et nimium felix ſæpe timenda fuit.
Suſtine (Epiſtetus dicebat) & abſtine. oportet
  Multa pati, illicitis abſ̃q, tenere manus.
Sic ducis imperium vinſtus fert poplite taurus
  In dextro: ſic ſe continet à grauidis.

D Vobus his verbis, ἀνέχε κỳ ἀπέχε , Philoſopho Epiſteto *Philoſo-*
  familiaribus, tota bene viuendi ratio comprehendi poteſt. *phia Epi-*
Primò ſiquidem ad patientiam adhortabatur, qua quiſque diſce- *ſteti duo-*
ret tum aduerſos fortunæ caſus, tum etiam laborem æquo ani- *bus com-*
                                                              prehenſa
                                                              verbis.
mo

FIGURE 7 Emblem on temperance, from Andrea Alciato, *Omnia Emblemata* (Antwerp, 1581), no. 34, '*Sustine et abstine*' [Bear and forbear]. Queens' College Library, M.7.36.

up, a very particular sort of meantime. As Celia says to Rosalind and Touchstone at the beginning of the scene, 'I pray you bear with me' (2.4.9). The other form of duration represented in the play is similarly thrown to waste, in the parallel scene: when Orlando leaves Duke Senior and Jaques to go fetch Adam, charging them again to 'forbear' their 'fruit', the Duke assures him that 'we will nothing waste till you return' (2.7.134). Despite the use of 'till', this is not the bearing of a time meantime, but the forbearance of time altogether; the 'nothing' that the Duke offers to waste is itself a waste. The resort in both scenes to the idea of waste is important because it shows how the Forest of Arden provides, in two possible senses, an escape from the real waste to which both Orlando and Rosalind (through her father) have been subject: deferral ('bearing') or denial ('forbearing'). For the daughters, waste becomes a temporary escape from fruition and consequence, something to be borne awhile; for the men, by contrast, the feudal fantasy of a wholesale rejection of ownership makes possible the true 'waste' of total dispossession: common property and the golden world.

The temporal project of *As You Like It* is to find a way to import the meantimeness of the Forest of Arden into the courtly, inland world from which the conditionality of as-relations has, by Frederick's usurpation and Oliver's default, been banished. To some degree this is merely a sophisticated way of saying what all Shakespeare comedies do (and perhaps all comedies do), in the cultivation of ironic models of the self somewhere between the painful sincerity of a catastrophic beginning and the no less painful assimilation of the new, socialized self into a pageant of justice at the play's conclusion. The particularly intensive focus of *As You Like It* on the as-relation, though, is signalled by the play's middle scenes, in which Rosalind allows Orlando to woo her in her own person, and by her own name, the only difference from reality being the 'as if' relation itself – an artificial imposition of the smallest possible increment of hypothesis (that is, mere hypothesis itself). By the end of the play, it is no accident that a number of characters tend to disappear or become marginalized – Adam, Celia, Frederick, Oliver, and, finally, Jaques himself – because their identity had always been, like the Fool in *King Lear*, hypothetical, or in the conceptual language of the play, 'conditional'. Like the temporary condition under which the money in an obligation or bond was considered owing which, once cancelled, removes the debt, the 'back-friends' (3.2.155) are exhausted by the court's return inland: for the court to return, repossessing its right place and discharging its outstanding payments (in estates and time), is to delete the 'foil' endorsed on the bond's 'backside', or verso, and cancel the condition of the obligation.[22]

The conclusion of the play thus returns with a sense of unresolved two-mindedness to the temporality of condition and the *cum/*'as' clauses that have defined the language of the characters throughout. Touchstone's long disquisition on the lie seven times removed appears, crucially, just before the entrance of Hymen with the two brides – an entrance that finally resolves the as-ifness of the play by disclosing Rosalind for the woman that she is (at least temporarily). The 'degrees of the lie' twice enumerated by Touchstone bear more than a passing resemblance to the seven degrees stipulated for the exchange of claims in the formal pleading of a case at common law: count (or *narratio*, narration), bar (or plea), replication, rejoinder, surrejoinder, rebutter, and surrebutter.[23] The fact that Touchstone's catalogue of lies fixes on seven degrees or stages is probably enough to advertise it as a parody of pleading, but the legal import of the passage hardly stops there. As Touchstone concludes:

> I knew when seven justices could not take up a quarrel, but when the parties were met themselves, one of them thought but of an If, as, 'If you said so, then I said so'. And they shook hands and swore brothers. Your If is the only peacemaker: much virtue in If.
>
> (5.4.96–101)

The 'seven justices' to whom Touchstone here alludes are faced with a 'courtly' quarrel of a different kind than we might at first expect: the 'lie' here becomes a 'counter' for the disagreement between two parties in a legal contest over the statement of the facts as set out in the pleading on the case. The seven stages of medieval pleading had evolved to reach the 'issue' (*exitus*) upon which the case could be tried – usually a question of fact averred of one party and denied of the other, though sometimes (in the case of a demurrer) a point of law.[24] In

Touchstone's example, the seven justices are not able to agree on the judgment on the issue; the only possible way in which this impasse could come about, by the medieval conventions of pleading, would be by demurrer, the arguments over which had subsequently proved inconclusive. In the rare cases where this result occurred – cases of legal *aporia* – the only route was to back up from the attempted resolution, and try to reach a different issue. This is exactly the situation that Touchstone succinctly describes: the parties, meeting, decide to transform the entire seven-stage process, after the fact, into a hypothetical.

Frederic Maitland, the great legal historian, dubbed this probative consideration of hypothetical points – legal argument conducted 'as-if' – 'tentative pleading'.[25] Before committing the formal pleading in a case to writing (in Latin), lawyers conducted oral pleading in Law French at the bar of the court, trying out possible positions; while these 'oral pleadings' were sometimes committed to paper (again, in Law French), unlike the formal entries they might always be subsequently amended. This had provided during the medieval period the usual route for discussion of points of law, as lawyers could agree on the fundamental points of law underpinning the decisions taken in pleading, and only commit the pleading itself to formal articulation once these points had been settled.[26] Consensus on the nature of such points of law thus developed organically during the medieval period, and was recorded in the manuscript year-books of the medieval period; year-books subsequently developed into the authored 'reports' of celebrated lawyers, who in the Tudor period began to publish their notes on cases in a print format (the most celebrated, of course, being the nine volumes compiled by Sir Edward Coke).[27] By the late sixteenth century, though, a substantial change had taken place in the way in which the issue in a case was reached. The 1540 Statute of Jeofails, which attempted to prevent the spurious quashing of verdicts on the basis of trivial formal errors in pleading, reserved such objections to the demurrer, requiring litigants who wished to take formal exceptions to stake their whole case on the alleged formal error.[28] Because this led to a rapid increase in the numbers of demurrers, judges became wary of prejudicing their opinions in the demurrer by commenting on tentative pleadings, and the latter were increasingly disallowed. With no opportunity to 'try out' points of law before the written pleadings, by the late sixteenth century lawyers had to rely increasingly on the (Latin) written books of entries, the first of which had been published in 1510, but the more recent of which – William Rastell's *A collection of entrees* – had appeared in 1574, and ran to over six hundred folios. Touchstone twice elaborates the seven degrees of the 'lie direct' at the end of *As You Like It* exactly because of this shift that had taken place, in recent memory, from tentative to formal pleading. In the first instance (5.4.68–80), he gives an account of the case wherein he reached the 'Lie Circumstantial and the Lie Direct' after he 'dislike[d] the cut of a certain courtier's beard' (5.4.69). In the second instance, by contrast, he 'nominate[s] the degrees of the lie' according to a printed source:

> TOUCHSTONE   O sir, we quarrel in print, by the book; as you have books for good manners. I will name you the degrees. The first, the Retort Courteous; the second, the Quip Modest; the third, the Reply Churlish; the fourth, the Reproof Valiant; the fifth, the Countercheck Quarrelsome; the sixth, the Lie with Circumstance; the seventh, the Lie Direct. All these you may avoid but the Lie Direct; and you may avoid that too, with an If.
>
> (5.4.88–96)

The shift from an instance of quarrelling to a form for quarrelling reflects the shift that took place in pleading in common-law courts during the sixteenth century. Touchstone drives home the reference with the use of 'avoid' – the formal Law French term for one of the most common responses in pleading.[29] Touchstone's emphasis on the 'if' – on the conditionality of the pleading as a whole – attempts to backtrack from the fixed, written formulae to which his second rehearsal of the stages of a lie direct has committed him, back to a hypothetical world in which no action is necessarily meaningful, because all actions are tentative, and all pleas avoidable.

The appearance of Hymen at exactly this moment, with the revelation of Rosalind's real identity, acts immediately to undermine the tentativity of Touchstone's legal lesson about pleading. The emblematics of Hymen's speech present a fantasy of active and realizable truth:

> HYMEN   Then is there mirth in heaven,
> When earthly things made even
> Atone together.
> Good Duke receive thy daughter,
> Hymen from heaven brought her,
> Yea brought her hither,
> That thou mightst join her hand with his
> Whose heart within his bosom is.
>
> (5.4.106–13)

Rosalind's hand, the symbol of agency and performance, is here joined to Orlando's intention (the 'heart within his bosom'). Orlando has revealed to Rosalind, through the tentative and hypothetical pleadings of their forest exchanges, the nature of his real intention in love; this Rosalind, now issuing in her true form, can join to real performance. The return of Jaques de Boys at this moment is necessary to the plot – with its *deus ex machina* resolution of the bitter enmity between the Dukes – but it is also conceptually consequent on the revelation of Rosalind's real self. The forest world can no longer persist as a place of anything more than deferral of the truth, as the hypothetical has, with the appearance of Hymen, been cancelled. The men's attempt to live in the Forest of Arden in a feudal golden age, to pursue a philosophy not of bearing but of forbearance, is exposed for its folly: even Frederick (who sees very little) sees that the dyad of possession/dispossession is always unstable, and that Duke Senior's fantasy of a seasonless life beyond 'the penalty of Adam' (2.1.5) is untenable. It is at the moment of Hymen's arrival that the last of the conditional characters – Jaques – makes his departure. Though Duke Senior calls for a 'stay . . . stay', the judgment is by this point inexorable. Jaques had earlier spoken, by an ostensibly theatrical metaphor, of the way in which all people have their 'exits and their entrances' (2.7.139–66); here the exit (*exitus*, 'issue') has finally been reached, and the case is ready for entrance (or 'entry').

The intrusion of the 'inland' and its court prospects into the Forest of Arden immediately transforms the significance of the happiness of the 'golden world'. Duke Senior's attempt to convince the host 'meantime [to] forget' the news from court, and to 'fall into our rustic revelry' sounds, as Jaques insists, like a hollow feint. No longer constrained by necessity, the forest sports have become mere frivolity. When all the meantimeness of the play has been diminished and reduced to mere 'pastime', and Jaques has departed, Duke Senior closes the play with a simple couplet that takes in all of the play's diverse formulations of the legal construction of conditionality and temporality:

> Proceed, proceed. We will begin these rights
> As we do trust they'll end, in true delights.
>
> (5.4.195–96)

The play's superior judge, momentarily stayed by Jaques's warning (recalling by a macaronic pun the *cave* of Roman law – forbearance, avoidance, refusal of the issue), once again sets the proceedings in motion – as much legal as dancing 'measures'. Jaques's parting act of sentencing, in which he gives to each of the primary protagonists what he or she 'deserve[s]', completes the conditional suspension of the 'as' relation, restoring wastes, discharging obligations, and concluding pleading (or, in Touchstone's case, temporarily concluding them). This has the effect of restoring the trust in obligations – in the conditionality of meantimes – that has been lacking in the ethical and political ruptures of the main plot, such that Duke Senior's final couplet is able to join beginnings to ends by trust. I have tendentiously mispelled 'rites' in my quotation of the couplet above, in order to emphasize what, to the reader as to the audience, must appear a slippery *sententia*: the performance of marriage, as always in Shakespeare's comedies, stands synecdochically for the whole bag of ethical and political obligations that will now, in a socially reconstituted world, remain reliable. To commence a rite, at the end of a Shakespeare comedy, is to enter into a right. Here, again, the syntactically ambiguous nature of the 'as' clause marries together the four different relations that conditionality creates:

1 Causal: we will begin these rights because we trust they will end in true delights.
2 Correlative: we will begin these rights in the same way that they will end, namely in true delights.
3 Temporal: we will begin these rights so long as we trust that they will end in true delights.
4 Conjurative: by the faith we have in the delightful end of these rites, we will begin them.

As Hymen has coupled the four couples, so Duke Senior restores the time: meantimeness creates the conditions for cause, significance, and trust. That Shakespeare fully intended this four-way syntactical knot to tie off the play is made plainly clear by Rosalind's short epilogue, in which she quickly runs through temporality (a lady at the end, a lord at the beginning), correlativity (wine needs no bush, yet good wine always has a good bush), and causality ('good plays prove the better by the help of good Epilogues'), before turning to the conjurative 'as'. In this final set-piece of grammar-made-moral-philosophy, Rosalind re-asserts the conditionality of her perfomativity (she is a he, after all), and both 'charge[s]' and 'conjure[s]' the audience, on the bases, respectively, of their love, and of her 'offer' to kiss the men, to show their appreciation.

PROSPEROUS OATHS

If the conclusion of *As You Like It* presents a social world reconciled to the ethical and political situation of a conditional temporality, it also leaves us (as all of Shakespeare's comedies do, and as comedy must) with a swallowed anguish. The straight-talking man of melancholy integrity, Jaques, has abandoned the scene, and a threatening pall of future fulfilment hangs over the final measures. Orlando had extolled the faithful Adam, early in the play, for his dutiful adherence to an ethical obligation rooted in the past, and not in the future; real honour and service – that of the golden age, in Orlando's estimation – is that which serves for a past duty or an obligation already sworn or promised, and not for a reward offered in the future:

ORLANDO   O good old man, how well in thee appears
                     The constant service of the antique world,
                     When service sweat for duty, not for meed.
                     Thou art not for the fashion of these times,
                     Where none will sweat but for promotion,
                     And having that, do choke their service up
                     Even with the having; it is not so with thee.
                                                                            (2.3.56–62)

Debt, in other words, is the preferred ethical relation for the good man, far superior to expectation of reward. For a benefit conferred in the past, rather than an expectation to be realized in the future, Adam continues to sweat. This model, an antique ideal from which the play's protagonists persistently swerve, has nonetheless not been completely marginalized by the play's close, and Jaques's 'bequeath[ing]' to the protagonists of their deserts and merits sounds less like a celebration and more like a condemnation. Surely it was convenient for Oliver to match himself to Celia, and gain her 'friends and allies'; surely it was politic for Orlando to fall in love with Rosalind, the daughter of the banished duke singled out for him after the wrestling by Le Beau. One might want to claim, for example, that Orlando fell in love with Rosalind before Le Beau entered, and that the retrospective interrogation was merely performed to shed light on his choice; but that would be to overlook Rosalind's curious gift of the chain, which she delivers with words designed to make it clear to Orlando that she is the daughter not of the incumbent but of the banished Duke. Orlando knows already which cousin is which, but pretends – for his own sake? for ours? – that he does not. The problem for the audience, and for the characters themselves, is that, short of Jaquean abstinence, they will never finally be able to distinguish between the genuinely virtuous love of a good man, and the self-interested and ambitious love of the careerist.

Shakespeare here anticipates an enlightenment approach to ethics that links moral action to law and the behaviour of individuals to universal categories. This peculiarly Kantian take on ethics – it forms the basis of Kant's discussion of the categorical imperative in *The Groundwork of the Metaphysics of Morals*[30] – is one with which

Shakespeare experimented repeatedly throughout this period of his career as a dramatist. Hamlet, for example, attempts an obfuscation of motive similar to Orlando's, just before the playing of the *The Murder of Gonzago*, when he insists to Horatio that their friendship is rooted in their shared commitment to a Stoic ethics – and must be so, because Hamlet stands to gain no future benefit from it:

> HAMLET   Nay, do not think I flatter,
> For what advancement may I hope from thee
> That no revenue hast but thy good spirits
> To feed and clothe thee? Why should the poor be flatter'd?
> No, let the candied tongue lick absurd pomp
> And crook the pregnant hinges of the knee
> Where thrift may follow fawning.
>
> (3.2.57–63)

Hamlet here resorts to a legal allusion – to the *negativa pregnans* of the canonists, by which a negative answer betrays an affirmative – in his attempt to reveal the hingedness of a bow to be not a mark of humility but rather a duplicity characteristic of flatterers. By a very impressive irony, as we have seen, Shakespeare turns the *negativa pregnans* back on Hamlet himself, for his 'nay' and 'no' only confirm for us the fact that, of course, he wouldn't want Horatio's money even if he had it, and values him only for his 'good spirits'.[31] Perhaps the clearest and most compelling example of this kind of thinking, though, comes from the second act of *Troilus and Cressida*, where Hector, Troilus, and Paris debate before Priam the question of whether or not to return Helen of Troy to the Greeks. The Greeks have promised the Trojans an oblivion if they should return Helen (see 2.2.1–7), effectively offering to forget the past, with 'all damage else', if only this one defect be made good. Hector allows his younger brothers the latitude to rehearse entry-level arguments out of the school primers of chivalric honour and moral philosophy before finally weighing in with the play's core ethical paradox. Telling Paris and Troilus that they 'have glozed – but superficially, not much / Unlike young men, whom Aristotle thought / unfit to hear moral philosophy' (2.2.165–67), he proceeds to demolish their arguments of 'pleasure and revenge' (2.2.171). Against their rash luxuriousness, Hector opposes the full force of natural and positive law:

HECTOR   Nature craves
                All dues be rendered to their owners. Now,
                What nearer debt in all humanity
                Than wife is to the husband? If this law
                Of nature be corrupted through affection,
                And that great minds, of partial indulgence
                To their benumbed wills, resist the same,
                There is a law in each well-ordered nation
                To curb those raging appetites that are
                Most disobedient and refractory.
                If Helen then be wife to Sparta's king,
                As it is known she is, these moral laws
                Of nature and of nations speak aloud
                To have her back returned. Thus to persist
                In doing wrong extenuates not wrong
                But makes it much more heavy.

                                        (2.2.163–88)

Hector's argument against Troilus and Paris distances the ethical obligation to 'nature' and 'law' from the affections – the 'wills' – that would keep Helen for some future advantage. To persist in the wrong of keeping her, by Hector's argument, is to exacerbate a crime against the 'near[est] debt in all humanity' that there is. If this is so, then why does Hector immediately change his mind, and throw in his lot with his brothers? Within a single line, he 'propend[s] … to keep Helen still; / For 'tis a cause that hath no mean dependence / Upon our joint and several dignities' (2.2.190–93). Where Paris and Troilus had celebrated Helen as something rich and valuable, Hector decries her worth; all the Trojans will gain by Helen in the future keeping of her, he claims, is shame and ignominy. But by an ethical paradox that only extends what we have seen already in *As You Like It* and in *Hamlet*, Hector finds that such shame is the only source of honour. Because the Trojans can hope for nothing at all by Helen's keeping – indeed, they maim themselves in keeping her – to keep her becomes the utmost act of self-dignification (or, in Shakespeare's usual parlance, self-gracing). They will die, as Cassandra's brief entrance in the middle of the scene assures us; they will do the greatest wrong, as Hector acknowledges; but because their future will be in every way cancelled, both in deed and in report, their total resistance to a total deletion will create for them unlimited dignity. The Greeks offer them restitution, and oblivion; the Trojans choose retention, and memory.

The way in which Hector's choice engages with ideas about temporality, redemption, law, and ethics provides a kind of answer to the problem posed by the conclusion of *As You Like It*. Jaques tries to stage a retreat from dogmatism and from certainty in the final moments of the play and, though he fails, Duke Senior does prorogue conclusiveness awhile even after Jaques's departure. But conclusiveness – reward for merit, just desert – will come for the characters of the play, for Jaques has promised it as his departure, and this satisfaction of conditionality and obligation will, presumably, leave the ethical and political relations of the play in the same bondless predicament in which we found them at the start. The 'chance of war' in *Troilus and Cressida*, similarly, joins conditionality to dignity: the greater the 'if', the greater the virtue. The heroes of *Troilus and Cressida*, for their part, should not return Helen to prevent Cassandra's doom; that would certainly be ignoble, and it would fail to show goodness, anyway. To make restitution and conform to the obligations of law and of nations, on the other hand, would be to do right, but such right-doing results only in oblivion: the good man cannot be distinguished from the type of the good man, and his 'free determination' (and here Hector anticipates Kant exactly) is such that it might be abstracted and universalized as a moral law. Indeed, Shakespeare parodies this process in the following act, when Troilus, Cressida, and Pandarus knowingly (and ironically) exchange their identities for categories (see 3.2.169–203). Similarly, one might argue for keeping Helen in order to achieve some sort of future pleasure or honour (the ends of Paris and Troilus, in their arguments), but profit here clouds the fame both of moral worth and of honour. Instead, Hector's choice pits the individuality of the self – 'dignity' – against the universals of law and ethics (knowns), but only once that individuality can be shorn of any suspicion of ambition. Dignity for Hector must be limitlessly self-defeating, a process of inscribing one's particularity indelibly on the past by reaching gigantically for an empty future, for a straw. In other words, Hector's argument creates absolute dignity by violating absolute obligation, but his choice is a tragic one inasmuch as it is made for all time.

At first, this paradoxical process of self-creating self-destruction might seem to have something to do with law only insofar as it utterly and constitutively opposes it. But the kind of law to which Hector refers in his closing arguments in the case of Helen of Troy is clearly the prescriptive, universal law of the classical world, and not the common law of early-modern England. Hector values himself by making himself – his particularity – an absolute, not by assimilating his nature to a pre-existent absolute; another way of putting this would be to say that Hector imagines himself to be an original to be imitated, rather than as an imitation or an instance. It is no accident that *As You Like It* spends so much time thinking about the attempt to regain an Edenic (or at least Adamic) liberty from women, property, and time; for its preoccupation with genesis-thought in relation to a conditional (or conjurative) self-possession is one that had exercised Shakespeare already, in a series of plays more directly and explicitly engaged with common law ideas. In the historical transition from *Richard II* to *Henry V*, England is seen to move from an Edenic garden-world to a military landscape of brutal economies; but the second tetralogy also charts the emergence of a precedential legal philosophy (much in the spirit of *King John*) from a divinely instituted legal order presumed to be entirely consistent with natural law. In the process it shows how the development of this legal philosophy requires us, as ethical subjects, to recognize that all authentic appeals to right imply self-deletion with reference either to the past (i.e. right by inheritance) or the future (i.e. right by conquest). The lineal descent to which Hal aspires to restore the monarchy stands in opposition to invasion – not only Ravenspurgh, but France – but this invasive model of self-construction, which is figured for Bolingroke in *Richard II* as the assertion of title, is closely linked in these plays, too, to market purchase and sale: receipts (reckonings), factors, theft, auction. The various engagements of these plays with the legal topics of feudalism, waste, prerogative, debt, and title lead Hal to take an attitude to law very similar, as I will argue, to Hamlet's, but the historical (rather than tragic, comic, or tragi-comic) frame pushes this legal interest towards a resolution of the temporal problem very different from that provided in *Hamlet*, *As You Like It*, or *Troilus and Cressida*. To put it bluntly, Hal cannot afford to live without a future; indeed, all his energy must be expended to secure the possibility of legitimate posterity. Celia and Rosalind can find faith in the temporary conditionality of their bond, a debt for which they stand surety to one another but which they are sure they will discharge; Hector can achieve dignity by obliviating his future; but Hal must at once both begin his own line, and delete – or at least mystify – that beginning.

The legal-temporal language by which the second tetralogy largely focuses its thinking about the relationship of present to future lies in an opposition between waste and oath. Oath-taking, and the breaking and fulfilling of oaths, occupies the historical narrative of these plays from the opening scenes of *Richard II* to the final lines of *Henry V*. The temporal character of the oath has an obvious relation to that of waste: where waste seeks to seize or realize in the present what should remain an ongoing condition or expectation in the future, the oath displaces into the future the sense and significance of a present utterance. The oath at the centre of *Richard II* is, of course, the oath of fealty, sworn during the act of homage by a feudal inferior to his lord. Upon this oath depended the entire structure of feudal relation, by which title (and thus identity) could be conferred, estates administered, social relations known, military ventures undertaken, and economic distribution regulated. Richard's opening lines, in the first scene of *Richard II*, stress the legal and temporal aspects of the fealty oath:

> RICHARD   Old John of Gaunt, time-honoured Lancaster,
> Hast thou according to thy oath and band
> Brought hither Henry Herford thy bold son,
> Here to make good the boist'rous late appeal,
> Which then our leisure would not let us hear,
> Against the Duke of Norfolk, Thomas Mowbray?
>
> (1.1.1–6)

The 'oath and band' which Richard here recalls is that of Gaunt's homage (*homagium ligeum*) to the crown, by which tie Gaunt is bound to return his son on a direct order from the king. It is important to observe that Richard does not use the words 'oath and bond' lightly, and that Gaunt recognizes the seriousness of the claim being made. It was common in feudal tenures for tenants to hold by 'homage' or by 'fealty'. Homage, as Thomas Littleton defined it in his *Tenores Novelli* (here in the English translation of the *New Tenures*):

> Homage is the most honorable seruice & most humble seruice of reuerence that a franktenant may do to his Lord. For when the tenaunt shal make homage to his Lorde he shal desend and hys head vncouered, & his Lorde shal sit, and the tenaunt shal kneele befeore him on both his knees, and holde his hands iointly together betweene the hands of his Lorde, and shal saye thus. I become your man from this day forward of life & limme & of earthly woorship & vnto you shal be true & faithfull, & beare you faith of the tenements that I clayme to holde of you sauing the faith that I owe vnto our soueraigne Lord the kinge. And the lord so syttyng shal kysse him. [32]

As Edward Coke explains in his commentary on Littleton's *Tenures*, however, 'as homage is the more honourable seruice, so Fealtie is a seruice more sacred because he is sworne thereunto'. [33] In fealty, the oath is paramount:

> Fealtie is as much to say as fidelitas in latine, and when a franktenaunt shall make fealtye vnto the Lorde hee shall hold his right hande vpon a booke and shal say thus. Heare you this my Lord, that I vnto you shal be faithful and true. and beare you faithe of the landes or tenenements that I clayme to holde of you. and truelye to you shall do the customes & seruices that I ought to do vnto you at termes assigned, as God me helpe & all his saintes, & then he kysseth the booke, But he shal not knele when he maketh his fealtie, nor shal make such humble reuerence as is aforesaide in homage. [34]

The combination of the sanctity of fealty and the reverence of homage, as Coke explains, could only be achieved in the oath of allegiance:

> And the reason wherefore the Tenant is not sworne to doing his homage to his Lord is, for that no subiect is sworne to another subiect to become his man of life and member but to the King only, and that is called the oath of Allegiance or *homagium ligeum*. And those words for that purpose are omitted out of Fealtie, which is to be done vpon oath.[35]

Cowell reprints in the *Interpreter* the usual form of the oath of allegiance, taken from the medieval *Praeludio Feudorum*: *Praestatur hoc Ligeum Homagium in manibus Regis vel imperatoris, genibus flexis, positis manibus iunctis in manibus Domini, dicendo: Ego iuro homagium tibi Dom[ini] vt a modo sim homo ligeus vester contra omnem hominem, qui potest viuere.*[36] The ceremony, then, was the same as that of homage, designed to produce a bond of reverence between lord and man; but the inclusion of the oath invested this subordination with a sanctity and a sense of exclusivity (*ego iuro homagium tibi Domini … contra omnem hominem*: 'I swear homage to your Lordship … against every man') not present in the lesser homage ceremony. This exclusivity has a diachronic as well as a synchronic function, for the inclusion of the words '*qui potest viuere*', though expressed in the present tense, import a future aspect. Richard's citation of the 'oath and bond', which takes in both fealty and homage, reminds Gaunt of the exclusive, future aspect of the *homagium ligeum*. This emphasis on the temporal requirements of the oath and bond presumably also motivates Richard's choice of the epithet 'time-honoured', as well as his emphasis on Gaunt's care for his son Herford, or Bolingbroke: Richard is reminding Gaunt that it is the perpetuation of homage and fealty over time that guarantees the bonds between generations, and the safe passage of tenure by succession.[37] Gaunt's answer acknowledges the claim – 'I have, my liege' (1.1.7) – and the subsequent exchange continues to point towards future performance, as Richard insists that the quarrel between Bolingbroke and Mowbray be on an 'apparent danger' 'aim'd' at the king, and no 'ancient' or 'inveterate malice'.[38] Access to Richard's 'presence' is only granted when Gaunt has satisfied the king that everything Bolingbroke has to say concerns not the past, but future obedience.

Richard attempts to assert the futurity of oath in this scene because, as readers of Raphael Holinshed's *Chronicles* will know, he fears too much attention to his past: the appeal of murder, a felony, which Bolingbroke lays to Mowbray's charge is to be traced, as the historical sources testify, directly to Richard's own instigation. Unfortunately for him, the past is exactly what Bolingbroke produces: a string of past crimes, including embezzlement, eighteen years of treasonous practices, and the death of the Duke of Gloucester, to which Richard can only reply by weakly ordering Mowbray and Bolingbroke to 'forget, forgive, conclude, and be agreed' (1.1.156). The gentlemen resist, and both Gaunt and Richard stress the necessity of a certain future guaranteed by allegiance and filial duty ('obedience bids'; 'there is no boot'); but both Mowbray and Bolingbroke insist that their own honours are dearer to them than their loyalty to the king, patently rejecting the oath of the *homagium ligeum*. Richard's crisis of futurity only deepens. Following the abortive trial by battle in 1.3 (in which Shakespeare follows Bracton's provision for combat upon appeal almost to the letter, with a special emphasis on Richard's dilatoriness in scheduling it[39]), Richard arrives at Gaunt's deathbed to appropriate his lands. Gaunt – like Hector now, a man without a future – prophesies without flattery the failure of Richard's reign in a 'blaze of riot' (2.1.33), a prediction of temporal compaction that he joins to a careful articulation of the legal means by which, as Holinshed notes, Richard perpetrated 'waste' on the crown estates. Gaunt's two key pronouncements on the issue come at the end of his (famous) long set-pieces, one delivered to York and the other to Richard:

> This land of such dear souls, this dear dear land,
> Dear for her reputation through the world,
> Is now leas'd out – I die pronouncing it –
> Like to a tenement or pelting farm.
> England, bound in with the triumphant sea,
> Whose rocky shore beats back the envious siege

Of wat'ry Neptune, is now bound in with shame,
With inky blots and rotten parchment bonds;
That England, that was wont to conquer others,
Hath made a shameful conquest of itself.

(2.1.57–66)

The 'parchment bonds' to which Gaunt alludes are those legal instruments by which Richard has aliened and 'leas'd out' the crown lands of the *fisc* – once the ample source of crown revenue – to his favourites. The financial arrangement was good policy: the king sought to generate a certain annual income, from a fixed money rent paid him by his 'farmers' – in exchange for the variable returns that had, in the past, been produced according to the vagaries of harvests and other economic conditions; in a sense, by aliening the crown lands, Richard sought to displace his risk by at least partially surrendering his prerogative.[40] Gaunt's claim, though, is that this financial arrangement has diminished the status of royal power:

A thousand flatterers sit within thy crown,
Whose compass is no bigger than thy head,
And yet, incaged in so small a verge,
The waste is no whit lesser than thy land.
O, had thy grandsire with a prophet's eye
Seen how his son's son should destroy his sons,
From forth thy reach he would have laid thy shame,
Deposing thee before thou wert possess'd,
Which art possess'd now to depose thyself.
Why, cousin, wert thou regent of the world,
It were a shame to let this land by lease;
But for thy world enjoying but this land,
Is it not more than shame to shame it so?
Landlord of England art thou now, not king,
Thy state of law is bondslave to the law,
And thou –

(2.1.100–1)

Gaunt's argument ties temporality in knots, as the mention of 'waste' in Shakespeare is always likely to do. In seeking to assure his future, Gaunt claims, Richard has made it a 'waste' – deposing himself by means of his own self-possession. This is a temporal paradox we have seen before, in the impatient ambition of Duke Frederick, and will see again, in the acquisitive desire of Tarquin; but here Gaunt ties it to the epistemological security that in other plays (*King John*, for example) law has been lionized for assuring. For Gaunt in these two speeches, the law represents a limiting and debasing power, one with which Richard has only newly tied his hands, and its primacy represents an importing of the future into the present, symbolized by waste. The emergence in these speeches of a new kind of law – one of contract, bargain, obliga- tion, and 'conquest' (the early-modern legal term for a purchase of title to land[41]), and 'lease' – reinforces this transition to a reified, epistemo- logically secure, but ethically bankrupt form of valuation.

Moreover, the temporal paradox occasioned by Richard's crimes, in Gaunt's account, has clear relation to one of the more arcane points of medieval legal philosophy, the theory of the king's two bodies. In his famous study of this topic, Ernst Kantorowicz devotes a chapter to the English reception of classical Roman ideas about the 'fisc' – originally the imperial treasury, but in English hands something far more elastic and, to use Kantorowicz's word, 'weird'. It was a standard English legal principle from the thirteenth century that the king did not have the right to 'alienate' certain things that were considered to be joined indis- solubly to the crown. As Kantorowicz has it,

Henry II created a *de facto* inalienable complex of rights and lands which later, in the thirteenth century, came to be known as the 'ancient demesne' and which formed, in the language of Roman Law, the *bona publica* or fiscal property of the realm. Moreover, the sheer existence of the 'ancient demesne' – a supra-personal compound of right and lands which was separate from the individual king and definitely not his personal property – gave substance ot the notion of an impersonal 'Crown' which developed simultaneously.[42]

The inalienability of the fisc, thus constituted, became for Bracton a material ground of the king's claim, in the crown, to sempiternity. Bracton calls the fisc a '*quasi*-sacred' thing which 'cannot be given or sold or transferred to another by the prince or reigning king', for 'such things constitute the crown itself and concern the common welfare'.[43] In relation to these matters, Bracton writes, *nullum enim tempus currit contra [regem]*: 'time does not run against the king'.[44] The implication in English legal philosophy after Bracton is clear: it is the undying nature of the fisc – not merely a treasury, but a heterogeneous amalgamation of rights, property, and powers – that confers on the English monarch his sempiternal body. According to Kantorowicz, Bracton's argument converted the king from a *vicarius Christi* to a *vicarius Fisci*: 'that is, the perpetuality of the supra-personal king began to depend also on the perpetuality of the impersonal public sphere to which the fisc belonged'.[45] For Shakespeare's John of Gaunt, the subjection of the king to law, in both his persons, could mean only one thing: Richard had dispossessed himself of his claim to sempiternity.

Richard's attempt to 'waste' time results, as Gaunt had predicted, in total temporal dispossession – he runs out of time. Shakespeare doesn't allow us to view the process of wasting as an apt metaphor for, or abstract construction of, his despotic attempt to control futurity. When, in an act of tyrannical appropriation worthy of Duke Frederick, Richard cuts off the inheritance of 'time-honoured Lancaster' and seizes into crown possession the Duchy of Lancaster with all its capital assets and revenue, we are presented with a violation that cuts straight to the core of the feudal order. The response from Gaunt's brother York is immediate and comprehensive, and much in the spirit of Bracton:

> How long shall I be patient? ah, how long
> Shall tender duty make me suffer wrong?
> [...]
> Pardon me, if you please; if not, I pleas'd
> Not to be pardoned, am content withal.
> Seek you to seize and grip into your hands
> The royalties and rights of banish'd Herford?

> Is not Gaunt dead? and doth not Herford live?
> Was not Gaunt just? and is not Harry true?
> Did not the one deserve to have an heir?
> Is not his heir a well-deserving son?
> Take Herford's rights away, and take from time
> His charters, and his customary rights;
> Let not to-morrow then ensue to-day:
> Be not thyself. For how art thou a king
> But by fair sequence and succession?
> Now afore God – God forbid I say true! –
> If you do wrongfully seize Herford's rights,
> Call in the letters patents that he hath
> By his attorneys-general to sue
> His livery, and deny his off'red homage,
> You pluck a thousand dangers on your head,
> You lose a thousand well-disposed hearts,
> And prick my tender patience to those thoughts
> Which honor and allegiance cannot think.
>
> (2.1.163–64, 187–208)

According to York, Richard risks throwing not only the entire feudal order into disarray, but the psychological, temporal, and perhaps even ontological assumptions that underpin it, too. The king's respect for inheritance is here made not only an emblem of the natural, political, ethical, and ontological structures that, working by succession, seem to emulate it. By the assumption of a radical position on the causal force of the example, York suggests that Richard's interference in the sacred custom and mystery of primogeniture will, itself, unseat time. While this is rhetorical hyperbole, York isn't necessarily wrong to fear a catastrophic exemplarity: because the king had occupied such an absolute and centric position in Plantagenet political order, and because that position was fundamentally tied (as he argues) to the very principle Richard has here undermined, his self-destruction could lead to the kind of total collapse that only a binary system can generate. *Richard II* may work best as a politic critique of absolutism on exactly these terms.

Richard's most famous discourse on time and 'waste' occurs in his final scene of the play, following his deposition, and produces a set of arguments that positions Hal's subsequent redress, in the three later plays of the tetralogy, of the temporal rupture created by (Richard's own) regicide. Here again we find Richard connecting the two versions of waste – a feudal and a commercial construction – to his temporal condition. Richard here scripts and produces a self-theatricalization that reveals the extent to which his deposition – in its full divorce of the name of 'Richard' from the kingship – has created the potential for self-awareness, irony, and even dissimulation in his performance of himself to himself. In an irrational pun worthy of Donne's first paradox, Richard promises that his copulative soul will produce 'still-breeding thoughts' (5.5.8), a contradiction that demonstrates the 'contentless-ness' of proliferation, or the emptiness of a future without a present. (This is a thought Richard formulates as his inability to make one's way into heaven: 'It is as hard to come as for a camel / To thread the postern of a small needle's eye' (5.5.16–17). As for Kant, the seeking of the good is the loss of it.) The experimentation with theatricalization of the self leads to a second version of the misconstruction of the relation between anticipation and experience:

> Music do I hear?
> Ha, ha! keep time – how sour sweet music is
> When time is broke and no proportion kept!
> So is it in the music of men's lives.
> And here have I the daintiness of ear
> To check time broke in a disordered string;
> But for the concord of my state and time,
> Had not an ear to hear my true time broke:
> I wasted time, and now doth time waste me ...
>
> (5.5.41–49)

What makes music unpleasant, when it does not 'keep time', is the misfit between expectation and experience, a relation Richard calls 'proportion'. The musical / financial puns on 'check' and 'concord' prepare the final, emphatic connection between waste and temporality, by which once again we find a protagonist struggling with an empty future after an attempt to anticipate or realize the future in the present. It is fitting, in this sense, that Richard concludes his soliloquy by picturing himself as a broken timepiece, unable either to tell the present time, or to make any forward advance.

Hal makes no secret, in the first part of *Henry IV*, that he plans to structure his bid for the kingship – a place that, contrary to reason, he must succeed in inheriting from a usurper – on a financial model. In his soliloquy at the end of 1.2, he promises that in 'redeeming time' he will make himself eligible and appropriate for an office for which, on the face of things, he seems peculiarly unsuited. The aptness of the place to the kind of education Hal requires, though, will emerge with a retrospective logic as the play goes on: Hal promises to make poor oaths precisely so that he can outperform them, informing the audience that 'by how much better than my word I am, / By so much shall I falsify men's hopes' (1.2.205–06). The *tantum . . . quantum* ('by how much . . . by so much') syntactical construction here plays jarringly against the falsification of hopes, exposing the paradox of a promise that will be kept by being broken. Slumming in Eastcheap is thus disclosed, as early as the second scene of the play, as a calculated strategy to debase his value, so that, when in the fulness of time he reforms himself, his reformation will 'show more goodly, and attract more eyes / Than that which hath no foil to set it off' (1.2.209–10). This combination of theatrical with financial metaphor Hal takes further in 3.2, where, upon a sharp rebuke from his father, he fully divulges the details of his intention. Like any well-meaning but clueless father, Henry gives Hal an earful about the ways in which, in his day, one went about establishing legitimacy to a usurped throne: a bit of careful theatricalization, mixed with an economic sense of when to withhold and when to supply the view of one's person – a trick designed to whet the appetites of the popular power base ('opinion, that did help me to the crown', 3.2.42), and keep them slavering. By contrast, Henry informs Hal, the prince's current tavern antics remind him of nothing so much as of Richard himself – so much so, in fact, that they seem to be patterned on Richard's precedent:

> PRINCE I shall hereafter, my thrice gracious lord,
> Be more myself.

KING   For all the world
             As thou art to this hour was Richard then
             When I from France set foot at Ravenspurgh,
             And even as I was then is Percy now.
             Now by my sceptre, and my soul to boot,
             He hath more worthy interest to the state
             Than thou the shadow of succession.
             For of no right, nor colour like to right,
             He doth fill fields with harness in the realm,
             Turns head against the lion's armed jaws,
             And being no more in debt to years than thou
             Leads ancient lords and reverend bishops on
             To bloody battles, and to bruising arms.
                                        (3.2.92–105)

Henry's logic is one that we have seen before, though to Elizabethan
audiences it would have been new. It is Hector's logic. Hotspur can
challenge a 'worthy interest' – a dignified claim – to the government of
England precisely because he enjoys 'no right, nor colour like to right'.
In throwing away all respects of loyalty and allegiance, and marching
in arms even against the king whom his own family created, Hotspur
creates worth from absolute transgression – trespass not only political,
but even rational and natural (on top of everything he is, as Henry
remarks, too young for all of this).

     The king plays directly into his son's hands here, by basing the
substance of his appeal and anxiety upon precedent. Although
Hotspur takes Hector's paradoxical line of argument, he does so in a
way that recreates Henry's own history; it is both heroically transgressive, and yet historically justified. Where Henry and Hotspur look to the
past for justification for their honour, though, Hal (like Celia and
Rosalind) looks intrepidly forward, and all his thoughts still tend to
redemption:

             I will redeem all this on Percy's head,
             And in the closing of some glorious day
             Be bold to tell you that I am your son,

When I will wear a garment all of blood,
And stain my favours in a bloody mask,
Which, wash'd away, shall scour my shame with it;
And that shall be the day, whene'er it lights,
That this same child of honour and renown,
This gallant Hotspur, this all-praised knight,
And your unthought-of Harry chance to meet.
For every honour sitting on his helm,
Would they were multitudes, and on my head
My shames redoubled! For the time will come
That I shall make this northern youth exchange
His glorious deeds for my indignities.
Percy is but my factor, good my lord,
To engross up glorious deeds on my behalf,
And I will call him to so strict account
That he shall render every glory up,
Yea, even the slightest worship of his time,
Or I will tear the reckoning from his heart.

(3.2.132–52)

In the new honour market of fiscal feudalism, worship can be bought and sold like any other tradeable commodity, and here Hal imagines that his long forbearance only gives Percy more and more lavish opportunity to 'engross up' glorious deeds as if they were goods in a public exchange, creating a potential differential between the two youths that Hal will use to dazzle the audience to his scene. His self-abasement is indispensable to this new twist on the financial cultivation of value in person: by how much greater the gap between Hal and Hotspur grows, by so much will Hal rise, upon the reversal, to steal Hotspur's glory. Hal conspicuously retains the emphasis on a fiscal theatricality that his father had introduced into the cultivation of the spectacle of majesty, basing his metaphor of redemption on the action of account by which a lord could sue his steward or factor for the production and satisfaction of his accounts, obligations, and payments.[46] But the key difference between the king's accusation and the prince's response is the difference in temporal focus: where Henry is preoccupied with the

precedent of the past, Hal is determined to do something unprecedented, and thus his 'I am your son' is enclosed within an 'I will'. It is
only natural, with this in mind, that he should conclude his speech
with the most elaborate oath-swearing of the tetralogy:

> This in the name of God I promise here,
> The which if He be pleas'd I shall perform,
> I do beseech your Majesty may salve
> The long-grown wounds of my intemperance:
> If not, the end of life cancels all bands,
> And I will die a hundred thousand deaths
> Ere break the smallest parcel of this vow.
>
> (3.2.153–59)

The hyperbolic quality of Hal's oath may distract from the pointed
logical inconsistency that complicates its representation of futurity. Hal
makes a show of swearing by God, and attributing to the divine the
power of legitimating or invalidating his oath; but instead of leaving it
there, he goes on to say, first, that the end of life will cancel his bond (a
legal commonplace), and second, that he will die a hundred thousand
deaths before breaking a 'parcel' – a 'piece', but also in contemporary
usage 'an item in an account', or 'a sum of money'[47] – of his oath. Hal
appeals to God's final judgment only immediately to undermine that
appeal, and then acknowledges the power of law to cancel the force of
his promise only immediately to deny that power. It is as if Hal gets as far
as 'cancels all bands' – a formulaic expression that suddenly reminds
him of the legal cast of his challenge to Hotspur – and immediately the
language of account ('parcel', 'vow') surges back into his self-defining,
hyperbolically felt, and intensely future-oriented thinking.

Hal is not entirely innocent of precedential thinking; like Hamlet, he
concerns himself with repetition and the forms of self-construction
that it enables, but with a strong emphasis on the ways in which his
actions might look forward to later repetition, rather than backward to
earlier originals. A typical example is the robbery on Gad's Hill, where
Hal and Poins mask themselves to double-cross their confederates,
robbing Falstaff and the other thieves, and then return to the tavern to

let him brag and to bait him with his cowardice. The financial over-
tones and aggressive humiliation of the escapade – robbing a thief, and
then ridiculing a braggart – make it obvious that Hal is in some sense
rehearsing here for the similar ambush he will later perform on
Hotspur at the battle of Shrewsbury. The other odd espisode from the
Eastcheap matter, Hal's and Poins's inscrutable victimization of Francis
the Drawer, similarly looks forward to Hal's intentions for Hotspur. Hal
makes a series of increasingly bizarre and unintelligible demands of
Francis, all the time cueing Poins to call for the servant's attention from
the other room. The result is that Francis, farcically distracted every
time that he should answer the prince, can only find the words 'Anon,
sir'. And yet Francis is so attracted by the promises that Hal seems to
make him – an offer of employment, a promise of substantial
patronage – that he cannot quite tear himself away to attend to Poins's
offstage summonses, and his professions of immediacy become, rather,
testaments to his dilatoriness. When we pay closer attention to the
nature of the questions Hal is asking, it becomes clear that he is rumi-
nating on the distinction between Hotspur and himself – ruminations
that tend, with brutal contempt, to his own favour. His first line of
questioning concerns Francis's indenture as an apprentice, and his
hypothetical willingness to abandon it; the second an offer to exchange
a thousand pounds for a lump of sugar (i.e. something valuable, like
Hotspur's glory, for something worthless, like Hal's intemperance); and
the third Francis's readiness to rob a man who sounds like a caricature
of vanity and arrogance. Francis's willingness to break his servitude,
seizing his time before the period has run its course, does not count in
his favour; Hal's and Poins's comic timing stands in critical opposition
to Francis' ambitious prolepsis. Francis appears (through Hal's manip-
ulative rhetoric) to demonstrate a similar impatience for the prince's
offer of a thousand pounds, but it is in the final question – whether he
will rob the braggart – that Hal decisively crushes him, for Francis is so
focused on identifying the target of the prince's satire ('O Lord, sir, who
do you mean?) that he misses his opportunity to profit when it comes.
After the incident, upon Poins's questioning, Hal reveals that he had
Hotspur before his mind throughout this 'cunning jest of the drawer'
(2.4.89–90) for, like Hotspur, Francis's 'industry is up-stairs and

down-stairs' but 'his eloquence the parcel of a reckoning' (2.4.99–100). Hal's motivation for this kind of rhetorical abuse lies in his chafing frustration at the stupidity and gullibility of his friends – evident here even when, as usual, Hal conspicuously fails to bother to answer Poins's direct question about the jest – but, even more so, in his overriding obsession with the desire to punish Percy for precisely that excellence that Hal's plan has afforded him. The anxiety betrayed by the routine rhetorical and ethical abuse to which Hal submits almost everyone around him – and particularly Falstaff – is an anxiety fundamentally characterized by timeliness, by a desire – despite the frustration – to wait for just the right moment to strike. That this preoccupation with timeliness is driven by a desire to create oneself as the original, in a legal sense, is evident from the way that Hal introduces the Francis jest to Poins: 'Step aside, and I'll show thee a precedent' (2.4.32–33).

Hal's politic need to be unprecedented, of course, remains intractably at odds with the precedent that he must, if he is to found the dynasty his father has enabled (for dynasties are always founded by the heir), set for his own children. As Spenser's Mutabilitie had claimed, nothing can be permanent that has a beginning. Shakespeare's solution to this logical problem is to drive Hal's narrative further into the philosophical preoccupations of medieval common law. In the autumn of 1562, Elizabeth asked her chief judges to assemble and consider the law in a case currently depending between her and several of her subjects. The Tudors, as inheritors of the Lancaster blood and thus lords of the Duchy of Lancaster in their personal right (rather than by virtue of their possession of the crown, with its 'ancient demesne', part of the fisc), had with the Duchy inherited a tangled history of legal decisions and actions pertaining to it. Edward VI had made a lease out of the Duchy lands during his nonage – i.e. while he was still under the age of twenty-one. Elizabeth, like her sister Mary before her, sought to know whether it was law that she should be bound by this lease, or whether she were free to reassign the title of the land in question, on the grounds that, her brother being under-age at the time of the grant, it could not legally stand. The judges had convened to discuss the case during Mary's reign, and Sir Robert Catlin, Chief Judge of the King's

Bench, had convened discussions on it twice before during Elizabeth's reign, once at Serjeants' Inn (1560) and once at Spooner's Hall (1561). He now being ill, Sir James Dyer CJ convened several of the judges, including Edmund Plowden in his capacity as one of the judges of the Duchy court, to look afresh into the matter. Their summary argument in favour of the lease's validity, though famous, requires brief rehearsal:

> And the greatest Part of them then, and all of them now assembled, except *Ruswel* (who had but little Time to consider the Matter) unanimously agreed that the Queen should not avoid the Lease made by King *Edward* her Brother, by reason of his nonage. For first of all they agreed, that by the common Law no Act which the King does as King shall be defeated by his nonage. For the King has in him two Bodies, *viz.* a Body natural, and a Body politic. His Body natural (if it be considered in itself) is a Body mortal, subject to all Infirmities that come by Nature or Accident, to the Imbecillity of Infancy or old Age, and to the like Defects that happen to the natural Bodies of other People. But his Body politic is a Body that cannot be seen or handled, consisting of Policy and Government, and constituted for the Direction of the People, and the Management of the public-weal, and this Body is utterly void of Infancy, and old Age, and other natural Defects and Imbecillities which the Body natural is subject to, and for this Cause what the King does in his Body politic cannot be invalidated or frustrated by any Disability in his natural Body. And therefore his Letters-patent which give Authority or Jurisdiction, or which give Lands or Tenements that he has as King, shall not be avoided by reason of his nonage.[48]

The doctrine to which the judges here appealed, commonly known (since Ernst Kantorowicz's famous study[49]) as 'the king's two bodies', could more accurately be described as 'the king's two temporalities'. The king's body politic, according to this mystical idea, is 'utterly void of Infancy, and old Age', and thus arguments over legal actions taken by Edward VI during his nonage are not only unsound – like the width of a line, or the volume of a square, these arguments simply do not exist. With this passage in mind, the entire subject – so extensively treated in Shakespeare's second tetralogy – of the body of the prince becomes invested with legal significance. The corpulent superfluity of Falstaff's body becomes, in this context, an emblem not only of low comedy, the transient, and the disreputable, but an emblem of the mortality that, once he becomes king, Hal must (in the sense of, has no choice but to) put off for ever. It is fitting, then, that Falstaff's first line is a demand to know the time of the day (*Henry IV Part One*, 1.2.1), and that Hal's reply stresses Falstaff's association with time, but not with days – rather, with nights, governed by the changeable moon. The 'doctrine' of the king's two bodies is reified, in the two parts of *Henry IV*, by Hal's caught suspension between the gross mortal body of the fat knight, on the one hand, and on the other the serene and day-lit body of the politic king.[50]

In a similar way, the lingering presence of Falstaff's ageing and diseased body in the second part of *Henry IV* not only doubles the king's own failing health, but – in Falstaff's politic attempts to make provision for himself, and guarantee his future (see, e.g., *Henry IV Part 2*, 1.2.228–49) – may allegorize the 'politic' anxieties of which lawyers like Plowden suspected Henry IV in his older age. For Henry IV never entirely accepted the mystical union of his two bodies, despite the confidence of later legal theorists that the politic body had force to assimilate his mortal body, completely and irrevocably. Instead he compelled Parliament to pass a charter reserving to him and to his heirs their personal rights in the Duchy of Lancaster, permanently disjoined from their rights in the crown estates:

> Which Separation, Division, and Severance of the Dutchy from the Crown, and from the Receipt and Order of the Possessions of the Crown, seemed to the Judges and other the Counsellors abovementioned to be a politic Scheme of King *Henry 4*. who well knew that he had the Dutchy of *Lancaster* upon a good and indefeasible Title, and that his Title to the Crown was not so good, and therefore having some Distrust that in Time to come the Crown might be taken from him or his Heirs, and being desirous nevertheless that the Dutchy should be mixed with the Possessions

of the Crown, and not be notoriously cut and dissevered from the Possessions of the Crown, it might be a Means of causing the Dutchy the sooner to be taken away from him or his Heirs, or at least he or his Heirs would receive no good by their being mixed with the Possessions of the Crown, if the Crown should be taken from him or his Heirs, for these Reasons he made the said Charter by the Authority of Parliament, whereby the said Separation is made as is shewn before.[51]

Such meticulous, doubting care for the title of the Duchy of Lancaster may help to explain, too, why Shakespeare makes so much, in Hotspur's and in Worcester's speeches of defiance at Shrewsbury, of the distinction between Henry's lineal right in Lancaster (on John of Gaunt's death) versus the 'gripe[d] . . . general sway' of the crown (see *Henry IV Part 1*, 4.3.52–88, 5.1.30–71). Henry, then, mistrusted the security of his assumption of the dignity royal; but the theory of the body politic, as it was developed in Shakesepare's time, was adamant on the seamless conjoining of the two estates:

> To this natural Body is conjoined his Body politic, which contains his royal Estate and Dignity, and the Body politic includes the Body natural, but the Body natural is the lesser, and with this the Body politic is consolidated. So that he has a Body natural adorned and invested with the Estate and Dignity royal, and he has not a Body natural distinct and divided by itself from the Office and Dignity royal, but a Body natural and a Body politic together indivisible, and these two Bodies are incorporated in one Person, and make one Body and not divers, that is the Body corporate in the Body natural *et e contra* the Body natural in the Body corporate.[52]

As Plowden later goes on to insist, 'his Body politic which is annexed to his Body natural takes away the Imbecillity of his Body natural, and draws the Body natural, which is the lesser, and all the Effects thereof to itself which is the greater, *quia magis dignum trahit ad se minus dignum*'. The problem with the philosophy of the king's two bodies, for the Lancastrians as for the Tudors (and eventually for Charles I), was that it could be forced, amphibolously, in either direction: either the conjoining of the two bodies, and the assimilation of the natural by the politic, led to an inviolably sacred kingship; or the severability of the two bodies made it possible to reinvest the sacred politic nature in a new body. So close to the execution of Richard II, the latter possibility represented a real threat for Hal.

In Shakespeare's solution to the problem – in which he sums the tetralogy's continuous preoccupations with temporality, oaths, and precedent – the young Henry V finally surrenders the problem to the judges. Earlier in the play, Hal had been imprisoned for striking the Chief Justice in the street; now, upon the death of Henry IV, the judge along with the other chief ministers and courtiers attends on the successor, but with trepidation. Hal's initial engagement with the Chief Justice is hostile:

KING   You are, I think, assur'd I love you not.
CHIEF JUSTICE   I am assur'd, if I be measur'd rightly,
                 Your Majesty hath no just cause to hate me.
KING   No?
                 How might a prince of my great hopes forget
                 So great indignities you laid upon me?
                 What! rate, rebuke, and roughly send to prison
                 Th'immediate heir of England? Was this easy?
                                                  (5.3.64–71)

The Chief Justice's apology for his conduct relies on the commonplace political argument that, in striking him, Hal struck not the man, but the office; not the Chief Justice, but the 'image of the King whom I presented' (5.2.79). The Chief Justice can thus claim that he was acting for the king – in the 'person', the 'image', and the 'administration' of the king, against his son. While of course this constitutes a slightly different argument from that of the king's two bodies, nonetheless it leads directly to it, as the Chief Justice recognizes:

                 Your Highness pleased to forget my place,
                 The majesty and power of law and justice,

> The image of the King whom I presented,
> And struck me in my very seat of judgment;
> Whereon, as an offender to your father,
> I gave bold way to my authority
> And did commit you. If the deed were ill,
> Be you contented, wearing now the garland,
> To have a son set your decrees at naught?
> To pluck down justice from your aweful bench?
> To trip the course of law, and blunt the sword
> That guards the peace and safety of your person?
> Nay more, to spurn at your most royal image,
> And mock your workings in a second body?
>
> (*Henry IV, Part 2*, 5.3.77–90)

The judge's imprisonment of the body of the prince here stands in opposition to the 'image' and 'workings' of the king's politic body – 'a second body' – which in this account, at least, is the primary *corpus*. In this radical re-imagination of the two bodies argument, the Chief Justice sees the sempiternal royal body as completely distributed; it has become the corporate body of the law. The consequent translation of the maxim *nullum tempus occurrit regi* ('time does not run against the king') to *nullum tempus occurrit legi* makes it possible for the Chief Justice to offer Hal the moot case that he has, all along, desired: 'Behold yourself so by a son disdained', suggests the judge, an opportunity that Hal realizes is too useful to resist. He immediately re-commissions the Chief Justice, willing him to serve long enough to see Hal's own son offend similarly against him. Hal makes the judge his new 'father', and promises to live by his direction, so long as the Chief Justice uses the same 'bold, just, and impartial spirit' as he did in censuring Hal (5.3.116). Hal has finally succeeded in his sleight of hand by welding an originary, future-oriented temporality to a lineal succession, creating himself as precedent, but without thereby exposing his own actions to the critique of the past. This is possible because, at a stroke, the Chief Justice becomes both his chastising 'father', and the man who now acts in his 'person': the mortal body, which is resistant to law, is joined to the 'void' and ageless body, which is law itself. Kant claims in the *Groundwork* that '*duty is the necessity of an action from respect for law*', and futher that 'an action from duty is to put aside entirely the influence of inclination and with every object of the will; hence there is left for the will nothing that could determine it except objectively the *law* and subjectively *pure respect* for this practical law'.[53] Hal's self-subordination to the Chief Justice at the end of *2 Henry IV* represents just such an ethical manoeuvre, designed to put his nobility and court at ease. But the paradox of his enduring, bodily individuality ('when men least think *I will*') persists, for – unlike Kant's theory of an ethical dignity – Hal continues to derive his worth and honour from his chivalric, exemplary particularity. *Henry V* will continue to expose these temporal and ethical paradoxes: from the way in which arguments over the Salic law in the first act anticipate Plowden's comments on Henry VII's claims to the throne in his *Comentaries*, to the proxy ridicule of the mercenary Williams in the final act. But always Hal's very duplicity, the legacy of Richard's Adamic fall from a paradisal feudalism, endows him with a sempiternality that absorbs, but never daunts, his transgressive pastness. Thus *Henry V* concludes not with 'oaths well kept and prosperous' (5.2.369), but with the promise of them. Law emerges in the second tetralogy not as a force that, with Gaunt and Kant, must undermine the sovereignty of the self, but as a precedential and thus never-quite-fulfilled universal, the promise of a promise.

Chapter Five

REX V. LEX, OR, THE PROUD ISSUE OF A KING

The debates over the nature of English equity in the 1590s, like those over the status of the court of Chancery in 1616, represent – at least in part – proxy battles for another ideological conflict that simmered threateningly between the reigns of Henry VIII and Charles I: the relationship of the crown to the common law. This was a debate that exercised some of the great minds of the period, from Thomas More and John Skelton, to Edmund Spenser, Edward Coke, Francis Bacon, and John Milton. Shakespeare's participation in the contest has usually been hung on one of two pegs, both based in his history plays: the legal-mystical theory of the king's two bodies, discussed briefly by Edmund Plowden in his *Comentaries*[1] and, according to Ernst Kantorowicz and Marie Axton, operative in *Richard II*, raises possible questions about the sanctity of royal power and the deposability of individual monarchs, while the supposed topicality of plays like *Richard II* and the two parts of *Henry IV* have been connected to the abortive Essex revolt of 1601.[2] But what has increasingly become apparent in historical studies of the monarch's fiscal, religious, and administrative policies – that Tudor and Stuart sovereigns attempted to consolidate their power first by manipulating, and later by contesting, common-law traditions – offers an important interpretative challenge to readings of Shakespeare's poetry and plays. From *The Rape of Lucrece* to *Richard II* and *Hamlet*, from *King John* to *Macbeth* and *King Lear*, Shakespeare takes up the problem of the authority of kings, the basis of rule or *dominium*, and the founding of political order; the decidedly legal character of the recurrent treatment of these issues in Shakespeare's work suggests that he was interested in more than just the grandeur of historical monument, or of catastrophic tragic reversal. This chapter will set out some of the ways in which Shakespeare's legal preoccupations with the limits of royal power reflect on, and challenge, the various arguments and even events that marked the evolution of the famous English mixed constitution; but it will also address the ways in which this ideological conflict continued to throw up epistemological and ethical arguments of various kinds. The texts on which I will focus, *The Rape of Lucrece* and *King John*, take up the relation of the king to the law, of law to equity, in relation to the individual's self-definition and self-publication within the social. Both texts also chronicle the foundation of a political order: *The Rape of Lucrece* records the origins of the Roman republic with the expulsion of the Tarquins by Lucius Junius Brutus, while *King John* chronicles the birth of an English nation loosed from papal authority, untethered from its French moorings, and newly conversant with a standard of consensual, or even constitutional, government. In their mutual focus on rape, on epistemology, and above all on common-law ideas of right, possession, negligence, and duty, these texts form a pair within Shakespeare's work as a whole, and a pair that, together, make important contributions to our understanding of Shakespeare's approach to the idea and practice of law.

'THIS PROUD ISSUE OF A KING': THE EPISTEMOLOGY OF LAW IN *THE RAPE OF LUCRECE*

The formal debate over the political and legal relation of crown to law began with the ascendancy of Thomas Wolsey, Lord Chancellor under Henry VIII.[3] Wolsey antagonized the common-law judges of King's Bench and the Common Pleas – as Ellesmere would later do under James I – by reversing common-law judgments in the court of Chancery.[4] A disgruntled plaintiff who had not, as he thought, received justice, or at the least a favourable verdict, in one of the two royal courts, by complaint to Wolsey could reopen the matter in Chancery, effectively turning the Chancery into a court of appeal. Because the Chancellor's judicial power was exercised by virtue of his appointment as the king's deputy, such review of common-law judgments essentially put the crown's prerogative above the common law as meted out in the royal courts. Common lawyers exclaimed against this unfettered use of the prerogative, and the encroachment of the Chancery on their jurisdictions at a time when the courts – whose officers relied on fees for their incomes – were suffering from a decline in business. The poet John Skelton, for one, attacked Wolsey for his supervenience in his satirical poem *Collyn Clout* – a poem that would go on to have a significantly influential afterlife in the 1590s.[5] Skelton vividly, and in precise technical language, evokes the jurisdictional conflict produced by Wolsey's tampering with common-law judgments. In their greed for fee-generating business, Collyn Clout alleges, Wolsey and his bishops have drawn business to the church courts and to Chancery, where they judge cases not by law but by 'wyll'. The common-law judges in return threaten the bishops with writs of 'praemunire', prohibiting them from handling common-law matters in alien (and particularly spiritual) jurisdictions, arguing that they have 'prescriptions', or immemorial grants, against the legal 'fictions' upon which the divines base their judicial power.[6] As Collyn goes on later to exclaim, Wolsey and the bishops should enjoy their 'lyberte', but only 'as it is *res certa /* Conteyned in *Magna Carta*' (718–19).

Among the lawyers themselves, Christopher St German's famous and learned treatise on equity *Doctor and Student* was written partly in response to Wolsey's innovatory expansion of prerogative-based Chancery jurisdiction under Henry VIII, and occasioned a controversial pamphlet war on prerogative power with Wolsey's successor, Thomas More. St German's stunning success at reducing the *jus non scriptum* to a rational set of hierarchically ordered governing principles put the common law on a footing with the respected, amply glossed, and painstakingly studied laws of Europe's *corpus juris civilis*.[7] His own purpose in drafting the dialogues seems to have been something of an intellectual propaganda exercise: unusually for a legal text of the time, the dialogues were composed and printed in Latin and English, rather than in Law French, and they were immediately issued in large numbers in competing editions – both characteristic of texts meant to reach the widest possible readership. St German's subsequent career as a royal polemicist, taking the crown's position against More's defence of the Church's jurisdictions and practices, suggests that his earliest and most famous dialogues – *Doctor and Student* – were part of the same effort to limit courts of 'conscience' like Chancery within a framework described by common-law principles. Sir Thomas More, conspicuously the first common lawyer ever appointed Lord Chancellor, recognized the danger when he began to take up – in his disarmingly wry and self-mocking way – the argument against St German. In a now famous story recounted by his son-in-law and biographer William Roper, More challenged the common-law judges to surrender their independence by admitting an equitable function to their judgments. When the judges of Common Pleas and King's Bench had complained that, as Chancellor, More continued to interfere with their authority by offering equitable remedies for litigants unfairly treated in common-law suits, More invited them to dinner and offered them the opportunity to work with him to reform the law. As he afterwards confided to Roper, the judges depended upon the supposed indifference of common-law judgment, and its valorizing of the jury role in deciding questions of fact – for 'they may by the verdicte of the Jurye cast of all quarrells from them selves uppon them, which they accompte their cheif defens'.[8] More's riposte to St German insisted on the quasi-federal subordination of English law to the internationalist and conscience-based oversight of Chancery, in opposition to an automaticity in jury trials that he saw as unconscionably and impractically indifferent. The constitutional shock of Henry VIII's break with Rome left the Chancery as something of a conundrum, and bequeathed to Elizabeth's reign a set of unresolved and mutable problems about the relation of the monarch to the common-law courts. Despite the claims and counter-claims made by More and St German, among others, the common lawyers who sat as Chancellors under Elizabeth had no unimpeachable basis upon which to ground their equitable power, and during the repeated political and religious crises that studded the opening decades of Elizabeth's reign, the nature and rights of the monarchy came under the almost constant scrutiny of lawyers.[9]

Basic to Shakespeare's early explorations into the sovereignty of the king against the law was the practical issue of what might be called legal epistemology. The legal polity of a pure monarchy might be distinguished from that of the pure republic by the degree to which the processes and standards of justice are knowable and known. Shakespeare's interest in the knowability of the law, with its costs and benefits, may well have derived from contemporary comparative legal study. *Ex facto ius oritur*, runs the celebrated maxim of civil jurisprudence: from the facts of the case, from what has been done, the law arises. No judgment can be given in a case where the evidence of an action, with all its attendant circumstances, has not been fully and searchingly presented and weighed, challenged, debated, and agreed. On this principle, civil lawyers opened a matter at law by the administration of interrogatories, lists of forensically pointed questions designed to solicit from the interested parties, and from reliable witnesses or experts, such answers as would make the task of the judge – judgment – more securely just. As Sir Thomas Smith (an English civilian) writes in his 1564 *De Republica Anglorum*, in 'the civill lawe . . . first the fact is examined by witnesses, iudices, tormentes and such like probations to finde out the truth thereof, and that doone the advocats doe dispute of the lawe to make of it what they can'.[10] The facts of the case, as determined by the process of inquest or examination, propel the lawyers handling a case towards the appropriate provisions of the law; the movement from inquest to judgment is driven by the fitting of the law to the facts at hand. The medieval English common law had, as we have seen, developed a form of judicial process founded not on fact, but on a process called pleading. 'Heere,' as Smith writes, 'the Sergeantes or counsellers before the Judges doe in passing forewarde with their pleading determine and agree upon the lawe, and for the most part and in manner all actions as well criminal as civill, come to the issue and state of some fact which is denied of the one partie, and averred of the other: which fact being tried by the xij men as they find, so the action is wonne or lost.'[11] The English trial process was able to forgo, in most instances, the expense of time and resources necessary to a full examination of the case, by reducing the matter in contention to a single disputed point of fact (L. *quaestio facti*).

It is no exaggeration to say that upon this distinction in the relation of fact to law stood the ancient liberty of the English subject, protected by Magna Carta from the possible tyranny of an absolute monarch. The common lawyers writing and practising after Bracton supposed the law antecedent to any given fact, and thus beyond the prerogative power of the king in his judicial function. Although the judges were appointed by the crown, they did not, like the king's ministers in their prerogative courts, judge *ad personam*, but rather by the law, standing apart from the power vested in them as servants of the crown, *ad rem*. As Sir Edward Coke was forced, in a politically explosive moment in 1606, to remind James VI and I, '*Ipse autem rex non debet esse sub homine sed sub deo et sub lege, quia lex facit regem. Attribuat igitur rex legi, quod lex attribuit ei, videlicet dominationem et potestatem. Non est enim rex ubi dominatur voluntas et non lex*' [The king must not be under man but under God and under the law, because law makes the king. Let him therefore bestow upon the law what the law bestows upon him, namely, rule and power. For there is no king where will rules rather than law].[12] The process of pleading, in its privileging of the consensual submission of all parties to the known law before the trial of fact, instantiates the division of the royal power of the king in his own person from his judicial power – vested in his judges – which might, in a given suit, act against him.

The priority of law and the trial of fact in the English common-law tradition gave rise to, and were protected by, the institution of pleading. At the core of this institution lay the issue, the material point – usually a single point of fact – upon which the competing claims of plaintiff and defendant in a common-law trial would be staked, and won or lost. The association between joinder of issue in pleading, and the disclosure of a *quaestio facti* that the jury might easily and securely grasp and efficiently judge, was not perceived by Shakespeare's contemporaries to be casual, but rather structural and necessary. In Sir Thomas Smith's formulation, this marriage of reduction to disclosure inheres in the very word 'issue' itself:

[In the courts, the judges] heare the pleading of all matters which doe come before them: and in civill matters where the pleading is for money or land or possession, part by writing, and part by declaration and altercation of the advocates the one with thother, it doeth so proceede before them till it doe come to the issue, which the latines doe call *statum causæ*, I doe not meane *contestationem litis*, but as the Rhetoritians doe call *statum*, we doe most properly call it the issue, for there is the place where the debate and strife (as a water held in a close and darke vessel can issue out and be voided and emptied) and no where else: that stroke well stricken is the departing of all the quarrelles.[13]

England's common law proves superior, in Smith's account, to other forms of European jurisprudence precisely for the efficiency and explicitness of the issue: as voiding is emptying, and strokes strike, so the joinder of issue results in the automatic 'departing' of the quarrel. 'Having seene both in Fraunce and other places manie devises, edictes and ordinaunces howe to abridge proces and to finde howe that long suites in law might be made shorter: I have not perceived nor reade as yet so wise, so just, and so well devised a meane found out by any man among us in Europe.'[14]

At the epicentre of *The Rape of Lucrece* is the idea of 'sovereignty': it is the 'boast of Lucrece' sov'reignty' (l. 36) that leads to her destruction, and the sovereignty of Sextus Tarquinius and his family that is, by the end of the poem, destroyed. And while the boast of beauty's and virtue's sovereignty incites Sextus first to covet and then to seize Lucrece for himself, there is another way in which it 'suggest[s] this proud issue of a king' (l. 37), 'for by our ears our hearts oft tainted be' (l. 38). The issue, or *exitus*, upon which the narrative will eventually come to turn will be precisely the status of perceptual claims – what ears and eyes can observe – against that of beliefs, intentions, and consciences. At stake is the legitimacy of this monarchy, and of monarchy as an institution, in the sense that monarchy can only be a just form of government in that polity where the king's external representation (or political action) truly reflects his internal self-regulation (or ethical composition). More: because the monarch governs by will, monarchy can only succeed, as Machiavelli observed, where the subjects believe in the virtue of their prince. In *The Rape of Lucrece*, the son (issue) of a king is tried by the issue (topic) of beauty and virtue, in order to determine whether virtue issues (is manifest) in beauty; upon this issue (point of contention, *exitus*) the various pleadings of the narrative will be determined. The poem presents an analysis of the relation between private and public, evaluating the claims of the monarchy for a human justice against those of the republic for a knowable one.

The epistemological problem in the poem begins and ends with Lucrece's own conscience. Augustine was the first to turn the 'history' of Lucrece's rape and suicide into a quasi-forensic debate about her consent and culpability. (For the sake of consistency, I will continue to call her 'Lucrece', rather than, as Augustine and many others knew her, 'Lucretia'.) As a key element in his defence of a convent of nuns ravished during Alaric's sack of Rome in AD 410, Augustine exposed the apparent hypocrisy and futility of the Stoic self-importance that had, in the canonical version of the Lucrece story, led the violated Roman matron to take her own life. Augustine was particularly concerned to impose a bar between the depraved lust of an aggressor, and the patience of the helpless victim; in the eighteenth chapter of the first book of *The City of God*, he takes up the problem of whether 'lust will defile even when it is another's':

> It will not defile, if it is another's; and if it defiles, it is not another's. Modesty is a virtue of the soul, and has as its companion a fortitude which resolves to endure any evil whatsoever rather than consent to evil. But no one, no matter how high-minded and modest, has power to control what is done to the flesh, but only what the mind will consent to or refuse. Who of sane mind, therefore, will suppose that purity is lost if it so happens that the flesh is seized and overpowered, and another's lust exercised and satisfied on it?[15]

Turning late Stoic arguments back upon themselves, Augustine figures purity as a virtue or freedom of the rational soul, the direction and control of which remains impregnable to assaults on the flesh. Basic to this line of argument is the assumption that the mind, including those problematic entities intention and conscience, can remain distinct from the body, and indeed – in a set of subtle logical distinctions naturally reminiscent of the *Discourses* of Epictetus – Augustine goes on to argue that because it is the rational soul that interprets and judges the acts and passions of the body, it is the judgments themselves that cause us pain, joy, shame, and so on.[16] A midwife may manually examine the womb of an unmarried virgin, or a surgeon perform a necessary operation upon her, and she remains chaste; but a harlot on her way to debauch herself, 'already corrupted in mind, violating the pledge which she has vowed to God', has already lost the 'sanctity of her body'.[17]

When Augustine turns explicitly to the case of Lucrece in the ensuing chapter, the division between body and mind upon which he has insisted becomes the basis for his famous, and highly influential, analysis of Lucrece's culpability. It had been traditional, according to Augustine – as it was apparently argued in a specific source no longer extant – to insist upon Lucrece's innocence and virtue in the face of Sextus's brutal attack, 'considering not the union of their members, but the separateness of their minds'.[18] But if she was innocent of Tarquin's lust, Augustine points out, she need not have executed upon herself the most extreme of judicial penalties by putting herself to death. If we consider the possibility that Lucrece was, in fact, executing deserved justice upon herself for her own culpable consent – 'seduced by her own lust', in Augustine's words – it becomes obvious that her prior passivity is not consistent with her later action:

> The case is reduced to a dilemma. For if she is acquitted of murder, she is convicted of adultery; and if she is acquitted of adultery, then she is convicted of murder. It is not possible to find a way out of this dilemma. One can only ask: If she was an adulteress, why is she praised? If she was pure, why was she slain?[19]

Augustine's famous analysis of the case puts Lucrece's consent to Sextus's lust on trial: if she did not consent, her mind remains clear and she is wrong to kill herself, but if she did consent, the execution is as just as the adultery was evil. In Augustine's account, Lucrece must either become an adulteress or a suicide; either way, she is not to be revered as a model, either of chastity or honour.

Then going beyond this legal dilemma, Augustine acknowledges
that Lucrece's suicide may not have arisen out of a love of purity and a
need to castigate herself for her own or another's contamination of
that purity, but because of 'a weakness arising from shame'.[20]
Augustine essentially shifts the concern from one of substance to one
of appearance: rather than attempting to purify herself by suicide,
Lucrece perhaps killed herself to demonstrate to others the state of her
uncontaminated and 'separate' mind:

> Being a Roman lady excessively eager for praise, she feared that, if
> she remained alive, she would be thought to have enjoyed
> suffering the violence that she had suffered when she lived. Hence,
> she judged that she must use self-punishment to exhibit the state
> of her mind to the eyes of men to whom she could not show her
> conscience. She blushed, indeed, to think that, if she were to bear
> patiently the infamy that another had inflicted upon her, she
> would be believed to have been an accomplice to it.[21]

Here Augustine carefully shifts the significance of Lucrece's suicide from
a demonstration of the real state of her mind – consenting or complicit –
to a demonstration of her concern for the good repute of society. The
meticulous attention in this passage to the idea of observation drives this
point home: 'she would be thought', 'to exhibit', 'she would be believed'.
What Lucrece means by her suicide is not that she is free of contamination by Sextus' lust, but that she wants to be seen to be free of that
contamination. The difference between Lucrece's case and that of the
Roman nuns who did not, after violation, lay hands upon their lives, is
that Lucrece had only human witness to assess the freedom of her
unspotted conscience, whereas the nuns, Augustine notes emphatically,
remained chaste 'in the sight of God', unconcerned with 'the scandal of
human suspicion'.[22] The almost giddy irony of Augustine's forceful
public attempt to exonerate the nuns from just that scandal by denying
its importance seems, incredibly, to have been lost on him.

The influence of Augustine's account of Lucrece's dilemma in *The
City of God* upon Shakespeare's telling of the story in *The Rape of
Lucrece* must not be underestimated. Either directly from source or indi-

rectly through intermediary versions, Shakespeare assimilated all the major elements of Augustine's formulation of the quasi-legal problem of her consent, represented them, and in most cases challenged them. Most salient among these influential elements is certainly Augustine's

FIGURE 8a, recto. The rape of Lucrece: a) Hans Holbein the Elder (1460–1524), *The Rape of Lucrece*. British Museum Rowlands 301. Both versions of Holbein's drawing show how the earlier scene of the rape figures visually in Lucrece's suicide, effectively superimposing Tarquin's guilt on Lucrece's self-destruction. b) Heinrich Aldegrever (1501/2–1555/61), *The Rape of Lucrece*. British Museum New Hollstein 64. This print of Tarquin's rape of Lucrece has been annotated, in a contemporary hand, with the caption *Lucretia à S[exto] Tarq[uinio] co[n]stuprata amore pudicitiae seipsam confodit* ('Having been raped by Sextus Tarquinius, for love of her chastity Lucrece stabs herself'). Again, the reception of the image confounds Lucrece's rape with her suicide, blurring distinctions between Tarquin's culpability for her rape and Lucrece's culpability for her death.

insistence that the story foregrounds an evidentiary problem, that the relation of the first crime – the rape – to the second crime – the murder – depends entirely on the status of Lucrece's conscience; the subsequent distinction in Augustine's argument between human and divine witness implies that the quality of a human conscience is ultimately unknowable except to a divine omniscience, and that Lucrece's history therefore exemplifies a problem that human institutions designed to police legal and ethical codes will always, necessarily, face in the assessment and judgment of criminal acts. But, whereas for Augustine Lucrece's suicide had been an incompatible insoluble that would not, by any construction, fit with her supposed innocence of Sextus' rape, Shakespeare harnesses English common law, in his version of the story,

FIGURE 8a verso

Lucretia à S. Tarqᵒ eǯtuprata amore pudicitiæ ſeipſam confodit.

FIGURE 8b

to draw Lucrece out of the dilemma of culpable consent and back to
virtue. And because he reintroduces to the story its political edge, characteristic of Livy's original but entirely stripped from Augustine's
highly psychological account, Shakespeare's emphasis on a common-
law solution to Lucrece's dilemma becomes by association a highly
charged celebration of constitutional liberty. For, finally, the story of
the rape of Lucrece is the story of the founding of the Roman republic –

more, of republicanism as a concept, even, of all subsequent republics tracing their lineage to Rome. In a highly characteristic moment of hubris, Shakespeare reached for an originary and aetiological tale – here, about the origins of no less an institution than a free society – and impregnated it with an anachronistic Englishness, such that England's own (idealized?) practice of constitutional monarchy under the Tudors comes, by a reading of *The Rape of Lucrece*, to be the prophetic fulfilment of an ancient Roman promise. Indispensable to this brilliant example of Tudor historiographical polychronicism is Lucrece's common-law defence.

It is crucial to recognize (as Shakespeare did) that upon the question of Lucrece's consent, for interpreters of some cultures and periods, may possibly hang the character of Tarquin's own culpability: if Lucrece consented, or even encouraged Tarquin's advance, he may not himself be solely, and summarily, guilty of the rape. This is a very slippery argument, both ethically and (in our own rightly careful age) politically speaking; and it is important that I be exactly clear. However dangerous or pernicious we may find the argument in practical terms, logically speaking the culpability for the crime of which Sextus stands accused is the more firmly located in him the more Lucrece can be freed of consent up to and during the violation. The legal problem is that it is impossible to know, or to demonstrate, what Lucrece's state of mind was at any given time; even she may not be a sufficient witness to her intentions. This is not to say that Tarquin would be less guilty of the rape if Lucrece could be shown to have consented in her conscience; of course, an inquest would consider Tarquin's guilt mitigated only by Lucrece's reliable communication, prior to the rape, of her consent. On the other hand, negligence might be alleged as a form of complicity in a case where the victim clearly knew the perils consequent on the non-performance of reasonable precautions; and it is here that Shakespeare's version of the story, for better or for worse, begins to complicate the plain legend out of Livy.

The status of Shakespeare's 'Argument' to *The Rape of Lucrece* is debated, and ambiguous: a synthesis of the history of Lucrece presented in sources from Ovid and Livy to William Painter's Elizabethan account, Shakespeare's argument seems to summarize his own ensuing narrative poem, but subtly to vary its emphases.[23] Some points of contact – such as the insistence of the 'Argument' on the culmination of Lucrece's history in the constitutional translation of Rome from monarchy to republic – have justly provoked critical judgments of *The Rape of Lucrece* as a poem decisively engaged in political philosophy, but few interpretations have rigorously studied the way Shakespeare deploys the 'Argument' as a kind of *coperto*, or even legend, guiding the interpretation of the poem it contains. An important and overlooked connection between the two texts is the way Shakespeare uses the word 'possession' in the opening of each, a parallel that gives the reader of the poem her first lesson in an ongoing Shakespearean exercise in exposition and superposition:

> Lucius Tarquinius (for his excessive pride surnamed Superbus), after he had caused his own father-in-law Servius Tullius to be cruelly murdered, and, contrary to the Roman laws and customs, not requiring or staying for the people's suffrages had possessed himself of the kingdom, went accompanied with his sons and other noblemen of Rome to besiege Ardea, during which siege the principal men of the army meeting one evening at the tent of Sextus Tarquinius, the King's son, in their discourses after supper everyone commended the virtues of his own wife, among whom Collatinus extolled the incomparable chastity of his wife, Lucretia.

This first sentence of the 'Argument', in its highly artificial Latinate syntax, advertises several things about Shakespeare's purpose in the poem as a whole, and his purpose in the 'Argument' in particular. First among which, this prose preface must not be considered dispensable to the poem, superfluous, slapdash, or the addition of a printer. The balance of the opening sentence (or in the proper Latin terminology, *colon*), in the way that it moves syntactically from 'Lucius Tarquinius' through 'Sextus Tarquinius' to 'Lucretia', illustrates with positional fidelity the entanglement of the two plots of the history, one political and the other sexual. But the *colon* also, with more precision, juxtaposes in parallel the two main verbal actions of the otherwise confusing mass of clauses: 'went ... to besiege Ardea' and 'commended' or 'extolled ... Lucretia'. All of the other verbal actions of the passage are subordinated, temporally and grammatically, to these two main verbs in the past tense, which are themselves connected by the preposition '... during ...'. The king's insecure 'possession' of Rome is thus carefully brought into parallel with Collatine's vulnerable 'possession' of Lucretia, her 'incomparable chastity' is set aside the king's proud cognomen 'Superbus', and both the political and the sexual possession are threatened by a siege, focused on the 'tent' of the king's son, Sextus Tarquinius.[24] Looking with the benefit of hindsight (as this story has probably always been encountered): if Ardea were to fall by the siege of Sextus Tarquinius, the monarchy would be confirmed; if Lucrece's chastity were to fall to the siege of Sextus Tarquinius, the monarchy would be, by contrast, undermined and destroyed. That the only physical location of the main actions described in this opening sentence are 'Ardea' and a 'tent' is probably neither fortuitous nor accidental; Shakespeare would have known the etymological connections in both Latin and English between 'tent' and 'attent', 'intent', and the Latin verb *tendo, tendere* ('to reach, to intend, to aim'), and the similarity of 'Ardea' to Latin *ardere* and *ardor*, or English 'ardour' ('head of passion or desire', or 'lust').

Given the careful parallel construction of the political and sexual plots of the narrative in the opening of the 'Argument', it is not at all surprising that Shakespeare should open the poem itself with a series of stanzas on the same subject of Collatine's 'possession' of Lucrece. The narrative opens, as in Livy, with the Roman captains enjoying a camp dinner during the siege of the city of Ardea. Sextus Tarquinius, son of the king, along with his kinsmen Tarquinius Collatinus and the other young men of the camp, debate the excellence of the virtue of their wives. Collatine, maintaining the chastity and modesty of Lucrece over all contenders, suggests a test: they should all ride to Rome, surprise their wives, and judge the result for themselves. It is, naturally, the sight of Lucrece's authentic and superexcellent modesty that, in all versions of the story, first and sustainingly inflames Sextus's predatory passion. Shakespeare's narrator turns the plaintive criticism of his suspense-building foreknowledge on Collatine:

> For he the night before in Tarquin's tent
> Unlocked the treasure of his happy state,
> What priceless wealth the heavens had him lent
> In the possession of his beauteous mate,
> Reck'ning his fortune at such high-proud rate
>   That kings might be espoused to more fame,
>   But king nor peer to such a peerless dame.
>
> O happiness enjoyed but of a few,
> And, if possessed, as soon decayed and done
> As is the morning's silver melting dew
> Against the golden splendour of the sun,
> An expired date cancelled ere well begun!
>   Honour and beauty in the owner's arms
>   Are weakly fortressed from a world of harms.
>
> Beauty itself doth of itself persuade
> The eyes of men without an orator.
> What needeth then apology be made
> To set forth that which is so singular?
> Or why is Collatine the publisher
>   Of that rich jewel he should keep unknown
>   From thievish ears, because it is his own?
>
>   (ll. 15–35)

Shakespeare's insistence here on Collatine's 'possession' of Lucrece is remarkable for several reasons. First, and most obviously, the 'priceless wealth' of her beauty and self, this 'rich jewel', likens Collatine's marriage to Lucrece to the custody of some valuable chattel. This is typical of the lyric tradition in which Shakespeare, like Spenser and Donne, wrote, and plays directly into the concept of ravishment as abduction or larceny discussed earlier. More subtly, Shakespeare seems to emphasize the idea of Collatine's 'possession' as a 'publishing', suggesting that Collatine only possesses Lucrece as 'his own' when he sets her forth, which is also the same moment that, necessarily, he loses her; Lucrece's beauty is like the dew, destroyed by the operation of the same body – the sun – that reveals it. The use of the conditional clause in the second line of the second quoted stanza ('And, if possessed . . .'), like the appositive locative of the sixth ('in the owner's arms'), establish possession as the condition of dispossession; but the subsequent stanza makes it clear that declared possession is not merely the condition, but the cause of the dispossession. The narrator suggests that the jewel is rich for being known by thievish ears, but at the same time under an inevitably-to-be-realized threat from those same thievish ears. The oddly dangling final clause, 'because it is his own', almost serves as an answer to the question, rather than as the question itself. To own something, in this formulation, is not to be possessed, but rather dispossessed, of it. This logic the narrator then extends to Tarquin's experience of desire:

> Those that much covet are with gain so fond
> That what they have not, that which they possess,
> They scatter and unloose it from their bond,
> And so by hoping more they have but less;
> Or, gaining more, the profit of excess
> Is but to surfeit and such griefs sustain
> That they prove bankrupt in this poor-rich gain.
>
> (ll. 134–40)

The inevitable forfeiture of the possessed, for both Tarquin and Collatine, seems to be the result of their ambition; the recognition of possession – that which certifies the possession – turns out to be a covetous stage beyond the mere possession itself, and is made as much a fault in Collatine as Tarquin. To have is to be happy; but to have much is already to have begun that process of quantification the end result of which is the discovery of defect:

> So that, in vent'ring ill, we leave to be
> The things we are for that which we expect;
> And this ambitious foul infirmity
> In having much, torments us with defect
> Of that we have; so then we do neglect

> The thing we have, and, all for want of wit
> Make something nothing by augmenting it.
>
> (ll. 148–54)

Both Collatine and Tarquin suffer equally from this paradox of possession, and both attract the reproof of the narrator as Lucrece's terrible
history begins.

Here Shakespeare draws on a peculiarly English legal understanding of 'possession', to be distinguished from the common use of
the word. As early as Bracton's *De legibus*, lawyers distinguished
between possession in law and possession in fact (or actual possession);
as Bracton writes:

> What is possession? It is clear that possession is the detention
> *corpore* and *animo* of a corporeal thing, with the concurrent
> support of right. Of a 'corporeal' thing, it is said, because
> incorporeal things cannot be possessed or be the subjects of
> usucapion or be transferred apart from some corporeal thing,
> since they do not admit of livery by themselves. They therefore are
> said to be *quasi*-possessed [and] can be transferred or *quasi*-
> transferred by acquiescence and use. Possession is also said to be
> 'the detention' of a thing, because it is held naturally by him who
> has it, that is, physically...When one is in possession and we
> dispute it against him, the dispute involves either that there be
> restored to us what is ours but we do not possess, as where we have
> been wrongfully ejected from our own possession, or another's, as
> that of our ancestors, or that (by interdict) we be allowed to retain
> (freely and quietly, properly and peacefully) what we do possess.[25]

Bracton goes on to clarify the concept of possession as 'detention
corpore and *animo*' in a way that suggests more exactly the lines along
which Shakespeare adapted common-law theories of possession to his
subject matter in *Lucrece*.

> Possession is divided into civil and natural possession. Civil is that
> retained by intention alone, natural by physical occupation, and

[thus] it is sometimes rightful, sometimes wrongful. One may possess in both ways, *animo* and *corpore*, [or in either, but] one cannot acquire possession except both *animo* and *corpore*, neither *corpore* alone nor *animo* alone. And just as it cannot be acquired except *animo* and *corpore*, so it cannot be lost unless both [are lost], and, since it is acquired by both, though it is lost *corpore* it may be retained by intention alone. [*Dividitur autem possessio sic: possessionum alia civilis, alia naturalis. Civilis autem est quae animo tantum retinetur. Naturalis, quae corpore, et aliquando iusta est et aliquando iniusta. Et potest quis utroque modo possidere, scilicet animo et corpore, ita quod neque corpore per se, neque animo per se, et adquirere nemo potest possessionem nisi utroque animo et corpore, et sicut non potest possessio nisi animo et corpore adquiri, sic non potest nisi utroque amitti, et cum utroque adquiratur licet corpore amittatur, animo solo poterit retineri.*][26]

Possession in law – civil possession, a kind of possession in *animo* – is here distinguished from possession in fact – actual or natural possession, possession in *corpore*. In order for possession to exist in its fullest sense, the thing possessed must be held by intention and in fact, and its possession must be ratified by right. A man who actually holds lands or parcels of land, of the existence of which he is ignorant, cannot then be said to possess them in the full sense, although he possesses them in fact and may have a right to them. Disputes of possession can thus be represented as attempts to harmonize these three aspects of full possession: actual possession should be recognized (i.e. confirmed), and should be supported by right. In other words, the common law recognizes the complex and divided nature of full possession, and – although Bracton himself continues to use the word slightly ambiguously – insists on the presence of all three elements in any perfect claim to possess a thing. Collatine's possession of Lucrece and her chastity, like Tarquinius Superbus' possession of Rome, only imperfectly satisfies the legal requirements for possession in this full sense.

In order to make his ownership of Lucrece secure and complete, Collatine 'publishe[s]' her worthiness, exposing his possession to public view so that by acknowledging that possession he may attest to his right.

In the language of the poem, he goes from being in 'possession' to being 'the owner', and attempts to appropriate Lucrece's virtue and beauty by incorporating them into 'his own arms'. Shakespeare's immediate resort to a lexis of the loan ('lent'), with its 'expired date cancelled', will not make sense unless the technical legal approach to the idea of possession in this passage is fully exposed. In effect, Shakespeare provides Tarquin with what a sixteenth-century lawyer might have called a 'colorable' right to approach Lucrece, through Collatine's mishandling of his own possession. Collatine asserts intention (*animo*) and right, but does not effect actual (*corpore*) possession. If by Shakespeare's language in this passage of loan and 'expired date' we may justifiably think of Collatine's right to Lucrece as conditional, the comments of the narrator in these stanzas seem to suggest that he has defaulted, at least partially, on these conditions ('cancelled'). While we have no reason for thinking Sextus to have a valid claim to Lucrece, in the legal terms of the period Collatine's neglect to 'enter' on his possession – to take it up *corpore* as well as *animo* – leaves the trover with certain opportunities, if not rights.

The legal diction in the passage surrounding Shakespeare's equivocal presentation of Collatine's 'possession' of Lucrece is echoed by another resort to the same concepts and language, occurring only a few stanzas on. As Tarquin wrestles in his bed with his conscience, Shakespeare's narrator supplies a brief discursion on covetousness:

> Those that much covet are with gain so fond
> That what they have not – that which they possess –
> They scatter and unloose it from their bond,
> And so by hoping more they have but less,
> Or gaining more, the profit of excess
> Is but to surfeit, and such griefs sustain,
> That they prove backrupt in this poor-rich gain.
>
> (ll. 134–40)

The contrast Shakespeare sets up here between what is 'had' and what is 'possessed' depends, again, on the distinction between possession as detention *corpore* and detention *animo*. What is 'had' here seems to correspond to possession *animo*, those things that the possessor covets, or expects to gain; while what is 'possessed' seems to refer to those things that are detained *corpore*, here squandered ('scattered') and released from security for the sake of expectation. Tarquin's fault of will, then, seems in legal terms to mirror Collatine's own insecurity; in publishing Lucrece's incomparable chastity in order to acknowledge and fully 'possess' her (adding *animo* to *corpore*), Collatine loses the possession that he had, while Tarquin, seeking to possess *corpore* what he already possesses *animo*, similarly exchanges one for the other. In this sense, *The Rape of Lucrece* might be considered a tragedy of complete possession.

The effect of the opening comments on Collatine's possession, when interpreted in light not only of Superbus's 'possession' of Rome in the 'Argument', but of his son Tarquin's *animo* 'possession' of Lucrece in stanza 20, is to spread the guilt of the rape across a number of complicit parties. Superbus has set the wrong political tone in the state at large, by grounding his 'possession' of the kingdom not on law, but on will; Collatine has made his possession vulnerable by publishing it in a bid to secure an insecurable ownership; and Sextus has proven himself a wilful prince whose grasp of possession is decidedly shaky. These early reflections on the paradox of possession tend to obscure and confuse any attempt to assign culpability for the rape that follows, and prepare the ground for more technical legal meditations on responsibility. For example, the structure of the narrative leading up to Tarquin's crime emphasize his guilt by giving him clear *mens rea*, and yet in various ways, from diction to narrative structure, they also delay and distribute that guilt again. So Shakespeare presents Tarquin, between lines 127 and 301, 'revolving' in his mind the act and its consequences in a form and language that shows him fully premeditant and aware of the deed and the deed's meaning. Although Shakespeare presents us with a Tarquin who, in lines 120–21, is 'intending weariness with heavy sprite', a later stanza makes it clear that this apparent intent is only superficial:

> Here pale with fear he doth premeditate
> The dangers of his loathsome enterprise,
> And in his inward mind he doth debate
> What following sorrow may on this arise.
>
> (ll. 183–86)

The distinction between an 'intending', which can be disguised by outward representation, and a moving premeditation, conducted in his 'inward mind', seems clear enough; and it is only a few stanzas further on that we find Sextus disclaiming the care of 'th'eternal power', who he recognizes cannot sanction this 'blackest sin' (ll. 344–57): he acts on his own authority, without sanction or defence. Similarly, as he confronts the newly awakened Lucrece, he communicates to her the process of inward debate that led him to her chamber:

> 'I see what crosses my attempt will bring,
> I know what thorns the growing rose defends;
> I think the honey guarded with a sting;
> All this beforehand counsel comprehends
> [...]
> I have debated even in my soul
> What wrong, what shame, what sorrow I shall breed;
> But nothing can affection's course control,
> Or stop the headlong fury of his speed.
> I know repentant tears ensue the deed,
> Reproach, disdain, and deadly enmity,
> Yet strive I to embrace mine infamy.'
>
> (ll. 491–95, 498–504)

Shakespeare seems to go to great lengths to ensure that Sextus, Lucrece, and the reader all know that he has premeditated and carefully considered the consequences of his action. In this respect, he cannot be supposed a casual offender, or one caught up in a crime by unthinking passion. Even his pretence of 'intending' fatigue damns him, for the feigning more clearly demonstrates his real purpose.

The knowing and counsel-conferring way in which Sextus approaches Lucrece and the rape is particularly important because, by the end of the narrative, he stands to be accused not only of rape, but of murder, and in the case of murder malice prepense enjoyed in early modern England an important and much-discussed legal status. Edward Coke writes in the *Third Part of the Institutes of the Laws of England* that:

Malice prepensed is when one compasseth to kill, wound, or beat another, & doth it *sedato animo*. This is said in law to be malice forethought, prepensed, *malitia praecogitata*. This malice is odious in law, as though it be intended against one, it shall be extended towards another.[27]

The choice that Sextus offers Lucrece – to satisfy his lust secretly, or to be killed and defamed publicly – demonstrates the sedateness of his soul at the moment of the crime's commission. Perhaps more importantly, it demonstrates his intention – or at least his conditional intention – to kill her:

> 'Lucrece', quoth he, 'this night I must enjoy thee.
> If thou deny, then force must work my way,
> For in thy bed I purpose to destroy thee.
> That done, some worthless slave of thine I'll slay
> To kill thine honour with thy life's decay;
> And in thy dead arms do I mean to place him,
> Swearing I slew him seeing thee embrace him.
>
> (ll. 512–18)

As Coke attests, malice prepense was of such force in the law of felony that it persisted through certain obstructions to and alterations of the intended crime. 'For if A command B, to kill C, and B by mistaking killeth D in stead of C, this is murder in B because he did the act: and it sprang out of the root of malice, and the law shall couple the event to the cause.' In *The Rape of Lucrece* Shakespeare takes special pains at the end of the narrative to link Lucrece's suicide back to the scene of the rape, notionally coupling the event to the cause:

> But more than he her poor tongue could not speak,
> Till after many accents and delays,
> Untimely breathings, sick and short essays,
> She utters this: 'He, he, fair lords, 'tis he
> That guides this hand to give this wound to me.'
>
> (ll. 1718–22)

The modern editorial problem of whether or not to place the 'he' of line 1718 in quotation marks perfectly reflects the parallel problems of self and identity basic to the question of culpability at this point in the poem: given that the 'he' is Sextus, Lucrece either finds herself unable to say more than 'he', or to say more than Sextus himself has already said, leaving her constrained either by his name or by his declared intentions. Shakespeare's Lucrece resists Augustine's condemnation by figuring herself at most as the accessary to Sextus's crime, now fulfilling the final part of the act initiated by his rape. Just as he had raised his hand to shake 'aloft' his sword before offering her the fatal choice (ll. 505–11), now Lucrece drives not her own hand and sword, but his, into her heart. Sextus' malice prepense comes to function, in this final act of Lucrece's life, as a commanding authority that relieves her of responsibility and thus culpability in her death.[28]

Shakespeare's attempts to distribute responsibility for both the rape and the murder of Lucrece do not merely serve to inculpate Sextus and exonerate Lucrece. In the approach to her chamber, Sextus encounters a number of material bars to his progress – the locked doors (ll. 302–05), the wind (ll. 309–15), Lucrece's glove (ll. 316–22) – that give him pause and opportunity to 'regard' and reconfirm his intentions. In misinterpreting these impediments as whets rather than judgments on his desires, he parodies a common-law maxim on the construction of evidence, and in this sense his behaviour continues to reveal his law-breaking culpability.[29] On the other hand, the last of these bars, the 'latch ' of Lucrece's door, seems to lead in a different direction:

> Now is he come unto the chamber door
> That shuts him from the heaven of his thought,
> Which with a yielding latch, and with no more,
> Hath barred him from the blessed thing he sought.
> (ll. 337–40)

Lucrece's dropped glove has already admitted some confusion into this scene of evidential interpretation – in Marlowe's near contemporary epyllion *Hero and Leander*, Hero's dropped glove more traditionally represents an invitation, rather than an obstacle, to the achievement of the mistress's private chamber and her body. But the 'yielding latch' seems even stranger; where the other doors had been locked, and had required forcing, now Sextus pauses over an unlocked door, 'with no more' than a latch not resistant, but 'yielding'. The emphasis that this conundrum throws on the word 'latch' privileges it, and especially given its close collocation with both 'barred' (in the succeeding line) and 'solicited' (in the following stanza), the word readily takes colour from a contemporary legal term now defunct:

> *Laches* or *Lasches* is as some thinke, an old French word that signifies slacknesse or negligence, and true it is that that is the signification of it, as it appeares, M. *Littl. sect.* 403. & 726. where Laches of entry is nothing else but a neglect in the infant to enter. So that I think it may be an old English word. And when we say, There is Laches of entry, it is as much as to say, There lacke is of entry or there is lacke of entry. And yet I finde that (*Lascher*) in French is to loyter, and (*Lasche*) signifies one that is idle or lazie: and therefore it may also come from the French. For Etymologies are divers, and many times *ad placitum*.[30]

Lasches was used widely in the technical legal discourse of Shakespeare's period to mean 'negligence', which is of course exactly what this 'yielding latch' symbolizes at this moment in Lucrece's narrative. It was, moreover, particularly associated with the law of possession, and especially with the need (for the heir or reversioner) to 'enter on', or take possession of, his or her land upon the death of the previous tenant, or the expiry of his or her lease.[31] While Shakespeare hasn't created a precise pun, the orthography of the two words shared enough overlap in the sixteenth century for one to invoke the other, especially in a context – as here – where the sense and the surrounding diction conduce to the effect. The imputed negligence hovering over this passage might be attached to the 'eternal power' whom Sextus leaves off importuning; to Collatine, who has failed to 'enter' on the possession of his wife and so debar the claims of an intruder; or to Lucrece herself, who has no more securely provided for her own safety. The surrounding passage would seem to support the first, the earlier stanzas on possession and ownership the second; but the subsequent narrative tends towards the third, in a way that makes uncomfortable reading for the ethical reader.

When Sextus first approaches the groggy Lucrece, she demands to know 'under what colour he commits this ill' (l. 476). It is a curious moment because it is so psychologically unwarranted: instead of immediately accusing Sextus of the wrong he is committing and will commit, Lucrece entertains the possibility that he has some legal right to perform this wrong. A 'colour', to a sixteenth-century readership, was a legal fiction or justification, some legally sound argument that could be alleged to justify an action or a claim in a court of law.[32] Strange that Lucrece's intuition should veer this way, certainly, but more importantly, she gives Sextus a rhetorical opportunity to shift the blame, which he immediately takes:

> Thus he replies: 'The colour in thy face,
> That even for anger makes the lily pale
> And the red rose blush at her own disgrace,
> Shall plead for me and tell my loving tale.
> Under that colour am I come to scale
> Thy never-conquered fort. The fault is thine,
> For those thine eyes betray thee unto mine.
>
> (ll. 477–83)

The reader cannot dismiss Sextus' preposterous attempt to shift the blame onto Lucrece for the same reason that Lucrece cannot ultimately reconcile herself – at least publicly – to her own innocence. Shakespeare shifts the meaning of 'colour' from its legal ('shall plead for me . . .') to its military application ('under the colour am I come to scale / Thy never-conquered fort'), suggesting the transition in Sextus' thought from right to conquest even as it betrays his aggressive intentions. This pun masks another ambiguity, which goes back to the moment Sextus first arrived at Collatium, to find white and red striving in Lucrece's face. In the opening stanzas of the poem, the red of Lucrece's face had metonymized her beauty, and the white her virtue; here, instead, the white tokens anger, and the red shame. Having been primed by the extraordinary excursus on colour at the opening of the poem, the reader cannot help but map the anger to virtue, the shame to beauty – and it is the beauty that, Sextus tells Lucrece, 'hath ensnared thee to this night' (l. 485). Sextus' 'colour' is Lucrece's 'colour' and, like the legal 'colours' from which it is derived, it is an ambiguous thing: why should Lucrece blush, if not for complicity? Or, more properly, Lucrece's 'colour' derives from Sextus'.

Given the way the narrative unfolds, the suspicion of Lucrece's complicity is only compounded, rather than relieved. The choice Sextus offers her – between public dishonour for a trespass she did not commit, on the one hand, and on the other private dishonour for a trespass she did – makes Lucrece the arbiter of her own fate. One might well ask why Sextus gives her such a choice in the first place; presumably, if rape is his intention, he might merely use his sword and strength to force her. But if what Sextus finds beautiful about Lucrece is her shame, then the success of his erotic achievement depends on her complicity; the more she is made responsible for her own fate, the more shame she will feel. This may help to explain why Shakespeare has him repeat the terms of the choice (ll. 668–72) just before he stamps out the light and buries her face in her linen. It may also help to explain why he gives Lucrece such rhetorical scope in her own defence; as Sextus notes, her impassioned pleas only serve to stimulate, rather than dampen, his desire, and for this reason the net result of her arguments is to demonstrate the degree to which her beautiful shame prevails over her virtuous anger. It is crucial to recognize, though, that Lucrece's problem is not necessarily her complicity, but the uncommunicable nature of her inward resistance. By the erotic conventions that governed Ovidian narratives like *The Rape of Lucrece*, it was impossible to gauge the sincerity of a woman's shame; as a social performance, shame could be manipulated, and Lucrece is ironically not afforded the luxury of Sextus' 'inward mind' in her pleas. By contrast, even, the arguments Shakespeare does allow her are without exception socially rather than personally motivated. At no point does she make an appeal to his humanity, asking him not to wrong her; instead she appeals to the bonds of hospitality (ll. 575–81), to the rights of her husband (l. 582), and to Sextus' own reputation as a prince and future king (ll.

596–644, 652–666). Lucrece's performance of resistance, in its commonplace and social character, tends to inculpate rather than to clear her, leading to the authentic psychological and emotional force of her lengthy self-study in the centre of the poem.

A new reader of the poem will find unexpected this central distension of Lucrece's story, in which Shakespeare distorts the summarized narrative of the Argument in order to foreground Lucrece's mental state and its relation to both the power of art and the political consequences of ravishment. It is most remarkable for the way it explicitly draws the import of the poem away from its dramatic narrative towards the epistemological preoccupations that, as we have seen, have been lurking only obscurely in its incident and language; again, the movement towards epistemology is yoked to a preoccupation with legal ideas. In the second part of this middle section, Lucrece contemplates a painting of the fall of Troy, in which the key actors of the *Iliad* are represented. Lucrece immediately recognizes the painting as the figuring of a rape, and longs to 'spen[d] her eyes' on two figures, Hecuba (whom she sees and condoles) and Helen (whom she neither sees, nor names, calling her simply 'the strumpet that began this stir'). Along the way Lucrece confronts the 'art / of physiognomy' in the 'ciphered' pictures of Ajax, Ulysses, and Nestor, whose depictions perfectly character their manners; the metonymized Achilles, represented by his spear; and the perjured Sinon, whose face betrays no indication of the perfidious betrayal he is about to execute. The varying degrees of correspondence between visual representation and psychological experience – from the exact relation in Ajax, to the radical disjunction between the outer and inward man in Sinon – drive Lucrece into an epistemological crisis, where doubt so much perplexes her regard that she resolves never again to trust her superficial perceptions:

> 'It cannot be,' quoth she, 'that so much guile' –
> She would have said 'can lurk in such a look',
> But Tarquin's shape came in her mind the while,
> And from her tongue 'can lurk' from 'cannot' took.
> 'It cannot be' she in that sense forsook,

> And turned it thus: 'It cannot be, I find,
> But such a face should bear a wicked mind.'
>
> (ll. 1534–40)

The trauma of Sextus' assault has by this point so undermined Lucrece's faith in the perceptible that she concludes not that perceptions are unreliable, but, more rigorously, that they are always wrong. The unknowability of the private mind has led Lucrece not to the tranquility of a radical sceptic, but to the cynicism of a pessimist.

This transition in her psychology draws, at the centre of this scene, on the early-modern English law of ravishment. As we have seen, the law governing and redressing the rape of a woman was ambiguous in this period, for all the attempts of Edward Coke, in his *Third Part of the Institutes of the Laws of England*, to spell it out in categorical terms. Much has been written on the statutes and penal codes governing ravishment and rape, in their relation to Shakespeare's narrative poem, but few have acknowledged the important and unresolved ambiguities at the heart of legislation and practice.[33] Of the two major ambiguities in the law, the first concerns the difference between sexual assault and abduction, between which the statutory law did not clearly distinguish until the nineteenth century.[34] This law recognized women of all ages, boys (especially heirs), and nuns as potential victims of a crime indiscriminately known as ravishment; while the statute provided for 'iudgement of life and of member' where the ravishment was of an unconsenting woman, with lesser penalties for crimes against consenting women and nuns, the overall effect of the statute is clearly to assimilate an understanding of ravishment as an assault to an explicit discussion of ravishment as abduction.[35] The wording of the statutes providing redress for this crime make it clear that such an abduction was considered a breach of the king's peace and not merely a private matter, apparently because (as in the opening scene of *A Midsummer Night's Dream*) the defiance of legitimate patriarchal authority tended to the undermining not only of the household, but of the state. The political consequences of such an unseating of the patriarch are everywhere evident in *The Rape of Lucrece*, such as in Lucrece's complaint about the very absent Helen of Troy:

'Why should the private pleasure of someone
Become the public plague of many more?
Let sin alone committed light alone
Upon his head that hath transgressed so;
Let guiltless souls be freed from guilty woe.
For one's offence why should so many fall,
To plague a private sin in general?'

(ll. 1478–84)

Lucrece's complaint cuts directly to the heart of the ambiguity in English statutory law governing rape and ravishment: Helen of Troy's absence from the painting reflects the absence from the legislation of any concern with the woman victim's suffering, and Lucrece's response reflects the transition from the reality of a private, probably passionate, and certainly traumatic crime to a public, general redress. Contemporary law was fundamentally uninterested in what happened to the woman ravished; an abducted woman, apparently, was legally assumed to have been raped.

More important here is the second important ambiguity in the English law governing rape and ravishment, that concerning consent of the woman. Although this statute provides for different legal remedies in cases distinguished by the level of consent of the 'victim', the yoking together of such manifestly different situations in one legal instrument demonstrates that the law did not distinguish between cases where a woman had consentingly absconded with her paramour, on the one hand, and on the other cases where she had been violently seized and possibly assaulted against her will. By focusing its attention on the abduction rather than the rape, the second statute of Westminster makes a rhetorical display of distinction, but essentially throws up its hands up in despair over the possibility of knowing the victim's intentions at any time – before, during, or after the abduction. Lawmakers also recognized that social security could be re-established after the crime without necessarily achieving the woman's consent to a match which satisfied her amerced 'lover' and propitiated father, brother, or other guardian; such a positive social outcome, being more important than the happiness of a single woman, was to be preferred to the execution of a pyrrhic justice. In its radically cynical approach to the redress of a real and traumatic crime, the English law of rape and ravishment exploited the political insignificance of women in order to secure a general remedy at the expense of the particular suffering (or not) of any given victim. In this context, Lucrece's outrage at the general suffering caused by Paris's rape of Helen of Sparta reads instead as a lyrical lament for the particularity of a woman's experience. Rather than an attack on Helen of Troy, that is, Lucrece's stanza reads equally convincingly as a lament for Helen of Sparta. Where is she?

The long middle section of *The Rape of Lucrece*, in its first part, also concludes with a legally inflected gesture toward the epistemological security of action over intention. In her distressed deliberations over what to do next, Shakespeare brings Lucrece to a curiously lyric moment, in which, despite the distraction in her aspect, she manages a complicated lyric conceit worthy of John Donne. Sextus had, in the earlier part of the poem, made 'will' the subject of his introspection and the engine of his desire and action; subsequently it was to his will that Lucrece addressed herself in her remonstrations with him before the rape. Now it is to a different kind of will that Lucrece turns. Having resolved to 'bequeath' her blood to Tarquin and her honour to the knife, she promises to Collatine for a 'legacy' her resolution; then, to drive home the point, Shakespeare both repeats and more pointedly clarifies the meaning of her action:

> 'This brief abridgement of my will I make:
> My soul and body to the skies and ground;
> My resolution, husband, do thou take;
> Mine honour be the knife's that makes my wound;
> My shame be his that did my fame confound;
> And all my fame that lives disbursed be
> To those that live and think no shame of me.
>
> 'Thou, Collatine, shalt oversee this will.'
>
> (ll. 1198–205)

The making of a testament and its execution were in Shakespeare's day matters for the probate courts, and not for the common law; but, for reasons already discussed, since the Statute of Wills in 1540 the personal will as a legal instrument had become associated with the subject's rights in the face of the monarch's privilege.[36] The development in Lucrece's conceit here from a psychological experience to a written instrument mirrors the overall tendency in this part of the poem to move from unknowable interiors to performed, evidentially secure public demonstrations. Lucrece goes so far, in the appointment of Collatine as her executor, to place the arbitration of her intentions in the hands of a third party. The link that Shakespeare creates between this reification of the inward, on the one hand, and on the other the common-law right of the will, pushes the reader towards the inevitable confounding of private trauma and political revolution with which the poem ends.

Ironically, from one way of looking at it, Lucrece's gift to Collatine – her resolution – fails: he does not take the revenge on Sextus to which her resolve, she imagined, would steel him. Instead the conclusion of the poem, as in the source, becomes the property of Lucius Junius Brutus, the wise fool who, long having bided his time in a feigned madness, now seizes his opportunity to expel the Tarquins from Rome and establish a free republic. While Sextus in his expulsion does not feel the full extent of the revenge Lucrece had imagined for him, the change in polity does reflect her wishes – or, perhaps more precisely, her actions – in a more profound way. She makes her innocence explicit to Collatine, Lucretius, and Brutus shortly before her death:

> 'O teach me how to make mine own excuse,
> Or at the least this refuge let me find:
> Though my gross blood be stained with this abuse,
> Immaculate and spotless is my mind.
> That was not forced, that never was inclined
> To accessory yieldings, but still pure
> Doth in her poisoned closet yet endure.'

(ll. 1653–59)

Lucrece manifestly here denies the inward soul's consent to rape that, on the part of the virgin nuns, Augustine had also denied; Lucrece demonstrates her Stoic security. But she goes beyond Augustine in also demonstrating that Stoic determination for self-release in suicide; however, her reasons are not those of which Augustine convicts her. While she recognizes the ability of her 'pure mind' to 'dispense' with the 'foul act', she nonetheless resolves upon her death for another, quite different, reason:

> 'No, no,' quoth she, 'no dame hereafter living
> By my excuse shall claim excuse's giving.'

Shakespeare's Lucrece's suicide is not motivated, as Augustine would have it, by her own infected conscience, but by her recognition that the intentions of the victim of a ravishment are finally unknowable, and that therefore (by her pessimistic logic) the law can and must seize only upon that which is done. To avoid the inconvenience of future harlots pleading a Lucretian defence, she elects the mischief of her own unjust execution. Lucrece's final resolution for death is thus motivated not by personal responsibility, but by social circumspection; she has entirely internalized the logic of the painting against which she exclaimed, and has razed Helen of Sparta from her own communicable experience. In recognizing her actions as a precedent, and in the implicit election of a political model that practically equates ethical with legal behaviour, Lucrece has already effectively invented Stoic ideology – an invention that Brutus only acts to implement in political terms. The transition to an epistemologically secure legal and political structure, no longer governed by will but by known laws regulating manifest actions, is that from a monarchy to a republic.

Shakespeare's *The Rape of Lucrece* has been called a republican poem, as if its story presented a triumph celebrating the foundation of a political system that righted the wrongs of the earlier, despotic regime.[37] To call this poem republican is to ignore its tragedy; the extremity from which, in political terms, it flies does not warrant the extremity to which it flees, and Lucrece is as pessimistic a thinker as Sextus. If anything, it might justly be considered, in political terms, a monitory *fabula* in the Aristotelian vein. The insistent technical legal register of the poem – from its earliest narrative sections, through its long and psychologically dense middle part, to its overtly politicized conclusion – suggests a different kind of ideology lying obliquely behind the poem's composition. It would be foolish to suggest that Shakespeare champions any position in a poem that works so effectively as a challenging thinking piece, yet at the same time it is difficult to ignore the irrefragable link created here between personal sacrifice and social security. In the spirit of More's *Utopia*, perhaps, Shakespeare offers to the reader here a model of personal and social identity that sees social goods purchased at the price of individual freedom and authenticity. Stoicism and republicanism emerge from this poem not as part of a triumphant ideology served up to the ambitious and chivalric Essex circle, but rather as a pure form of government beset not only by problems, but by tragedy. In practical terms, ambiguity cannot survive Lucrece's denominator; but neither, in any socially consequent sense, can the will.

'THE WINKING OF AUTHORITY': TYRANNY, COMMODITY, AND EQUITY IN *KING JOHN*

Shakespeare's *King John* is not a play about Magna Carta, despite the fact that it narrates events both before and after the nobility's successful limitation of John's power within articulated bounds. Though Magna Carta could never have been far from Shakespeare's or his audience's minds, the play instead focuses on three other stories, all of which bind together ideas about nationalism, common law, and the limitation of the king's powers: the loss of the Plantagenets' French holdings (Poitou, Anjou, Touraine, Maine), which left them largely bounded to England; John's usurpation of the crown and barring of the claims of his nephews Arthur and the bastard Philip Falconbridge; and the break with Rome, over the appointment of Stephen Langton as Archbishop of Canterbury, that established, in patriotic English imaginations, the precedent for Henry VIII's later Reformation. In its presentation of an England on the brink of geographical definition and imperial autonomy, it thus functions as a politically aetiological narrative in much the same way as *The*

Rape of Lucrece, supplying to its audience the kind of historical evidence of foundation with which Pocock was so rightly impressed. But within this overall historical and documentary thrust, Shakespeare's play also wrestles with the problems of legal epistemology that he first raised in *The Rape of Lucrece*, again associating monarchical power with instability and unknowability.

The affinity of this play with *The Rape of Lucrece* first becomes clear in the first scene of the second act, when John meets King Philip of France before the gates of the town of Angers. Philip has been prevailed upon to challenge John by Constance, widow to John's elder brother Geoffrey, on behalf of Constance's son Arthur – who by strict primogeniture holds the better right to the throne of England and its dependent territories. Backing John's claim are his mother, Eleanor of Acquitaine, and the newly recognized bastard son of Richard Coeur-de-Lion – another of John's elder brothers and his predecessor on the throne. Backing him also, by the messenger Chatillon's report, come other men:

> . . . all th' unsettled humours of the land –
> Rash, inconsiderate, fiery voluntaries,
> With ladies' faces and fierce dragons' spleens –
> Have sold their fortunes at their native homes,
> Bearing their birthrights proudly on their backs,
> To make a hazard of new fortunes here.
>
> (2.1.66–71)

John's attempt, by the French report at least, unabashedly represents the case of merit against that of right. The men who support him, having cashed and disowned their patrimony, seek to achieve honour and status – 'new fortunes' – on their own 'hazard'. They will not inherit, but rather purchase, their honours. Philip aptly greets this host, and this king, by reminding him of his duty to preserve the right, in terms both resonant and prophetic:

> This toil of ours should be a work of thine;
> But thou from loving England art so far
> That thou hast underwrought his lawful king,

> Cut off the sequence of posterity,
> Outfaced infant state, and done a rape
> Upon the maiden virtue of the crown.
>   (2.1.93–98)

These lines smack of York's wrist-slapping reprimand to Richard II, in a play Shakespeare had probably only just completed when he undertook the rewriting of *The Troublesome Reign of John, King of England*; but they are prophetic in a different way. The charge of rape – in the early-modern English legal sense – is not casual: later Arthur's mother, Constance, will enter raving, with her hair down about her shoulders; and, more importantly, John will capture Arthur in battle and convey him back to England – removing the infant ward from the custody of his guardian, his mother. Philip's accusation raises the now familiar problem of the relation of a public duty to a private interest, the unseating of patriarchal authority (here, lineage) in favour of personal gain (here, the crown). Fittingly, John's forces are distinctive not only for their self-making nature, but for the incompatibility between their external presentation ('ladies' faces') and their internal constitution ('fierce dragons' spleens'). The unknowability of the wilful monarch, confounding the public in the personal interest, suddenly emerges into view as a primary preoccupation of this play.

The rape of which Philip accuses John is not the first of the play; at the end of the first act, the newly recognized Bastard meets his mother, with James Gurney, in court. Having come to defend her honour, Lady Falconbridge finds she is too late, and can only confirm Philip's suspicion that he was conceived out of wedlock, the product of her adultery with Richard Coeur-de-Lion. While this confession, following after Philip's recognition and knighting, accomplishes a number of ends, one of its chief ends is to demonstrate that the Plantagenet style of kingship is a wilful and irresistible one:

LADY   King Richard Coeur-de-lion was thy father.
FALCONBRIDGE   By long and vehement suit I was seduced
                To make room for him in my husband's bed.
                Heaven lay not my transgression to my charge!

> Thou art the issue of my dear offence,
> Which was so strongly urged past my defence.
>
> (1.1.253–58)

The moral of this story, for the ebullient Philip, is that submission to the
royal will is right; as he says, 'If thou hadst said him nay, it had been
sin. / Who says it was, he lies: I say 'twas not' (1.1.275–76). By
preparing John's 'rape' of the crown with this more conventional rape
of Lady Falconbridge, Shakespeare places substantial emphasis on the
wilfulness of the early Platagenet monarchs, and puts John into the
very shoes of Sextus Tarquinius. To an Elizabethan, the associations of
Platagenet wilfulness with tyrannical government temporarily shorn
of the 'ancient constitution', or the unwritten, immemorial *lex terrae*,
would have been obvious. Robert Snagge observes in the treatise
derived from his 1581 Middle Temple reading:

[A]fter the Conquest there were divers Insurrections not only of
the people, that did rise without Reason, but of divers of the
Nobility of the best sort, who endured Famin, (and that so far as
they did eat the vilest vermin) yea, and the utter overthrow of their
Houses and Posterity; And all their cause was, but to be restored
to their antient Laws & Liberties. And that civil dissention
continued long for that cause, and the Nobility, without restitution
of them, would not yield to their Kings, as men that shewed
themselves to be made of the right *English* mould, ready to endure
any pain and loss, rather than the loss of their native Laws &
Liberties, and to subject themselves to the Will-government of
their new Lords, and new Law, that the Conqueror brought in, and
the pleasures, and oftentimes the displeasures of their Kings, who
did all, and took all, as pleased themselves, under pretence of their
Prerogative; which Prerogative rightly used, and truly understood,
is a thing most honorable to the Crown, and not prejudicial to the
Law, nor hurtful to the Realm, nor any Subjects lawful Interest, or
Liberty. But that Will-government in the Kings, discontententment
in the Nobility, & continual Wars within the Realm, continued
until K. *Henry* the 3. who (being by that time by divers descents

purged and purified by our *English* Air, and by Education after the
order of our Nation, and so become *English*, and of a better nature
than the Aliens, and their offspring) of love to his subjects, was
content to allow *Englishmen* their *English Laws*.[38]

Shakespeare's careful plotting in the opening acts of *King John* creates
an emblem of the 'will-government' that contemporary political
history associated with Plantagenet rulers following on the conqueror,
a tyrannical approach to rule founded not on right, but on conquest. Its
associations with prerogative authority, rather than consensual or
constitutional rule, make it for Snagge an aberrant period in English
legal history, the only period in which Englishmen were, if only for a
time, not governed by their ancient customs, their 'Laws & Liberties'.
Snagge's belief that this period of 'will-government' concluded in the
reign not of John, but of his son Henry III, perhaps explains why
Shakespeare's play takes John's death, and not Magna Carta, as the
inaugural moment of a new, constitutional era.

In this context of will, right, and conquest, it is not surprising to find
that possession *animo* and *corpore*, again, structure the legal dispute at
the centre of the play, in a far more direct and explicit way than in *The
Rape of Lucrece*. Following the embassy of Chatillon in the first scene,
John attempts to shore up himself and his mother by telling her, 'Our
strong possession and our right for us', to which Eleanor replies, 'Your
strong possession much more than your right' (1.1.39–40). And
indeed, the three possible claimants to the throne of England – John,
Arthur, and Falconbridge – are divided by their respective claims on
animo and *corpore*. John holds the crown, with its lands, in fact, but has
no right; Arthur holds the right, but lives in exile in France; while
Falconbridge has neither right nor possession, but of the three, for his
virtue and valour is clearly the most fit for the position. The play's
action can only conclude when, following both Arthur's and John's
deaths, John's son Henry is again able to unite right with possession. A
parallel – or perhaps parodic – dichotomy plays out in the opening,
more comic scene between Philip Falconbridge and his younger half-
brother Robert, the legitimate Falconbridge heir, who come to court to
resolve their own inheritance dispute. This case, too, turns on primo-

geniture, but because of Philip's alleged bastardy, even as the elder son he will not inherit, and it is left to John and Eleanor to validate his claim to Plantagenet blood in order – ironically – to preserve primogeniture intact. Old Sir Robert Falconbridge, knowing his son Philip for a bastard, by will devised his lands at his death to his second and natural son, creating a matter in equity to be resolved by appeal to the royal conscience. Philip's detention of the land *corpore* subsequently gives way to his brother's possession *animo*, in return for the elevation in honour he receives by recognition of his paternity. It seems that justice has been done, and yet both Eleanor and John seem strangely eager to recognize Philip as Richard's lost bastard, presumably because they see the advantage of amassing a faction on their own party – and especially a faction with such clear military advantages for their forthcoming French campaign: Richard Coeur-de-Lion still retained a mythical status as a soldier across the Christian world, and both John and Eleanor instantaneously fix on Philip's stature and strength, finding them 'perfect Richard'. Moreover, custody of a pretender in the male line – even an illegitimate one – will give John a stronger case in facing down the claim of Geoffrey's son.[39] This is only the first of countless suggestions in *King John* that a legal decision might be swayed by the commodity not of one of the parties, but of the judge, and it sets the tone for the disputes over possession that will follow.

The almost comic nature of the first scene of the second act, in which John and Philip of France, along with all their attendants, hold a fruitless parley, derives from the inability on either side to produce a legitimate authority to decide the matter. Because every participant to the treaty has an interest in their own position, their appeals to right sound not only hollow, but shrill:

JOHN	From whom has thou this great commission, France,
	To draw my answer from thy articles?
PHILIP	From that supernal judge that stirs good thoughts
	In any breast of strong authority
	To look into the blots and stains of right.
	That judge hath made me guardian to this boy,

	Under whose warrant I impeach thy wrong
	And by whose help I mean to chastise it.
JOHN	Alack, thou dost usurp authority.
PHILIP	Excuse it is to beat usurping down.
ELEANOR	Who is it thou dost call usurper, France?
CONSTANCE	Let me make answer: thy usurping son.
ELEANOR	Out, insolent! Thy bastard shall be king
	That thou mayst be a queen and check the world.
CONSTANCE	My bed was ever to thy son as true
	As thine was to thy husband; and this boy
	Liker in feature to his father Geoffrey
	Than thou and John in manners, being as like
	As rain to water, or devil to his dam.
	My boy a bastard? By my soul I think
	His father never was so true begot.
	It cannot be, an if thou wert his mother.

(2.1.110–31)

John attempts to foreclose Philip's challenge by appealing to the lexis of the common law: his implicit argument is that, because he currently holds the office and power of the crown, any inquest into his possession must derive from a commission issued on his own authority. Philip seizes on John's rhetorical ploy, introducing more intensively the lexis of the English common law (judge, right, guardian, warrant, impeach), even as he leapfrogs John's authority by appeal to a divine mandate. When John claims that mandate for himself, the exchange quickly degenerates to farce: first Eleanor accuses Constance of the adultery that would make Arthur a bastard (cannily reducing his claim to the status of Philip Falconbridge's), but then Constance accuses Eleanor not only of adultery, but of incest with her son. In another abortive attempt to disinherit Arthur later in the scene, Eleanor also claims to possess a will that bars Arthur's title; playing on the word 'will', Constance quickly exposes this for the ploy it is. The Bastard takes the true temperature of the negotiations when he begins to play the fool, baiting the Duke of Austria over his lion-skin mantle; his suggestion that the marks of sovereignty (the lion-skin) do not reflect sovereign worth is one neither king can tolerate, and the conference immediately breaks down into a satire on politic self-interest, only resolved when all parties suddenly realize they can profit one another mutually, without battle, by a dynastic marriage. The Bastard's famous concluding speech on 'commodity' provides the moralitas for the scene's moral farce, in which law has been reduced to a lion-skin.

John's parallel encounter with Pandolf, legate of Pope Innocent, occupies the centre of the following scene. The same issues of right and authority surface here, though the conditioning of the earlier scene can only make the audience less patient with, and more cynical about, the righteous claims Pandolf rehearses. John's impatient reply is charged with the popular English anti-Catholic sentiment of the early 1590s, but also with the frustration of his earlier interchanges with Philip:

> JOHN What earthy name to interrogatories
>   Can task the free breath of a sacred king?
>   Thou canst not, Cardinal, devise a name
>   So slight, unworthy, and ridiculous
>   To charge me to an answer, as the Pope.
>   Tell him this tale, and from the mouth of England
>   Add thus much more: that not Italian priest
>   Shall tithe or toll in our dominions;
>   But as we, under God, are supreme head,
>   So, under him, that great supremacy
>   Where we do reign we will alone uphold
>   Without th'assistance of a mortal hand.
>   So tell the Pope, all reverence set apart
>   To him and his usurped authority.
>
> (3.1.73–86)

If John's rhetoric here looks back (particularly in the use of 'interrogatories' and 'usurped authority') to the language of the previous scene, it is because he is eager to diminish the standing of the Pope's legate by equating his claims with those, now exploded, advanced by Philip and himself for the throne of England. For a moment this tactic works, as Constances engages Pandolf in a curiously bathetic sideshow:

CONSTANCE   O lawful let it be
             That I have room with Rome to curse awhile.
             Good Father Cardinal, cry thou 'Amen'
             To my keen curses, for without my wrong
             There is no tongue hath power to curse him right.
PANDOLF   There's law and warrant, lady, for my curse.
CONSTANCE   And for mine too. When law can do no right,
             Let it be lawful that law bar no wrong.
             Law cannot give my child his kingdom here,
             For he that holds the kingdom holds the law.
             Therefore, since law itself is perfect wrong,
             How can the law forbid my tongue to curse?
                                        (3.1.105–16)

Constance's insistence on 'law' as a mortal and 'earthy' code, now in the hands of a corrupt judge, serves to accomplish the disparagement begun by John. Pandolf is at first patient in disassociating himself from her attack on John, but her second salvo, in which she invokes the example of her son's disinheritance to undermine the integrity of law as a whole, leaves Pandolf exposed. When he offers to extend the excommunication to Philip for his refusal to oppose John, the scene turns more recognizably into a contest between human and divine bases for temporal power. King Philip pleads commodity, but Pandolf remains firm: 'All form is formless, order orderless, / Save what is opposite to England's love' (3.1.179–80). This leaves Philip to choose between a 'civil war' of allegiances, caught as Pandolf notes having made 'faith an enemy to faith'. Where John had chosen the epistemologically insecure human basis, consistent with his commodity, Philip ultimately chooses Pandolf.

The epistemological morass into which John has cast himself by the rejection of some supernatural standard leads to the one real tragedy of the play – the death of Arthur of Brittany. Like the rape of Lucrece, it remains unclear even at the end of the play who is responsible for

Arthur's death, though Shakespeare's careful repetition of a few conspicuous rhetorical tropes suggest that it is John's default on legal epistemology that is to blame. In a narrative twist familiar from the end of *Richard II* (and from Elizabeth's tortuous machinations in the issuing of a warrant for the death of Mary Queen of Scots), John seeks both to order Arthur's death and to deny responsibility for it; but unlike Henry IV's repentance, John's indicts not himself but the office and state of kingship, on precisely those grounds of unknowability to which he himself has reduced the royal will. When he first approaches Hubert to commit the murder, in Act 3 Scene 3, John's solicitation pauses over Hubert's ability to know his purpose:

> JOHN   ... Or if that thou couldst see me without eyes,
> Hear me without thine ears, and make reply
> Without a tongue, using conceit alone,
> Without eyes, ears, and harmful sound of words;
> Then in despite of broad-eyed watchful day
> I would into thy bosom pour my thoughts.
> But, ah, I will not. Yet I love thee well,
> And by my troth, I think thou lov'st me well.
>
> (3.348–55)

John here fantasizes about the possibility of a direct communication with Hubert, the forging of a communion so immediate that Hubert might know his purpose without the interposition of sense, perception, or the phenomenal world. Though John comes near to asking Hubert to kill Arthur, he never actually utters the command; instead, he concludes with, 'Well, I'll not say what I intend for thee' – a promise of reward punningly contingent on Hubert's ability to act on unexpressed orders. When Hubert returns to John in Act 4 Scene 2, having baulked at his resolve to kill Arthur, but determined to pretend to the murder in order to chasten and perhaps soften John, the king deflects Hubert's accusation:

> JOHN   Why seek'st thou to possess me with these fears?
> Why urgest thou so oft young Arthur's death?

> Thy hand hath murdered him. I had a mighty cause
> To wish him dead, but thou hadst none to kill him.
> HUBERT No had, my lord? Why, did you not provoke me?
> JOHN It is the curse of kings to be attended
> By slaves that take their humours for a warrant
> To break within the bloody house of life,
> And on the winking of authority
> To understand a law, to know the meaning
> Of dangerous majesty, when perchance it frowns
> More upon humour than advised respect.
>
> (4.2.204–15)

In the peevish madness that now begins to engulf him, John reaches for all the key diction of his earlier confrontations with Philip of France and Pandolf: 'warrant', 'authority', and 'advised respect' all feature pivotally in those earlier scenes in which John first contested and then abandoned the customs and bases, both human and divine, upon which he might have grounded some intelligible, knowable structure of rule and law. Now he recites them in a stinging rebuke to court construal that rebounds upon his own office: the will of the king, caught chaotically between 'humour' and 'advised respect', is not knowable precisely because it is neither personal nor political, but some turbulent confluence of the two.

When Hubert protests that he has a legal instrument – 'your hand and seal' – to warrant his supposed murder, John produces a more impassioned condemnation of court intriguers and flatters, the full extension of which takes in not only the understanders, but the practice of interpretation itself:

> JOHN Hadst thou but shook thy head or made a pause
> When I spake darkly what I purposed,
> Or turned an eye of doubt upon my face,
> As bid me tell my tale in express words,
> Deep shame had struck me dumb, made me break off,
> And those thy fears might have wrought fears in me.
> But thou didst understand me by my signs,

> And didst in signs again parley with sin;
> Yea, without stop, didst let thy heart consent,
> And consequently thy rude hand to act
> The deed which both our tongues held vile to name.
>
> (4.2.232–42)

John's indirect indictment of the state of kingship is based on its need of 'signs', and the culture it creates of interpretation and supposal, which in turn permits it to effect ends that a more public, more accountable political structure would shame to perform. By avoiding the need for open acknowledgment ('darkly'), he claims, kingship and its creatures fall inevitably into unethical behaviours. Because of the way that this exchange develops out of the spiralling political and ethical confusion created by John's defection from all standards but the fact of his own possession of political authority, its significance to the play as a whole is seminal. Arthur's death – an accident, but one occasioned by John's dark purposes – both ends the conditions that led to the play's great jurisdictional conflicts, and brings about John's fall. The unknowability of the king's will unseats the understanding of law, and puts all possession in doubt.

John's final moments in Act 5 provide a kind of coda to this meditation on the legal epistemology of an unfettered monarch, but a coda that again accuses him for his detachment of kingship from the law that should legitimate it. Having been poisoned by a monk, John lies dying of a fever as his revolted lords, his son prince Henry, and the Bastard return to his side. Two of his final speeches recall his history as a prince who attempted to rule by possession, without right. Speaking to his son and lords of his fever, he tells them:

> JOHN   I am a scribbled form, drawn with a pen
>   Upon a parchment, and against this fire
>   Do I shrink up.
>
> (5.7.32–34)

Salisbury has only just finished telling Prince Henry that upon his accession he will 'set a form upon that indigest' left by his father; here

John reduces the idea of form from Salisbury's imagined political extent to a single parchment instrument – a deed, probably of possession. John's claim on power had only ever amounted to a personal possession *corpore*, unjustified by right and contemptuous of law and honour; the fever that kills his body must also therefore destroy his kingship. But it is in his last speech that his words – though unwittingly – betray the abiding importance for this play of Arthur, and the tragedy of his confused, unnecessary end:

> JOHN   The tackle of my heart is cracked and burnt,
> And all the shrouds wherewith my life should sail
> Are turned to one thread, one little hair;
> My heart hath one poor string to stay it by,
> Which holds but till thy news be uttered,
> And then all this thou seest is but a clod
> And module of confounded royalty.
>
> (5.7.52–58)

In his last words, John recalls the words spoken by the Bastard, in the previous act, to Hubert, upon the discovery of Arthur's body:

> BASTARD   If thou didst but consent
> To this most cruel act, do but despair;
> And if thou want'st a cord, the smallest thread
> That ever spider twisted from her womb
> Will serve to strangle thee; a rush will be a beam
> To hang thee on; or wouldst thou drown thyself,
> Put but a little water in a spoon
> And it shall be, as all the ocean,
> Enough to stifle such a villain up.
>
> (4.3.126–34)

The careful way in which Shakespeare echoes this speech in John's final words seems to impeach him, finally, of the tragedy of Arthur's death; John, reduced to a 'thread', breaks. Arthur mistaking took a leap he could not sustain; but that leap would never have been necessary had John not already disjoined possession from right, and sought to govern without law. In the closing verses of the play, Salisbury, Pembroke, and the Bastard take command of the negotiations with the Dauphin, ordering the Prince to attend his father's funeral, but they also kneel to him in subjection, even as he sheds tears of gratitude. John's dying promise to be a 'clod / And module' – the traditional item exchanged in a lord's enfeofment of a feudal tenant in an estate – points the way towards a restoration of the political order, as a balance of law and royal power; but, along with the 'scribbled form', the image of the clod also reduces John to the mere fact of his seisin, or possession, of the land of England. In his final, almost confessional, expostulations, John acknowledges obliquely, but with well-worn legal imagery, the lack of right which has proved to be his downfall. It is fitting that, in concluding the play, the Bastard stops the princes' tears for John, reminding them that the days of the 'proud foot of a conqueror' are now over.

In different ways, both *The Rape of Lucrece* and *King John* take up the problem of the relation between the king and the law; in *The Rape of Lucrece*, Shakespeare weighs the promise of republican law against the monarch's will, while in *King John* the tragedy of a conqueror's absolutism sees no respite within the relentless disorder of the play itself. Yet both works use legal ideas about possession and rape to investigate the epistemology of law, problematizing consent and culpability in a way that drives a wedge between ethical and legal judgment, while also, paradoxically, insisting on the fundamental importance not only of the fact of possession, but of right. Lucrece may die innocent, a willing sacrifice for the pessimistic political order she has come to idealize; John by contrast certainly dies guilty, but the vigour and beauty of his 'signs' die with him, and the 'truth' with which the Bastard closes the play may represent an impoverished, as well as a secure, epistemological conclusion. Shakespeare probably cannot be said to have contributed to the debates on the relation between sovereign and law that convulsed Europe between Jean Bodin and Louis XIV, but with this play and poem he seems to place the significant power of art in a tense deadlock with the extreme forms of republic and monarchical thought that undermine it – where the will of a king is unknowable, the will of a republican is irrelevant. Somewhere in between these two enormities, the literary and ethical conversation between inwardness and outwardness may flourish.

Chapter Six

THE REPORT OF THE CAUSE OF HAMLET

Hamlet, the prince of Denmark, faces and passionately endures a problem that lies at the nexus of ancient, but intractable, philosophical speculation. Some readers of the play call it a problem of action, others a problem of knowledge, others a problem of being; some an ethical, some a political, problem; some a crisis of faith, others one of aesthetics. Really it is all of these: expressed in abstracted, sometimes symbolic terms, it wins by its ambiguous expression, and ambiguous conception, that capacious extensibility into all provinces of thought and feeling which only the most fundamental questions can achieve. Hamlet asks, 'Can I be?' which is tantamount to asking, 'How can I be?' In the Aristotelian ethical, political, epistemological, and metaphysical traditions into which Shakespeare had been, by his birth and schooling, inducted, it was considered axiomatic that a man[1] could fulfil his nature through striving for ethical and political perfection, with the end (as Philip Sidney had observed, following Aristotle) of well doing, and not of well knowing only. To act the part of a good man, though, was to achieve nothing unless one had the knowledge of that good. This good was to be apprehended through the operation of reason, the exercise of which required a careful configuration of the powers of the soul. Here, though, the Aristotelian philosopher-man reaches an impassable paradox, for a man's suppression of beastly passion and the subordination of the self to the universal rule of reason eliminates in that man exactly those qualities that make *him* the agent of the identity that he seeks. Put simply, one cannot simultaneously both be, and know, oneself. Hamlet's problem is that of the theatre; it is also that of the law.

Aristotle himself makes it clear, in passages from the *Nicomachean Ethics* and the *Politics*, how theatre and the law offer the same unanswerable challenge to any unified theory of the self, knowledge, and the good. According to Socrates, as Aristotle acknowledges, it would be impossible for a man to do evil who knew the nature of the good; but Aristotle interrogates this claim before accepting it, and notes one particularly intransigent kind of problem with it. The word 'know' (ἐπίστασθαι) is used, he claims, in two senses:

> A man who has knowledge but is not exercising it is said to know, and so is a man who is actually exercising his knowledge. It will make a difference whether a man does wrong having the knowledge that it is wrong but not consciously thinking of his knowledge, or with the knowledge consciously present to his mind.[2]

In order to understand how a man can have knowledge of the good, but not keep it present to his mind at any given moment of choice, it is necessary (Aristotle claims) to understand the implicit syllogistic reasoning that must obtain in any application of a general principle to a particular case. In every ethical judgment, this man must allow the major, universal premise (e.g. All good men prefer the claims of virtue in such a case) to govern the minor, particular premise (e.g. I am such a man, or this is such a case).

> Now it is quite possible for a man to act against knowledge when he knows both premises but is only exercising his knowledge of the universal premise and not of the particular; for action has to do with particular things. Moreover, there is a distinction as regards the universal term; one universal is predicated of the man himself, the other of the thing; for example, he may know and be conscious of the knowledge that dry food is good for every man and that he himself is a man, or even that food of a certain kind is dry, but either not possess or not be actualizing the knowledge

whether the particular food before him is food of that kind. Now clearly the distinction between these two ways of knowing will make all the difference in the world.

(VII.iii.6)

Anyone unable to accept the instance of a particular thing as a manifestation of a general type, in other words, will be unable to apply general perceptions about the good, and so unable to act well. Similarly, anyone unable to accept *himself* as an instance of a general type will be unable to apply general perceptions of the good; and, as Aristotle suggests, there are a number of ordinary cases in which these suspensions of self-knowledge take place, all of which he sees (as the play *Hamlet* also sees them) as versions of theatricality:

> Again, it is possible for men to 'have knowledge' in yet another way besides those just discussed; for even in the state of having knowledge without exercising it we can observe a distinction: a man may in a sense both have it and not have it; for instance, when he is asleep, or mad, or drunk. But persons under the influence of passion are in the same condition; for it is evident that anger, sexual desire, and certain other passions, actually alter the state of the body, and in some cases even cause madness. It is clear therefore that we must pronounce the unrestrained to 'have knowledge' only in the same way as men who are asleep or mad or drunk. Their using the language of knowledge is no proof that they possess it. Persons in the states mentioned repeat propositions of geometry and verses of Empedocles; students who have just begun a subject reel off its formulae, though they do not yet know their meaning, for knowledge has to become part of the tissue of the mind, and this takes time. Hence we must conceive that men who fail in self-restraint talk in the same way as actors speaking a part.
>
> (VII.iii.7–8)

Sleep, drunkenness, madness, and emotion all here become forms of theatricality, in which the self becomes divided, the acting self dissociated from the knowing self. Moreover, anyone who does not recognize that this chair is a chair, like in some essential respect all other chairs, also participates in the theatrical ontology. (Another more general version of the same argument, as we will see, is that raised by Polonius in Act 2 Scene 2 of *Hamlet*: 'take this [particular] from this [universal], if this [instance] be otherwise'.) A man caught in this theatrical ontology, divided from himself and thus from the world, cannot seek out the good, and therefore can neither be fully human, nor be in any complete sense at all.

In the *Politics* Aristotle deals with a complementary formulation of the problem, that of law. The starting point of his inquiry into the nature of kingship and monarchy, he says, is 'whether it is more advantageous to be ruled by the best men or by the best laws'.[3] The answer proves complicated because of the generality of law and the particularity of the individual cases to which it must be applied: law in and of itself is better than personal judgment, Aristotle reasons, so long as it is deployed by someone who can adjust it equitably when, because of its generality, it would do harm. This is the solution Aristotle also adopts in the *Nicomachean Ethics*,[4] a solution which in both works proved extremely influential in early-modern legal thinking, especially in England. But in the *Politics* Aristotle goes a little further, and suggests what kind of thinking a king, or judge, would have to do in order to discharge this equitable function: he must become indistinguishable from the law itself, purging himself exactly of those characteristics that make him particular.

> The law first specially educates the magistrates for the purpose and then commissions them to decide and administer the matters that it leaves over 'according to the best of their judgement', and furthermore it allows them to introduce for themselves any amendment that experience leads them to think better than the established code. He therefore that recommends that the law shall govern seems to recommend that God and reason alone shall govern, but he that would have man govern adds a wild animal also; for appetite is like a wild animal, and also passion warps the rule even of the best men. Therefore the law is wisdom [νοῦς] without desire. And there seems to be no truth in the analogy

which argues from the arts that it is a bad thing to doctor oneself
by book, but preferable to employ the experts in the arts . . . [For]
certainly physicians themselves call in other physicians to treat
them when they are ill, and gymnastic trainers put themselves
under other trainers when they are doing exercises, believing that
they are unable to judge truly because they are judging about their
own cases and when they are under the influence of feeling.
Hence it is clear that when men seek for what is just they seek for
what is impartial [τὸ μέσον]; for the law is that which is impartial.
                                                            (III.xi.3–6)

The word translated here as 'wisdom' is Aristotle's νοῦς – not reason,
exactly, but mind or intellect, that organ of the soul that deploys
reason; and the word translated here as 'impartial' is Aristotle's τὸ
μέσον – which carries the force of 'impartiality', but literally means 'the
middle, the mean'. Aristotle's analogy of the physician or gymnastic
trainer suggests why the 'common mind' understanding of law makes
sense: when we appeal to this 'common mind', we appeal to a self that
is outside of our own, and at the moment of self-treatment, when bias
is most dangerous, we can no longer be trusted to make that motion. In
other words, law – to live and act by the law – requires a prince to judge
'according to the best of his judgment', but that judgment is not his,
but the law's. At the moment when he achieves the good, the prince
loses himself, subordinating himself to the law.

While it is true that Aristotle makes these arguments in several
places, and in several treatises on several subjects, the ideas slip easily
into conversation because, in both the *Nicomachean Ethics* and the
Politics, the man striving to achieve the good – whether in his own soul,
or in the polis – has to negotiate the same rift between universals (duty,
the law) and particulars (this temptation, that case). In both the ethical
and the political predicament, the same combination of epistemological and ontological problems confronts him: either the prince refuses
to accept the application of the universal to the particular, and is faced
with the unstable and unknowable world of theatrical seeming, or he
accepts the application only to discover that his νοῦς has become ὁ
νόμος (law) and τὸ μέσον (common). When we first see Hamlet in Act 1,

Scene 2 of *Hamlet, Prince of Denmark*, this is exactly his condition. Gertrude recalls the 'common' end of humanity in death, and demands of Hamlet why it 'seems [...] so particular' with him. His famous reply runs exactly into the ground that Aristotle had sketched in the *Nicomachean Ethics*, situating him in the theatrical ontology in which the divided self cannot be reconciled to the world:

> Seems, madam? Nat it is, I know not 'seems'.
> 'Tis not alone my inky cloak, good mother,
> Nor customary suits of solemn black,
> Nor windy suspiration of forced breath,
> No, nor the fruitful river in the eye,
> Nor the dejected haviour of the visage,
> Together with all forms, moods, shows of grief,
> That can denote me truly. These indeed seem,
> For they are actions that a man might play;
> But I have that within which passeth show –
> These but the trappings and the suits of woe.
>
> (1.2.76–86)

Hamlet struggles away from a world of seeming, but his sure conviction in his own inexpressible, undemonstrable particularity forces him right back into the theatrical ontology he desires to escape. The existence of 'trappings' and 'suits', of 'actions that a man might play', of the 'common' world that Gertrude both represents and articulates, offers an invasive threat to Hamlet's yearning for absolute self-knowledge. Is the self socially constructed (in 'common'), or personally authorized ('so particular')? But Shakespeare, like Aristotle, carefully juxtaposes Hamlet's intractable thrashing in the theatrical ontology with the exposition of a parallel problem in the nature of law. Fortinbras of Norway has sent to the king of Denmark, Claudius, demanding restitution of lands he claims were illegally surrendered by his father to Old Hamlet. These lands he will have restored, or he threatens invasion. In making this claim, Fortinbras pits a natural form of entry into possession (inheritance, right) against a conventional one (contract, conquest), and in so doing constructs a jurisprudential version of the dilemma facing Hamlet himself: do we submit to the law because it is right, or is the law right because we have submitted to it? In *Hamlet*, Shakespeare frames these paired legal and ontological problems by a recurring opposition between invasion and inheritance – between the breeding, penetrative son/sun, and the dutiful, accommodating heir/air. In a series of set-piece dialogues so philosophically elaborate that their very thought betrays, even constructs, the frenzied obsessiveness of his passionate ontological crisis, Hamlet tries to negotiate a solution between a theatrical, evasive particular self and a dutiful, invasive universal office. While the enquiry may lead only to the recedent aporia of Hamlet's own silenced voice, the mode of the enquiry evidences a close confection of philosophical speculation with English common-law concepts – so close, indeed, that as the play closes we must ask whether Hamlet's fate is not the tragedy of early-modern common law itself.

For if Hamlet's crisis and end exemplify or particularize a common or universal experience, they also reflect a very topical set of political and legal arguments active in London and Westminster at the turn of the seventeenth century. Before turning to *Hamlet*, it will be helpful to pass briefly through the evidence of another of Shakespeare's plays from about the same time, like *Hamlet* preoccupied with the distinction between 'common' laws and 'particular' judgments: *Measure for Measure*. In the extended meditation of this play on equity and the power of the prince to abrogate, qualify, interpret, or apply the law emerges in another form the central epistemological question at stake in early-modern jurisprudential debate: what does the judge know, and how? A judge informed by a divinely warranted rational capacity, and led by God's hand, may presume to know all, and consider himself to be responsible, in turn, to an omniscient judge; but a judge informed by evidentiary conventions, whose 'knowledge' is not that of a man, but of his office, is constructed by and himself constructs a law not of divine, but of conventional, human warrant. In both *Measure for Measure* and *Hamlet*, the possibility of a disinterested and universal, the possibility of a divine, right disappears into the primacy of the 'record' – the written account of the proceedings of a case at law.[5]

THIEVES PASSING ON THIEVES

The Duke of Vienna, Vincentio, makes a clear distinction at the beginning of *Measure for Measure* between the two commissions he gives to Escalus and Angelo, deputies in his supposed remove from the city. Although he says nothing about what the commissions themselves contain, the comments he makes during the course of the grants betray something about his perceptions of the two men. Escalus is a judge in the professional sense, a man whose 'science' in the 'properties' of government is richer than Vincentio's own. But more than this, Angelo believes that Escalus's profound learning in the laws will lead to a kind of certainty to his execution of justice, which Vincentio can prescribe with confidence:

> Then no more remains
> But that, to your sufficiency, as your worth is able,
> And let them work. The nature of our people,
> Our city's institutions, and the terms
> For common justice, y'are as pregnant in
> As art and practice hath enriched any
> That we remember. There is our commission,
> From which we would not have you warp.
>
> (1.1.7–14)

'Common justice' here signals the regular law, grounded on the customs, institutions, and language of the law as usually practised. The anacolouthon of the first sentence here, the grammar of which breaks down (hypermetrically) on 'that', is important: where we expect the subordinate clause to introduce a new subject – the agent of the action who will do the 'work' – instead it avoids one, opting rather for two independent clauses followed by a hortatory but impersonal subjunctive.[6] It is of course apt that Vincentio should remove the subject from his injunction because the law, as he describes it here, has no administrative agent: Escalus's learning is so complete, and the terms of reference of his commission so clear, that the discharge of his office will be, in a sense, automatic.

Vincentio's grant of commission to Angelo is quite different. Angelo, the Duke tells Escalus, has been selected for a more personal and primary position:

> For you must know, we have with special soul
> Elected him our absence to supply;
> Lent him our terror, drest him with our love,
> And given his deputation all the organs
> Of our own power.
>
> (1.1.17–21)

Angelo will serve as Vincentio's deputy proper, and will discharge the powers of 'mortality and mercy in Vienna'. His judicial role will not be 'common' like that of Escalus, but 'special', a distinction in terms familiar in the judicial controversies of the Elizabethan period, in which 'special actions', 'special remedies', and 'special verdicts' began to encroach – not without resistance – on the courts of common law.[7] Angelo's attempt to evade the honour and responsibility of the position is unsurprising, since Vincentio makes it clear by his preamble that Angelo has developed a 'character' in his life of such perfect consistency and transparency that it has, effectively, wiped clean any touch of inwardness. What the Duke enjoins him to do – 'enforce or qualify the laws / As to your soul seems good' (1.1.65–66) – represents exactly that which Angelo must most fear, inasmuch as his character, like a 'metal', rather wants to be 'stamp'd' than made the measure by which other matters might be valued.[8] The distinction that Vincentio makes between the commissions for the two men, then, is that between the monarch's powers of *jus dicere* (speaking the law, enforcing it) and *jus dare* (giving the law, or making it). One is a legal commission, the other an extra-legal power.

When Vincentio divides in two his commission for the governing of Vienna, the distinction he makes between Escalus and Angelo reflects an important rift in the English common-law justice of Shakespeare's age. As we have seen, English government was subject between the accession of Henry VIII and the Civil War to serious and recurring constitutional shocks,[9] and it is in the context of these larger historical tendencies that, from the middle years of Elizabeth's reign, some English lawyers began to write exploratory discourses on the relations of the courts, and the idea of equity as practised in Chancery as well as in other aspects and places of the common law. Fundamental to the debates over equity was the jurisdictional disposition of common law versus prerogative (or conciliar) courts in the English constitution. Theorists like Sir Thomas Smith in his *De republica Anglorum* (first published in 1583) might describe and even celebrate the various and mutually limiting bases and sources of legislative and judicial power in English government,[10] and such celebration certainly did have a prescriptive effect – even if only to help solidify a constitutionalist ideology among English gentlemen, parliamentarians, and lawyers. But from the 1590s, influenced by the writings of St German, Plowden, and Jean Bodin, lawyers like William Lambarde and Edward Hake began to take up in innovative and pointed ways longstanding questions about the relation between the crown and the judges. Forced to couch their discourses cautiously in indirect discussion, both men directed their attention to the role of the Chancery as a court of equity within the common law, and focused on its relations to the jurisdictions of other courts.[11]

Lambarde and Hake might seem to have taken opposing views: Lambarde contested that the king (or queen) must reserve some residual power in himself or herself, after the distribution of authority and effective power to the royal judges, by which he or she was not only able, but was expected and required to intervene in the process of common law for the purposes of review and appeal. In a complex adaptation of passages from Bracton's *De legibus et consuetudinibus Angliae*, Lambarde 'confirme[s] by proofes drawn out of our Countrie *Lawes*, and *Lawyers*' that the widest possible 'general *jurisdiction*' is retained by the kings of England:

> Master *Henry Bracton*, that lived in the time of King *Henry* the third, hath in the *ninth* and *tenth Chapter* of his Booke, these words following: *Rex (& non alius) debet judicare, si solus ad id sufficere possit: cum ad hoc per veritatem sacramenti teneatur astrictus. Excercere igitur debet Rex potestatem Iuris, sicut Dei Vicarius, &*

Minister in terra. Sin Dominus Rex ad singulas causas determinandas non sufficiat, ut levior sit illi labor in plures personas, partito onere eligere debet viros sapientes, & timentes Deum, & ex illis constituere Iusticiarios.[12] [The king (and not another) should act as judge, if alone he were able to supply the place, for to that he is held bound by virtue of his oath. Therefore the king ought to exercise the power of justice, as the Vicar and Minister of God on earth. But since the Lord king is not capable of the determination of all causes, in order that his labour may be lessened, the burden being divided among many people, he must choose wise and God-fearing men, and make justices of them.]

The words doe prove two things serviceable for this purpose: First, That the King ought onely to be the *Iudge* of his people, (if he alone were able to performe that *Office*) as well because hee is within his owne *Kingdome* the *Vice-roy* of *God,* (the supreme *Iudge* of the World) as also for that hee is thereunto bounden by *Oath,* taken at the *Coronation.* The second, That albeit he doe (for the multitude of *Causes*) substitute others underneath him, yet is hee not thereby discharged himselfe: for it is done, *ut levior sit illi labor,* that his labour be the lighter; not, that he should sit unoccupied. And lest you should doubt, that so much is not comprised in that *Oath* of his, one *question* therein, amongst others, is this, *Facies fieri in omnibus Iudiciis tuis æquam, & rectam Iustitiam, & discretionem in misericordia & veritate secundum vires tuas:* [Will you see that in all of your judgments equity and right justice are administered, and discretion in mercy and truth to your people?] To the which hee answereth, *faciam* [I will]: wherein the words, *Iudiciis tuis, & vires tuas,* doe more properly denote his owne doing, than the doing of his subalterne *Iustices;* albeit their *Iudgement* be after a certaine manner, the *Iudgement* of the King himselfe also, from whence their *Authoritie* is derived.[13]

The purpose of this passage is to locate not only the power of *jus dare,* but equally the power of *jus dicere* firmly in the person of the king, whose delegation to ministers and judges is described (by Lambarde) as a matter of administrative necessity, but not of substance. Lambarde

studiously ignores several key passages of Bracton's *De legibus* occurring between the three phrases he selects for special citation, including
one in which Bracton specifically enjoins the king to 'put on the bridle
of temperance and the reins of moderation', and acknowledges that
the king, 'since he is the minister and vicar of God on earth, can do
nothing save what he can do *de jure*'.[14] In this selective recourse to
Bracton Lambarde creates a strong justification for the two conciliar
courts, one criminal (Star Chamber) and one civil (Chancery), that
derive their authority from the king's own residual judicial power. Of
the Chancery itself, where this power is discharged in its corrective
function, Lambarde follows Aristotle on the need to adapt general
remedies to particular circumstances, using Aristotle's famous analogy
of the leaden rule of the Lesbian builders; but he also adapts the work
of the French political philosopher Jean Bodin, who in his 1576 *Six
livres de la République* had coined the phrase 'justice harmonical' to
describe the happy unity of a lawful government managed by an effectively absolute prince:

> And therfore, although the *written Law* be generally good, and just;
> yet in some speciall case, it may have need of Correction, by reason
> of some considerable Circumstance falling out afterwards, which
> at the time of the Law-making was not fore-seene: Whereas
> otherwise, to apply one generall Law to all particular cases, were
> to make all *Shooes* by one *Last*, or to cut one *Glove* for all *Hands*,
> which how unfit it would prove, every man may readily perceive.
> And hereof this *Equitie* hath the name in *Greek* epieikia, of επι
> *secundum* ['according to'], and εικος *conveniens* ['what is fitting'],
> *vel rationi consentaneum* ['or agreeable to reason']; because it doth
> not onely weigh what is generally meet for the most part, but doth
> also consider, the person, time, place, and other circumstances in
> every singular case that commeth in question, and doth thereof
> frame such judgement as is convenient and agreeable to the same:
> So that in sum the *written Law* is like to a stiffe rule of *Steel*, or *Iron*,
> which will not be applied to the fashion of the *Stone* or *Timber*
> whereunto it is laid: And *Equitie* (as *Aristotle* saith well) is like to
> the leaden rule of the *Lesbian Artificers*, which they might at

pleasure bend, and bow to every stone of whatsoever fashion . . .
Equitie should not bee appealed unto but only in rare and
extraordinary matters, lest on the one side, if the *Iudge* in *Equitie*
should take *Iurisdiction* over all, it should come to passe (as
Aristotle saith) that a *Beast* should beare the rule: For so hee calleth
man, whose *Iudgement*, if it bee not restrained by the Chaine of
Law, is commonly carried away, with unruly affections. And on
the other side, if onely streight Law should bee administred, the
helpe of *GOD* which speaketh in that *Oracle* of *Equitie*, should be
denyed unto men that neede it. And therefore even as two *Herbes*
being in extremitie of heate, or cold, bee by themselves so many
poysons, and if they bee skilfully contempered, will make a
wholesome *Medicine*: So also would it come to passe, if either this
Arithmeticall Governement, (as they call it) by rigour of *Law* onely,
or this *Geometricall Iudgement* at the pleasure of the *Chancellour* or
Prætor onely should bee admitted; and yet if they bee well
compounded together, a most sweete and harmonicall *Iustice* will
follow of them.[15]

Lambarde's account of the Chancery and the Chancellor sounds much
more conciliatory and constitutional than his later discussion of the
residual judicial power of the king, but even here, he stops well short of
agreeing with St German that the Chancellor ought to 'rule' his
conscience by the grounds of the common law. Instead, the Chancellor
inherits from the king, whose authority he represents, the ability to
intervene in common-law justice as and when he chooses, and in what
manner he thinks fit; but, he says, 'a good *Chancellour* will permit the
Common Law to hold her just honour, and not make such violent irrup-
tion upon her borders, but will so moderate his power, and provide, that
the Gate of *Mercie* may bee opened in all Calamitie of Suit: to the end,
(where need shall bee) the Rigour of *Law* may bee amended, and the
short measure thereof extended by the true consideration of *Iustice* and
Equitie'.[16] England, he concludes, has cause to thank heaven that,
during Elizabeth's reign, it has had such a learned Chancellor, 'a man
no lesse learned in the *Common Lawes* of this Realme, than accomplished with the skill of this *Moderation* for *Equitie*'.[17] Lambarde

distinctly leaves open the possibility that the Chancellor's position could be notoriously abused.[18]

By contrast, Edward Hake appears to insist in *Epieikeia* on the fact that equity is a principle inhering in the law itself, and not in the mind of the prince's deputy. Matching Lambarde's resort to Bracton, he writes:

> First, it is agreed of all parts that *Equity* is a correction adhibited or put to a lawe generally made. Secondly, I agree with *Ferus* that hereunto is neede of the wisest men that can be had. Nowe the onely matter in question betwene us is this, whether the *Equity* thus adhybited be the righteousnes of the judge or expositor of the lawe, or of the lawe itself. And, for myne owne opinion, I conceive it somewhat cleere that if the lawe we speake of be a good lawe and well grounded, then the *Equity* that must be used to the correction of the generalitye thereof cannot be said to be the *Equitye* of the judge, but of the lawe, for otherwise the lawe muste be a lawe without *Equitye*, which weare indeede to be a lawe without justice, and so (uppon the matter) to be no lawe but a meare tyranicall constytution, for as *Bracton* sayeth, in his first booke entituled *De rerum diuisione: A justitia quasi a fonte quodam omnia jura emanant et quod vult justitia idem jus prosequitur.* [From justice, as from a fountain-head, all rights arise and what justice commands *jus* provides.][19]

Hake's distinction between the equity of the judge and the equity of the law is not exactly the same as St German's. St German had argued that the Chancellor, in Chancery, should act like a common-law judge – ordering and ruling his judgment after the known bases of the common law – with a single distinction, that the Chancellor referred his judgment to a larger range of bases than the common-law judge (i.e. including reason, general customs, etc.).[20] Hake argues, by contrast, that the principle of any law's equitable construction inheres in the law itself, and that no judge – neither the Chancellor nor any of the common law judges – has a need to refer his decision to any external or distinct ground or rule. But this form of equity – in the exposition of a law – is distinct from the equity provided in a court like Chancery, where the 'circumstances' examinable are not those of the case, but 'withowte or beside the case':

> Although a man may saie that the *Equity* of the Chauncery is an *Equity* that helpeth where the Common lawe helpeth not, yet wee may not saye that the lawe helpeth not for that it is defectyve in the case, for then shold wee saye there were need of so many newe lawes as there are cases wherein the Common lawe helpeth not, which is not to be thoughte; but rather wee may saie that the cause why the lawe helpeth not is indeed for that it will not helpe, neyther wolde it ever have bine the minde of the lawmaker to have holpen in such a case if the case had bine foreseene unto him.[21]

In an abrupt departure from the earlier part of his treatise, Hake contests that the equity of the Chancery is an entirely extra-legal power, one that seeks not to apply reason or the law of God to the intention of the lawmaker, but that seeks to go beyond the remit of the statute, maxim, or custom at hand in order to redress an offence to reason or to God *absolutely*. And it is in this word, 'absolute', that Hake finally reveals his treatise to be a firmly residualist text: 'As the courte of Starre Chamber is by the absolute power of the Prince knowne to the Common lawe for causes cryminall, so the courte of Chauncery is by the absolute power of the Prince knowen also to the Common lawe for causes civile.'[22]

The manuscript treatises of Lambarde and Hake, composed in the delicate years of posturing and preparation before the accession of James VI and I, approach and articulate the doctrine of residualism through a discussion of jurisdictions and the relation of common to equitable justice in the English constitution. Absent here is the direct and explicit confrontation over the king's power that would surface in the debates between Sir Edward Coke and Lord Chancellor Ellesmere between 1607 and 1616. Coke would go on to claim that the crown's ancient distribution of judicial power to the judges had created, through the accretion of centuries of case and statute law, an unbridgeable rift between the king's natural reason and the judges' 'artificial reason'; no longer could the king intervene personally in legal decisions, simply because he was not learned enough. So Coke reports in his *Prohibitions del Roy* of 1607 that 'the King was informed, that ... the judges are but the delegates of the King, and that the King may take what causes he shall please to determine, from the determination of the Judges, and may determine them himself'.[23] Coke claims to have answered, 'in the presence, and with the clear consent of all the Judges of England, and the Barons of the Exchequer', that James was wrong, and that only in the upper house of Parliament could the king, sitting among the Lords, as in a court of error reverse the judgments of the court of King's Bench. James, 'greatly offended', protested that 'he thought the law was founded upon reason, and that he and others had reason, as well as the Judges'. Coke replied that, though this was true, nonetheless:

> His Majesty was not learned in the laws of his realm of England, and causes which concern the life, or inheritance, or goods, or fortunes of his subjects, are not to be decided by natural reason but by the artificial reason and judgment of law, which law is an act which requires long study and experience, before that a man can attain to the cognizance of it: and that the law was the golden met-wand and measure to try the causes of the subjects; and which protected his Majesty in safety and peace.[24]

Coke's position on the irrevocable distribution of judicial authority would eventually be contested by Lord Chancellor Ellesmere, whose position in support of the king's residual and absolute prerogative was no less severe than Coke's against it. Ellesmere stated bluntly in the 1607 case of the *Post-nati* that:

> I make no doubt, but that as God ordained kings, and hath given Lawes to kings themselves, so hee hath authorized and given power to kings to give Lawes to their subjects; and so kings did first make lawes, and then ruled by their lawes, and altered and changed their Lawes from time to time, as they sawe occasion, for the good of themselves, and their subjects.[25]

In his forceful assertion of the residualist position, Ellesmere dispensed entirely with the complicated historical arguments adduced by Bodin,[26] and with the rational enquiry, based on jurisdictional negotiation, pursued by both Lambarde and Hake, basing his argument instead upon patristic authority, the civil law, and a strained reading of Bracton's *De legibus et consuetudinibus Angliae*.[27] By the time of Coke and Ellesmere, the contest over the king's authority had come out into the open, and could be expressed in its true terms. Before 1607, by contrast, the problem of the monarch's residual power – the existence of the seed of tyranny, for some – still lay couched, darkly, in a debate over the limits of the jurisdictions of the various common-law and prerogative courts.

It is in the spirit of Lambarde and Hake, then, that Shakespeare figures a separation, in *Measure for Measure*, between the common and equitable functions of the law. An uncertainty pervades the play from the moment that Escalus and Angelo receive their commissions, and demand clarity of one another:

ESCALUS	I shall desire you, sir, to give me leave
	To have free speech with you; and it concerns me
	To look into the bottom of my place.
	A power I have, but of what strength and nature,
	I am not yet instructed.
ANGELO	'Tis so with me. Let us withdraw together,
	And we may soon our satisfaction have
	Touching that point.

(1.1.76–83)

Angelo's epistemic optimism here is of course the joke, and the problem, of the play: whereas Vincentio has instructed him to exercise his own authority and judgment personal in all affairs of state, instead Angelo quickly demonstrates that he will deliver justice 'by the book': that is, rather than put his own conscience on the line, he prefers to judge all matters as strictly as possible according to the letter of the written law. By contrast, Escalus – whose commission requires him to play the role of common-law, book-learned justicer – immediately emerges as the champion of equitable mollification. Their first case, *Rex v. Claudio et Julietta*, exposes their differences with simple clarity:

ANGELO We must not make a scarecrow of the law,
        Setting it up to fear the birds of prey,
        And let it keep one shape till custom make it
        Their perch, and not their terror.

ESCALUS   Ay, but yet
        Let us be keen, and rather cut a little,
        Than fall, and bruise to death. Alas, this gentleman,
        Whom I would save, had a most noble father.
        Let but your honour know –
        Whom I believe to be most strait in virtue –
        That in the workings of your own affections,
        Had time coher'd with place, or place with wishing,
        Or that the resolute acting of your blood
        Could have attain'd th' effect of your own purpose,
        Whether you had not sometime in your life
        Err'd in this point, which now you censure him,
        And pull'd the law upon you.

                                        (2.1.1–16)

Here again Shakespeare resorts to his device of the demonstrative pronoun, 'that'. The first word of line 10 is superfluous to the grammar; Escalus might simply have said, 'Let but your honour know, in the workings of your own affections ... whether you had not ... err'd ... and pull'd the law upon you.' Instead he begins by asking about 'that' – that is, about a specific, resistant circumstance, some fact, some detail. In 'that' lies the whole mystery of equitable interpretation. Escalus never questions the purpose of the law, nor the justice of the sentence Angelo proposes. He simply wants to save Claudio, and thinks it might be done by a 'that'. But Angelo is rigid:

        'Tis one thing to be tempted, Escalus,
        Another thing to fall. I not deny
        The jury passing on the prisoner's life

> May in the sworn twelve have a thief, or two,
> Guiltier than him they try. What's open made to justice,
> That justice seizes. What know the laws
> That thieves do pass on thieves?
>
> (2.1.17–23)

Angelo here makes an implicit analogy between (a) the distinction between his thoughts and Claudio's actions, and (b) the distinction between the unknown crimes of a juryman and an accused thief at trial. His thoughts, in other words, are like the furtive acts of a seeming honest man – and so also would his acts be, so long as they remained unknown to the law. Escalus seeks a conscientious dispensation for Claudio based on Angelo's conscience; Angelo, in return, denies the relevance of his conscience, or even of his deeds, to the execution of the law. Because the law is, for Angelo, at all times *im*personal, its 'knowledge' is equivalent not to what the judge knows, but to what is on record. As he tells Isabella in Act 2, Scene 2, 'mine were the very cipher of a function / To fine the faults, whose find stands in record, / And let go by the actor' (2.2.39–41). Angelo again refers to himself as a common-law judge – 'the voice of the recorded law' – at 2.4.61.

Angelo's unfitness for equitable judgment – his fetishization of the record – descends, ironically, into the theatrical ontology of which Aristotle had warned: he plays the part of the lechour with Isabella, but continues to seem the austere and unsoiled justice to the public. This may at first seem a paradox: how can the absolute respect for law beget exactly that theatricality which is its opposite? It is possible because, as Angelo insists to Isabella at the end of the second act, what the law knows is only what certain men allow it to know: 'As for you, / Say what you can: my false o'erweighs your true' (2.4.168–69). Just as a thieving juryman may pass judgment on a thief, and the law be never the wiser, so the absolute dissociation between the judge's person and his office must result in hypocrisy. This hypocrisy is the result of Vincentio's 14-year lapse of princely rule. Although, as he tells the Friar in the play's third scene, he has an 'absolute power' (1.3.13) in Vienna, for a period of 14 years he has played the part of 'an o'ergrown lion in a cave / That goes not out to prey' (1.3.22–23). As Lever first noted, this reference to Horace's *Epistles* invokes not an inactive predator, but one that has reversed the normal narrative of the hunt: Horace's lion invites its prey to visit the cave, saving itself the burden of discovery.[28] This little emblem of constitutional justice, which imagines the lion-judge as a sedentary arbiter not of the truth, but of 'what's open made to justice', explains why Angelo is unable to comprehend the nature of the equitable office imposed upon him: he has never seen a prerogative justice, a truly inquiring justice, a justice not *ad rem* but *ad personam*, in action. Equity in a limited sense has meanwhile survived in Vienna: Escalus engages in various forms of Hakean equity when he tries Pompey Bum, not only in holding an interrogative trial (following the English Chancery process), but by allowing himself latitude in the construction of the prostitution statute, and by using the occasion as an opportunity to replace the bumbling constable Elbow. Above all, Escalus appeals to equitable principles when he discriminates between Pompey, a low-life, and Froth, a man of 'four-score pounds a year': Froth he dismisses with a warning, but Pompey a threat (and ultimately, upon re-trial, a punishment). This weaker form of equity, which informs the construction and application of the statute laws, persists in Vienna; the kind of equity missing from the city is that of the absolute prince, that of residual prerogative power, and without it the city slips into Angelo's theatrical nightmare – an ontological chaos and a political tyranny.

At first sight, the only possible route out of the theatrical ontology, as out of the political tyranny, may seem to lie in faith. If the king's prerogative can be accepted to derive from, and be answerable to, divine judgment, it can be trusted to act justly. When Coke stood up to James in 1607, claiming that the king had reason but not learning ample enough to intercede in English common law, he was responding directly to a challenge from the Church. According to Coke's *Reports*, James had been set on in the case by Archbishop Bancroft, and grounded his justifications for intervention upon arguments Bancroft had supplied. These arguments for the king's residual prerogative power derived from scripture: 'The King may take what causes he shall please to determine . . . And the Archbishop said, that this was clear in divinity, that such authority belongs to the King by the word of God in the Scripture.'[29] Similarly, in order to justify his claims about residual prerogative power Ellesmere frequently made resort, as in the case of the *Post-Nati*, to passages in the Old Testament. With this in mind, it seems particularly pointed that, in *Measure for Measure*, figures of religious authority – friars, nuns – only appear in contexts in which their authority is to be usurped by actors desiring to impersonate them. In the third and fourth scenes of the first act, in particular, both Vincentio and Isabella appear determined to take on the roles, merely, of religious persons. As the Duke importunes the Friar:

> Therefore, I prithee,
> Supply me with the habit, and instruct me
> How I may formally in person bear
> Like a true friar.
>
> (1.3.45–48)

In the opening of the following scene Isabella, equally, shows a marked emphasis on the 'privileges' and 'restraint[s]' of the nuns of St Clare; like Vincentio, she is most concerned with the 'formal' aspects of her new identity. When in Act 5 Lucio cites the relevant proverb, *cucullus non facit monachum* ('a habit does not make a monk'), the ironies of Vincentio's godly ministrations in the prison, like those of Isabella's godly sermonizing on chastity, are thrown into relief. What if the reverence accorded to the traditional divine warrant for law is nothing other than another of the law's customs?

In the manuscript revisions to Bracton's treatise on law Shakespeare might well have found a compromise that suited his own comic requirements. The treatise we know by Bracton's name was probably originally the work of another man, his master William of Raleigh. After additions and corrections added in Bracton's time, the manuscript passed in many copies into many hands, and was over the centuries altered, often with polemical significance. Key passages on the relation of the king to the laws appear to be particularly corrupt, probably evidence of the attempts by later owners of the manuscript treatise to reconstrue the relation in ways that suited the demands of their own times or convictions. One such passage is that in which

Bracton's text acknowledges the king's limitations: 'The king has a superior, namely, God. Also the law by which he is made king.' [30] Elsewhere in the treatise the word *superior* appears to much different effect: for example, *rex parem non habet, nec vicinum, nec superiorem* ['the king has no equal, no neighbour, no superior'];[31] *parem autem habere non debet nec multo fortius superiorem maxime in iustitia exhibenda* ['he ought to have no peer, much less a superior, especially in the doing of justice'].[32] Bracton's treatise appears to argue that the king's duty to divine authority is expressed by submission to legal authority, and that the king who acts with the advice of his barons, and according to the form of the law, acknowledges in doing so his own answerability to God. What Bracton's text does not appear to know is how one may, finally, distinguish between a prince who divinely wills such submission, and a prince who is bound by legal convention. What kind of habit does Vincentio wear? For *Measure for Measure*, the crux seems to come in Act 4, Scene 3, where 'heaven provides' by 'accident' the head of a notorious pirate, Ragozine, that will save Claudio from the block (4.3.77). For a moment it seemed that Vincentio might be forced to secure his political and sexual ends by the destruction of the soul of the unprepared Barnardine – a mortal sin for the Duke, for 'to transport [i.e. execute] him in the mind he is / Were damnable' (4.3.68–69). God's apparent intervention in the head-trick seems all the more significant to the play's meditation on legal authority because it comes at the end of two scenes very much preoccupied with the furnishing of the 'warrant': Vincentio supplies ducal authority to the Provost (4.2.180–208), Abhorson takes a 'warrant' to Barnardine, (4. 3. 41–42) and Vincentio gives Isabella a 'token', a 'sacred vow', and a 'holy order' to confirm her in the justice of the (dubious) course to which he sets her (4.3.138–49).

But if all these instances of 'warrantize' appear to be underwritten by God's intervention in the supply of Ragozine's head, the final duping of Isabella – which Vincentio defers until the end of the play – seems to gesture in a different direction. Promising to make her 'heavenly comforts of despair / When it is least expected' (4.3.110–11), Vincentio neglects to tell Isabella that Claudio has been saved. When he finally does reveal Claudio's deliverance, the revelation induces in

Isabella not joy but rather terror – a terror which Vincentio exploits in order to secure the girl, with one single breath, as his wife:

> If he be like your brother, for his sake
> Is he pardon'd; and for your lovely sake
> Give me your hand and say you will be mine.
> (5.1.487–89)

Isabella dares not refuse Vincentio at this moment – dares not even speak – because she has just been subjected to a masterclass in manipulation, one which has resulted in her absolute subjection. For a few brief moments, all that stood between Isabella and an inexpungible accusation of fornication was the word of the Duke himself. In his determination to drive Isabella to despair – first by seeming to abandon her in the resolution of the bed-trick, and then by keeping her in the dark over the head-trick – Vincentio demonstrates to her his power not as ruler, but as controller of the record. Justice cannot seize that which has not been made open; in reserving to himself the power to determine what facts to admit to judgment, Vincentio demonstrates a prerogative power that goes far beyond the equitable interventions made by Escalus earlier in the play. Moreover, Shakespeare takes careful pains in this scene to assert the importance of this control to the contemporary struggles over residual prerogative power, the jurisdiction of the Chancery, and the supposed 'warrant' of law in divinely instituted reason. Immediately after his 'judgments' of Angelo and Isabella, the Duke pauses to utter an odd aside, as if to himself: 'I find an apt remission in myself' (5.1.495). The word 'remission' may well simply mean 'relaxation', as if Vincentio is testifying to the ease and calm he feels at the conclusion of a complex, comic game with considerable personal and political stakes. But 'remission' is also a calque for the Latin law term *remissio*, from *remittere*, and here translates the familiar English common-law word 'remitter'. In this sense, as Cowell has it, remission 'signifieth in our common law, a restitution of one that hath two titles to lands or tenements, and is seised of them by his later title, vnto his title that is more auncient'.[33] Vincentio experiences, by his resolution of the play's comic entanglements, that reversion to the ancient condition of his princely government of Vienna of which, in Act 1 Scene 3, he had told the Friar – the condition of absolute power. But the word 'apt' hides a further complexity. A tenant's right to 'remission' was grounded, as St German had famously discussed it in *Doctor and Student*, upon a maxim of the law. Maxims, in turn, were grounded upon that reason instituted in humanity by God. Or were they?

> Maxymes / haue ben alwayes taken for law in this realme / so that it is not lawfull for none that is lernyd to denye them / for euery one of those maxymes is suffycyent auctorytie to hym selfe to such an extent that it is fruitless to argue with those who deny them . . . And it nedyth not to assygne any reason or consideration why they were fyrste receyued for maxymes for it suffyseth that they be not agaynst the lawe of reason nor the law of god in any respect / & that they haue alway be taken for lawe. And suche maxymes be not onlye holden for lawe / but also other cases lyke vnto them / and all thyngis that necessaryly foloweth vpon the same / ar to be reduced to lyke lawe. And therfore most commenly there be assygned some reasons or consyderacyon why such maxymes be resonable and ought reasonably to be observed as maxims to the intent that other cases lyke may the more conuenyently be applyed to them and judged by the same law.[34]

The Student, whose task it is in the dialogue to explain to the Doctor the nature and bases of English common law, admits himself to be in real doubt about the legal authority of maxims. The best that can be said, he suggests, is that reasons are usually offered to justify the maxims *in order that they may be conveniently applied to other cases.* In other words, the Student acknowledges that the learned judges accept maxims, and go through a sham process of reasonable justification of them, for the sake of 'convenience'. In the original Latin of the dialogue, St German's word for 'conuenyently' – the linchpin of the whole argument about maxims, of which remission is a conspicuous example – is *apte*.

The momentary congruency between St German's and Shakespeare's texts may be fortuitous – though I suspect it isn't – but there is no denying that the aptness of Vincentio's remitted, absolute title in Vienna leaves open the fundamental question of political theory posed by the opening of the play. At the play's conclusion we are no closer to knowing whether the prince enjoys a divinely sanctioned, residual prerogative in matters judicial, or by contrast can only manipulate the record in order to ensure that constitutional justice continues to suit his interests. The record bears no mark of a prerogative intervention: Claudio's 'crime' in sleeping with his 'wife' Juliet pardons itself, once Angelo's 'marriage' to Mariana has set the precedent for *sponsalia*; Angelo's punishment – to be published to the world as the husband of a woman he thought he had raped – is in conscience, not in law; and Isabella's attempt to convey herself into a nunnery, so denying the prince the right of her wardship, collapses when Vincentio 'ravishes' her, and awards the fine, in marrying her, to himself. But if Shakespeare's play appears not to take a position on the prerogative power of the prince, it nonetheless asserts the importance, in both political and theatrical terms, of the record. Vienna's Duke had never promised to improve on Angelo's constitutionalist uncomprehension of equity; it was Vincentio, we may remember, who told the Friar he preferred to impose the office of reform on a deputy, 'and yet my nature never in the fight / To do in slander' (1.3.42–43). The one person Vincentio hesitates to leave unpardoned, as the play closes, is the slanderer Lucio; moreover, Lucio recognizes that his punishment, like his crime, turns on the record. Vincentio eventually insists that Lucio marry Kate Keepdown, a punishment that Lucio likens to 'pressing to death' (5.1.519). Pressing to death, or *peine forte et dure*, was the traditional punishment assigned to felons, usually traitors, who refused to be tried by the laws of England – that is, defendants who refused to allow their cases to be entered on the record.[35] It was a grisly fate a traitor sometimes chose in order to prevent his treason from being recognized in law, thus protecting his family from corruption of the blood, and loss of their estates. By weighting the prisoner's chest with heavy stones, the king's executioners made him as 'mute' as he had been when he stood, without an answer, before the judges – actually crushing the breath from his body. Let the people believe what they like about the basis of my power, Vincentio reasons, but I will determine what they say.

77

Perſecutiones aduerſus Catholicos à Proteſtanti-
bus Caluiniſtis excitæ in Anglia.

Et tua femineum commendat gloria ſexum,
Dura nec in ſummis animo demiſſa virago
Supplicỹs, teneràmque tui non pondera molem
Corporis, inieĉti non turbauère molares:
Quin, ait, his totos membris imponite montes,
Spiritus innocua tranſcendet ad aſtra ruina.

K 3   P RES-

FIGURE 9 *Peine forte et dure* ('Persecutiones aduersus Catholicos à
Protestantibus Caluinistis excitæ in Anglia'), from Richard Verstegan [Richard
Rowland], *Theatrum Crudelitatum Hæreticorum Nostri Temporis* (Antwerp: apud
Adrianum Huberti, 1592). Cambridge University Library, G.10.26.

INHERITANCE AND INVASION:
NATURALISM, CONVENTIONALISM,
AND THE LAW IN *HAMLET*

Hamlet, Prince of Denmark takes up these same problems, in strikingly similar terms, and comes to a startlingly parallel conclusion – most startling, of course, because Hamlet's story is not a comedy but (we are told) a tragedy. Inheritance and invasion are the two paradigms for self-construction, and self-destruction, facing Hamlet throughout his play, the echo of Aristotle's opposition between a theatrical ontology and a legal 'common mind'. As the son of another Hamlet, and a man whom his mother, at least, fully expects to go on to become the father of another Hamlet,[36] Hamlet stands by dint of primogeniture at the cruel crossroads of an infinite chain of twinning relations. In taking up his name, 'Hamlet', and the office of king that goes with it, he can imp his identity, twinningly, upon that of his own father; but in doing so he will only perpetuate a process that, in its endless iteration of further Hamlets, will crowd his own custody of the name and title – his own particular being – to its limit of nothing. Moreover, Hamlet makes a rash vow, accentuating this crowding, in 1.5 of the play, where he promises his father that he will wipe from his brain 'all trivial fond records, / All saws of books, all forms, all pressures past / That youth and observation copied there', so that his father's 'commandment all alone shall live / Within the book and volume of my brain, / Unmix'd with baser matter' (1.5.99–104). Hamlet therefore might like to think twice before assuming, under his father's name, the place his father occupied. The other threat that Hamlet faces is invasion. We learn in the first scene of the play that another man – Fortinbras, prince of Norway – intends to invade Denmark and substitute himself for Hamlet, both as prince and as revenger. Hamlet himself might well beat this prince of Norway to the punch, and himself displace the usurper Claudius, his uncle; so Hamlet would become not an inheritor, but an invader, and indeed Claudius's interposition as avuncular usurper seems designed to place Hamlet in exactly this predicament. Hamlet must kill Claudius, but everything depends on the significance of the act. If it is done in the memory of his father, Hamlet will cede his identity to evacuative inheritance; if it is done in his own right, Hamlet will thereby admit the comparable right (of conquest, of substitution, of the invader) claimed by Fortinbras.

The opening few lines of *Hamlet* introduce the paired princely predicaments of inheritance and invasion. They provoke questions about authority, truth, and identity, but they also demonstrate how the structure of Hamlet's dilemma extends into, and is created by, language itself. The first words of the play, which belong to the sentry Barnardo, present a peculiar paronomasia,[37] which leads, in turn, to the first of the play's doublets:

> BARNARDO   Who's there?
> FRANCISCO   Nay, answer me. Stand and unfold yourself.
> BARNARDO   Long live the king!
> FRANCISCO   Barnardo?
> BANARDO   He.

The paronomasia, or pun, in the opening line is easily overlooked when not read with an informed hindsight. 'Who's th'heir?' Barnardo asks; to which the correct answer would, presumably, be 'Hamlet'. But instead of answering either of the two questions he has just been asked, Francisco replies with another question, inverting the triadic structure of the pun by presenting Barnardo with a hendiadys of sorts. The inverse relation between paronomasia and doublet is elemental to this play, and can best be seen graphically:

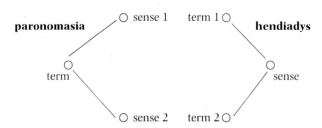

The paronomasia is constructed of a single signifier (e.g. 'Hamlet'), which has two referents ('Old Hamlet' and 'Young Hamlet'). The hendiadys (Greek, 'one through two') is constructed of two signifiers with a single referent. To 'stand' and to 'unfold yourself' are not quite equivalent actions, and Francisco does not exactly mean either one of them, precisely because he means both of them; what he means is some third term, which remains unexpressed (and perhaps inexpressible) – a meaning triangulated by the two expressed terms, but sufficiently contained in neither of them.[38] The paronomasia and the hendiadys represent, in the simplest form possible, a challenge to the idea that a fundamental and straightforward relation – what I will hereafter call a 'natural' relation – might exist between a single word and the thing that it names. In structural terms, then, the opening few lines seem to lay down the pattern for a play the rhetoric of which will be dominated by these two, mirrored distortions of a natural relation between words and things.

A recognition of the nature of these two rhetorical figures does not, of course, exhaust the importance of these opening lines. Not only the fact of these figures, but the purpose to which they are deployed, matters to the developing pattern. Francisco and Barnardo are jumpy partly because they have, on previous nights, seen a ghost on the Elsinore ramparts, but partly too, as we soon learn, because Denmark is preparing for war. Paronomasia is here linked with inheritance ('Who's th'heir?'), possibly the most important of the means by which legal title to estates was passed in early-modern England, and one under painful scrutiny in a play where the protagonist has been elbowed out of the political order by an uncle effectively pleading *casus belli*. The other means by which property might be transferred was by a transaction *inter vivos*, either passively (gift) or actively (purchase or, by the early modern term, 'conquest'). This kind of transaction the play imagines as invasion, for reasons I will discuss below, and invasion is, of course, that to which Francisco alludes in his doublet, 'stand and unfold yourself': what he has added to 'who's there' is the note of defiance and fear; no longer simply an enquiry ('who's there' ends with a question mark), Francisco's retort is a jussive command, the challenge of a sentry fearing attack. One curious feature of this exchange is that, even after Francisco has turned the questioning around to his advantage, Barnardo still resists answering directly. The structure of the beginning of the conversation would seem to work like this:

QUESTION	[Who's there?]
COMMAND	[Nay, answer me. Stand and unfold yourself.]
DEFLECTION	[Long live the king!]
QUESTION	[Barnardo?]
ANSWER	[He.]

This description of the structure is actually (though usefully) incorrect. What is important about Francisco's question ('Barnardo?') is not that he is *asking* it – this is not the reason he gets an answer. What matters about his question is that, from his perspective, it is superfluous: he already knows, by this point, that he is talking to Barnardo. The reason that he bothers to ask Barnardo whether it is, indeed, he, is rather because he wants Barnardo to know that it is Francisco asking; his question is in fact a statement. Only Francisco would know to expect Barnardo, so only Francisco could at that moment ask for Barnardo; hence Barnardo knows he is safe. The question then becomes, how does Francisco learn (not guess – he can guess well enough that he is speaking to the man due to relieve him at this hour – what he needs here is *proof*) that he is speaking to his friend? The answer lies in Barnardo's deflection, the watchword 'long live the king', which is the middle term of a syllogism. Barnardo and Francisco have agreed beforehand that, when one of them demands of the other, 'stand and unfold yourself', the other should answer, 'long live the king'. Like the question that follows, this phrase does not mean what it seems to mean; instead, it means, 'I am the one who knows to say, "long live the king"'. Francisco then performs a brief mental calculation: 1. anyone who knows to say 'long live the king' in answer to 'stand and unfold yourself' is Barnardo; 2. this man knows to say 'long live the king' in answer to 'stand and unfold yourself'; 3. ergo this man is Barnardo. The two syllogisms that depend from Francisco's doublet-challenge should not, however, surprise us, for 'unfold' was the usual English translation, in the handbooks of logic current in the Elizabethan period, for the Latin logical term *explicare*, which gives us the English word (also used in logic) 'explicate'. To 'explicate' a syllogism – to 'unfold' it – is to analyse and expound it, proposition by proposition.[39] Fittingly enough, 'stand' in its substantive usage was sometimes, during this period, apparently used as a synonym for 'argument' or logical 'proposition'.[40]

The importance of the syllogistical reply to the paronomastic query is, of course, the way in which it further emphasizes the triangulated structure of significance relations to the thought of the play to come. Refractions of both fundamental structures proliferate in *Hamlet*. Shakespeare rarely lets up from punning ('son'/'sun' is only the most important), and the huge incidence of hendiadys and other forms of doubletting in the play has become, since George T. Wright's study,[41] a critical commonplace. Twins abound – Cornelius and Voltemand, Rosencrantz and Guildenstern, Hamlet and Old Hamlet, Fortinbras and Old Fortinbras – and nearly every scene features some conspicuous example of (in Polonius's words) the 'indirections' used to 'find directions out': 'catching' and 'angling' are Shakespeare's preferred metaphors (as in *The Winter's Tale*) for an empirical strategy of laying out bait (the first term) in order to provoke some response (the middle term) that can then be used to reach an epistemologically secure conclusion about the nature of Hamlet's dangerous ethical and political predicament.[42] This leads to large and central plot structures like the Mousetrap (baiting), ancillary episodes like the entrapment of Laertes by Reynaldo (angling), and repeated conversations in which the play's characters struggle with the paradoxical nature of a linguistic and rhetorical medium that, because of its baitedness, reveals more about the interpreters than it does about the speakers – as in this ironic moment in the fortunes of the apparently guilty-minded Gertrude:

GERTRUDE I will not speak with her.
HORATIO   She is importunate,
                  Indeed distract. Her mood will needs be pitied.
GERTRUDE What would she have?
HORATIO She speaks much of her father, says she hears
                  There's tricks i' th' world, and hems, and beats her heart,
                  Spurns enviously at straws, speaks things in doubt
                  That carry but half sense. Her speech is nothing;
                  Yet the unshaped use of it doth move

>   The hearers to collection. They aim at it,
>   And botch the words up fit to their own thoughts,
>   Which, as her winks and nods and gestures yield them,
>   Indeed would make one think there might be thought,
>   Though nothing sure, yet much unhappily.
> GERTRUDE 'Twere good she were spoken with, for she may strew
>   Dangerous conjectures in ill-breeding minds.
>
>   (4.5.1–15)

It is often assumed that Gertrude admits to guilt here (just as it is, equally erroneously, assumed that Claudius admits to guilt in his chapel confession in 3.3); in fact what she says is far stranger, and suggests why the 'invasion' aspect of syllogistic meaning in this play is so threatening to Hamlet. Horatio describes a familiar phenomenon: someone approaches us, speaks something unintelligible to us in an awkward way that demands a response, and before we know it we have said something that, to an observer, seems to reveal more about our presuppositions than about our questioner's meaning. An example of a man and woman, speaking at a noisy party, may help:

> WOMAN   Do you often come to this place?
> MAN   Now? I mean, sure, I'd love to!
> WOMAN   No, I said, do you often come here?

Within a few minutes of this awkward exchange, the woman has carefully disentangled herself from this too-eager conversationalist. Gertrude fears that Ophelia will induce her to make a similar kind of slip: the 'unshaped' quality of her speech, like the noise in the crowded room, makes her words just unintelligible enough that any response will have to apply some form of construction to the initial words in order to qualify *as* a response; the 'botch[ing] ... up' of the words, the 'aim[ing]', might well lead the listener to betray her apparent intentions. The most interesting aspect of this phenomenon is the temporal paradox it creates: the man in the scenario above perhaps never intended – at least not coherently, not choately – to try to seduce the woman, but her perceived invitation led him to acknowledge a potentiality in the social situation that, for him, had so far remained unrealized. Regardless of the fictional or mistaken nature of the prompt that led to this acknowledgment, the woman's witness of it gives her some real information about a hypothetical that, perhaps, she would have preferred not to know – her interlocutor here is more interested in her than she believed, or before knew. But this knowledge is, though undeniable, in a way false – the man never would have had the thought had he not been incited to it, and so his retrospectively created intention – though now witnessed by both and imputed to him – remains in some sense a paradox. In effect, the woman's ambiguity has imputed an intention to the man that he did not have, or that he may not have had, creating something *in the past* from a position in the present. Ophelia's madness acts on Gertrude not merely as a burden, but as an invasionary threat, one that might not only cause her to leak or let slip an existent intention or guilt that she would rather keep silent, but one that might – in some real sense – create the existence of that guilty intention (that is, create the *having been* of that psychological state) even while revealing it. Gertrude rightly fears what is, in simple terms, an invasive threat to the most secure part of her nature, her willing consciousness.

Horatio's account of Ophelia's madness, and Gertrude's response to it, sketch out the linguistic basis of an invasive epistemology that, as we shall shortly see, unnerves Hamlet throughout the play; but before I turn to Hamlet's negotiation of this conceptual problem, the temporal and ontological catastrophes it creates, and their relation to a set of legal ideas with which we have already become familiar, I want to pause over one further lexical detail in Horatio's report. It is often the case that a single unusual word, or sometimes even an odd syntactical construction, in a passage of Shakespeare's writing will suggest an intertextual allusion, and something of the kind happens here. 'She says she hears there's tricks i' th' world', Horatio informs Gertrude – what kind of tricks? Hears from whom? It might have made more sense if Ophelia had said she'd heard there were, say, 'fools i' th' world', but who has been speaking to her about 'tricks'? Hamlet has; and Ophelia can be forgiven for taking some time to understand him, for he has been doing it in Greek:

POLONIUS   [*Reads.*] *To the celestial, and my soul's idol, the most*
                      beautified Ophelia – That's an ill phrase, a vile phrase,
                      'beautified' is a vile phrase. But you shall hear –
                      these; in her excellent white bosom, these, etc.
GERTRUDE   Came this from Hamlet to her?
POLONIUS   Good madam, stay awhile, I will be faithful.
                      Doubt thou the stars are fire,
                      Doubt that the sun doth move,
                      Doubt truth to be a liar,
                      But never doubt I love.
O dear Ophelia, I am ill at these numbers. I have not art to reckon my
groans. But that I love thee best, O most best, believe it. Adieu.
    Thine evermore, most dear lady, whilst this machine is to him,
    Hamlet.

                                                    (2.2.109–23)

Hamlet's letter to Ophelia has a number of strange features, all of
which go back to Plato's *Cratylus* – an intertext richly active in this
letter, as in the play generally. The last, but perhaps most important, of
these strange features is the word 'machine'. It is never adequately
glossed in modern editions, nor do editors ever have much insight into
why Hamlet chooses that extraordinary syntactical structure for his
subscription, answering Ophelia's possessive pronoun ('thine', a geni-
tive relation) with a dative of interest ('whilst this machine is to him').
'Machine' here has been variously taken to mean 'fabric of the
universe', or 'engine', as if Hamlet were promising Ophelia to be hers
during life. But 'machine' – while not quite a neologism, for it had
specialized uses in early-modern English before Shakespeare – was new
in this kind of literary, personal context, and here invokes its Latin figu-
rative usage, as well as its Latin literal usage. *Machina* in Latin, a
transliterated borrowing of Greek μηχανή, meant for Virgil not only
'engine' but also 'contrivance, strategy, trick'. This is the sense in which
the Greek original is both analysed (at length) and then playfully used
by Socrates in the *Cratylus*.

    Before thinking about why Shakespeare might appeal to this sense,
and to this passage of the *Cratylus*, it will be necessary to stand back a

moment and fill in the background of the passage's allusions. First of all, why does Polonius call 'beautified' a 'phrase'? It wasn't entirely unknown for sixteenth-century English grammarians to use this term with reference to a single word, but nor was it common, and Shakespeare seems to insist, through Polonius's repetition, that we should notice him doing so.[43] There is just the possibility that Polonius actually meant the word in its more usual sense, as 'a group or sequence of words expressing an idea'; but in what sense could 'beautified' fulfil this definition? The *Cratylus* is Plato's dialogue about names and language, and concerns the debate between conventionalists, like Socrates' interlocutor Hermogenes, who believe that all linguistic signs mean what they do only by convention, and naturalists like Cratylus, who believe that all linguistic signs ultimately derive (sometimes marred by historical change) from some original and true association between an apt, mimetic rendering, on the one hand, and the thing itself, on the other. During his long discussion of the naturalist position, Socrates indulges playfully (and deeply sarcastically) in a series of fanciful etymologies, in which simple words are revealed to be elliptical forms of longer phrases composed of supposedly simpler, ancienter (and thus purer) language.[44] It might seem ridiculous to suppose that Polonius pauses briefly here to consider 'beautified' as the product of the phrase 'beauty if eyed', but such a notional phrasal etymology is exactly consistent with the sense and the wordplay of the words immediately preceding. 'Celestial' points us to the sky, where 'soul' becomes 'sol' becomes 'sun' becomes 'son'; 'idol' easily yields 'idle', and Hamlet is once again complaining of his filial undutifulness. Perhaps more importantly, to praise Ophelia is in this way ('celestial', 'soul's idol') is to make her divinity apparent – an idol is a *visible* god, as opposed to the kind of divinity that lurks in bushes on mountains. If I praise you, Hamlet reasons, and make you an idol, then I have made you beautiful; this is a constructive theory of language based on conventionalism; Hamlet says nothing of Ophelia herself, except that epithets are being attached to her name. By contrast, at the end of the letter he makes the opposite move: 'But that I love thee best, O most best, believe it.' Here the reverse motion obtains: Ophelia's nature as 'most best' is prior to, and causes, Hamlet's hyperbolical love. Here the world and its use of language responds to the real nature of things, in a naturalist gesture at language. But perhaps the most important allusions to *Cratylus* in this passage come in the central poem, where Hamlet connects the stars to fire, the sun to motion, and truth to falsehood. The grammatical ambiguity of this poem is its central rhetorical ploy, of course, but the choice of the particular subjects – stars, the sun, truth – bears scrutiny, for these are terms for which Socrates presents elaborate false etymologies during his playful argument in defence of natural language.[45] Moreover, the false etymologies that he creates for these words touch on exactly those qualities that Hamlet 'doubts' in his poem – the stars, Socrates claims, are made of fire, the sun called Ἥλιος because it is always turning, and truth (ἀλήθεια) is always 'wandering' in a way that seems to make it change place with falsehood itself (ψεῦδος, 'the opposite of motion'). Finally, Socrates' long mock-defence of the naturalist argument concludes in a triumphant discussion of the clinching case for the conventionalist argument – 'numbers':

> SOCRATES [...] For, my friend, if you will just turn your attention to numbers, where do you think you can possibly get names to apply to each individual number on the principle of likeness, unless you allow agreement and convention on your part to control the correctness of names? I myself prefer the theory that names are, so far as is possible, like the things named; but really this attractive force of likeness is, as Hermogenes says, a poor thing, and we are compelled to employ in addition this commonplace expedient, convention, to establish the correctness of names.[46]

To be 'ill at these numbers' is to be a bad poet (where 'numbers' means 'verses'); but by this phrase Hamlet also means that the triumph of conventionalist language – by which Socrates may ridicule the naturalist etymologies of star, sun, and truth, and cast doubt upon the *Cratylus'* fundamental association of fluidity and motion with goodness, and stasis with evil – causes him to feel ill. The crisis of which he informs Ophelia in his letter is of course the epistemological malaise that readers have long seen in his ambiguous use of the word 'doubt', with his references to a Copernican astronomy, and the best that Ophelia can do is to 'believe it'; but another aspect of this crisis is that created by his meditation on the *Cratylus*: not only is the world unknowable, but that unknowability is intimately tied to our inability to communicate by means of a language secured on anything firmer than convention.[47]

With this in mind, we may revisit the last, troubling line of Hamlet's letter, its subscription. The use of 'machine' here cuts right to the heart of Socrates' argument in the *Cratylus*, and indeed, to the heart of his method. For μηχανή occupies a very privileged place among the words for which Socrates develops false etymologies during his long mock apology for naturalism, as it is the site of a pun lying at the basis of the irony of the whole dialogue. μηχανή, Socrates claims, sits at 'the loftiest height' of his enquiry, intimately involved with the nature of the words ἀρετή and κακία (virtue and wickedness). μηχανή itself seems to derive from the words μῆκος (length) and ἄνειν (to accomplish), and so indicates 'a great accomplishment', while ἀρετή is shown to arise from ἀεὶ ῥέον, suggesting that it is 'always flowing', or always in motion. By contrast, Socrates demonstrates that many terms associated with κακία, 'wickedness', seem to invoke impediments to motion, lethargy, and stillness. But when he has finished his etymological fugue of naturalism, Hermogenes exposes the conventionalist 'trick' lying at the centre of this central discussion:

[SOCRATES]	Perhaps you will say this is another invention of mine; but I say if what I said just now about κακία is right, this about the name of ἀρετή is right too.
HERMOGENES	But what is the meaning of the word κακόν which you used in many of your derivations?
SOCRATES	By Zeus, I think it is a strange word and hard to understand; so I apply to it that contrivance [μηχανή] of mine.
HERMOGENES	What contrivance?
SOCRATES	The claim of foreign origin, which I advance in this case as in those others.[48]

It is here –at the 'loftiest height' of Socrates' discussion in the dialogue – that all of the main strands of the ironic treatment of naturalism come together. It is clear from this passage how – as elsewhere in the dialogue – Socrates associates virtue with flow and vice or evil with stasis; this emphasis of the dialogue, which reaches its height here, might, of itself, have suggested the importance of the *Cratylus* to a poet writing *Hamlet*. It is in this passage, too, that the word used throughout the dialogue to describe the irony, or 'strategy' of the Socratic method – μηχανή – is itself given the etymologizing treatment. It is of considerable importance to the intertextual dependence of *Hamlet* on *Cratylus* that Socrates should here associate μηχανή with 'great accomplishment', and that he should then go on to establish this very word as the means by which, at the end of this passage as elsewhere in the dialogue, he evades naturalist argument. When Hermogenes demands of Socrates where the word κακόν, 'evil', comes from, Socrates resorts to his 'trick' by claiming it is a 'βαρβαρικόν', a word of foreign origin. In other words, Socrates argues that words can either be inherited from original, mimetic forms that held a true relation to things-as-they-are (naturalism), or be borrowed into Greek (as into English) by a 'trick', as invaders (conventionalism). The invasion of words from other tongues is for Socrates a 'trick', naturally, because it conceals the way in which inheritance or natural origin must have operated in the foreign origin, no matter by how many successive borrowings the word was eventually traduced into the language at hand. When Hamlet promises Ophelia that he will be hers 'whilst this machine is to him', he thus promises to remain her lover not during life, but during the persistence of a conventional language relation; at least part of the cause of her eventual descent into madness must, then, be her recognition of this 'trick'.[49] We can recognize this convention as exactly that of Francisco and Barnardo, who agreed the meaning of 'long live the king' before the first scene of the first act; conventionalism depends on retrospection, and as a result, for Hamlet, every meaningful experience he has in the play is secondary, belated, or retrospective. Similarly, this retrospectiveness of meaning is the point of Hamlet's abusive play on honesty and bawdry, virtue and relish in the nunnery scene; as he says to Ophelia there, in a conversation packed with re-wordings (re-membrances, re-deliveries, re-ceivings), time by its consummations 'translates' honest intentions into the 'sanctified bawds' of which Polonius had earlier warned his daughter. Conventionalism is also fundamentally defenceless against loan words – words with no history, no memory – just as 'stand and unfold yourself' is a question that might receive any number of possible, agreed answers (or middle terms), all of which – under the right circumstances – could be correct.

Cratylus has one more important idea to offer to Shakespeare's play. When Socrates and Hermogenes first take up the problem of the nature of language, Socrates asks Hermogenes who it is who provides names (or words) in the first place:

SOCRATES	And can you not tell this, either, who gives us the names we use?
HERMOGENES	No.
SOCRATES	Do you not think it is the law that gives them to us?
HERMOGENES	Very likely.
SOCRATES	Then the teacher, when he uses a name, will be using the work of a lawgiver?
HERMOGENES	I think so.
SOCRATES	Do you think every man is a lawgiver, or only he who has the skill?
HERMOGENES	He who has the skill.
SOCRATES	Then it is not for every man, Hermogenes, to give names, but for him who may be called the name-maker; and he, it appears, is the lawgiver, who is of all the artisans among men the rarest.[50]

At first it may seem odd to suppose that it is the law [νόμος] and the lawgiver [νομοθέτης] who give names to speakers of a language. But a little reflection makes it clear why this parallel is so attractive. Law, like language, was traditionally thought to arise from one of two sources (or, like language, from a complex combination of the two): either a natural impulse implanted in humanity by some divine power, or the time-hardened practice of convention, agreed by people from time immemorial.[51] Again we face the dichotomy of naturalism versus conventionalism. That this relation has been considered more than a simple parallel is suggested by a diverse range of traditions in the early modern period – from the historical arguments that the earliest judges were, like the Irish *brehon*, also bards,[52] to the emblematic tradition of Hercules Gallicus,[53] to the Christian association, through the Greek word λόγος of the New Testament, between reason as natural law and reason as the 'word'. In *Hamlet* the association between a conventionalist account of language and legal custom is made clear in several episodes, not least in the latter part of the first scene, directly following the curious exchange between Barnardo and Francisco discussed above. Here Horatio sits down to explain to Marcellus just why it is that invasion is such a threat to Denmark; in answer to Marcellus's question, Horatio rehearses the history of a legal agreement:

> HORATIO   [...] At least the whisper goes so: our last king
> Whose image even but now appeared to us,
> Was, as you know, by Fortinbras of Norway,
> Thereto pricked on by a most emulate pride,
> Dared to the combat; in which our valiant Hamlet –
> For so this side of our known world esteemed him –
> Did slay this Fortinbras, who by a sealed compact
> Well ratified by law and heraldry,
> Did forfeit, with his life, all those his lands
> Which he stood seized on to the conqueror;
> Against the which a moiety competent
> Was gaged by our King, which had returned
> To the inheritance of Fortinbras,
> Had he been vanquisher; as, by the same cov'nant
> And carriage of the article designed,
> His fell to Hamlet.
>
> (1.1.80–95)

The threat of Norway's invasion of Denmark, which hangs over the entire play and effectively becomes, in the final scene, its structuring revenge plot, is tied from the beginning to a conventionalist account of law: here, Horatio recounts how Old Hamlet and Old Fortinbras agreed a 'compact' (L *conventio*) so that the outcome of their single combat could be properly and securely interpreted. The result was, naturally, to wipe out the claims of 'inheritance' in one or the other of the countries, in favour of the 'conqueror'; what the two kings did not, perhaps, predict was that this would necessarily have the consequence (because of the threat of Fortinbras's revenge) of deprecating inheritance in favour of *conventio* in the conquering country, too: Claudius notes in his maiden speech to the court, in 1.2, that his conventionalist claim to power has been at least partly based on 'your better wisdoms, which have freely gone / With this affair along' (1.2.15–16). But Claudius's conventionalist usurpation only exposes (retrospectively) the originary and defining convention (or *conventio*) of the play, one that we discover from the Sexton in 5.1 (ll. 136–40) is exactly – to the day – synchronous with Hamlet's life.

STICKING IN THE HEIR:
EQUITY AND MISOGYNY

The association Plato makes between the conventionalism of language and the conventionalism of law is one, then, that Shakespeare echoes in the first scene of *Hamlet*. The basic problem of law – to create universal remedies for irregular circumstances – is similarly the problem of language, which must also apply universals (names, words) to subjective experience and the irregular instances of an ordinary person's life. For the speaker who wishes to communicate a genuinely idiomatic thought or experience by a significant word, neither the heritable (natural) nor the invasionary (conventional) model of language offers much hope: if one assumes the meaning of a word as it is given, one must inevitably to some degree cut one's thought or experience according to the available cloth; to insist on a new definition is to open the Pandora's box of an infinite proliferation of authorizable meanings.[54] The same is true of law: a system of law based on an absolute and divine dispensation, for example, will admit no reform, whereas a system of law based entirely on convention stands – as we have seen in *King John* and *Measure for Measure* – vulnerable to supplantation. As we might expect, Hamlet goes on through the play agonizing in various rhetorical forms about the claims and frustrations of both the inheritance and the invasion models of speech, in ways that continue to draw a close connection between language and law. One obvious manifestation of this rhetoricized anxiety is Hamlet's constant return, in almost every of his scenes, to the word 'air'. In a sublimated paronomasia that occasionally breaks through into explicitness, he invokes and provokes discussion about air at nearly every opportunity. Perhaps the most elaborate of these allusions – the Player's recital of the moment where Pyrrhus's sword 'seem'd i' th' air [i.e. heir] to stick – may serve to indicate the obsessive elaboration of the play's wordplay. In Marlowe's and Nashe's *Dido Queen of Carthage*, the source of the Pyrrhus speech, Pyrrhus had famously 'whisked' his sword about, dispatching Priam in a casual gesture. In Shakespeare, the operative role of the air in Priam's death is absurdly enhanced, as Priam swings wide, 'but with the whiff and wind of his fell sword / Th' unnerved father falls' (2.2.464–65). Not only does Priam die by whoosh, but the whole of Troy, 'seeming to feel this [non-] blow' (2.2.466), crashes to the ground. What Shakespeare does not repeat from Marlowe's original is the moment where Hecuba, gripping Pyrrhus by the eyelids, is hauled off by soldiers and swung through the air. This detail in Marlowe reflects an older, macabre tradition in which Pyrrhus was said to have killed Priam not with his sword, but by bludgeoning him to death with the body of his grandson, Hector's son and the heir of Troy, Astyanax. This heir appears nowhere in the player's account of the death of Priam, but Shakespeare's dramatic (and absurdly hyperbolic) pause on the familiar 'air'/'heir' pun makes the dead body conspicuous by its absence. It is of course exactly this instrumentality that Hamlet fears – and sublimates.

Hamlet (or *Hamlet*) may fear assimilation as just another heir of the revenge ur-narrative, but the play also fears the invasion of other stories about invasion, and above all that of Jephthah. Polonius advertises himself to Gertrude and Claudius as the kind of 'assistant to a state' who can get past 'circumstances' to 'find / Where truth is hid, though it were hid indeed / Within the centre' (2.2.157–59). He can do this, he suggests, because he always has; and if he cannot, precedent itself shall fail:

FIGURE 10 Attic amphora of the late sixth century BC. Musée du Louvre. Canino collection, F222. This vase shows Neoptolemus (Pyrrhus) bludgeoning King Priam of Troy with the body of Astyanax, Hector's son.

POLONIUS Hath there been such a time – I would fain know that –
                      That I have positively said ''Tis so',
                      When it prov'd otherwise?
CLAUDIUS Not that I know.

POLONIUS   Take this from this, if this be otherwise.
                                         (2.2.153–56)

Polonius uses the demonstrative 'that' to refer to past experiences of his wisdom and perspicuity; the subordinated clause ('That I have positively said "'Tis so"') repeats the word, which Claudius, again, repeats ('Not that I know'). In modern editions of *Hamlet*, editors often insert a stage direction before the next line in an attempt to make sense of it, suggesting to the reader that Polonius perhaps points to his head and then his shoulders while he speaks it; but the text is much more effective without such intervention. Polonius is applying a past rule to a present circumstance – 'that' to 'this' – and promises that the present ('this') will be just like the past ('that'). If it isn't, he suggests that 'this' should be taken from 'this' – that is, that 'this' should be considered meaningless unless it is 'that'.

Given Polonius's assurance that he can read the past to predict the future, it is striking that he does not see the threat posed by Fortinbras. Hamlet certainly does. When the ambassadors return from Norway in 2.2 with their fair reply, Hamlet cannot be far away, for the details of their exchange with Claudius structure Hamlet's conversation with Polonius later in the scene. The news they bring from Norway is ostensibly good: the bed-rid uncle of Fortinbras has given them a favourable audience, and has seemed to act to restrain his nephew, sending out 'arrests' and giving him a 'rebuke'. For his part, Fortinbras makes auspicious undertakings:

> [. . .] Fortinbras . . . in brief, obeys,
> Receives rebuke from Norway, and, in fine,
> Makes vow before his uncle never more
> To give th'assay of arms against your majesty.
> Whereon old Norway, overcome with joy,
> Gives him three thousand crowns in annual fee
> And his commission to employ those soldiers,
> So levied as before, against the Polack,
> With an entreaty, herein further shown,
> That it might please you to give quiet pass

> Through your dominions for his enterprise,
> On such regards of safety and allowance
> As therein are set down.
>
> (2.2.68–80)

Incredibly, Claudius immediately agrees to this transparently dissimulative proposal:

> It likes us well;
> And at our most considered time we'll read,
> Answer, and think upon this business.
>
> (2.2.80–82)

Claudius has apparently achieved peace in our time, but the illusion to any discerning eye is very thin indeed. For one thing, Denmark is hardly on the way between Norway and Poland; Fortinbras's 'warlike' arrival at the end of the play – to Elsinore, in the far southwest of the country – gives the lie to his supposed intention of marching eastwards. For another, the idea of a king allowing a foreign army leave to travel through his kingdom – under any 'regards of safety and allowance' whatsoever – was by sixteenth-century standards, plainly absurd. Queen Elizabeth had in 1588 told her own assembled troops at Tilbury that she had been warned by her counsellors not to commit herself to 'armed multitudes' – and these were her own forces.[55] The privy council's anxiety about the density of unemployed English soldiers (mixed in the legislation of the time indiscriminately with 'vagabonds' and 'masterless men') residing in London, near to the court, led to a series of proclamations against them throughout the Elizabethan period,[56] and government fears nearly proved prescient when, in 1599, the Earl of Essex returned without warrant from his commission in Ireland, or again, in 1601, when he tried to raise a popular force against the Cecils.[57] The idea that Denmark would allow a hereditary enemy – and one with a grievance – to pass through its territory unchecked, under any conditions, would have struck contemporary audiences not only as absurd, but (very likely) as slightly topical.

Hamlet, for his part, is under no illusion about Fortinbras's intentions, and betrays as much to the careful audience before the scene is out. When he finally comes on stage, he enters reading a book. Polonius immediately enquires as to the matter that he is reading and, after some contentious quibbling, Hamlet claims to be reading 'slanders':

> For the satirical rogue says here that old men have gray beards, that their faces are wrinkled, their eyes purging thick amber and plum-tree gum, and that they have a plentiful lack of wit, together with most weak hams – all which, sir, though I most powerfully and potently believe, yet I hold it not honesty to have it thus set down.

> (2.2.196–202)

In Claudius's initial account of his 'business' with Norway, in 1.2, he played upon Norway's invalid status, noting that the feebleness of Norway's legs ('bed-rid') had exposed him to ignorance of his nephew Fortinbras's 'gait' in the preparation for war with Denmark. In playing further upon the 'weak hams' of old men, here, Hamlet stresses the way in which Norway has persisted in his ignorance, and argues that Norway – perhaps like Claudius – cannot see the real intentions of Fortinbras.

If this seems a weak supposal, Hamlet's other conversation with Polonius in this scene drives home much more explicitly his impatience with Claudius's and Polonius's lack of policy, and makes it clear that Hamlet has been spying on them:

HAMLET	O Jephthah, judge of Israel, what a treasure hadst thou!
POLONIUS	What a treasure had he, my lord?
HAMLET	Why,
	'One fair daughter, and no more,
	The which he loved passing well.'
POLONIUS	Still on my daughter.
HAMLET	Am I not i' th' right, old Jephthah?
POLONIUS	If you call me Jephthah, my lord, I have a daughter I love passing well.

HAMLET	Nay, that follows not.
POLONIUS	What follows then, my lord?
HAMLET	Why,

       'As by lot, God wot',

   and then you know,

       'It came to pass, as most like it was' –

   the first row of the pious chanson will show you

   more; for look where my abridgements come.

                 (2.2.404–21)

There is no question that Hamlet's abrupt allusion to the story of Jephthah in Judges 11 is motivated by the important narrative parallel between Ophelia and Jephthah's daughter. Before leading the host of Israel against the Ammonites, Jephthah had sworn to God in prayer that, if Israel were victorious, he would sacrifice the first living creature he encountered upon his homecoming; God having given him the victory, and Jephthah having returned home to the sight of his daughter, coming out of the house to greet him, he fulfilled his vow. Polonius, obtuse as ever, seems not to draw the moral of the allusion – namely, that Hamlet has overheard Polonius's recent conversation with Claudius (2.2.159–67), and expects him to sacrifice his daughter (i.e. by using her as bait to trap Hamlet). But the allusion also has considerable significance for Hamlet, as he might in a similar sense be thought a child whose father was bent on sacrificing him: Old Hamlet's ghost has required a vow of Hamlet to perform a revenge that will, inevitably, result in Hamlet's death; moreover, in achieving his revenge, Hamlet's totalizing act of memory ('thy commandment all alone shall live / Within the book and volume of my brain') will consecrate the entire significance of his life to the rehabilitation of his father's soul. The allusion to Jephthah might thus be read, too, as a plaintive expostulation against the waste of Hamlet's own life – a waste he is beginning to fear inevitable. For a moment, the threat of the erasure of the inheritance relation rears, again.[58]

But the linguistic detail of Hamlet's allusion tell a third story, and it is here that we return to the prince's preoccupation with invasion. For Hamlet's allusion to the Jephthah narrative is much more complete than editors or critics have allowed, and points us not only to the fate of Jephthah's daughter, but to the history of Jephthah himself.[59] As the son of Gilead by a harlot, Jephthah was initially driven out of Israel into Tob, where 'gathered idle fellowes to Iphtah' – a ragtag army over which he served, successfully and famously, as a general. When his legitimate brothers faced invasion from the Ammonites, they sent to Jephthah to return and lead them in battle. He agreed; but instead of marching directly out against the enemy, he instead sent messengers to give the Ammonites a brief history lesson: when Israel first came out of Egypt, it sought to 'pass' through Edom, through Moab, and by Heshbon, but the kings of these several lands refused them, whereupon Israel fought with Sihon and Jahaz, and destroyed him, possessing the fertile lands of these nations from the river Arnon to the river Jabbok. Jephthah's point is that the Israelites have once already been granted the possession of these lands by their God; why put their right to the test again? Hamlet's allusion to the story cites its precedent for a different purpose: Israel begged passage through these lands, but the request (as Sihon saw) was a pretext, and within short time the Israelites had conquered and possessed the countries. The language of the Geneva translation of the Bible is quite specifically at play in 2.2 of *Hamlet*: if we take a second look at the moment that the ambassadors return and report back to Claudius, we find that they too have reported Fortinbras's request for 'quiet pass', an appeal that Claudius admits 'likes us well'. To the obsessive prince spying on the scene, two words stick fast in the contemptuous consciousness: pass, well; pass, well. It is thus no surprise to find Hamlet harping not on Polonius's daughter, but on the idea of passing, and of Claudius's politically inept response: '... The which he loved passing well.' Hamlet has good cause for ridiculing Polonius's ability to judge state matters by appeals to precedent, for he has only just witnessed (as we have) Polonius declaring to Claudius, with absolute self-possession, that there has never been a time when he has positively said ''Tis so', when it proved otherwise – and then Hamlet has watched him, as we have, make that exemplary switch from 'that' to 'this'. To add insult to injury, Polonius has with his usual hyperbole put his identity on the line: 'If he love her not, / And be not from his reason fallen thereon, / Let me be no assistant for a state, /

But keep a farm and carters' (2.2.164–67). In the allusion to the Jephthah story, then, Hamlet compasses not only Ophelia's developing fate (her life literally sacrificed to her father's position as 'assistant for a state'), nor his own predicament (the child sacrificed to the glory and honour of a soldier father), but also – by precise verbal allusion and a little sarcastic lesson in exemplary history – the impending threat of a dissimulative military invasion. Hamlet has been spying; unlike the gum-eyed greybeards, he knows what Fortinbras is planning; and Hamlet cannot escape the frustration and anger that drives him to an obsessive, witty abuse of the incompetent advisor to the king over whose machinations, Hamlet knows, he may by even casual intelligence prevail.

One other aspect of the Jephthah allusion should give us further brief pause. Jephthah, like Hamlet (or so Hamlet says), is the son of a harlot, and thus Jephthah is a man brought into disrepute and barred from his birthright. Hamlet goes to great pains to make us think that Gertrude is, similarly, an unchaste, faithless, and mutable woman. In the most awkwardly sexual terms, Hamlet expostulates against the perfidy of his mother's unseemly haste in marrying her dead husband's brother. Hamlet's large and lavish expressions of anger and revulsion constitute one of the most serious crimes committed in the play for, of course, we have no independent testimony or evidence, whatsoever, that Gertrude is anything but modest, chaste, and dutiful. Indeed, Shakespeare goes to considerable pains to insert a scene – Act 1 Scene 3 – into the play's plot before the ghost appears to Hamlet, the whole function of which is to show us the way in which the Danish court treats its women. Polonius's straight handling of Ophelia – 'Come your ways' – pretty much sums it up. The court at Elsinore requires of women absolute and unquestioning obedience to paternal and fraternal authority; Ophelia's gestures at a kind of insinuating and knowing ethical parity with Laertes, early in the scene, are ruthlessly crushed by what can only be seen as Polonius's cruel decisiveness at the scene's close. With this in mind, Gertrude's later lines, and particularly her acknowledgment that the cause of Hamlet's lunacy is likely 'no other but the main, / His father's death and our o'er-hasty marriage' (2.2.56–57), read more like reproaches of Claudius's heavy-handedness, than complicit wantonness. As I have suggested above, it is nothing short of careless to suppose that Gertrude confesses to complicity with or passion for Claudius – or worse – in her exchanges with Hamlet or with Horatio in Acts 3 and 4. When Gertrude confesses to Hamlet, 'thou turn'st my eyes into my very soul', she might well be saying that his emphasis on seeing ('Ha, have you eyes?') has trans-formed her soul into sight, and nothing more; this is why it has 'black and grained spots' (i.e. pupils) in it.

The question then remains: if it is not Gertrude's behaviours, nor yet her intentions, that provoke Hamlet's revulsion, why is he so incensed against her? The metaphysical anxiety that both nauseates and enrages Hamlet stems from her identity as mother, and is rooted in an ancient allegorical identification, preserved in Aristotelian physi-ology as well as in the etymological links between several key terms in several languages, such as those between mother (*mater*) and matter (*materia*).[60] What Hamlet imagines as Gertrude's lust and inconstancy is her passivity and weakness, her inability to resist the new man (*pater*, 'pattern') whose identity deletes the memory of his predecessor. That Hamlet imagines this weakness as a metaphysical problem is indicated by his frequent conflation of sex and conception, on the one hand, with illness and death on the other. Maggots breeding in a dead dog – the emblem that Hamlet provides for Polonius at 2.2.181–82 – provide us with a typical conflation of the site of birth (maggots) and death (the dog), making a grotesque out of the commonplace of Aristotelian metaphysics, that all sublunary things are born into the conditions of their own destruction – further, that their birth is the sign of their death. The tradition of viewing *materia* as a harlot-wife whose constant sexual appetite for new men causes her to put on form after form in an insatiable riot of change, is one Shakespeare certainly knew from Proverbs;[61] his use of the association in *Hamlet* echoes the emphasis of the erotic lyric poetry of John Donne, among others, and points us back towards the *Cratylus* – a dialogue on names and words that concludes in the *aporia* of Heraclitean flux.[62] Socrates' argument at the end of *Cratylus* is that any attempt to come to an understanding of the nature of words will suffer from the unstable and diseased state of mortal experience of, and situation in, the transient phenomenal world – for how can words imitate the nature of reality, when reality itself cannot hold its shape? Hamlet's problem with communication and significance, then, finds itself undermined at a level more basal and radical than we might first have supposed: even the very nature of things is contaminated by the instability of a slippery referentiality that looks (for all the world) linguistic. It is not for nothing that the maggots in a dead dog are a 'kissing carrion': corruptive generation takes place not in the womb, but in the mouth.[63]

The importance of Gertrude's symbolism for Hamlet's anxiety about invasion, inheritance, and language should not be underestimated. In his first few moments in the play, Hamlet makes it clear that, despite his inability to express his nature ('that within which passeth show'), nonetheless he is firmly convinced of the reality, existence, and thus stability of that nature ('that within') (1.2.77–86). Even if the whole of this inner being reduces to simple choice, as Hamlet perhaps feigningly suggests to Horatio in the 'heart of heart' passage, nonetheless he continues to assert that some identity persists, and persists constantly. The metaphysical landmine which Socrates indicates at the end of the *Cratylus* is the danger that the problem of linguistic arbitrariness may extend all the way to the nature of reality itself; then the seeker after truth (in metaphysical as well as epistemological terms) would be faced not only with the problem of formulation and communication of ideas about that truth, not only with the difficulty of apprehending securely a perceptually compromised reality, but with a fundamentally unstable reality. Aristotle's theatrical ontology is, in other words, also a linguistic ontology, a kind of being in which 'that' never maps onto 'this' and the world is defined by a failure of the 'carriage of the article designed' – that is, of the effectiveness of the demonstrative pronoun.[64] Hamlet's attempt to appeal beyond language thus depends on isolating and defusing the threat posed by Gertrude's nature as a woman who has been remarried to another man, a woman whose womb – in its production of Hamlets – deletes Hamlets. To Hamlet's anxious thought, what is at stake is exactly the absence at the centre of Gertrude's nature, the part of her that is incapable of resisting new impression, because it gives way.

Hamlet's configuration of anxieties about language, sex, metaphysical instability, knowledge, and a theatrical ontology exposes what to us must seem a damning indictment of early-modern English law. In his abusive rant at Ophelia in the nunnery scene, Hamlet makes it clear that the metaphysical decay represented by a woman's *materia* is equivalent to her 'nicknaming' of 'God's creatures'; as Gertrude later says, '*her* words may strew dangerous conjectures in ill-breeding minds'. The systematic misogyny of sixteenth-century English common law – like that of contemporary nations across Europe – excluded most women from most kinds of legal identity and power. The basis of this exclusion was rarely articulated, probably because it rested upon fundamental shared assumptions and prejudices of a social nature, the relevance of which to legal categories and axioms would have been considered too obvious to justify articulation. But clues survive. In an excellent article on the legal status of women, equitable legal interpretation, and *Hamlet*, Carolyn Sale has drawn attention to a few curious passages in Edmund Plowden's *Comentaries*, including Tudor justice James Hale's explanation for a particularly misogynist statute passed during the reign of Henry VII:

> For the Makers of the Statute considered the Frailty and Inconstancy of Women, who might easily by flattering Words be deluded and enticed to Covin, and therefore they ordained against them a Penalty, as a Bridle to their Inconstancy, and would not make them, who have so little Discretion, Judges of the Goodness or Badness of the Titles of Actions, but prohibited their Covin.[65]

The 1496 act of which Hales was speaking sought to prevent ductile widows from colluding with their male relatives, or engaging in 'covin', in order to gain control over their deceased husbands' estates – a pernicious practice that, the statute held, defrauded the eventual heirs of their inheritance. For her part, Sale is well aware that Gertrude plays the role of just such a conniving 'jointress', out to practise with her brother–husband to disinherit her son. But *Hamlet* as a play does not so much indict Gertrude as it does the position taken by James Hales above. Hales accuses women of exactly that undiscerning attention to outwardness, to appearance, to the shells of words, for which Hamlet holds Gertrude and Ophelia responsible. This tendency to privilege words over the import of words (which opens the door to flatterers) is fundamentally opposed to equity, as Plowden discusses it. In his consideration of the judgment given in *Eyston* v. *Studd*, Plowden notes that:

> It is not the Words of the Law but the internal Sense of it that makes the Law, and our Law (like all others) consists of two Parts, *viz.* of Body and Soul, the Letter of the Law is the Body of the Law, and the Sense and Reason of the Law is the Soul of the Law, *quia ratio legis est anima legis.* And the Law may be resembled to a Nut, which has a Shell and Kernel within, the Letter of the Law represents the Shell, and the Sense of it the Kernel, and as you will be no better for the Nut if you make Use only of the Shell, so you will receive no Benefit of the Law, if you rely only upon the Letter, and as the Fruit and Profit of the Nut lies in the Kernel, and not in the Shell, so the Fruit and Profit of the Law consists in the Sense more than in the Letter. And it often happens that when you know the Letter, you know not the Sense, for sometimes the Sense is more confined and contracted than the Letter, and sometimes it is more large and extensive. And Equity, which in Latin is called *Equitas*, enlarges or diminishes the Letter according to its Discretion.[66]

There is no question that, in the legal culture of Elizabethan London, the association of nutshells with both words and women was proverbial; witness Donne's laddish Inns of Court lyric, 'Community', which concludes in a biting couplet by insisting on the fungible quality of women: 'And when he hath the kernel eat, / Who doth not fling away the shell?' In this context, Hamlet's near-readiness to be 'bounded in a nutshell' reads as an ambiguous glance simultaneously at the instability of language, of women, and of law. For while Plowden may argue for the privileged and noble place of discretion in the improvement of English law, the security of the discretion's operation will only rectify deficient justice (as we have seen) if the reason upon which it is based is, truly, universal. Plowden records Serjeant Catlin, in the report of *Browning* v. *Beston*, as claiming that 'our Law, which is the most reasonable Law upon Earth, regards the Effect and Substance of Words more than the Form of them, and takes the Substance of Words to imply the Form thereof'.[67] Both Catlin's and Plowden's own claims about legal interpretation, though, privilege reason by concealing the role of the judges. Sixteenth-century common law may well have been the world's most reasonable, but its execution – as Hamlet knows – lay in the mouths of men.

THE REPORT OF THE CAUSE OF HAMLET

The escape from arbitrariness in language becomes clarified, in *Cratylus*, as a far larger problem: the nature of the origin of all law (including not only that of reason, but that that binds together all things). Hamlet makes the same transition, and is preoccupied with no less total a concern. Like Socrates' *nomothetes*, and like Vincentio, Hamlet can make at best a dubious appeal for a divine warrant to authorize his language and his nature. The transformation of the legal to the metaphysical in *Cratylus* would not have seemed at all foreign to an early-modern intellectual readership. Richard Hooker makes this connection with painstaking care in the opening book of *Of the Lawes of Ecclesiastical Politie* (1598), and lawyers of the period found similar kinds of reflection in the basic introductions to *synderesis* and conscience in Christopher St German's dialogue on equity *Doctor and Student*.[68] Both St German and Hooker, of course, root their understanding of legal order in a divine warrant – a move that Hamlet, bound by two competing claims of justice, cannot easily make; but even if he had been allowed some reprieve from the Hegelian ethical bind of the tragic hero,[69] it seems unlikely that Hamlet would happily have embraced the assimilation of the individual into the divine universal any more contentedly than, say, the narrator of Donne's holy poetry. Shakespeare's figuration of Hamlet's metaphysical crisis in the legally inflected terms of inheritance and invasion may have been prompted by the structure of the *Cratylus* and the models furnished by Pyrrhus and Jephthah, but the play's way of thinking through the problem drives much more intimately towards early-modern English common law. While Shakespeare cannot be said to offer a solution, in any certain sense, to the intractable problem of mutability mooted by Socrates at the end of the *Cratylus*. Hamlet's exploitation of common-law learning raises some fascinating complexities for thinking about the problem.

It is by now critical common knowledge that Shakespeare made resort, in the later parts of *Hamlet*, to some precise textual allusions to law cases reported in Edmund Plowden's *Comentaries* of 1571. The scholarship of both Luke Wilson and Carolyn Sale has shown how Shakespeare's meditation on act, intention, crime, and guilt is focused, in *Hamlet*, through an engagement with two cases especially, those of *Rex v. Saunders* and *Hales v. Petit*.[70] Plowden's *Comentaries* provide as philosophical an account of common law as one could imagine: his reports record the discussions and debates of leading judges concerning ambiguous points of law raised by complicated cases, discussions which quickly lead back to the fundamental rational principles upon which English common law was held to be based. Thus when debating *Hales v. Petit*, the judges passed from the superficial contest over land between Margaret Hales and Cyriack Petit, to the philosophical nub at the basis of the dispute between them: whether or not Margaret's late husband, Sir James Hales, who had drowned himself several years earlier, could be considered to have killed himself knowingly and purposefully. Similarly, when debating *Rex v. Saunders*, the judges needed to decide whether Saunders, who had accidentally killed his daughter with a poisoned apple intended for his hated wife, could be said to have shown some sort of culpable 'transferred intent' in the death of the girl – a decision upon which his conviction for the felony of murder would rest. Both of these cases have clear substantive consequences for thinking about intention and responsibility in *Hamlet*: Ophelia's suicide prompts the gravediggers in 5.1 to allude directly to *Hales v. Petit*, as they weigh the degree of her culpability in a crime that could threaten the state of her immortal soul (and, similarly, Hamlet is perplexed throughout the play as to whether the achievement of his revenge is tantamount to suicide); while Claudius may prove guilty of the murder not only of Gertrude and Laertes, but even of himself, as a result of the debates on transferred intent in *Rex v. Saunders*. Wilson and Sale are certainly right to insist on the way in which Shakespeare's

allusions to Plowden in the closing act of *Hamlet* suggest an engagement with thinking about intention and the nature of an act, in a play
so conspicuously focused on the problems and potentials of action, and
its consequences for the agent's sense of self.

But these two particular cases are significant among Plowden's
discussions for another reason: they both demonstrate how senior
judges were prepared to manipulate the record of a case to serve extra-
legal interests. In the report of *Rex* v. *Saunders and Archer*, Plowden
makes it clear how the judges avoided settling the matter of the guilt of
Archer, the accomplice who supplied the poison (though for a different
intended crime), precisely because they wanted to avoid putting his
eventual release on record.[71] But the drama of *Hales* v. *Petit* is far more
revealing. Margaret Hales began an action in law against Cyriack Petit
for a trespass she claimed took place on 21 November 1560, when Petit
supposedly drove his animals onto her land at Graveney Marsh in Kent,
allegedly causing her up to 100 marks of damage.[72] The action was
built on a series of fictions. By common convention, Hales claimed ficti-
tiously that Petit had entered the land *vi et armis* (by force and arms)
because this allowed her to style the offence as a trespass, and to force
Petit to appear before the court of Common Pleas in Westminster; the
alternative, to admit that the matter was one of right to title over land,
would have required a *praecipe* writ, to which Petit might have
answered in a local court, and by simple non-performance. It was
crucial for Hales to compel Petit to answer a charge in the Common
Pleas because, her late husband having been a judge of the court, she
could hope for a sympathetic reception from his former colleagues, who
might be expected to condole the plight of a woman left widowed by
suicide. Hales's position was grim: because suicide was considered a
felony against the self (and an unpardonable crime against God), all of
her husband's lands had at his death been escheated, or forfeited,
leaving her with nothing. It was apparently important to her solvency
to claim survivorship in a piece of land – the estate at Graveney Marsh
– in which she claimed to have held a joint tenancy with her husband.
By bringing a fictitious case of trespass against Petit, Hales forced Petit
to admit that he had, indeed, driven his animals onto the land at that
day and time, but that nonetheless her case did not amount to a case in

law against him, because he denied the premise upon which she claimed the survivorship. He demurring, the judges retired to discuss the question of whether Margaret Hales could inherit the sole right to a lease upon the death of her husband, a *felo de se* (or suicide). Upon that demurral arose the series of questions – about agency, the temporal sequence of intention and performance, and the nature of action – which exercised the judges so philosophically that Shakespeare, famously, borrowed from their deliberations for his play.

The land Hales claimed in survivorship of her husband Sir James, the marsh at Graveney, had been leased jointly to Sir James Hales and his father, John Hales, by the Archbishop of Canterbury, Thomas Cranmer, for a period of twenty years beginning after the feast of St Michael (i.e. on 1 October) in 1540. John Hales appears to have died almost immediately after the lease came into effect. Cranmer himself went to the stake in 1553; according to Plowden's report, he confirmed his lease to James Hales just before his death, and further extended it, this time jointly to both Sir James Hales and to his wife Margaret, for twelve further years from the feast of St Michael, 1560 (i.e. from a date seven years in the future). James Hales, by all accounts a committed Protestant whose crisis of conscience and ultimate suicide were provoked by the zealous Counter-Reformation of Mary I and her marriage to Philip of Spain in 1554, killed himself in August of that year. Crucially, Margaret Hales took no formal contestatory action over Graveney Marsh – which passed with the rest of Hales's goods into crown control, and was then granted by letters patent to the possession of Cyriack Petit and one John Webb (who subsequently died) – until 1560, when the extension of the lease (the one turning it into a jointenancy) – had been due to come into effect. Margaret Hales immediately commenced her action against Petit, the record of which, as Plowden's notes make clear, *'appears amongst the Records of* Trinity *Term 3* Elizabeth' (June–July 1561).[73] The attempt by John Goldwell, Hales's attorney, is clear; though James Hales had been dead almost seven years, Goldwell sought to convince the judges that Margaret Hales's right by Cranmer's lease had survived the death both of the Archbishop and of her husband, and that immediately upon the renewal of the lease, with its provision for jointenancy, in October

1560, Margaret Hales, though until then only retaining a future right, had come to be possessed of a present right. The fiction upon which the claim was based was that, though the jointenancy had been only a future condition at the time of James Hales's death in 1554, the expectation of that future right had in some sense passed into his wife even then, and made her capable, even if only in the future, of repossessing the lease of the land. It is obvious why this case should have interested Shakespeare in the writing of *Hamlet*; Goldwell was effectively arguing that a future right inhered proleptically in Margaret Hales's condition at the time of the death of her husband, enough so that it could, upon its activation in 1560, delete the intervening events and rights of the preceding six years. From the perspective of the present, the future would come to have changed the past.

In order to argue their case for Margaret Hales, Serjeants Southcote and Puttrell devised elaborate, even absurd, reasonings. For example, Puttrell claimed that in the moment of Sir James Hales's death, both his forfeiture of his estates and his death (including his guilt for his death, and thus the escheat of his lands to the crown) occurred in an instant; and yet in that instant the law considered his wife's full seizure in the jointenancy to take place before the escheat of his lands to the crown, 'for every Instant contains the End of one Time, and the Commencement of another'.[74] But Dyer CJ established the better position, that Hales's forfeiture of his goods to the crown had relation to the moment of his feloniously throwing himself into the river, and not to the moment of his death, so that the crown obtained title through escheat before the moment of Margaret Hales's full survivorship in the jointenancy: 'by this Relation of the Forfeiture which has a Retrospect to the Act done, the Law inflicts a Punishment upon the living Man for the Act done in his Lifetime, which was the Cause of his Death afterwards'.[75] This reasoning, however, created an anomaly in the record of the case, because, as Brown J argued, the crime could not appear of record during the criminal's life:

> And although the Act, by which he has avoided the Trial and
> Judgment of the Law, does not appear of Record in his Lifetime . . .
> the Reason thereof is, because there is no Possibility of its being

found in his Lifetime, for until the Death there is no Cause of Forfeiture. And he himself is the Cause why he cannot be arraigned for the Offence, and why the Offence cannot be otherwise inquired in his Lifetime.[76]

But in showing themselves ready to amend the record to see justice done in this case, the judges opened up the possibility of three further exceptions in the case, all of which would tend to the insufficiency of Petit's plea in bar, and thus of Margaret Hales's right to her action (and the land). First, Brown noticed that at no point had Cyriack Petit explicitly claimed that Cranmer was alive, and because his lease to James and Margaret had not been confirmed, it must be thought to have expired with his death. Second, the record did not show that Sir James Hales was in possession of both of Cranmer's leases at the time of his death, thus preventing the crown from receiving the escheat of the lands. But last he noted:

... that the Day of the Trespass is assigned the 21st Day of *November* in the *second* Year of the reign of the present Queen, which Day is in *anno Domini* 1559. And the new Lease made to the Plaintiff and her Husband did not commence until *Michaelmas* 1560, which is the *Michaelmas* after the Trespass assigned, so that the Plaintiff has assigned the Trespass before the Commencement of the new Lease, and yet the Defendant has not given her any Colour, for the new Lease which was not then commenced is no Colour to her, and therefore they had no Cause to argue the Matter in Law which they had argued, For which three Causes the Plaintiff ought to recover for the Insufficiency of the Bar.

The whole case, Brown J claims, was a mistake, for Hales's attorney Goldwell, in entering the first plea on the record, had made a simple mistake with the dates. A monarch's regnal year is deemed to have begun on the day of the death of his or her predecessor, but it only comes to have done so once that monarch's reign is ratified by a coronation. Mary died on 17 November 1558, and Elizabeth was crowned on 15 January 1559. In his declaration (the plaintiff's formal presentation of the case, which could not afterwards be traversed), Goldwell seems to have slipped by supposing 21 November to have been before, rather than after, the beginning of the regnal year; he thus dated Petit's entry into Graveney Marsh as occurring on 'the *twentieth* Day of *November* in the *second* Year of the Reign of the Lady the Queen now' – not 1560 but, as Brown J remarked, 1559. Margaret Hales had not, in November 1559, yet come into possession of the suspended joint lease – in other words, the future that might affect the past, changing the nature of the significance of Hales's death in 1554, had not yet come to pass *at the moment of the complaint* (by 1561, of course, it had; but that fact could not now change the fixed and dated quality of the complaint as it had been made, with reference to the – incorrect – earlier date of 1559). On top of it all, Goldwell's mistake with the regnal year, by drawing attention to the way in which a coronation acts retrospectively to create a day of accession, partakes of the same logic. The case, as it came to be concluded in 1562–3, was beset by evidence and arguments themselves riven by the same temporal paradoxes that had characterized it from the start.

In this context, it is not surprising to find that Plowden records Dyer CJ's short and apparently exasperated response to Browne J's alleged exceptions. Dyer CJ's conclusions make it clear that the case had become a farce of the record:

> To which it was answered by the Lord *Dyer*, that for any thing shewn in the Record it might be that the Bishop was alive. And if he was not, a Lease made by him who has the Fee simple is not determined by his Death, as a Lease of Tenant for Life is, but it is only voidable, and until it be avoided it is good, for which reason it shall be intended to continue until the Avoidance be shewn. As to the second Point, it is pleaded in Fact that Sir *James* was possessed of both the Estates at the Time of drowning himself. And if the Plea and the Office, which finds both the Leases, be put together, it will appear manifestly to the Court that he was possessed of them at the Time of drowning himself. As to the third Point, he said that if the Plaintiff's Lease was not commenced at the Time of the Trespass supposed, from thence it follows that she had no Title,

and was not able to punish this or any other Trespass. And tho' Colour is not given by the Defendant, yet if it appears to the Court that the Plaintiff has no Title, it would be hard that she should have Judgment.[77]

Dyer CJ's responses make it clear that the only thing that matters to judgment in the case is the record of the case itself. Petit and Hales had joined issue on an agreed version of the fact, which made no mention of the state of Cranmer, who at law could thus be deemed living – for all that the judges knew him to be dead. Similarly, although his indentured lease (to Hales and his wife) had been 'avoided' by his arrest under charges of treason, and subsequent execution in 1553, Petit had shown no proof of this in the case, and so his lease must, for the purposes of the discussion, be considered to have remained in force. In other words, Dyer CJ noted that the act that had taken place in the future to undo the force of the grant made in the past had not been noted, and so remained – to their cognisance – as if it had not been done. And yet for all that, Margaret Hales might have been granted her action on the basis of the mistake made by Goldwell, except that – by this point – the Chief Justice had become impatient with the manifest nonsense of the much-abused record.

These arguments are important to *Hamlet* not merely because Hamlet is, in Claudius' words, old Hamlet's 'survivor', the heir attempting to recover his father's estate by deleting the intervening period of usurpation by a third party. Nor are these arguments important simply because they demonstrate the complex temporal ironies of a case in which, at every turn, future events change the significance of past events – not merely apparently, but intrinsically – in the same way that, relentlessly, they do in *Hamlet*. Dyer CJ's arguments at the end of Plowden's reports matter to *Hamlet* precisely because they reveal the degree to which the entire substance of the argument on the case – which has, rightly, so exercised critics for its close parallels with *Hamlet* – is a series of moot points. Margaret Hales could never have recovered Graveney Marsh, not merely because the complex philosophical arguments she and her attorney provoked were at best tenuous, but because, at a very early stage in the declaration, the attorney had got the date wrong. The entire sequence of arguments, then, which took up a fair amount of the judges' time in 1562–63, was enclosed within an impossibility. In other words, while it is highly significant to readers of *Hamlet* that *Hales* v. *Petit* concerns intention, action, and the nature of temporal succession in common legal philosophy, it is similarly important that all of these points are, from start to finish, moot, and that the overriding substance of the case, as it was argued on both sides, was the desire of some of the judges to help the destitute wife of their lamented friend, who killed himself out of conscience while suffering under the reign of a Catholic monarch. The law of *Hales* v. *Petit* was neither equitable, nor pragmatic, but interested: for the memory and love of a single man, his fellow judges were prepared to manipulate the record to undermine the law.

Judges are appointed to administer the law and to form their judgments – even in cases of equity – upon the principles upon which the customary or written law itself is based. In *Hales* v. *Petit*, at least some of the judges sought to undo the law to answer to a different impulse – one which had nothing to do with justice. The allusion to *Hales* v. *Petit* in 5.1 of *Hamlet* functions, like the earlier allusion to the Jephthah story, as an index to Hamlet's thinking at this point in the play. Perplexed by the deleting nature of the inheritance relation, Hamlet has struggled throughout the play to find a way both to keep his rash oath ('remember me') and yet to avoid his own erasure. There is no question that Shakespeare must have been attracted to Plowden's account of *Hales* v. *Petit* because of its preoccupation with action and temporality, but it seems likely, too, that Shakespeare noticed the essential pointlessness of the arguments in the case – the way in which all the hypothetical defences of Margaret Hales's position were predicated on a fiction of the case's viability, which was only sustained so long as her case was bound to fail. The tolerance and inventiveness of the judges, in their willingness to debate the strength of Hales's position, points to their human, rather than legal, concern with the case's outcome. Hamlet's position in Act 5 of his play is similar to that of Margaret Hales: he seeks a means by which to save himself, the 'survivor', from a 'filial obligation' that undermines his attempts to communicate and will shortly destroy him bodily, but the only escape lies in making himself an exception from the law. But Hamlet's case is like Margaret Hales's case in another sense, too. Lord Dyer pointed out in his closing arguments on the case that the parties on both sides had bound themselves to certain fictions, offensive to reason, by the way in which they had established the record of the case: for all the record contained, Cranmer might still have been alive in 1562, his deed unavoided, and the original trespass an event not of 1560, but of 1559. What mattered to the final judgment were not the realities of the situation, but the agreed nature of the case as it had developed – partly from error, partly from the strategies of the two sides in pleading – over the course of exchange leading to the demurrer. The overriding lesson of Plowden's report of this case is the primacy of the record.

When we begin to look at Hamlet's behaviour and speeches over the course of the play, with the retrospective intelligence of this allusion as our prism, the importance of the distance between record and reality leaps into critical focus. The play is marked by a number of scenes – some of which I have already discussed – in which characters seem to demonstrate, by their inculpatory actions or their speeches, earlier and culpable intentions. One such scene is Gertrude's apparent confession to Hamlet in her closet (3.4.88–91), which on more careful consideration must be acknowledged doubtful, if not plainly misleading; a similar moment is Gertrude's later admission to Horatio that she would prefer not to speak with Ophelia (4.5.1–20). The entire course of *The Murder of Gonzago* is another case of the same. Stanley Cavell has, rightly, asked why it is that Claudius can watch the dumbshow patiently, without betraying any sense of recognition of his alleged crime, but leap up later, as if on cue, when Lucianus poisons the Player King in the playlet.[78] The only difference between the two performances of the 'murder' is, of course, Hamlet's intervention in the latter part of the performance, as a 'chorus'. His signal contribution is to transform the nature of the playlet from a re-enactment of a past murder to the promise or threat of a future murder, which is done by a slip on a single word: as Lucianus takes the stage, ready to enact the poisoning, Hamlet introduces him not as the brother, but as 'nephew to the King' (3.2.246). Claudius only rises from his seat after this nephew commits the murder, and Hamlet has promised that 'the murderer gets the love of Gonzago's wife' (3.2.265–66). What Claudius perceives, then, is a threat against his life, rather than the rehearsal of a scene from his past – for Hamlet, like Lucianus, is the nephew. Whether or not he killed Old Hamlet, he betrays no evidence, one way or another, in this scene. And yet Hamlet, who has made a great show of enlisting Horatio's help, earlier in the scene, 'in censure of [Claudius'] seeming' (3.2.76–90), refuses to admit after the playlet that the trap has done anything but prove Claudius's guilt:

> HAMLET   O good Horatio, I'll take the ghost's word for a
>   thousand pound. Did'st perceive?
> HORATIO Very well, my lord.
> HAMLET   Upon the talk of the poisoning?
> HORATIO I did very well note him.
>
> (3.2.288–92)

Horatio's non-committal response to Hamlet's enthusiasm here has often been remarked, but apparently not by Hamlet, who fails to admit any miscarriage in his professed plan. What Hamlet has achieved is not the demonstration of Claudius's guilt, but rather the association of an action – Claudius's rising from the play – with a causal event – the representation of an alleged crime – for the interpretation of which we were earlier given a key. Our interpretation of Claudius's action has been every bit as conditioned – by the convention established between Hamlet and Horatio before the playlet – as Francisco's interpretation of Barnardo's 'Long live the king'. Furthermore, Horatio's failure to challenge explicitly Hamlet's blatant misconstruction of Claudius's behaviour allows the record to stand.

Similarly, we observe Claudius attempting to pray in the chapel in 3.3, just after *The Murder of Gonzago*. He appears to confess to the murder of Old Hamlet in no uncertain terms, and Hamlet's subsequent, scrupulous decision not to kill him conditions us, retrospectively, to think that Claudius is here praying for redemption from a crime already committed. But if we pause a little, and look at his language in the wrangling 'soliloquy' he delivers (the scare quotes betray my belief that Hamlet is, despite the lack of a stage direction, peering around the curtain of the tiring house), Claudius appears to be not finished with a crime, but caught in the very midst of one. 'My stronger guilt,' he says, 'defeats my strong intent':

> And, like a man to double business bound,
> stand in pause where I shall first begin,
> And both neglect. What if this cursed hand
> Were thicker than itself with brother's blood,
> Is there not rain enough in the sweet heavens
> To wash it white as snow? Whereto serves mercy
> But to confront the visage of offence?
> And what's in prayer but this twofold force,
> To be forestalled ere we come to fall
> Or pardon'd being down?
>
> (3.3.41–50)

It is generally assumed that, when Claudius speaks of pausing 'where I shall first begin', he is talking about the action of praying; but his emphasis later in the passage is as much on prayer that forestalls, as on prayer that pardons, 'being down'. The fact we must remember, in this context, is that Claudius has, in effect, just initiated the series of steps that will issue in 'a brother's murder'[79] – the scene in which this soliloquy occurs begins with Claudius speaking to Rosencrantz and Guildenstern, informing them of the need to travel to England: 'The terms of our estate,' Claudius tells them, 'may not endure / Hazard so near us as doth hourly grow / Out of his brows' (3.3.5–7). While it may be the case that Claudius killed Old Hamlet, and it may be the case that it is that crime to which he refers in his soliloquy in this scene, the circumstances of the scene, and the language of his soliloquy, do not quite convince. It might especially give us pause, as suspicious readers, to notice that, in the middle of Claudius's meditation, he considers the difference between an interested 'shuffling' in corrupt legal cases, and a heavenly judgment where causes cannot be misconstrued:

> But 'tis not so above:
> There is no shuffling, there the action lies

In his true nature, and we ourselves compell'd
Even to the teeth and forehead of our faults
To give in evidence.

(3.3.60–64)

It is often considered an irony that, had Hamlet killed Claudius in the chapel, Claudius might well have gone to hell, and not to heaven. But the greater irony of this scene may be that, had Hamlet killed Claudius while he was praying, he might have died guilty only of the intention to kill his nephew in the future – and that, as Claudius represents it in this very scene, merely in self-defence.

One further discrepancy between Hamlet's claims and his actions – at least in the Q2 text – bears mention here. When Hamlet returns from the sea voyage, after not quite making it to England, he recounts to Horatio in 5.2 a providential narrative so apparently thick with accidental serendipities of fortune that the prince becomes a convert to divine justice. Indeed, it is clear that the apparent sea-change in Hamlet's attitude to his vow and his destiny takes place as a result of his conviction, first experienced and acknowledged during the England voyage, that 'there's a divinity that shapes our ends, / Rough-hew them how we will' (5.2.10–11). This scene, which turns around a 'warrant' and apparently gives Hamlet the divine conviction he needs to guarantee his language and his action, is the parallel to Vincentio's supposed epiphany in Act 3 of *Measure for Measure*. But all of the supposed accidents of Hamlet's fortunate escape – from the midnight 'grop[ing]' that leads Hamlet to his friends' 'packet', to the discovery of his father's signet-ring in his purse – should probably be read not as providential coincidences, the evidence of some prevenient grace determined to marshal Hamlet's way to safety (and thence to revenge). Instead, we might remember Hamlet's words to Gertrude at the end of 3.4:

There's letters seal'd, and my two schoolfellows,
Whom I will trust as I will adders fang'd –
They bear the mandate, they must sweep my way
And marshal me to knavery. Let it work;

> For 'tis the sport to have the enginer
> Hoist with his own petard, and't shall go hard
> But I will delve one yard below their mines
> And blow them at the moon. O, 'tis most sweet
> When in one line two crafts directly meet.
>
> (3.4. 204–12)

Hamlet knows Claudius's intentions in sending him to England; he knows that Rosencrantz and Guildenstern are to have signed letters importing his death (even before they receive them); and he knows, already, that he will reverse upon their heads the fate to which they soon will carry him. This being the case, his later protestations of wonder at the intervention of divine providence, with its invisible hand guiding his sea-gown-scarfed face, sound not only hollow, but decidedly malicious. And who is the crucial witness not present when Hamlet admits to his mother that he knows Claudius's plans, or indeed in 4.3 when Hamlet tells Claudius that he sees 'a cherub that sees' Claudius' purposes (4.3.51)? Horatio.

And so it is that Hamlet calls upon Horatio, with his dying breath, to become a 'reporter': 'report me and my cause aright / To the unsatisfied' (5.2.346–47). The kind of 'reporting' that Shakespeare has Hamlet have in mind here is legal reporting, answering the legal 'records' – trivial fond records – that Hamlet wiped from his brain in 1.5 in order to replace them with a single, overriding commandment. To 'report' a 'cause' is to write the formal and precedent-forming account of an action and its associated judgments, and so to make it part of the incontrovertible record – tissue of the law. The thread of contingencies and contiguities with which Hamlet has presented us throughout the play amount to a record – the record of a legal case – made official by Horatio's undertaking, as the play closes, to 'report' it. All we can judge, as the audience called to the matter, is what is played before us – the record, and not the matter itself. Hamlet's subtle manipulation of expectation, cause, and action leads Claudius, Gertrude, Rosencrantz and Guildenstern, and even Ophelia and Polonius to seem to incriminate themselves. Are they really guilty? Is Gertrude a strumpet? Is Claudius the murderer of his brother? Did Rosencrantz

and Guildenstern make love to their employment? We can only judge
Hamlet's story on the basis of what we have seen; but Shakespeare
gives us enough evidence, perhaps, to suspect that our perspective on
the action of the play may not be completely innocent of contamination; why, for example, can we, like Hamlet – but not like Gertrude – see
the ghost in 3.4? We can know the names for things at the end of
Hamlet, Prince of Denmark, because Hamlet and Horatio have, it seems,
agreed upon the conventionalist account of the story; but we cannot
know the reality. It is striking that Horatio appeals to pragmatism in his
rush to tell Hamlet's story, as the play closes, 'even while men's minds
are wild, lest more mischance / On plots and errors happen' (5.2.401–
02). Hamlet appeals throughout the play to Serjeant Catlin's
indefeasible reason, and seems to present us with the kind of end-
shaping divinity whose subscription will warrant and authorize all
language, all form, all law. But as the play closes, and Horatio rushes to
report Hamlet's cause, we can only wonder whether his report will
contain enough of the right words.

Chapter Seven

CODICIL: THE MAXIM AND THE ANALOGY

Portia's judgment against Shylock in the penultimate act of *The Merchant of Venice* exposes not Shylock's hard-heartedness, nor his self-interestedness – quite the reverse. Is it hard-hearted for a man to notice, as Shylock does halfway through the trial of his bond, that Bassanio and Gratiano are callous perjurors in love? Or to wish that his daughter had married anyone but a Christian, so to have avoided their hypocrisy?

> These be the Christian husbands! I have a daughter –
> Would any of the stock of Barrabas
> Had been her husband, rather than a Christian.
>
> (4.1.293–95)

Nor is Shylock self-interested, as the Christians appear to claim in their pleas, their insults, and their jibes. If anything, Shylock has taken too little care of himself and his business, as is demonstrated by the ease with which Lorenzo steals away with – ravishes – his daughter Jessica.[1] If we turn to the technical legal language and concepts that structure the dialogue and arguments in this scene, this impression only becomes firmer. It has often been claimed that Portia victimizes Shylock on a technicality, exploiting the law – or selected legal positions – in order to bring down a man for whom she and all her peers have contempt. In fact the substance of her argument against Shylock, as it develops in the second part of the scene, relies on one of the most fundamental and firmly held of common law maxims,[2] *verba fortiùs accipiuntur contra proferentem* ['a man's words shall be taken most strongly against himself.'] – a maxim Francis Bacon discusses at length in his book of maxims (written during Elizabeth's reign, but first printed in 1630). Bacon's formulation and copious illustration of the maxim make it clear that the party beneficiary to any kind of legal instrument must take especial care in its formulation, for the law will construct its words against him with straight rigour.

Bacon's extended discussion of the maxim reveals a number of more particular ways in which it signifies resonantly with Shylock's and Antonio's 'merry bond' in *The Merchant of Venice*. Above all, as Bacon notes, the maxim promotes caution:

> This rule that a mans deedes and his words shall be taken strongliest against himselfe, though it bee one of the most common grounds of the law, it is notwithstanding a rule drawn out of the depth of reason; for first it is a Schoole-Master of wisdome & diligence in making men watchfull in their owne businesse, next it is author of much quiet and certainty, and that in two sorts; first, because it fauoureth acts and conueyances executed, taking them still beneficially for the grantees and possessors; and secondly, because it makes an end of many questions and doubts about construction of words: for if the labour were onely to picke out the intention of the parties, euery Iudge would haue a seuerall sense, whereas this rule doth giue them a sway to take the law more certainely one way.[3]

Shylock's watchfulness in his business is of core importance to Portia's judgment, as is made clear by several conspicuous markers in the text, both in this scene and earlier. Careful readers might be surprised to note that, though one document is read out in the Duke's court during the trial, it is not the 'merry bond' but Bellario's letter, and what the bond actually contains we never fully discover. But a careful reader might be surprised by one emphatic reference, made by both Shylock and Portia, to an element the bond certainly does contain. When Portia finally concedes the bond's validity, she directs Antonio to prepare himself:

PORTIA   Therefore lay bare your bosom.

SHYLOCK   Ay, his breast,

              So says the bond, doth it not noble judge?

              'Nearest his heart', those are the very words.

                               (4.1.250–52)

The problem with these 'very words' – which constitute one of the only direct quotations of the bond given us – is that they simply are not those the careful reader noticed Shylock using, in 1.3, when he directed Antonio to go to the notary and give him 'direction for this merry bond'. Shylock had been exact about an ambiguity:

          Go with me to a notary, seal me there

          Your single bond, and (in a merry sport)

          If you repay me not on such a day

          In such a place, such sum or sums as are

          Express'd in the condition, let the forfeit

          Be nominated for an equal pound

          Of your fair flesh, to be cut off and taken

          In what part of your body pleaseth me.

                        (1.3.143–50)

Had Shylock gone with Antonio to prepare the bond, he might have directed its wording according to this original formulation. Instead, he sent Antonio ahead of him, returning home to collect the ducats – home, where his house was all in disorder:

SHYLOCK   Then meet me forthwith at the notary's,

              Give him direction for this merry bond –

              And I will go and purse the ducats straight,

              See to my house left in the fearful guard

              Of an unthrifty knave: and presently

              I'll be with you.

                        (1.3.171–76)

It is often the case in Shakespeare's play that a contiguity or a contemporaneity of two actions signals their conceptual – sometimes even causal – connection. This is the kind of thinking and plotting that led to the bifold construction of Shakespeare's comic and some tragic plots (Lear and Gloucester, for example; or the nested mutually interpreting actions of *A Midsummer Night's Dream*), and it is the recognition of this contiguous-causal connection that enables us to make sense of, and criticize, the plays. Here this technique is broadcasting unmistakably that Shylock's trip to his house is a marker of his own unthriftiness, his unwatchfulness, just at the moment when Antonio is busy at the notary's commissioning the bond. Here, the text discloses, is the moment of Shylock's most important lapse: when he should be attending to the words of his legal instrument, the words that might one day be taken most strongly against himself.

Several ironies attend on Shakespeare's invocation of the *verba fortiùs* maxim at this point in the play, which help to explain its significance. At first, Bacon's extended discussion makes the maxim seem decidedly apt to Portia's purpose here:

> But now it is to bee noted, that this rule is the last to bee resorted to, and is neuer to bee relied vpon but where all other rules of exposition of words faile; and if any other come in place, this giueth place. And that is a point worthy to bee obserued generally in the rules of the law, that when they encounter and crosse one anothe[r] in any case, it bee vnderstood which the law holdeth worthier, and to bee preferred; and it is in this particular very notable to consider, that this being a rule of some strictnesse and rigour, doth not as it were it's [*sic*] office, but in absence of other rules which are of more equity and humanity; which rules you shall afterwards finde set downe with their expositions and limitations.[4]

This is the only maxim in Bacon's relatively comprehensive collection that he considers to be a guide of last resort. It is a trump card for legal interpretation – a kind of master switch that, when all other means have failed, can be relied upon to illuminate an ambiguous text. But Bacon considers it a guide of last resort precisely because it is a rule 'of some strictnesse and rigour', and indeed suggests that it should only be applied when other means 'of more equity and humanity' have been exhausted. Portia does exactly this, waiting until the very last possible moment before the knife dives in Antonio's chest before she halts it – and halts it, all other means being spent, by reading Shylock's words 'strongliest against himselfe'. The irony is that, had Shylock been more watchful of his interest in the bond – had he directed the bond to be written in the more ambiguous way that he originally conceived it – Portia's ploy could never have been successful. Shylock might have removed hair, teeth, veruccas, or anything bloodless, to the value of a pound. It is exactly the stipulation that the flesh be 'nearest his heart' that makes bloodlessness impossible, for Antonio's bosom is full of blood. Portia's escape becomes possible not because of an ambiguity, but because of a specificity. Shylock should have been more watchful of his interest, and he should have been less exact.

And yet Portia also twists the maxim to do something against which Bacon explicitly warns. The problem with her construal of the bond's import is not that she reads it strongly against its beneficiary, but rather that she reads it too strongly – so strongly that the penalty becomes a nonsense. Bacon writes:

> So it is a rule, that words are so to bee vnderstood, that they worke somewhat, and been not idle and friuolous: *verba aliquid operari debent, verba cum effectu sunt accipienda.* And therefore if I buy and sell you the fourth part of my manor of dale, and say not in how many parts to be diuided, this shall bee construed foure parts of fiue, and not of 6. nor 7. &c. because that it is the strongest against mee; but on the other side, it shall not bee intended foure parts of foure parts, or the whole or foure quarters, and yet that were strongest of all, but then the words were idle and of none effect.[5]

To write a bond that promises a penalty that simply cannot be exacted would be pointless, and so this cannot, even by the maxim, be taken for a true construction of the bond's intent. By Bacon's elaboration of its meaning, then, at least some equity persists in the maxim – enough to suppose that no one would knowingly draft a bond that was not, at least to some degree, in his own interest. In this sense, in Bacon's view, the law always retains some equitable awareness of the intents and ambitions of the individuals upon whom it passes judgment; it may not admit evidence of their individual circumstances, but it certainly supposes things about them as individuals – and among those things, a modicum of self-interest. This may be so; but in Shylock's case, Portia actually goes so far as to claim that the law is utterly innocent of the human interests upon which it rules:

> ANTONIO   Most heartily I do beseech the court
> To give the judgment.
> PORTIA   Why then thus it is, –
> You must prepare your bosom for the knife.
> SHYLOCK   O noble judge! O excellent young man!
> PORTIA   For the intent and purpose of the law
> Hath full relation to the penalty,
> Which here appeareth due upon the bond.
>
>   (4.1.241–47)

At first, or to a careless (or an eager) observer, it may seem as if Portia here simply states that the condition on the obligation has been exhausted, and the bond's penalty clause – until the failure of the condition, constrained – now fully activated. But by this point she has already conceded this (4.1.228–31); and in any case her words are too strange for such a simple meaning. 'The intent and purpose of the law', in an equitable system, is very different from 'the intent and purpose of the law' in a talionic system. In an equitable system, this 'intent and purpose' would be to uphold the right, by appeal to the principles on which written and customary forms of law were based or had developed. In a talionic system, by contrast, the intent and purpose of the law would be simple application. For Portia to say that 'the intent and purpose of the law / Hath full relation to the penalty', in short, is for her to say that law in Venice has just become a machine. We have met in this book already with judges who wished laws to work without reference to their executors (e.g. Angelo); here we witness a judge who wishes to apply the law without any reference – any reference at all – to the humanity of its subjects. This is law entirely stripped of equity, and all of its 'intent and purpose' lies in the penalty. One of the greatest ironies of this scene, then, is that the maxim of last resort should stop short of the failure of equity, because the failure of equity is a nonsense. Portia demonstrates so much to and by Shylock.

For Portia has another audience, besides Shylock himself, for whose benefit the drama of the 'devil's' law case is being staged. When the Duke of Venice sent to the old judge Bellario for his advice on Shylock's bond, Bellario was (so the fictional letter reads) in consultation with Balthasar, the 'young doctor of Rome', but their business was not law, but a 'loving visitation' (4.1.150–53). Someone else stands to gain by the forfeiture of Antonio's bond to Shylock, and that is Antonio. He, like Shylock (but unlike Bassanio, or Gratiano) pleads with Portia to deliver judgment against him; his reason, as he makes clear at the end of 3.3, is that he wants his sacrifice to be witnessed: 'Well gaoler, on, – pray God Bassanio come / To see me pay his debt, and then I care not' (3.3.35–36). His punning on 'heart' throughout this scene points to the circumstance that puzzled us earlier – why should he have altered the bond to read 'nearest his heart' in place of 'in what part of your body pleaseth me'? It seems that Antonio wanted his last sacrifice for his dearest love, Bassanio, to be a literal one:

> Give me your hand Bassanio, fare you well,
> Grieve not that I am fall'n to this for you:
> For herein Fortune shows herself more kind
> Than is her custom: it is still her use
> To let the wretched man outlive his wealth,
> To view with hollow eye and wrinkled brow
> An age of poverty: from which ling'ring penance
> Of such misery doth she cut me off.
> Commend me to your honourable wife,
> Tell her the process of Antonio's end,
> Say how I lov'd you, speak me fair in death:
> And when the tale is told, bid her be judge
> Whether Bassanio had not once a love:
> Repent but you that you shall lose your friend
> And he repents not that he pays your debt.

> For if the Jew do cut but deep enough,
> I'll pay it instantly with all my heart.
>
> (4.1.263–79)

Of course, Antonio is not merely consoled that he should get the chance to die for Bassanio; he rejoices at it and has desired it from the moment that Bassanio threatened to purchase himself, by Portia's means, out of Antonio's debt. This is why Antonio imagines himself, here, richest at the moment of his utter forfeiture. The irony of Antonio's injunction to 'bid her be judge' is cutting, because Portia happens to be judge not only of the fact of Antonio's significant sacrifice, but of his studious securing of it: he goes so far as to give Bassanio the script of his last triumph – what Bassanio should say when he reports Antonio's death to Portia, Antonio's only rival. Antonio (like Shylock) will get more justice than he wanted, for Portia's witness of his scheming reveals to her the way in which Antonio belies, by his 'final' words, the love that he claims for Bassanio. If indeed Antonio loved Bassanio all, his last words would, presumably, express that, and not his anxiety that that love should be related to Portia. It is not enough, in other words, that Antonio should die for Bassanio. Bassanio has to watch him do it; moreover, he has to tell Portia about it. Here we see that the bond – apparently the instrument of an obligation between Antonio and Shylock – is in fact an obligation between Antonio and Portia, the condition again being the failed payment of Shylock, and Antonio has demanded the forfeiture, which is Bassanio. To invoke the maxim *verba fortiùs accipiuntur contra proferentem* against Shylock, then, is also to invoke it against Antonio; but in this case, the agent is utterly self-interested, and the deployment of the maxim is designed to reduce his gain. Portia's grip on the situation very nearly slips when, subsequently, the Duke appears about to bestow all Shylock's wealth on Antonio, and her anxiety to disempower him explains why she leaps in to prevent the grant:

> DUKE   That thou shalt see the difference of our spirit
> I pardon thee thy life before thou ask it:
> For half thy wealth, it is Antonio's,

> The other half comes to the general state,
> Which humbleness may drive unto a fine.
>
> PORTIA Ay, for the state, not for Antonio.
>
> (4.1.366–71)

It is essential to Portia that Antonio be stripped of his means now, so that she may re-grant them to him later, precisely at the moment that she also reveals, by the return of the ring, her imposture (5.1.266–79). The court scene is as much a judgment on Antonio's literalism as it is on Shylock's, and he – a suitor for his own default – is cheated of his bond.

An important corollary of this conclusion relates to the degree of interestedness we may suppose in Shakespeare's 'use' of such legal elements in his writing. Taking for example the importance of the *verba fortiùs* maxim to the court scene in *The Merchant of Venice*, we can construct two opposed stories to account for its presence here. The first is an interested model: Shakespeare reads the maxim in a manuscript copy of Bacon's work, sees the potential of the interpretative razor that it encodes, and decides to harness it in order to bring down one of his villains in a paradoxically villainous way. The other model is disinterested: Shakespeare's plotting throws up ethical and interpretative problems, which come to a head in this scene, and the conclusion that he devises for the story independently recreates the force of the maxim, of the knowledge of which he is innocent. (Whether or not he also knows about the maxim is irrelevant; that is, an unintended use of the maxim is one example of a distinterested use.) The difference between the two models is not essential, but formal, in that the first model is exactly like the second except insofar as Shakespeare recognized, in the action of constructing the conceptual relations of the scene, the artificial nature of the maxim as a maxim. We cannot adjudicate between these two (extreme) models of the interestedness of composition, except probabilistically, and indeed there are many possible variations of both, lying somewhere on the spectrum between them, from which we might also conceivably choose. While these opposed accounts of a text's allusiveness might be possible in almost any circumstance, what makes this one special is that the allusion itself has consequences for the allusiveness. If we take the words 'strongliest' against Shakespeare, then of course he meant nothing by the allusion, and was not, in other words, aware of it; but to do so would be to take the text as a nonsense. It may involve meaning, but it cannot ultimately lead to significance. Shakespeare offers no solution to this problem except this allusion alluding to its own allusiveness. What we do with it, as Theseus concedes to Hippolyta (*MND*, 5.1.208–210), is up to us.

The court scene from *The Merchant of Venice* touches directly on every one of the legal problems and interpretative possibilities raised in this book, and is in some sense a summation of them all: the ravishment of Jessica hangs over Shylock's revenge; the obligation of Antonio's bond is a debt come due for discharging; Portia's justice moves decisively (but dissimulatively) away from prerogative mercy and toward the epistemological clarity of literalism. But the judgment of Shylock is representative in another sense, too. The way in which this scene analogizes the love-interest between Bassanio and Antonio, on the one hand, and the money interest between Shylock and Antonio, on the other, is similarly typical of the structures to which Shakespeare's use of legal language, concepts, and argument has led us, in every chapter of this book. The English common law of Shakespeare's day may have had, in St German's formulation, six principal grounds, but those six are really constituted by only two distinct kinds: rules or *regulae* to one side, and to the other examples. (Law is, in this, like poetry: it mediates between, and is defined by its mediation between, universals and particulars.) Every system of law functions to some degree by mediating between these two sources of legitimacy, but early-modern English common law gave unusual pre-eminence to custom and to the very purest form of the *regula*, the proverb or maxim – a form so close to reason itself that it hardly needs writing down, because it is always, palpably, on the tip of the mind's tongue. What is not often enough appreciated is that the maxim shares, by virtue of its universality, a kind of sympathy with custom and precedent that more specific forms of *regulae* – like statutes – do not. Custom and precedent authorize judgment or action by analogy. A maxim would seem to work slightly differently, though of course the basis of precedential thinking – *in consimili casu consimile debet esse remedium* ('like judgment in cases like') – can be expressed as a maxim. A maxim would seem to require application guided by reason, where a precedent invites imitation that works – given the basic parity between cases – automatically. And yet a common-law maxim, so close as it is to the rational principle that gives rise to it, has an analogical extensibility that looks very much like precedential logic, the only difference being that this precedence is not narrative, or temporal, but conceptual. Shakespeare's blurring, in his plot construction, of the relation between contiguity or contemporaneity, on the one hand, and causality or at least affinity on the other, suggests to us how we might see narrative precedentialism as a marker for conceptual precedentialism. Analogies work diachronically, like precedent in law; but they also work synchronically, by connecting ethics to politics, politics to metaphysics, metaphysics to epistemology, epistemology to the linguistic. This analogical extensibility, like precedential imitation, is an intellectual reflex, and one legacy of Shakespeare's legal humanism.

What makes law not only attractive but indispensable to an understanding of Shakespeare's dramatic and poetic works is not or not merely that it affords us this or that critical insight, nor that it helps to explain who sat in Shakespeare's audience, nor even that it gives us vantage on the positions or beliefs that Shakespeare himself held on topical questions like absolutism or legal reform. To stop at any one of these ends would be to mistake a thing for a thing that it imports. Legal language, legal concepts, and legal arguments permeate Shakespeare's writing because they are the structure through which he, and many of his contemporaries, conceived and organized the practical philosophical thinking for which their classical humanist educations had fitted them. It may be that this book takes a strong line on the precise verbal constructedness of Shakespeare's dramatic as well as poetic works; it may be that this book suggests the possibility of interpretations of Shakespeare's works that emphasize this or that metaphysical scheme, or this or that political model; it may be that this book helps us to see more deeply into six or seven passages of Shakespeare's plays and poems; and these are ends I have sought here. But the larger end to which these tributary ends all flow is, I hope, that of which these readings are not constitutive, but exemplary, and that is a recognition of a habit of mind in Shakespeare the plotter, Shakespeare the user of words, Shakespeare the reader of many books and of the world. This habit of mind – which he like all of his educated contemporaries absorbed in part from his education, and in part from the sustained intrusion of legal business and writing on his personal and professional experience – derived from the common law. Its major contours – the analogic *imitatio* of narrative precedent (inheritance), and the analogic extension of the maxim's *consimile* (invasion) – constantly pattern his writings, but no more fix a meaning or an interpretation than a bond stipulates the absence of everything that it does not stipulate. It would be foolish and idle to suppose that Shakespeare's works were not interested; but it would be wrong not to find them interesting.

NOTES

1: PREAMBLE: 'HOW SHALL I UNDERSTAND YOU?'

1. Studies of Shakespeare's legal knowledge have led some commentators and critics to the conclusion that he was a lawyer, and sometimes to the conclusion that he was Sir Francis Bacon. The writings of Sir G. George Greenwood, for example, argued with increasing insistence for Bacon's authorship; see *Is There a Shakespeare Problem?* (London: John Lane, 1916). Greenwood's position was contested by J. M. Robertson in *The Baconian Heresy* (London: H. Jenkins, 1913), but this one-sided controversy, if quieted, has hardly disappeared. The nineteenth- and early twentieth-century contributions of lawyers to the study of Shakespeare (and of Shakespeare to the practice of law) has been summarized and evaluated by O. Hood Phillips in *Shakespeare and the Lawyers* (London: Methuen, 1972); see esp. chs 10–12 (pp. 141–92).
2. See, e.g., Paul S. Clarkson and Clyde T. Warren, *The Law of Property in Shakespeare and the Elizabethan Drama* (Baltimore: Johns Hopkins University Press, 1942); and George W. Keeton, *Shakespeare's Legal and Political Background* (New York: Barnes and Noble, 1968).
3. Recent groundbreaking studies of legal ideas in Shakespeare's work (and that of his contemporaries) include Luke Wilson, *Theatres of Intention: Drama and the Law in Early Modern England* (Stanford: Stanford University Press, 2000); Karen Cunningham, *Imaginary Betrayals: Subjectivity and the Discourses of Treason in Early Modern England* (Philadelphia: University of Pennsylvania Press, 2002); Subha Mukherji, *Law and Representation in Early Modern Drama* (Cambridge: Cambridge University Press, 2006); Rebecca Lemon, *Treason by Words: Literature, Law and Rebellion in Shakespeare's England* (Ithaca: Cornell University Press, 2006); Bradin Cormack, *A Power to Do Justice: Jurisdiction, English Literature, and the Rise of the Common Law, 1590–1625* (Chicago: University of Chicago Press, 2007); and Lorna Hutson, *The Invention of Suspicion: Law and Mimesis in Shakespeare and Renaissance Drama* (Oxford: Oxford University Press, 2007). There are a number of excellent articles in Constance Jordan and Karen Cunningham, eds, *The Law in Shakespeare* (Houndmills: Palgrave Macmillan, 2007). The dictionary compiled by B. J. and Mary Sokol, *Shakespeare's Legal Language* (London: Athlone, 2000), provides a useful survey of topics in this area, and routes for further study.
4. Francis Bacon, 'Of Judicature', in *The Essayes or Counsels, Civill and Morall* (London: John Haviland for Hanna Barret, 1625), p. 324. The English translation is that of Bacon's source, 1 Timothy 1:8.
5. Bacon, 'Of Judicature', p. 324.
6. Bacon, 'Of Judicature', pp. 316–17.

7. 1 Timothy 1:5.

8. See *OED*, 'mere', *n.*[1] 1, 3; and 'mere', *n.*[2] 1a, b.

9. Even in Shakespeare's day, 'setting (something) down' had a range of meanings that included encamping a host (cf. *Coriolanus*, 5.3.1–2); putting (something) down on paper, or recording it (cf. *Hamlet*, 1.5.107–08); fixing (something) at a certain price or amount; and prescribing a rule or regulation, or giving a judgment (cf. *Cymbeline*, 1, 4, 165–68; *Hamlet*, 3.1.169–70). See *OED*, 'set', *v.* 143. All of these meanings are operative here, as the Soldier suggests that Timon's epitaph will be interpreted by Alcibiades – but also that Timon's epitaph will interpret Alcibiades, and in so doing reveal the limits of his power.

10. See instead Anne Barton, '"Wrying but a little": Marriage, Law, and Sexuality in the Plays of Shakespeare', in *Essays, Mainly Shakespearean* (Cambridge: Cambridge University Press, 1994), pp. 3–30; and B. J. and Mary Sokol, *Shakespeare, Law and Marriage* (Cambridge: Cambridge University Press, 2003).

11. Two provocative introductory studies of Shakespeare's reflection of, or participation in, ongoing contemporary debates over natural law are R. S. White, *Natural Law in English Renaissance Literature* (Cambridge: Cambridge University Press, 1996); and Ian Ward, *Shakespeare and the Legal Imagination* (London: Butterworths, 1999).

12. Sir Frederick Pollock, 'A Note on *Shylock v. Antonio*', *Law Quarterly Review*, 30 (1914), 175–77 (p. 175).

13. Pollock, 'A Note on *Shylock v. Antonio*', p. 176.

14. 'To thine and Albany's issues / Be these perpetual', he says to Goneril; and to Regan, 'To thee and thine hereditary ever / Remain this ample third of our fair kingdom.' (1.1.66–67, 79–80) The stipulation that succession to the lands should be restricted to Goneril's issue with Albany narrows the nature of the grant, transforming it into what early-modern lawyers called an 'entailed' estate, or a 'fee tail'. 'Perpetual' echoes so-called 'perpetuity clauses', by which donors sought to prevent their heirs from aliening the estate in the future, and dispossessing their heirs. On entailed estates in the period, see Baker, *OHLE 6*, pp. 692–701.

15. Charles Spinosa, '"The name and all th' addition": *King Lear*'s Opening Scene and the Common-Law Use', *Shakespeare Studies*, 23 (1995), 146–86. For an introduction to the medieval practice of making over estates to the legal ownership of 'feoffees to use', then occupying the estate as a *cestuy que use*, see Baker, *OHLE 6*, pp. 653–86.

16. See Ronald W. Cooley, 'Kent and Primogeniture in *King Lear*', *Studies in English Literature 1500–1800*, 48 (2008), 327–48.

17. Bracton, *De legibus*, II, p. 66. Henricus (or Henry) de Bracton (or Bratton, d. 1268) served as a legal clerk and later senior assize judge in the southwest of England. He was thought for centuries to have been the author of the legal treatise cited here, which has often simply gone by his surname, and was first published under that name by the Elizabethan legal printer Richard Tottell in 1569. In the twentieth century, some legal historians have argued that Bracton in fact only revised the text of the work now known as *De legibus et*

consuetudinibus Angliae (*On the Laws and Customs of England*), an earlier draft of which was probably originally compiled by his one-time master, the judge and Bishop of Winchester William of Raleigh (*d.*1250), or successively by a number of clerkly hands; for a discussion of the various authorship possibilities, and a judicious summary of the arguments made by S. E. Thorne, Bracton's great editor, see J. L. Barton, 'The Mystery of Bracton', *Journal of Legal History*, 14 (1993), 1–42. I follow early-modern practice in continuing to cite Bracton as the author of the treatise.

18. Bracton, *De legibus*, II, p. 68.

19. Bracton, *De legibus*, II, pp. 70–71.

20. Bracton, *De legibus*, II, pp. 67.

21. See Samuel Harsnett, *A declaration of egregious Popish impostures* (London: James Roberts, 1603), p. 48: '*Modu, Ma: Maynies* deuill, was a graund Commaunder, Muster-maister ouer the Captaines of the seauen deadly sinnes . . . The Exorcist asks *Maho, Saras* deuil, what company he had with him, and the deuil makes no bones, but tels him in flat termes, *all the deuils in hell.*' Harsnett (or his printer) confuses Modu for Mahu on the same page. Note, as my discussion continues, that Shakespeare has altered the spelling from *Modu* to *Modo* – this is not insignificant.

22. See Edmond Blunden, *Shakespeare's Significances* (London: Jonathan Cape, 1929); cited in Anne Bradby, *Shakespeare Criticism, 1919–35* (Oxford: Oxford University Press, 1936), pp. 276–77.

23. Horace Epistles, II. i. 208–13, in *Q. Horati Flacci Opera*, ed. Edward Wickham (Oxford: Clarendon Press, 1912).

24. Thomas Drant, *Horace his arte of Poetrie, pistles, and Satyrs Englished* (London: Thomas Marshe, 1567), sig. G7^r.

25. Note the Latin wordplay here: 'private' comes from L *privatus*, from the verb *privare*, 'to take away, remove'. To ask Poor Tom for a word *in private* is literally to ask him for a word under limitation (= *modo*).

2: SHAKESPEARE'S LEGAL LIFE

1. William Caxton, *Game and Play of the Chesse* (London: William Caxton, 1474), in Book 3, Chapter 3, 'Of the offices of notaryes aduocats skryueners and drapers or clothmakers'.

2. Caxton makes at least two other significant intrusions into his text: a complaint concerning England's political and military decay, with a prayer for its amendment (Book 3, Chapter 1); and at the conclusion of the work an exhortation to political reform and cultural renewal, commending the book to his patron.

3. See, for example, J. H. Baker, 'The English Legal Profession, 1450–1550', in *Lawyers in Early Modern Europe and America*, ed. by Wilfred Prest (London: Croom Helm, 1981), pp. 16–41 (pp. 16–17).

4. Sir John Fortescue, *De Laudibus Legum Angliae*, ed. by S. B. Chrimes (Cambridge: Cambridge University Press, 1942), cap. xv (pp. 36–37).

5. Sir Thomas Smith, *De Republica Anglorum*, ed. Mary Dewar (Cambridge: Cambridge University Press, 1982), Book 1, Chapter 5 (p. 52).

6. The four primary inns were supported by a collection of smaller inns – the Inns of Chancery – of less stable foundation. For a discussion of the establishments and privileges of these societies, see J. H. Baker, 'The Inns of Court and Chancery', *LPCL*, pp. 44–74.

7. 3 James VI and I, cap. 7. See *Statutes*, II, pp. 602–03.

8. For a full discussion of the origins, development, and practices of these two courts, see Baker, *IELH*, pp. 44–49.

9. For further discussion of the development of the bill of Middlesex and the *latitat*, see Baker, *IELH*, pp. 41–45; Marjorie Blatcher, *The Court of King's Bench: A Study in Self-Help* (London: Athlone, 1978); and N. G. Jones, 'The Bill of Middlesex and the Chancery 1556–1608', *The Journal of Legal History*, 22 (2002), 1–20.

10. On the development of *indebitatus assumpsit*, see Baker, *IELH*, pp. 341–45; and A. W. B. Simpson, *History of the Common Law of Contract: the Rise of Assumpsit* (Oxford: Clarendon Press, 1975).

11. J. H. Baker, *IELH*, p. 51. For a number of cautions on interpreting the significance of this expansion in the plea rolls, see S. F. C. Milsom, *Historical Foundations of the Common Law*, pp. 66–67.

12. 27. Eliz. 1. cap. 8; see *Statutes*, II, p. 291.

13. Thomas Wilson, *The Arte of Rhetorique* (London: George Robinson, 1585), p. 96.

14. See, e.g., Martin Ingram, *Church Courts, Sex and Marriage in England, 1570–1640* (Cambridge: Cambridge University Press, 1987).

15. For a contemporary description of these jurisdictions, including the Star Chamber, see William Lambarde, *Archeion, or, A discourse vpon the high courts of iustice in England* (London: E. Pursloe for Henry Seile, 1635).

16. See, e.g., Samuel Schoenbaum, *William Shakespeare: A Compact Documentary Life*, revised edn (Oxford: Oxford University Press, 1987), pp. 30–44; and Park Honan, *Shakespeare: A Life* (Oxford: Oxford University Press, 1999), pp. 25–42.

17. For an account of the duties of a constable in the period – such as the issuing of passports to labourers – see William Lambarde, *The Duties of Constables, Borsholders, Tything-men, and such other lowe Ministers of the Peace* (London: Roger Warde, 1582).

18. Cf. *Les Termes de la Ley*, f. 13ʳ: 'Affeerors are such as be appointed in Court leets, &c. to mulct such as have committed any fault which is arbitrably punishable, & for which no expresse penalty is prescribed by Statute.' Because such fines were assessed on the discretion of the affeeror, the office required an oath of impartiality, and was usually conferred upon men known for honest and fair dealing.

19. See Michael Dalton, *The Countrey Justice: Containing the Practice of the Justices of the Peace out of their Sessions* (London: William Rawlins and Samuel Roycroft, 1697). For an overview of the statutory provisions of the office in the period, see the entry for 'Iustices of the Peace' in 'A Repertory or Table Containing the Substance of all the materiall points, of those statutes at large ... as are now generally in force, and vse', in *Statutes*, II, pp. 42–46.

20. See Shakespeare Birthplace Trust Records Office (SBTRO), BRU 2/1 (Council Book A), p. 150.

21. See Samuel Schoenbaum, *William Shakespeare: A Compact Documentary Life*, revised edn (Oxford: Oxford University Press, 1987), pp. 32–33.

22. See Schoenbaum, *William Shakespeare*, pp. 39–40.

23. See Schoenbaum, *William Shakespeare*, p. 40.

24. For the original purchase of New Place in May 1597, see SBTRO ER 27/4a, the exemplification of fine that Shakespeare was given as a record of the sale. For the clearing of the title to New Place effected between Shakespeare and Hercules Underhill in 1602, see National Archives (PRO) Court of Common Pleas, Feet of Fines, C.P. 25 (2)/237, Michaelmas 44 & 45 Elizabeth I, no. 15.

25. For Shakespeare's suit in the Stratford Court of Record against Philip Rogers in July 1604 for a sum of thirty-five shilling and ten pence, see SBTRO ER 27/5. For his suit against John Addenbrooke in 1608–1609 for £7 4s, see SBTRO BRU 15/5/116, BRU 15/5/139, ER 27/6, and ER 27/7.

26. For the purchase of four yardlands of arable land in Old Stratford from John and William Combe, in May 1602, see SBTRO ER 27/1. Later that year Shakespeare also purchased the Dead Lane cottage in Stratford; see SBTRO ER 28/1.

27. Shakespeare derived a substantial income from his half-interest in the lease of tithes, reckoned in 1617 at £60 per annum. For this he paid in July 1605 £440 to Ralph Hubaud of Ipsley, as evident in the assignment of the moiety of tithes, SBTRO 27/2.

28. For the records of the case, see National Archives (PRO) REQ 4/1; the evidence has been recently sifted in Charles Nicholl's *The Lodger: Shakespeare on Silver Street* (London: Allen Lane, 2007).

29. Schoenbaum's treatment of the enclosure episode is typical; see *William Shakespeare*, pp. 281–85; see also Mark Eccles, *Shakespeare in Warwickshire* (Madison: University of Wisconsin Press, 1961), pp. 136–38; and E. K. Chambers, *William Shakespeare: A Study of Facts and Problems*, 2 vols (Oxford: Clarendon Press, 1930), II, pp. 141–52. Shakespeare compounded directly with William Replingham, Mainwaring's cousin and agent, to protect his financial interest in the land should the enclosure proceed; thereafter he stayed out of the long-running and sometimes violent dispute between the Corporation and Combe.

30. For an account of this nocturnal escapade, see Schoenbaum, *William Shakespeare*, pp. 206–09.

31. See Edward Arber, *A Transcript of the Stationers' Registers of London, 1557–1640*, 5 vols (London: 1875–94), I, p. 322.

32. For an excellent introduction to the importance of the Bishops' Ban to the production and interpretation of English literature in the early-modern period, see Cyndia Susan Clegg, *Press Censorship in Elizabethan England* (Cambridge: Cambridge University Press, 2004), ch. 9, 'The 1599 Bishops' Ban'.

33. A typical example is the entry in the Stationers' Register for *Hamlet, Prince of Denmark*. Although entered in July 1602, the 'good' quarto was not printed until 1604/5. See Arber, *Transcript*, III, p. 89. Strictly speaking, once the

company had sold the text to the printer, entering the copy was his responsibility; but in practice the company must have cooperated with the printer on securing the value of the text.

34. This scene first appears in the quarto of *Richard II* published by Matthew Law in 1608.

35. For an introduction to Renaissance humanism, see Jill Kraye, ed., *The Cambridge Companion to Renaissance Humanism* (Cambridge: Cambridge University Press, 1995), esp. Peter Mack, 'Humanist Rhetoric and Dialectic', pp. 82–99; and Daniel Wakelin, *Humanism, Reading, and English Literature 1430–1530* (Oxford: Oxford University Press, 2007).

36. On the fashion for scepticism at this time, see Richard Popkin, *The History of Scepticism From Savonarola to Bayle* (Oxford: Oxford University Press, 2003), pp. 3–79.

37. See Walter J. Ong, *Ramus, Method, and the Decay of Dialogue: From the Art of Discourse to the Art of Reason* (Chicago: University of Chicago Press, 2004); and Howard Hotson, *Commonplace Learning: Ramism and its German Ramifications, 1543–1630* (Oxford: Oxford University Press, 2007), pp. 51–67.

38. Desiderius Erasmus, *De ratione studii*, ed. by Craig R. Thompson, *Collected Works of Erasmus: Literary and Educational Writings 2: De Copia / De Ratione Studii* (Toronto: University of Toronto Press, 1978), p. 666.

39. Thomas Wilson, *The Arte of Rhetorique*, sig. Aij^v.

40. See *Gabriel Harvey's Marginalia*, ed. G. C. Moore Smith (Stratford-upon-Avon: Shakespeare Head Press, 1913), p. 122.

41. Thomas More, *A fruteful, and pleasaunt worke of the beste state of a publyque weale, and of the newe yle called Vtopia*, transl. Ralph Robinson (London: S. Mierdman for Abraham Vele, 1551), sig. ffv^r–ffv^v.

42. Epictetus, *Discourses*, ed. W. A. Oldfather (Cambridge: Harvard University Press, 1925), pp. 24–25.

43. Quintilian, *Institutio Oratoria*, 11. 1, trans. by H. E. Butler, 4 vols (London: Loeb, 1922), IV, pp. 155–57.

44. See George Puttenham, *The Arte of English Poesie* (London: Richard Field, 1589); especially 3. 23 ('What it is that generally makes our speach well pleasing and commendable, and of that which the Latines call Decorum'), 3. 24 ('Of decencie in behauiour which also belongs to the consideration of the Poet or maker'), and 3. 25 ('That the good Poet or maker ought to dissemble his arte, and in what cases the artificiall is more commended then the naturall, and contrariwise').

45. See my *Spenser's Legal Language: Law and Poetry in Early Modern England* (Cambridge: Boydell and Brewer, 2007), pp. 203–31.

46. Jasper Heywood, *The Seconde Tragedie of Seneca entituled Thyestes* (London: Thomas Barthelettes, 1560), preface, ll. 169–76.

47. Heywood, *Thyestes*, preface, ll. 205–08.

48. For details on this account of the *Gesta Grayorum*, see *Gesta Grayorum: Or, the History of the High and mighty Prince, Henry Prince of Purpoole*, etc. (London: W. Canning, 1688).

49. See *Gesta Grayorum*, pp. 20–23. I discuss the relationship of the play to the

revels in 'Consideration, Contract, and the End of *The Comedy of Errors*', *Law and Humanities*, 1 (2007), 145–65.

50. This performance is recorded in the diary of John Manningham, a member of the Middle Temple who was present at the play; see *The Diary of John Manningham of the Middle Temple, 1602–1603*, ed. R. P. Sorlien (Hanover, NH: University Press of New England, 1976).

51. Marie Axton has argued that the holiday revels were opportunities for students at the Inns not only to hone their theatrical skills, but to practise their courtly behaviour; citing Sir John Fortescue, she sees the Inns of Court as a university preparing its students for all the requirements of civic life, including the practical ones. See Marie Axton, *The Queen's Two Bodies: Drama and the Elizabethan Succession* (London: Royal Historical Society, 1977), pp. 3–10.

3: THE LOVE OF PERSONS: COMMON LAW AND THE EPISTEMOLOGY OF CONSCIENCE IN THE *SONNETS* AND *A LOVER'S COMPLAINT*

1. I quote here directly from the 1609 edition, in order to avoid the editorial changes normally made to the sonnet by modern editors, in diction and spelling. See *Shake-speares Sonnets* (London: Thomas Thorpe, 1609).

2. The allegorical and psychological effects made possible by hypallage were not available to classical rhetoricians, simply because neither Greek nor Latin establishes grammatical relation primarily through word order (as English does); shifting the place of a word, in English, will quickly create new grammatical relations, which in the hands of a skilled poet can complicate the linguistic representation or construction of the relations between people, or between people and things. Material objects can become ready symbols for interior psychological states, or (as here) the psychological experience of an individual can be subtly displaced onto universal aspects of space and time. The absence of discussion of transferred epithet in Henry Peacham's *The Garden of Eloquence* (London: H. Jackson, 1577), or in George Puttenham's *Arte of English Poesie* (London: Richard Field, 1589) suggests that Elizabethan poets were pioneering the various effects of this new figure at about this time. Sister Miriam Joseph has documented Shakespeare's use of this among other figures in her *Shakespeare and the Arts of Language* (New York: University of Columbia Press, 1947); for hypallage, see pp. 58–61.

3. See *Statutes*, II, pp. 248–51. English monarchs occasionally created such commissions of inquisition purely for financial gain: investigating the real nature and extent of lands and estates in a given area could expose 'concealed' lands and other irregularities, the discovery of which could substantially increase the royal rents and the money raised through parliamentary subsidies. A typical example is Henry VII's 1505 writ to a group of Yorkshire commissioners, charging them to enquire into 'concealed lands, wards, reliefs, escheats, treasure trove, goods of outlaws, felons and fugitives, forfeitures and concealments of officers, alienations in mortmain and entries without licence' (National Archives, C 142/19).

4. '*Escheat*, Eschaeta is a word of art, and deriued from the French word *Eschear* ... and signifieth properly when by accident the Lands fall to the Lord of whom they are holden, in which Case we say the fee is escheated' (Coke, *1 Institutes*, f. 13ʳ) And '*Escheatour* (*Escaetor*) commeth of (*Escheate*) and signifieth an officer that obserueth the *Escheates* of the king in the countie, whereof he is *Escheatour*, and certifieth them into the *Eschequer*'. See Cowell, *Interpreter*, sig. Cc2ᵛ.

5. 'Deed [*fait*] is a writing sealed and delivered, to prove & iustifie the agreement of the party, whose deed it is, to th'end contained in the Deed, as Deed of Feoffement is a proof of the livery of seisin, for the land passeth by the livery of seisin, but when the Deed and the Delivery are ioyned together that is a proofe of the livery, and that the feoffor is content that the feoffee shall have the land.' See *Les Termes de la Ley*, ff. 154v–155r. See also the entry for 'defeisance', f. 105r.

6. See *OED*, 'watchman', *n*. 5.

7. In making this abrupt passing claim for a paired 'absolutist' political and literary landscape in the late 1590s and early seventeenth century, I am mindful of the compelling work of historians from J. G. A. Pocock to Glenn Burgess, not all of whom have been convinced of the existence of an 'absolute' theory of kingship (much less of poetry) before the 1640s. Burgess, for example, points out that most sixteenth- and early seventeenth-century Englishmen seemed to consider a limited monarchy completely compatible with the 'irresistibility' of royal power; nonetheless, he acknowledges the desirability of retaining the term 'absolutist' to refer to those who were committed to the 'general freedom' of the monarch from parliamentary or other political control. See *Absolute Monarchy and the Stuart Constitution* (New Haven: Yale University Press, 1996), pp. 209–24. Regardless of one's stance on the concept or language of absolutism in the period, however, there is no question that the final decades of the sixteenth century and the early decades of the seventeenth witnessed key shifts toward political centralization and, in the minds of some legal and lay commentators, incipient tyranny: the rise of the Privy Council, the growth and consolidation of judicial power in the Chancery, the expansive granting of monopolies, and the emergence of the High Commission were just some of the more conspicuous battle-grounds on which parliamentarians and judges fought the crown, under both Elizabeth and James. In the court poetry of the period, as I have argued elsewhere, we see English poets grappling tenaciously with the consequences of this ideological shift for their own poetics – perhaps nowhere so urgently as in Edmund Spenser's *The Faerie Queene*, where the play of unity and plural error in literary interpretation becomes the central focus of the first book.

8. The allegorical quality of the rhetoric of lyric in English sonnets of the 1590s is often ignored, pejorized, or imperfectly recognized; but contemporary testimony suggests that poets considered it a main and vital part of their enterprise in this genre. A typical account is supplied by Giles Fletcher in the preface to his 1593 sequence, addressed to the eponymous Licia, where he playfully invites and resists allegorical identifications of his lyric subject:

If thou muse vvhat my *LICIA* is, take her to be some *Diana*, at the least chaste, or some *Minerva*, no *Venus*, fairer farre; it may be shee is Learnings image, or some heavenlie vvonder, vvhich the preciest may not mislike: perhaps under that name I have shadovved *Discipline*. It may be, I meane that kinde courtesie vvhich I found at the Patronesse of these Poems; it may bee some Colledge; it may bee my conceit, and portende nothing: vvwhatsoever it be, if thou like it, take it ...

See Giles Fletcher, *LICIA, or Poemes of Loue* (Cambridge: John Legatt, 1593), sig. B1ʳ.

9. A typical editorial emendation in sonnet 61 tells a tale: many editors alter 1609's 'tenure' to 'tenor', apparently because they are unconvinced of the importance of legal thinking to the sonnet. One recent editor who has resisted this particular change (and whose notes regularly foreground the importance of legal thinking in the poems) is Colin Burrow, in the Oxford Shakespeare edition of *The Complete Sonnets and Poems*.

10. Critical views differ on the authorship of *A Lover's Complaint*. A judicious critic will entertain them all but, I think, admit that the evidence of Shakespeare's authorship is both strong and, in light of the reading I give below, perhaps a little the stronger. Brian Vickers has recently contended on stylistic evidence that the poem is the work of John Davies of Hereford, a writing master working in London during the period; see his *Shakespeare, A Lover's Complaint, and John Davies of Hereford* (Cambridge: Cambridge University Press, 2007). As MacDonald P. Jackson pointed out in a review of Vickers's book, though, the value of Vickers's stylistic evidence is dubious because arbitrarily selected – certain words in *A Lover's Complaint* may point to Davies's authorship, but a different set of words might point to a different author (even Shakespeare, whose name appears on the first printed edition of the poem). See Macdonald P. Jackson's review in the *Review of English Studies*, 58 (2007), 723–25. As I argue below, stylistic differences between *A Lover's Complaint* and Shakespeare's other poetry are to be expected, in any case: it was considered the mark of a good poet, in the sixteenth century, to be able to vary one's style (including diction), and the abrupt conceptual departure of the *Complaint* from the *Sonnets* would seem to demand exactly such a variation.

11. For the emphasis on political allegory in *Astrophil and Stella, wherein the excellence of sweete poesie is concluded* (London: Thomas Newman, 1591), see, e.g., nos 14, 18, 21, 23, 30, 69, 107. It is not surprising to find these sonnets pushing towards a political register, given Sidney's claim, in *The Defence of Poesy*, that the end of poetry should be 'knowledge of a mans selfe, in the Ethicke and politick consideration'. See *The Defence of Poesy* (London: William Ponsonby, 1595), sig. D1ʳ.

12. The lover of Spenser's *Amoretti and Epithalamion* (London: William Ponsonby, 1595) calls his beloved a 'tyranesse', and frequently characterizes her in military terms (see, e.g., *Amoretti*, nos 11 and 12); even when the sequence eventually achieves erotic harmony, the lover still speaks in terms of being 'tyed', of 'captivity', and of being a 'thrall' (see nos 65 and 73). Daniel takes a much more explicitly legal approach in *Delia*, but by sonnet 24 we still find

him reduced to abjection: 'Yet my soules soueraigne, since I must resigne;
Reigne in my thoughts, my loue and life are thine.' See *Delia, Containing
certaine Sonnets: with the complaynt of Rosamond* (London: Simon Waterson,
1592), no. 24.

13. For an introduction to the succession controversy and the government's
attempts to contain it, see Cyndia Susan Clegg, *Press Censorship in Elizabethan
England* (Cambridge: Cambridge University Press, 1997), pp. 79–102.

14. Hughes and Larkin, *Tudor Royal Proclamations*, pp. 506–08.

15. See *Leicester's commonwealth: The Copy of a letter written by a master of art of
Cambridge (1584) and related documents*, ed. D. C. Peck (Athens: Ohio
University Press, 1985), pp. 104–08.

16. I have argued for the importance of the succession issue to Nashe's satire on
patronage in the early 1590s; see 'Getting it Back to Front in 1590: Spenser's
Dedications, Nashe's Insinuations, and Ralegh's Equivocations', *Studies in
the Literary Imagination*, 38 (2005), 173–98.

17. The upper house first raised the matter of Elizabeth's marriage and
succession in a petition of 1563. The Queen normally deputed her replies to
the Lord Keeper, but in this instance he read her personal reply, from a
prepared manuscript, in her presence, deflecting both petitions by a general
promise to keep the matter in her care. See d'Ewes, *Journal*, pp. 74–76. The
lower house also broached the issue, more directly, in the same parliament,
by means of a petition delivered to the Queen by Speaker Thomas Williams
on 28 January 1562/3, to which the Queen replied on 16 February and
again on 10 April 1563; see d'Ewes, *Journal*, pp. 81–83, 85, 91. On 5
November 1566, the Queen summoned a delegation of members of both
houses to Whitehall, where she was presented with a further petition, which
she again deflected; thereafter she wrote by Sir Edward Rogers and Sir
William Cecil to the House of Lords in no uncertain terms:

> [Her] Grace had signified to both Houses, by words of a Prince, that she
> by Gods Grace would Marry, and would have it therefore believed; and
> touching limitation for Succession, the perils be so great to her Person,
> and whereof she hath felt part in her Sisters time, that time will not yet
> suffer to treat of it. Whereupon all the House was silent.

See d'Ewes, *Journal*, pp. 105–08, 124, 127–30. The Commons pressed the
issue, and were instructed on 8 November 1566, by Sir Francis Knollys, that
'they should no further proceed in their Suit', and again on 12 November,
this time by a 'special Command from her Highness to this House' sent by
the Speaker, 'notwithstanding her first Commandment, that there should
not be further talk of that matter in the House . . . and if any person thought
himself not satisfied, but had further reasons, let him come before the Privy
Council, and there show them' (d'Ewes, *Journal*, p. 128). The queen later
relaxed her prohibition on the Commons' liberty of debate, but reproved the
house for pressing the matter with 'violent', almost daily suits throughout
November 1566 (d'Ewes, *Journal*, pp. 130–31). At the closing of the 1566
parliament, the Speaker of the Commons, Richard Onslow, again
admonished the queen of the dangers arising from her virginity and failure

to provide for the succession (d'Ewes, *Journal*, pp. 114–15), to which, 'not pleased with the doings of the House of Commons', reproved them 'for busying themselves in this Session, with matters which did not appertain at this time unto them' (d'Ewes, *Journal*, p. 135).

18. Mary Stuart was explicitly mentioned in the 1566 House of Lords discussion on the succession (see d'Ewes, *Journal*, p. 104). Her right to the succession was reaffirmed by John Leslie's 1584 *Treatise towching the right, title, and interest of the most excellent Princess Marie, Queene of Scotland, and of . . . Iames, her Graces sonne, to the succession of the croune of England* (Rouen: G. L'Oyselet, 1584), and was advanced too by Parsons in *Leicester's Commonwealth*.

19. Extant copies include Fletewoode's autograph, CUL MS Add. 9212. For more on this manuscript treatise and its importance, see J. H. Baker and Jayne Ringrose, *A Catalogue of English Legal Manuscripts in Cambridge University Library* (Cambridge: Boydell, 1996), pp. 652–53. Leslie answers the objections based on *De natis ultra mare* in his *Treatise*, ff. 22^r–39^v.

20. See *OED*, 'remove', *n*. 1a, 4a; and 'remove', *v*. 2b, 3b. The playfulness of Shakespeare's usage here spells in miniature the general ambiguity of the sequence on its own social and political pretensions. On the one hand, this line insists that the lover will prefer private leaves to public discourse, but on the other it accomplishes that insistence by recourse to a word that reeks of that seem public discourse. In other words, in resisting removal to new jurisdictions (or allegorical applications), the poem employs a metaphorical diction that activates exactly those applications.

21. Cowell, *Interpreter*, sig. Zzz3^r–Zzz3^v.

22. See 25 Edward 3 cap. xx (*Quia emptores terrarum*). For an introduction to the history of the use, and Henry VIII's successful war against it, see J. H. Baker, *IELH*, pp. 248–58.

23. See *IELH*, pp. 253–54.

24. *Re Lord Dacre of the South* (1535); see Baker and Milsom, no. 105.

25. 'An Act expressing an order for Vses and Willes', 27 Henry 8 cap. x; see *Statutes*, I, pp. 582–84.

26. Another politically important concept with which the use became aligned in the 1590s, which may well have as much to do with Shakespeare's musing on the use as it does with Spenser's at about the same time, is the Irish practice of tanistry. The tanist of an Irish sept – or designated successor to the chieftain or taoiseach – was appointed at the time of the chieftain's accession, such that the taoiseach was considered in political terms a kind of 'cestuy que use', and the tanist was, effectively, as important a partner to treaties and negotiations as his nominal lord. See Spenser's discussion of tanistry in *A view of the present state of Ireland* (1596) (Dublin: James Ware, 1633), pp. 5–7.

27. Thomas Littleton, *Tenures in Englishe* (London: Richard Tottel, 1576), sig. Biiij^r–Biiij^v.

28. See *OED*, 'use', n. 5.

29. See, e.g., 13 Elizabeth 1 cap. viij, 'An Act against Vsury', *Statutes*, II, pp. 150–51. The anonymous tract *The death of vsury, or, the disgrace of vsurers* (Cambridge: John Legatt, 1594) is typical of the popular animus against the

practice, as is a collection of six sermons by the populist preacher Miles
Mosse, entitled *The arraignment and conuiction of vsurie* (London: Widow
Orwin for Thomas Man, 1595). Shakespeare's illustration of the
conventional Elizabethan contempt for usury, and for usurers, can be seen
most clearly, of course, in *The Merchant of Venice* (esp. 1, 3, 98ff., where
Shylock remembers how Antonio has 'rated' him 'about my monies and my
usances').

30. *Les Termes de la Ley*, f. 288v.

31. Shakespeare's interest in the ethics and erotics of use and waste also appears
in *A Midsummer Night's Dream*, which begins with Theseus likening the
chaste moon to 'a step-dame or a dowager / Long withering out a young
man's revenue' (1.1.5–6). Because widows were accorded a life interest in
their dead husbands' estates, they were sometimes suspected of wasting the
estate's assets, to the prejudice of the heir or reversioner.

32. The opposition between a self-consuming waste of beauty (pure aesthetic
experience) and a self-discovering use of beauty (pure moral message)
animates the ironies of Thomas More's *Utopia* (1516), another text
preoccupied – though more menacingly – with the epistemology of an
interiorized legal code.

33. For the legal resonance of 'sessions', cf. William Lambarde's *Eirenarcha*
(London: 1588), pp. 374–75:

> I will (for this time) call *a Session of the Peace* An assemblie, of any two (or
> moe) Iustices of the Peace (one of them being of the *Quorum*) at a
> certaine day (and place within the limits of their Commission)
> appointed, to enquire by a Iurie (or otherwise to take knowledge) and
> thereupon to proceede to heare & determine according to their power,
> of causes within their Commission, & the Statutes referred to their
> charge.' Lambarde is at pains, too, to distinguish a sessions from a simple
> enquiry, 'in so much as to enquire, and not to heare and determine, is but
> a halfe doing, and not worthy the name of a Session of the Peace.

For 'summons', cf. Cowell, *The Interpreter*, sig.Ppp4ʳ: '*Sommons, alias Summons*
(*Summonitio*) commeth of the French (*semondre, i. vocare*) It signifieth in our
common law, as much as (*vocatio in ius*) or (*citatio*) among the Ciuilians.' The
proximity of 'summon' and 'remembrance' in this line is particularly
interesting because the offices of Clerk of the Summons and Remembrancer
(or 'Clerk of the Remembrance', as Cowell has it) were both positions in the
Exchequer, a court in Westminster Hall predominantly preoccupied with the
settling of accounts – both those of the king and those of the Lord Treasurer.

34. 2 Westminster, cap. 11, in *Statutes*, i, p. 33.

35. It is a commonplace of the sixteenth-century English erotic lyric that erotic
love is based on transgression, or the threat of transgression. The *locus
classicus* is the second song of Sidney's *Astrophil and Stella*, in which Astrophil
breaks his vow of good behaviour and kisses Stella while she is sleeping.
Sidney sharpened the scenario in *The Countess of Pembroke's Arcadia*, where
the prince Musidorus proves his love to Pamela by attempting to rape her
during her sleep: Pamela's ultimate response to the assault is relief – the relief

of discovering the Musidorus loves her enough to lose her. The erotic dynamics of transgression are unblinkingly anatomized in *The Rape of Lucrece*, where Tarquin repeatedly erects little barriers for his forward progress, then delights in toppling them, culminating in his famous dismissal of Lucrece's pleas for mercy: '"Have done," quoth he, "my uncontrolled tide / Turns not, but swells the higher by this let' (ll. 645–46). Competition and transgression are core elements in the erotic theory of Georges Bataille; see his *Eroticism*, transl. Mary Dalwood (London: Boyars, 1987).

36. See, e.g., Philip Sidney's 'slave-borne *Muscovite*' in *Astrophil and Stella*, 2, and sonnets 29 and 47; and Edmund Spenser, *Amoretti*, 65.

37. Eric Partridge, in *Shakespeare's Bawdy* (London: Routledge and Kegan Paul, 1968), pp. 221–22, compares the conclusion of *The Passionate Pilgrim*, where Venus warns Adonis of the threat of the boar:

> 'Once,' quoth she, 'did I see a fair sweet youth
> Here in these brakes deep wounded with a boar,
> Dee in the thigh, a spectacle of ruth.
> See in my thigh,' quoth she, 'here was the sore.'
> She showed hers; he saw more wounds than one,
> And blushing fled, and left her all alone.

Burrow, in Shakespeare's *Complete Sonnets and Poems* (pp. 79–80), is certainly right that this poem is not Shakespeare's, and is probably the work of Richard Barnfield; but the joke about Adonis's 'wound', of course, lies at the centre of the complicated play of androgyny in Shakespeare's own *Venus and Adonis*. A slightly more ironic bawdy joke emerges from the 'strong proof of constancy' Portia exhibits to Brutus in *Julius Caesar* – a 'voluntary wound, / Here in the thigh' (2.1.298–300).

38. See *OED*, 'engross', *v*, 9a and 10.

39. See *OED*, 'engross', *v*, 3, 4, and 5.

40. See *OED*, 'cross', *v*, 3; 'cancel', *v*, 1. That Shakespeare had 'cancel' in mind here becomes more clear as the sonnet continues: Latin *cancelli*, or 'cross-bars', was used in late Latin as the term for a 'lattice', or 'enclosure', including the enclosure where a prisoner was restrained in court. More suggestively, perhaps, William Lambarde writes of the office of chancellor in his *Archeion*:

> Our *French* word *Chancellier*, is fetched from the *Latine*, *Cancellarius*; and that, from *cancello*; and they all three framed out of the *Greeke καγκαλῶ* which signifieth properly, to make *Lattises*, *Grates*, or *Grosse-barres*, to enclose any thing withall; and *metaphorically*, to bound and containe any thing within certaine *barres* and *limits*.
>
>   And out of these two significations, two principall parts of his *Office* doe issue: For after the similitude to those *crossed Barres* or *Lattises*, he is said to *cancell, deface, to make void* a *Record*, because the *vacat* thereof is done, by drawing certaine crosse lines Lattise-wise with his Pen over it; whereby it is so inclosed and shut up, that from thenceforth no exemplification thereof may be given abroad.

> And likewise in his *Court of Equitie*, he doth (when the Case requireth)
> so *cancell* and *shut up* the *rigour* of the generall *Law*, that is shall not
> breake forth to the hurt of some one singular Case and person.
> (Lambarde, *Archeion*, pp. 46–47)

The 'crossing' of sonnet 133 might thus be thought to invoke not only cancelling, but the conscience of the Chancery – conscience opposed, naturally, to the 'rigour' of line 12.

41. See Burrow, *Complete Sonnets and Poems*, p. 646.

42. On balance, the regular (though not exclusive) attributions of 'fair' to the beloved, and 'true' to the lover, stand up: see, for example, the final couplet of 123 (to Time: 'This do I vow and this shall ever be:/ I will be true despite thy scythe and thee.'), and the final couplets of 147 and 152 ('For I have sworn thee fair . . .').

43. To 'cross' one number x with another number y is to take a line of x units and 'cross' it with a line of y units; the resulting two-dimensional space contains the product of that cross. 'Thrice threefold . . . crossed' thus represents not three by three (or nine), but rather three 'crossed' lines, drawn three times, creating a cube of twenty-seven. Shakespeare thus plays numerically between 'three and three and three' and 'three by three by three'.

44. The two most influential recent studies of the composition of Shakespeare's *Sonnets* use stylometric evidence to break the sequence into four blocs: 1–60 (1591–5, revised), 61–103 (1591–5, unrevised), 104–26 (1597–1603), and 127–54 (1591–5; thought to be the earliest). See A. Kent Hieatt, Charles W. Hieatt, and Anne Lake Prescott, 'When did Shakespeare Write *Sonnets* 1609?', *Studies in Philology*, 88 (1991), 69–109; MacDonald P. Jackson, 'Rhymes in Shakespeare's Sonnets: Evidence of Date of Composition', *Notes & Queries* (244), 1999, 213–19; and MacDonald P. Jackson, 'Vocabulary and chronology: the case of Shakespeare's sonnets', *Review of English Studies*, 52 (2001), 59–75. For a judicious overview of these and other studies, see Burrow, *Complete Sonnets and Poems*, pp. 103–11. While this scheme may in broad terms accurately describe the original composition of many of the poems contained in each group, interdependent close readings of sonnets such as this of 105 and 133 suggest that there is certainly more to the story than a haphazard agglomeration of largely independent groups. If Shakespeare continued to reorder and revise the sequence in the seventeenth century, there is no reason to think that he did not break up earlier blocs, revise and adjust individual sonnets to generate sequential patterns and effects, or even compose new material to replace or supply old defects. It is difficult to say what the process of 'composition' means, and thus to determine where it 'ended'.

45. Sir Edward Coke, *A Little Treatise of Baile and Maineprize* (London: William Cooke, 1635), p. 1.

46. Coke, *A Little Treatise of Baile and Maineprize*, pp. 2–3.

47. Coke, *A Little Treatise of Baile and Maineprize*, p. 30.

48. See for example Joel Fineman, *Shakespeare's Perjured Eye: The Invention of Poetic Subjectivity in the Sonnets* (Berkeley: University of California Press, 1986), esp. pp. 297–300.

49. See Aristotle, *Nicomachean Ethics*, V.x. 3–8.
50. Christopher St German had driven a decisive wedge between conscience and equity in his well-known dialogue on equity *Doctor and Student*. St German's project had been to liberate English common law, and in particular the Chancery, from the arbitrary 'conscientious' judgments of prelate Chancellors; at about the same time that he argued, in *Doctor and Student*, that equitable judgment in Chancery ought to be ordered 'after the rewles and groundes of the lawe of the realme', Henry VIII broke with tradition by appointing a common lawyer, Sir Thomas More, as Chancellor. See my discussion of St German's project and its Elizabethan legacy in *Spenser's Legal Language: Law and Poetry in Early Modern England* (Cambridge: Boydell and Brewer, 2007), pp. 125–38. But St German's campaign against conscience redefined rather than deprecated the term, and common lawyers continued in Elizabeth's reign to speak of equitable judgment as judgment by conscience.
51. On perjury and subornation to perjury, see Coke, *3 Institutes*, pp. 163–67. A statute from the reign of Henry VII ordered parties grieved to complain of perjury by bill to the justices of the court wherein the perjury had been committed; thereafter these justices should submit the matter to the Chancellor:

> And then the same Chanceller shall cause by Writ at the suite and costes of the partie complainant, all such person or persons, against whom the saide complaint is so made, to come afore the same Chanceller and Treasurer of England, the chiefe Justice of either Bench, and the Clerke of the Rolles for the time being, which shall haue full power and authoritie by this present Acte, by their discretion, to examine all such person or persons appearing before them, of all things comprised in the Bill of complaint, and to punish all and euery such person or persons, as by that examination shall be found offender or offenders, as well of periurie as other after their discretion. (11 Henry 7 cap. 25: *Statutes*, i. p. 373)

The discretionary authority of the Lord Chancellor in perjury cases was explicitly reaffirmed by Elizabeth's perjury act (5 Eliz. cap 9).

4: WASTING TIME: CONDITIONALITY AND PROSPERITY IN *AS YOU LIKE IT* AND THE SECOND TETRALOGY

1. It is probably not too much, in fact, to call *As You Like It* Shakespeare's primogeniture play, inasmuch as its comic predicament is based on the failure of two fraternal relationships, failures which represent the two social threats created by the primogeniture custom: the insolence of the assured heir and the ambition of the younger son. As Sir John Baker argues in *The Reports of Sir John Spelman* (vol. II, p. 208), primogeniture and the even stricter practice of 'entailing' lands inalienably to the customary heir 'subjected parents to the cradle, taking away a man's authority over his eldest son'. This was a

social evil of which Thomas Starkey had written in his *Dialogue Between Reginald Pole and Thomas Lupset* (*c.* 1536):

> This entailing, specially after such manner only to the eldest son in every base family, maketh many reckless heirs, causeth them little to regard nother learning nor virtue, inasmuch as they are sure to be inheritors to a great portion of entailed land, and so, by this assurance, they give themself to all vanity and pleasure, without respect; the which I think they would not do if they were in doubt of such possessions, and the whole inheritance to hang upon their behaviour and learning.

See Starkey, *Dialogue*, ed. Kathleen M. Burton (London: Chatto & Windus, 1948), pp. 105–09, 174–76. In its emphasis on this social problem, *As You Like It* is closely linked to *King Lear* which also, as I will argue below, turns on the scene of a father's blessing.

2. On 'stalling' as 'bringing to a stop', see *OED*, 'stall', *v.*, 11a, b. The 'th' suffix in Anglo-Saxon was applied to verbs to create abstract nouns of temporal state: so 'heal' gives 'health', 'die' 'death, and 'grow' 'growth' (see *OED*, '-th', *suffix*[1]). These abstract nouns are temporally non-finite in a different way from the infinitive form of the verb, and precisely as Orlando describes in this passage: an infinitive verbal form expresses potential not yet placed or instantiated by connection with a subject or an object; but the abstract substantive 'growth' is not potential but real ('stays . . . unkept', 'nothing . . . gives'), its non-finite quality a result of its indeterminate unrealizedness.

3. Two eighteenth-century editors, William Warburton and Thomas Hanmer, both add 'my father' to the impersonal clause; Alexander Dyce in his third edition of Shakespeare's works (1875–76) supplies 'he'.

4. Other contemporary, and important, examples of this technique include Hamlet's conversation with Horatio at the opening of 5.2 of *Hamlet* ('So much for this, sir. Now shall you see the other.'), and the opening of 2.1 of *Troilus and Cressida*, in which Ajax and Thersites walk on stage just after Ajax has asked Thersites the question, 'What's the matter from the general?'

5. The legal basis of Rowland de Boys' 'charge' is left vague in the play: it is not clear whether he placed the obligation on Oliver through his will (i.e. in a clause of his testament), or simply enjoined a promise of his eldest son at the moment of conferring his paternal blessing. Either way, though, the quasi-contractual nature of the exchange could not have been actionable in a common-law court. As Edward Coke notes in his discussion of 'Perjury or subornation of Perjury, and incidently of Oaths' in *Institutes 3* (pp. 163–67):

> If a man calleth another perjured man, he may have his Action upon his case, because it must be intended contrary to his Oath in a judiciall proceeding: and so it is termed in our statute of 5 Eliz. but for calling him a forsworne man, no Action doth lye: because the forswearing may be extrajudiciall. If the defendant perjureth himselfe in his answer in the Chancery, Exchequer Chamber, &c. he is not punishable by this statute, for it extendeth but to witnesses, but he may be punished in the Star chamber, &c. (p. 166)

Prerogative courts like Chancery, Requests, and (as Coke notes) the Star
Chamber were able to rule on cases of breach of promise, a jurisdiction they
had taken over from the old *laesio fidei* action of the church courts. The action
of another of Shakespeare's comedies, *The Comedy of Errors*, turns on breach
of promise; see my essay, 'Consideration, Contract, and the End of *The Comedy
of Errors*', *Law and Humanities*, 1 (2007), 145–65.

6. It is worth noting that we have seen this kind of thinking before: Lear
unwisely gives his eldest daughters all, too soon and without condition,
thereby licensing them to default and abuse him. With the parallel from *As
You Like It* before us, it is even possible to see how the opening of *King Lear*
performs a kind of disgavelling of Lear's British constitution, importing from
the primogeniture system its notorious flaw (i.e. the insolence of the heir).
The development of the legal theory of contract in the period showed a
similar kind of emphasis on the *consideratio*, or consideration: a sometimes
fictional allowance over and above the payment for goods or services, which
then allowed a defrauded creditor to sue the defaulter on an action of
assumpsit; for Shakespeare's careful use of 'the doctrine of consideration' in
The Comedy of Errors, see my 'Consideration, Contract, and *The Comedy of
Errors*', *Law and Humanities*, 1 (2007), 145–66.

7. Latin *cum* could be used prepositionally ('with'), but it is the conjunctive uses
(of *quom*, written *cum* from the time of Cicero) which shadow and inform the
English constructions of 'as': 'when', 'while', 'if', and with the correlative
tum, 'as ... so'. On the various Latin constructions with *cum*, see E. C.
Woodcock, *A New Latin Syntax* (London: Methuen, 1959), pp. 187–95. *Cum*
was, of course, intensively used in the technical syntactical formulae of early
modern Latin legal documents. Medieval statutes made regular use of *cum* in
the preambles to individual acts ('Whereas ...'), while commissions and
letters patents employed the word, in constructions of similar import, to
define the conditions of the issuing of the instrument. *Cum* did not, however,
have the conjurative force of English 'as', as in phrases like, 'As I hope in
heaven', etc.

8. See above, pp. 72–84.

9. This is the sense in which Shakespeare uses the idea in the opening lines of
A Midsummer Night's Dream, where Theseus compares the lingering moon
to a 'step-dame or a dowager, / Long withering out a young man's revenue'
(1.1.5–6).

10. Cowell, *Interpreter*, sig. Bbbb2ʳ.

11. Rastell, *Statutes*, f. 521ʳ.

12. See *OED*, 'foil', *n*¹, 3c. Shakespeare makes the same connection between the
cancelling of a debt (redemption) and foiling in *1 Henry IV*, 1.2.203–10.

13. This form of a condition is adapted from University of Nottingham Library,
MS Ne D 1567. A conditional obligation (a 'marriage bond') was taken out
on Shakespeare's marriage to Anne Hathaway on 28 November 1582; see
Worcestershire Record Office, X 797 BA 2783, which is printed (and
translated) in E. K. Chambers, *William Shakespeare: A Study of Facts and
Problems*, 2 vols (Oxford: Oxford University Press, 1930), II, pp. 41–42. For an
introduction to conditional bonds, see Baker, *IELH*, pp. 323–325, and A. W.

B. Simpson, *History of the Common Law of Contract: the Rise of Assumpsit* (Oxford: Clarendon Press, 1975).

14. Frederick's animosity towards Rowland de Boys, and his son Orlando, appears to be part and parcel of his anxieties about merit. His sudden anger at Rosalind stems from his belief that Rosalind outshines Celia in the people's estimation ('she robs thee of thy name, / And thou wilt show more right and seem more virtuous / When she is gone'; see 1.3.74–81), a perception that breaks upon him (in Le Beau's account) only *after* he has seen Orlando best Charles at wrestlng in the previous scene. Key to Frederick's 'humorous' change in this earlier scene is Orlando's announcement that his name is 'Orlando my liege, the youngest son of Sir Rowland de Boys' (1.2.212). Had Orlando been an heir, and not a dispossessed younger brother out to demonstrate his desert, Frederick would not have turned from him, nor turned upon Rosalind. Orlando, for his part, is well aware of the Starkeian cultural assumptions that inform Frederick's anger: 'I am more proud to be Sir Rowland's son, | His youngest son, and would not change that calling | To be adopted heir to Frederick' (1.2.221–23). In this context, the famous *deus ex machina* delivered by Jaques de Boys at the end of the play makes perfect sense: Frederick suddenly abandons the usurped dukedom because he realizes that, having become the legitimate ruler, all the 'men of great worth' must naturally fly to his disempowered brother (5.4.152–56). Whether he wins or loses in his planned assault on the Forest of Arden, his estimation will fall – so he abdicates.

15. For this legal use of 'waste', see Cowell, *Interpreter*, sig. Bbbb2ʳ: 'Waste in the second signification is taken for those parts of the Lords Demesne, that be not in any one mans occupation, but lye common for bounds or passages of the Lord and tenent from one place to another, and sometimes for all the Kings subiects. Which seemeth to be called waste, because the Lord cannot make such profit of it, as he doth of other of his land ...' In the strict use of the word, an early-modern English 'forest' was the peculiar domain of the king, and in that sense not necessarily 'waste' ground; but in *As You Like It*, it is precisely this issue that is under examination: does Frederick's ducal power extend to the exclusive ownership of this natural place, or does it resist possession, like waste ground? This is the point of Duke Senior's earliest exchange (in 2.1) with Amiens and the First Lord, where he calls the forest 'more free from peril than the envious court', and learns that Jaques thinks him a tyrannous usurper for hunting deer, the 'native burghers of this desert city', 'their own confines' (2.1.21–63). Later in the play (4.2) Jaques proposes to present the First Lord – the killer of the deer – 'to the Duke like a Roman conqueror', setting the deer's horns on his head 'for a branch of victory' (4.2.1–5); here Jaques's defiance of poaching regulations, by celebrating a subject who has asserted the principle of common hunting rights, drives again towards the idea of Arden as a 'common waste'.

16. See *OED*, 'feudary, feodary', *n.*, 1b. Corin reports to Touchstone in the following act that Rosalind is 'my new mistress's brother' (3.2.83–84).

17. Erasmus discusses 'sustine et abstine' in the *Adages*, II. vii. 13; see *Collected Works of Erasmus*, vol. 34: *Adages II.vii.1 to III.iii.100*, transl. Margaret Mann Phillips (Toronto: University of Toronto Press, 1982), p. 10.

18. Cowell, *Interpreter*, sig. Z3ʳ. 'Distress' is similarly operative in 3.5, where Rosalind and Celia eavesdrop on Phebe's cruelty to Silvius. Silvius asks for 'relief' from Phebe (3.5.86) for the distress she has caused him, so that his grief and her sorrow might be 'extermined'. When Phebe attempts to compound in a 'neighbourly' way with him by offering him love, Silvius raises the stakes by demanding her; but she is firm about her offer of 'recompense', and returns to thinking of her own transactional exchange with Rosalind (Ganymede), with the faux-legal maxim, 'omittance is no quittance' (3.5.133).

19. Oliver himself will suffer a literal distress in the immediately following scene (3.1), as Duke Frederick seizes into his hands the whole of the de Boys estate, pending Oliver's discovery of his brother. This distress is carried out in explicitly legal terms, as Frederick resorts to the language of tenurial law:

> Thy lands and all things that thou dost call thine,
> Worth seizure, do we seize into our hands,
> Till thou canst quit thee by thy brother's mouth
> Of what we think against thee.
>
> (3.1.9–12)

To 'quit' is to repay a debt (see *OED*, 'quit', *v.* 1a, b), while the modern senses of the verb 'seize' (and its derivatives) arise from its original legal sense, 'to put (a person) in legal possession of a feudal holding (see *OED*, 'seize', *v.* 1 a, b, c, and 2 a, b). The 'officers of such a nature' whom Frederick readily details to 'make an extent upon his house and lands' (3.1.16–17) are presumably those responsible for the appropriations mentioned in the play's first act.

20. See *OED*, 'inland', *n., a.,* and *adv.,* 1; and 'Demaine' in Cowell, *Interpreter,* sig. Y1v–Y2v. Rosalind's use of the word 'inland' at 3.2.338 cannot be innocent: either she has been spying on Orlando's meeting with Duke Senior (see 3.4.32–36), or she, like Orlando, recognizes the Forest of Arden as a feudal fantasy-land created by her father.

21. See *OED*, 'time', *n.* 15b.

22. Celia's use of 'back-friend' in 3.2 is not normally read with any sense of reference to the material bond of obligation, as I suggest here; but the only other time Shakespeare uses the compound – at 4.2.27 of *The Comedy of Errors* – it very clearly has this or a similar sense. There, Dromio of Syracuse is informing Adriana and Luciana that his master has been arrested by a 'backfriend, a shoulder-clapper' – the constable whose presence is promised by the back of an obligation, and whose hand seizes you, when you default, from the back. The conceptual beauty of the connections that Shakespeare makes here is that this 'back-friend' is also temporally a friend from the past, the promise of whose intrusion has been left depending since the signing of the bond.

23. For an introduction to these and other technical aspects of formal pleading, see Baker, *IELH,* pp. 76–79; and Baker, *OHLE 6,* pp. 335–49.

24. The formal process of pleading is concisely described in Sir Thomas Smith's *De republica Anglorum*. The matter to be decided at law is called an 'issue' or *exitus*; all 'issues ... in our lawe bee ordinarily two *facti* [of fact] or *juris* [of

points of law]'. As Smith writes, 'If the question be of the lawe, that is if both the parties doe agree upon the fact, and each doe claime that by lawe he ought to have it', it 'is called a demurre in the lawe', and 'all the Judges shall meete together, and what they shall pronounce to be the lawe, that is helde for right'. But 'in that case where the lawe is not doubtfull thus it is ended, that in the answere, replication, rejoinder, or triplication and so forth', such that 'each partie must grant to the other stil that in the fact which he cannot denie': and then 'the matter is concluded in the pleading'. See Smith, *De republica Anglorum*, p. 95.

25. See Frederic Maitland, ed., *Year Books of 3 Edward II (1309–1310)* (London: Selden Society, 1905), p. lxvii.

26. See J. H. Baker, 'Joinder of Issue: the Mechanics of Pleading', in *The Reports of Sir John Spelman*, 2 vols (London: Selden Society, 1978), II, pp. 92–103.

27. On the year books, see Baker, *IELH*, pp. 178–82. For named reports, see L. W. Abbott, *Law Reporting in England 1485–1585* (London: Athlone, 1973).

28. See 32 Hen. 8 cap. 30.

29. The defendant had four possible courses: to deny all the facts (a 'general traverse'), to deny a single fact (a 'special traverse'), to admit the facts but introduce a new fact (an 'avoidance'), or to admit the facts, but deny that they created a lawful case for the plaintiff ('demurrer'). See Baker, *IELH*, pp. 77–78.

30. See Immanuel Kant, *The Groundwork of the Metaphysics of Morals*, ed. and transl. Mary Gregor (Cambridge: Cambridge University Press, 1997), e.g. at p. 13: 'An action from duty has its moral worth *not in the purpose* to be attained by it but in the maxim in accordance with which it is decided upon, and therefore does not depend upon the realization of the object of the action but merely upon the *principle of volition* in accordance with which the action is done without regard for any object of the faculty of desire.'

31. See Luke Wilson, *Theatres of Intention*, pp. 134–74.

32. Thomas Littleton, *Tenures* (London: Richard Tottel, 1576), sig. Cij^v.

33. Coke, *Institutes 1*, f. 68^r.

34. Littleton, *Tenures*, sig. Ciij^v.

35. Coke, *Institutes 1*, f. 68^r.

36. Cowell, *Interpreter*, sig. Ss2^r.

37. Bracton emphasizes the danger to the tenant (here, Gaunt) in any violation of the bond of homage:

> The effect of homage is this, that if one has done homage to another, his true lord or a non-lord, he cannot withdraw from such lord or his homage without judgment, as long as he holds the tenement, either in demesne or in service, by which he is bound to do homage. Because of the bond of homage the tenant may do nothing to the disherison of his lord or his severe injury, nor conversely, may the lord so act toward the tenant. If either so acts homage is completely dissolved and extinguished, and the *nexus* and obligation of homage, since they act contrary to homage and the oath of fealty, and it will be a just judgment that they be punised with respect ot that in which they offend, that is, if it is the lord, that he lose his lordship: if the tenant, his tenement.

See Bracton, *De legibus*, II, p. 233. What Gaunt stands to lose, as Richard suggests, is his estate – 'time-honoured Lancaster'. By contrast, the only judge who can deprive Richard of *his* estate – the kingdom – is God himself, as Gaunt reminds the Duchess of Gloucester in the following scene.

38. Here 'apparent' provokes its usual collocation, 'heir', which will make curious subsequent intrusions into the language of the scene and play (see, e.g., 1.1.85); on 'ancient' (f. L. *ante*, 'before') and 'inveterate' (f. L. *inveterare*, 'to make old'), see *OED*.

39. For Bracton's discussion of the order of a trial by combat in cases of appeal of felony, see *De legibus*, II, pp. 381–402. Bracton gives special emphasis to the importance of holding the combat as soon as possible after the appeal: 'When he [the appellee] has elected to make his defence by his body and all the elements necessary for an appeal are in order, let the duel be waged at once [*statim*]' (*De legibus*, II, p. 391; see also p. 399, where he repeats this injunction). Richard puts off the appeal before the start of the play, attempts to quash it, and then ineptly delays the combat until St Lambert's day. Note too that, in normal practice, interruption of the trial by combat for any reason was prohibited. In Bracton's account, the *bannus regis* (king's ban) must be proclaimed immediately upon the exchange of oaths from the competitors: 'It is the command of the king and of his justices that none by so hardy or rash as to move or utter a word no matter what he may see or hear; if anyone acts to the contrary he shall be arrested and put in prison, to lie there for a year and a day until the lord king has expressed his will concerning him' (*De legibus*, II, p. 400). In *Richard II*, it is of course Richard himself who ineptly violates his own ban.

40. Holinshed's account of Richard's insolent financial dealings begins with the record of 'a new and strange subsidie or taske granted to be leuied for the kings vse' in 1380 (Holinshed, *Chronicles*, III, p. 427), which led to Wat Tyler's rebellion. Later, in 1399, Richard's council developed new expedients for raising money:

> But yet to content the kings mind, manie blanke charters were deuised, and brought into the citie, which manie of the substantiall and wealthie citizens were faine to seale, to their great charge, as in the end appeared. And the like charters were sent abroad into all shires within the realme, whereby great grudge and murmuring arose among the people: for when they were so sealed, the kings officers wrote in the same what liked them, as well for charging the parties with paiment of monie, as otherwise. (Holinshed, *Chronicles*, III, p. 496).

Richard specifically mentions these blank charters at 1.4.48, along with the 'farm[ing] of our royal realm, / The revenue whereof shall furnish us / For our affairs in hand' (1.4.45–47).

41. See *OED*, 'conquest', n. 6a, b, c. The *OED* claims that this was a Scots usage, but many early modern English poets pun on the relation between 'conquest' and the purchasing of estates; for example, see the final couplet of Shakespeare's sonnet 6: 'Be not self-willed, for thou art much too fair / To be death's conquest and make worms thine heir.'

42. Ernst Kantorowicz, *The King's Two Bodies :A Study in Mediaeval Political Theology* (Princeton: Princeton University Press, 1953), p. 167.

43. Bracton, *De legibus*, II, p. 58.

44. Bracton repeats this maxim twice, both times in direct connection with the relation between the king and the fisc: see *De legibus*, II, pp. 58, 167.

45. Kantorowicz, *The King's Two Bodies*, p. 191.

46. The writ for the action of account closely collocates *computum* ('account') and *reddat* ('render'), in the same way that Hal does: 'Rex vicecomiti N. salutem. Praecipe A. quod reddat B. rationabilem computum suum de tempore quo fuit receptor denariorum ipsium B. Et nisi fecerit &c.' See Anthony Fitzherbert, *Natura Brevium*, f. 117.

47. See *OED*, 'parcel', *n.* 3, 4.

48. Plowden, 'Case of the Dutchy of Lancaster, at Serjeant's-Inn', in *Commentaries*, p. 213.

49. For Kantorowicz's discussion of the case of the Duchy of Lancaster, see *The King's Two Bodies*, pp. 401–09.

50. Lorna Hutson has argued forcefully that the 'doctrine' of the king's two bodies, as reported in Plowden, was not as influential as has commonly been assumed; she claims, instead, that Plowden's Aristotelian understanding of equity was the revolutionary, lasting legacy of his *Commentaries*. See her 'Not the King's Two Bodies: Reading the "Body Politic" in Shakespeare's *Henry* IV, Parts 1 and 2', in Victora Kahn and Lorna Hutson, *Rhetoric and Law in Early Modern Europe* (New Haven: Yale University Press, 2001), pp. 166–98. Hutson appears to me to underestimate the importance of Christopher St German's *Doctor and Student*, which in both Latin and English editions was published in huge volume from the 1530s, and which contains a fully articulated account of Aristotelian equity, naturalized to the English context. While she is right to note that most contemporary lawyers seem to have dismissed the two-bodies argument – even in Plowden's text there are traces of ridicule – it certainly does not follow that Shakespeare would have left it alone.

51. Plowden, 'Case of the Dutchy of Lancaster, at Serjeant's-Inn', *Commentaries*, p. 215.

52. Plowden, 'Case of the Dutchy of Lancaster, at Serjeant's-Inn', *Commentaries*, p. 216.

53. Kant, *Groundwork of the Metaphysics of Morals*, pp. 13–14.

5: *REX V. LEX*, OR, THE PROUD ISSUE OF A KING

1. See 'Willion versus Berkley' in Plowden, *Commentaries*, pp. 223–52 (esp. pp. 234, 238); 'The Case of the Dutchy of Lancaster' in Plowden, *Commentaries*, pp. 212–23 (esp. p. 213, pp. 220–21).

2. See Ernst Kantorowicz, *The King's Two Bodies: A Study in Mediaeval Political Theology* (Princeton: Princeton University Press, 1957) and Marie Axton, *The Queen's Two Bodies* (London: Royal Historical Society, 1977). The traditional claim that a performance of *Richard II* was commissioned by the Earl of Essex's men on the night before his revolt in 1601 is rehearsed in most

standard biographies; it is often connected to Elizabeth I's supposed
(exasperated) protestation to William Lambarde, 'I am Richard II; know ye
not that?', and to the fact that the deposition scene – presumably politically
explosive during Elizabeth's reign – did not appear in any of the quarto
editions of *Richard II* printed before 1603, but first appeared in Q3, printed in
1607.

3. Historical study on this point is, in the age of dramatic television
reconstructions of Henry VIII's romantic and sexual exploits, slightly scruffy,
but it seems likely that the protest at Wolsey's quick and absolute ascendancy
under Henry VIII reflected years of less public disgruntlement over Henry
VII's centralizing fiscal and administrative policy. Thomas More was among
those who, in gratulating Henry VIII's accession to the throne in 1507, urged
him to rule in a style more attentive to his ancient counsel (the nobility), and
the swift execution of Edmund and Dudley – Henry VII's most notorious bag-
men – seems to have set the tone for a reign that would seem to devolve
power, while in reality concentrating it in a succession of expendable royal
deputies.

4. A well-known reaction to Wolsey's allegedly arbitrary judgments was the
anonymous *Replication of a Serjeant at Law*, a polemical tract that attacked
the Chancery as a court opposed to the common law, the law of reason, and
the law of God. See John Guy, ed., *St German on Chancery and Statute* (London:
Selden Society, 1985), pp. 99–105.

5. See John Skelton, *Collyn Clout*, ll. 92–114, in John Scattergood, ed., *John
Skelton: The Complete Poems* (Harmondsworth: Penguin, 1983).

6. *Les Termes de la Ley*, 221^r: '*Praemunire* is a Writ, & it lyeth where any man
sueth any other in the Spirituall Court, for any thing that is determinable in
the Kings Court.' *Les Termes de la Ley*, 222^r: '*Prescription* is when a man
claimeth any thing, for that he, his ancestors, or predecessors, or they whose
estate hee hath, have had, or used any thing all the time, whereof no mind
is to the contrary.'

7. For an analysis of the contemporary reception of St German's works, and
some hypotheses about his intentions in *Doctor and Student*, see John Guy,
'Thomas More and Christopher St German: The Battle of the Books', in
Alistair Fox and John Guy, *Reassessing the Henrician Age: Humanism, Politics
and Reform 1500–1550* (Oxford: Basil Blackwell, 1986), pp. 95–120. As Guy
argues (pp. 102–03), *Doctor and Student* 'created the impression that English
law was an homogeneous *corpus* . . . and it enhanced vastly the status of the
English common law with regard to other species of law, especially canon
law and papal law'.

8. See William Roper, *The lyfe of Sir Thomas Moore, knighte*, ed. Elsie Vaughan
Hitchcock (1935), pp. 44–45.

9. Informal and written Inns of Court debate over the queen's prerogative
power, and the general relation of the crown to Parliament and the courts,
ran under several general heads. Historical accounts of Magna Carta or the
statute *prerogativa regis*, such as those presented in Inns of Court readings
(lectures) by senior lawyers, often touched on the contested boundary
between crown and common law; examples include Robert Snagg's 1581

Middle Temple reading on Magna Carta and the Chancery, published in 1654 as *The antiquity and original of the court of Chancery and authority of the Lord Chancellor of England* (London: Henry Seile, 1654); and a notebook containing readings on statutes, probably compiled by William Fletewood (CUL MS Gg.6.18), which includes a treatise on Magna Carta, a reading of the first chapter (*De pace*) of the first Statute of Westminster, and notes on a reading on *Prerogativa Regis*. Another important focus for these debates was the status of the court of Chancery and the power of the Chancellor: William Lambarde compiled a well-known manuscript (BL MS Stowe 415) for Sir Thomas Egerton (later Elizabeth's Lord Chancellor) during the late 1590s, including records, readings, cases, and other evidence relevant to the relation between crown prerogative power and common-law jurisdiction. A third focus for this kind of debate was, during Elizabeth's reign, the problem of the succession; the dialogue treatise on *De natis ultra mare* ('Certaine errors'; see, e.g., CUL MS Add. 9212) often attributed to William Fletewood, which deals with the common-law limitations on aliens' rights of inheritance, was designed to examine, and bar, the claim of Mary Queen of Scots to the English throne.

10. Sir Thomas Smith, *De Republica Anglorum*, ed. by Mary Dewar (Cambridge: Cambridge University Press, 1982), p. 96.
11. Smith, *De Republica Anglorum*, ed. Mary Dewar, p. 96
12. Bracton, *De legibus*, II, p. 33.
13. Smith, *De Republica Anglorum*, pp. 94–95.
14. Smith, *De Republica Anglorum*, p. 96.
15. Augustine, *The City of God against the Pagans*, ed. and transl. by R. W. Dyson (Cambridge: Cambridge University Press, 1998), p. 27.
16. For the Stoic arguments on rational freedom adapted (with obvious irony) by Augustine in this chapter of *The City of God*, see Epictetus, *Discourses*, 1.2; 1.17; 1.29; 3.24; and 4.1.
17. Augustine, *The City of God*, p. 28.
18. Augustine, *The City of God*, p. 29.
19. Augustine, *The City of God*, pp. 30–31.
20. Augustine, *The City of God*, p. 31.
21. Augustine, *The City of God*, p. 31.
22. Augustine, *The City of God*, p. 31.
23. For the sources of the Lucrece narrative, see Ovid, *Fasti*, 2.711–852; Livy, *History of Rome*, 1.57–59; and William Painter, *The First Tome of the Palace of Pleasure* (London: Thomas Marshe, 1575), ff. 5r–7r.
24. As Livy makes clear in his account of the siege of (the opulently wealthy) Ardea, Tarquinius Superbus turned his forces on the city because the Roman people – exhausted, impoverished, and mutinous after the forced construction of the Temple of Jupiter on the Tarpeian mount and of the Great Sewer running beneath the city – could only be appeased by distraction and the spoils of war. Tarquinius Superbus thus gambled the security of his kingship on the success of the siege. See Livy, *Roman History*, 1.55–57, and particularly 1.57.1–2: *Ardeam Rutuli habebant, gens ut in ea regione atque in ea aetate divitiis praepollens. Eaque ipsa causa belli fuit, quod rex Romanus cup*

> *ipse ditari, exhaustus magnificentia publicorum operum, tum praeda delenire*
> *popularium animos studebat, praeter aliam superbiam regno infestos etiam quod se*
> *in fabrorum ministeriis ac servili tam diu habitos opere ab rege indignabantur.*

25. Bracton, *De legibus*, II, pp. 121–22.
26. Bracton, *De legibus*, II, p. 122.
27. Coke, *Institutes 3*, p. 51.
28. Coke treats explicitly the circumstances in which a commanded murder is executed by means other than those specified:

> Another diversity there is, when the commandement extends expresly to the killing of another, and for the better accomplishment thereof prescribeth a mean; that is, to kill him by poyson, and he killeth him with a Gun, he is accessory: for the commandement was to kill, which ensued, though the mean was not followed & *finis rei attendendus est.* And the substance of the commandement, *viz.* [to kill] is pursued: and the same offence, that was commanded, is committed. (Coke, *Institutes 3*, p. 51)

By this logic, Lucrece's delay of the murder until after the rape is immaterial to its causation; either way, Tarquin's subornation of the crime remains continuous and effective.

29. Of these impediments the narrator comments, 'He in the worst sense consters their denial.' The legal maxim *in mitiori sensu* (evidence should be construed in the weakest or best sense possible) was commonly invoked, especially in defamation trials from the late sixteenth century onwards, to guide the construction of parol evidence. See Baker, *IELH*, pp. 441–42.
30. *Les Termes de la Ley*, ff. 193r–93v.
31. Cf. Littleton's *Tenures*, where he discusses 'lasches of entry' in the infant heir or reversioner; see Coke, *Institutes 1*, ff. 246r–246v, 308ʳ–308ᵛ. Coke writes that 'Laches signifieth in the Common Law, rechlesnesse or negligence, *Et negligentia semper habet infortunium comitem*' (f. 246v).
32. Cf. Cowell, *The Interpreter*: 'Colour *(color)* signifieth in the common law, a probable plee, but in truth false, and hath this end, to draw the triall of the cause from the Iury to the Iudges' (sig. Q1v). The entry in *Les Termes de la Ley* is roughly similar, calling colour 'a fained matter, which the defendant or tenant useth in his barre, when an action of trespasse or an Assise is brought against him, in which hee giveth the demandant or plaintiffe a shew of the first sight, that hee hath good cause of action, where in troth it is no just cause' (f. 58v). *Les Termes de la Ley* also includes an entry for 'colour of office', which for its lexical overlap with this part of the poem warrants attention: 'Colour of Office is always taken in the worst part, and signifies an act evilly done by the countenance of an Office, and it beareth a dissembling face of the right Office, whereas the Office is but a vaile to the falshood, and the thing is grounded upon vice, and the Office is as a shadow to it' (f. 59r).
33. Critical studies of the poem touching on the law of rape and ravishment include Ian Donaldson, *The Rapes of Lucretia: A Myth and Its Transformations* (Oxford: Clarendon Press, 1982); Stephanie Jed, *Chaste Thinking: The Rape of Lucretia and the Birth of Humanism* (Bloomington: Indiana University Press, 1989); B. J. Sokol and Mary Sokol, *Shakespeare's Legal Language: A Dictionary*

(London: Athlone, 2000), pp. 319–24; and Barbara J. Baines, 'Effacing Rape in Early Modern Representation', *ELH*, 65 (1998), 69–98.

34. 2 Westminster (13 Edw. 1), cap. 33, in *Statutes*, p. 37.

35. The writ specified by the statute for redress in cases of ravishment makes this assimilation clear in its collocation *rapuit et adduxit*, 'ravished and abducted'. See *Statutes*, p. 37.

36. Lucrece's initial assignment of her possessions – blood, honour, and resolution – to Sextus, the knife, and Collatine, may also reflect the presence of the Statute of Wills. That statute, which governed the rights of landowners to devise their estates by will, allowed them to transmit up to a third of their real property as they chose, leaving the rest to be passed by the custom of primogeniture, and assessed according to the revived feudal incidents that Henry VIII had reinstated. By English common law, the murder weapon, as a deodand, would become the property of the crown, so that Lucrece effectively consigns two-thirds of her possessions to Sextus, leaving only the third part, her resolution, to her husband. This loosely invoked parallel between Tudor legislation and the structure of this passage merely serves to accentuate the opposition between a sovereign monarchical state and a knowable model of the social self.

37. See, for example, Andrew Hadfield, *Shakespeare and Republicanism* (Cambridge: Cambridge University Press, 2005), ch. 4 ('The beginning of the republic: *Venus* and *Lucrece*'), pp. 130–53.

38. Robert Snagg, *Antiquity & Original of the Court of Chancery, and Authority of the Lord Chancellor of England*, pp. 6–9.

39. Indeed, when Philip of France produces Arthur of Brittany in Act 2 Scene 1, he goes through the same theatrical presentation of 'these eyes, these brows ... this little abstract ... which died in Geoffrey' (2.1.101–02).

6: THE REPORT OF THE CAUSE OF HAMLET

1. Following Aristotle and thinking forward towards Hamlet, I will use the male pronoun throughout this section. The problems are universal, but they were originally figured as those of male princes.

2. Aristotle, *Nicomachean Ethics*, trans. H. Rackham, rev. edn (Cambridge: Harvard University Press, 1934), 7.3.5.

3. Aristotle, *Politics*, transl. H. Rackham (Cambridge: Harvard University Press, 1932), 3.10.3.

4. See the *Nicomachean Ethics*, 5.10.3–8 (1137b11–1138a4).

5. See *OED*, 'record', *n.*[1] and *adj.* 2; and Cowell, *Interpreter*, sig. Iii1ᵛ–Iii2ᵛ.

6. The text is almost certainly not corrupt at this point in the play. Shakespeare seems to have intended the words 'But that' to form an abortive line, probably indicating a pause or some kind of brief lapse in the actor's delivery, signalling the shift in syntax that deletes the agent.

7. The word 'special' was commonly used by English lawyers during this period in two connections, both of them related to legal innovation and development. The special action or remedy, or 'action on the case', exploded during the Tudor period as common lawyers sought to adapt the law to new

economic and social pressures, and to revive the fortunes of the royal courts. During the second half of the sixteenth century, common-law courts also began to tolerate 'special verdicts', in which the jury 'merely prayed the court's discretion whether judgment should given for the plaintiff or the defendant'. In both the action on the case and the special verdict, judges were called upon to use their discretion, either by setting the conditions under which a new or modified form of action could be allowed, or by reaching a judgment on the evidence and resolving the jury's indecision. On special actions, see Baker, *OHLE 6*, pp. 751–53, and Baker, *IELH*, pp. 61–64. As Thomas Walmsley J noted during the arguments over a 1595 case, the nature of special actions on the case is that they should only be available when other remedies fail; if a case is actionable in debt, therefore, it should not be allowed in *assumpsit*:

> Action on the case is so called from *cadendo*, because something happens in it which does not happen in other cases. For where you have an ordinary action of debt, you may not have action on the case unless upon special cause. As, in this case, if the money were payable at Michaelmas and for non-payment of it the other will forfeit his bond of £20, or such similar *casual* or special thing, action on the case lies. Otherwise not.

See Walmsley's argument in *Paramour v. Payne*, BL MS Harleian 4552, f. 92, transl. and cited by J. H. Baker, 'New Light on Slade's Case', in Baker, *LPCL*, p. 413.

8. Shakespeare's allusion here is to the leaden rule of the Lesbian builders, first discussed by Aristotle in the *Nicomachean Ethics*, and thereafter a standard metaphor for equitable redress of rigorous law. Angelo wants his 'metal' to be given a rigid form and shape, rather than made an instrument flexible enough to apply to circumstance.
9. See above, pp. 154–156.
10. This is the general topic of the second book of Smith's treatise, which begins with a celebration of the integrity and legitimacy of the English monarch ruling through Parliament; and then passes to a description of 'how this head doth distribute his authoritie and power to the rest of the members for the gouernment of his realme, and the common wealth of the politique bodie of England.' See Smith, *De republica Anglorum*, pp. 34–87 (p. 47).
11. Significantly, despite their indirection, both treatises appear to have been considered too controversial to reach print. Lambarde's *Archeion* was not published until 1635, when the political climate had changed enough that the council could not be embarrassed by the tame absolutism of some of Lambarde's points; and Hake's *Epieikeia* did not appear in print until 1953.
12. This quotation is a selection from three distinct passages in Bracton, *De legibus*, pp. 304, 305, 306. The modern collated text reads slightly differently in these locations, but the sense is unchanged; but see caveats below.
13. William Lambarde, *Archeion, Or, A Discourse upon the High Courts of Iustice in England* (London: E. P. for Henry Seile, 1635), pp. 95–98.
14. Bracton, *De legibus*, p. 305.

15. Lambarde, *Archeion*, pp. 69–72. For Aristotle's discussion of the equity and the leaden rule of the Lesbian builders, see *Nicomachean Ethics*, transl. H. Rackham (Cambridge: Harvard University Press, 1934), 5.10 (pp. 313–17). For Bodin's 'harmonicall' mediation between 'the inflexible straightnesse of *Polycletus* his rule' and 'the vncertaine pliantnesse of the Lesbian rule', see *The six bookes of a Commonweale*, transl. R. Knollys (London: A. Islip and G. Bishop, 1606), p. 760.

16. Lambarde, *Archeion*, p. 73.

17. Lambarde, *Archeion*, p. 74.

18. As we have seen (see pp. 34–35 and 216–218), the conflict between Sir Edward Coke CJ and Thomas Egerton, Baron Ellesmere LC in 1616, concerning the limits of the prerogative jurisdiction of Chancery, would explicitly articulate this danger. As Timothy Tourneur noted after James VI and I's intervention in the dispute – on the Chancery's part – the Chancellors threatened to 'enthral the common law (which yeilds all due prerogative), and by consequence the liberty of the subjects of England will be taken away, and no law practised on them but prerogative, which will be such that no one will know the extent thereof'. See BL MS Add. 35957, f. 55^v, transl. in Baker, 'The Common Lawyers and the Chancery: 1616', *LPCL*, pp. 205–29 (p. 222).

19. Edward Hake, *Epieikeia*, ed. D. E. C. Yale (New Haven: Yale Univeristy Press, 1953), p. 11. The cited passage, and translation, are from Bracton, *De legibus*, p. 22.

20. See Christopher St German, *Doctor and Student*, ed. T. F. T. Plucknett and J. L. Barton (London: Selden Society, 1974), pp. 30–31, 101–05.

21. Hake, *Epieikeia*, p. 126.

22. Hake, *Epieikeia*, pp. 139–40.

23. Coke, *Reports*, XII, pp. 280–81.

24. Coke, *Reports*, XII, p. 282.

25. 'The Speech of the Lord Chancellor of England, in the Eschequer Chamber, Touching the *Post-Nati*' (1608), in Louis Knafla, *Law and Politics in Jacobean England: The Tracts of Lord Chancellor Ellesmere* (Cambridge: Cambridge University Press, 1977), pp. 202–53 (p. 248).

26. See Ellesmere, 'Touching the *Post-Nati*', in Knafla, *Law and Politics in Jacobean England*, p. 247.

27. Ellesmere cited from Bracton, *De legibus*, ii, pp. 109–10, concerning the inability of 'private persons' or justices to 'question the acts of kings'. This passage argues that, in the case of a charter or act made by the king, the king's opinion should be sought on any ambiguities or uncertainties in its interpretation; but it also argues that 'the king has a superior, namely, God. Also the law by which he is made king. Also his *curia*, namely, the earls and barons, because if he is without bridle, that is without law, they ought to put the bridle on him.' Indeed, Bracton warns the nobility and judges that, if they do not restrain the king, they shall themselves be adjudged to hell with *fletus et stridor dentium*' [wailing and gnashing of teeth]. See Bracton, *De legibus*, II, pp. 109–10.

28. See Horace, I.i.70–75, in *Q. Horati Flacci Opera*, ed. Edward Wickham (Oxford: Clarendon Press, 1912).

29. Coke, *Reports*, XII, pp. 280–81.

30. Bracton, *De legibus*, II, p. 110.

31. Bracton, *De legibus*, II, p. 157.

32. Bracton, *De legibus*, II, p. 305.

33. Cowell, *Interpreter*, sig. Lll1[r].

34. Christopher St German, *Doctor and Student*, ed. T. F. T. Plucknett and J. L. Barton (London: Selden Society, 1974), pp. 58–59.

35. On *peine forte et dure*, see Baker, *IELH*, pp. 508–09.

36. Speaking of the iterated palimpsest of paternity that besets the inheritance model of identity, Claudius tells Hamlet in 1. 2 that 'you must know your father lost a father; / That father lost, lost his . . .' (1.2.89–90); Gertrude later says over Ophelia's grave that 'I hop'd thou shouldst have been my Hamlet's wife' (5.2.242).

37. This figure (fittingly) goes under different names, the variety of which reflect different attitudes toward its essential function. We know it as the pun. George Puttenham in *The Arte of English Poesie* (London: Richard Field, 1589) calls it 'prosonomasia', emphasizing rather the propinquity – even to illusion – of two distinct forms, than the amphibolous significance of the paronomasia proper. For Puttenham it is a figure 'by which ye play with a couple of words or names much resembling', where 'one seemes to answere th' other by manner of illusion' (p. 212); while paronomasia, a kind of limit case, describes the prosonomasia where the resemblance or illusion between the terms has become complete (the distinction in the senses, of course, persists). Hamlet's anxiety about the gap between paronomasia and prosonomasia, as I shall argue below, emerges when he accuses Ophelia of 'nicknam[ing] God's creatures' at 3.1.145; 'the nicknamer' is Puttenham's English name for prosonomasia.

38. The theory – almost in itself a philosophical argument – of the hendiadic relation is developed by George T. Wright in his essay on the figure in *The New Princeton Encyclopedia of Poetry and Poetics* (Princeton: Princeton University Press, 1993), pp. 515–16. While common versions of the figure (e.g. 'gold and cup' for 'golden cup') are (apparently) comparatively innocuous, the figure can easily become complicated by a more vexed pairing of explicit terms. For example, here 'stand and unfold' means both 'don't move' but also 'reveal your identity'; the implication seems to be that a static passivity ('stands') is a divulging posture.

39. See, for example, Thomas Spencer, *The Art of Logick* (London: John Dawson for Nicholas Bourne, 1628), c. 51 (p. 269). 'Of an explicate Syllogisme in generall': 'A Syllogisme is then explicate, when the proposition, assumption, and conclusion, are orderly framed together.' Opposed to the explicate are the 'contracted Syllogismes'; if the sentries on the ramparts in *Hamlet* are anxious to 'unfold' themselves, the court, by contrast, is 'contracted in one brow of woe' (1.2.4).

40. See *OED*, 'stand', *n.*[1], 2c.

41. George T. Wright, 'Hendiadys and *Hamlet*', *PMLA*, 96 (1981), 168–93.

42. The most famous example of this kind of 'fetch' occurs in Polonius's instructions to Reynoldo in 2.1, where he counsels him on the feints he will need to use to gain information about his son's behaviour in France:

> See you now,
> Your bait of falsehood takes this carp of truth:
> And thus do we of wisdom and of reach,
> With windlasses and with assays of bias,
> By indirections find directions out.

(2.1.61–65)

Polonius also describes false vows to Ophelia as 'springes to catch woodcocks' (3.1.115) and 'tenders' (3.1.101–09), 'brokers' (3.1.127), and 'mere implorators of unholy suits' (3.1.129); all of these words cast Hamlet's supposedly sincere protestations as middle terms in arguments/transactions designed to achieve surreptitious ends (as at 3.1.128: 'not of the dye which their investments show'). Hamlet takes a similar approach to *The Murder of Gonzago*, of which he famously (and unsettlingly) also uses the word 'catch' (2.2.594); the play is figured as a form of (fictional!) bait designed to lure Claudius into revealing himself.

43. See *OED*, 'phrase', *n.*, 2a, b.

44. For example, see Plato, *Cratylus*, 421A, where Socrates etymologizes the word ὄνομα by recourse to the verb μαιέσθαι ('to search'): 'The word ὄνομα seems to be a word composed from a sentence signifying "this is a being about which our search is". You can recognize that more readily in the adjective ὀνομάστον, for that says clearly that this is ὄν οὑ μάσμα ἐστίν (being of which the search is).'

45. See Plato, *Cratylus*, 408E–409A, 409C, and 420E–421B.

46. Plato, *Cratylus*, 435B–435C.

47. The opposition I here suggest between naturalism and conventionalism begins with Plato, but was taken up energetically during the medieval period, especially in the controversy over nominalism, where the two terms remained antithetically opposed. For a recent caution about the reductive nature of this binarism, see Peter T. Struck, *Birth of the Symbol: Ancient Readers at the Limits of Their Texts* (Princeton: Princeton University Press, 2004), pp. 88–90.

48. Plato, *Cratylus*, 415A–416A.

49. The association in *Hamlet* between 'trick' (for μηχανή) and the unetymologizable words of *Cratylus* runs deeper than the language of Hamlet's letter. A similar passage occurs, for example, upon Laertes's discovery of Ophelia's death in 4.7, where the key terms of the debate, and the circumstantial terms of Socrates' discussion, are again all present. Laertes laments, 'Too much of water hast thou, poor Ophelia, / And therefore I forbid my tears. But yet / It is our trick; nature her custom holds, / Let shame say what it will' (4.7.160–63). 'Custom' is here allowed to prevail a little upon 'nature', as the 'trick' holds; as if to drive the intertextual reference home, Shakespeare immediately has Laertes make recourse to one of the key unetymologizables, πῦρ, as if it were a touchstone for Laertes's inability to

achieve naturalism in his language and gesture: 'I have a speech of fire that fain would blaze. / But that this folly doubts it' (4.7.165–66). The punning on 'fain'/'feign' and 'doubt'/'dout' (i.e. 'extinguish') here reinforces the collapse of naturalism into conventionalism.

50. Plato, *Cratylus*, 388D–389A.

51. These are the sources identified, for example, by Bracton in the introductory sections to *De legibus et consuetudinibus Angliae* (see pp. 22–28). For Bracton 'auctor iustitiae est deus' ('the author of justice is God'), but 'consuetudo vero quandoque pro lege observatur ... vicem legis obtinet' ('custom truly sometimes is observed as law ... and takes the place of law') (p. 22). Bracton's distinction between natural law (p. 26) and civil law (p. 27) tends to a similar end.

52. See, for example, the suggestive discussion of the antiquity of poetry in Philip Sidney, *A Defence of Poetry*, in *Miscellaneous Prose of Sir Philip Sidney*, ed. Katherine Duncan-Jones and Jan van Dorsten (Oxford: Clarendon Press, 1973), pp. 74–76. Edmund Spenser also links the historical practices of the Irish bards and brehons in *A view of the present state of Ireland* (1596), in *A Variorum Edition of the Works of Edmund Spenser*, ed. Edwin Greenlaw et al., 11 vols (Baltimore: Johns Hopkins University Press, 1947–53), x, ll. 118–33, 2256–344.

53. In the sixteenth-century emblematic tradition, Hercules in his later age was figured as an orator whose eloquence bound and ordered civil society; a good example appears in the 1550 edition of Andrea Alciato's *Emblematum Liber*. This civilizing power of speech was similarly emphasized in emblematic representations of Orpheus and other mythical poets; see Sean Keilen, *Vulgar Eloquence: On the Renaissance Invention of English Literature* (New Haven: Yale University Press, 2006), pp. 32–88.

54. Sextus Empiricus in his *Hypotyposes* or *Outlines of Pyrrhonism* reduces all fallacious dogmatic positions on knowledge to these two predicaments, and then shows that they both present an epistemological impasse. The first fails because it is arbitrarily axiomatic (on what basis can we establish the authority of those 'true' words we have inherited?), the second because it provokes an infinite regression (in order to agree the definition of one word, we must use other words; in order to agree the nature of those words, we must use yet other words; etc.). See the discussion of the Two Modes, in Sextus Empiricus, *Outlines of Pyrrhonism*, transl. R. G. Bury (Cambridge, Mass.: Harvard University Press, 1933), 1. 178–79 (pp. 101–03).

55. See *Elizabeth I: Collected Works*, ed. Leah Marcus, Janel Mueller, and Mary Beth Rose (Chicago: University of Chicago Press, 2000), pp. 325–26.

56. Regular proclamations were issued against 'vagabonds, and against vnlawfull assemblies in and about London' throughout Elizabeth's reign, as they had been in the reigns of Henry VIII, Edward VI, and Mary; these were occasionally associated with proclamations directed specifically against soldiers or traitors, making it clear that the Privy Council considered them parallel, and often connected, threats to public order. From the later years of the reign, see, e.g., Humfrey Dyson, ed., *A Booke Containing All Such*

Proclamations, as were publised during the Raigne of the late Queene Elizabeth (London: Bonham Norton, 1618), f. 300 ('against vagrant soldiers and idle persons', 5 November 1591), f. 324 ('for suppressing of the multitude of idle vagabonds, and auoyding of certaine mischieuous dangerous persons from her Maiesties Court', 21 February 1594), f. 356 (27 September 1598), f. 383 (15 February 1601).

57. A proclamation was issued 'concerning the practises of the Earles of Essex, Rutland, and Southampton' on 9 February 1601; see Dyson, ed., *Proclamations . . . [of] Elizabeth*, f. 382.

58. The connection between Judges 11 and the plights of both Ophelia and Hamlet are made more explicit by the temporal scheme of the play. Jephthah affords his daughter two months to go with her maids into the mountains to bewail her virginity, after which he sacrifices her; Hamlet, similarly, repeatedly comments on the elapsed period of two months, or (in Ophelia's account, 'twice two months') since his father's death. See 1.2.138 ('but two months dead') and 3.2.130–32 ('twice two months', 'two months'). In a freakish parallel, Claudius tells Laertes (at 4.7.81) that a French gentleman called 'Lamord' ('death') visited the court at Elsinore 'two months since'.

59. See Judges 11:12–23.

60. Aristotle claimed in the *De generatione animalium* [*On the generation of animals*] that in mammals, including humans, the father contributed the sexually active *pneuma*, or pattern, in the form of semen, while the mother contributed the passive material on which the *pneuma* was to work; see *De generatione animalium*, 1. 20. Form and pattern (from L. *pater*) are literally 'father-stuff', while material and its English derivative 'matter' are literally 'mother-stuff'.

61. See Proverbs 6:20–35; this section of Proverbs seems to have been important to Shakespeare at about this time, for the concerns it raises over harlotry seem very active in *Troilus and Cressida*, in the first scene of which Troilus is (by the play's misogynistic logic) 'by means of a whorish woman . . . brought to a piece of bread'. The philosophical tradition of reading this chapter of Proverbs as a metaphysical allegory for instability of the phenomenal world begins with Moses Maimonides in *The Guide of the Perplexed*, ed. Schlomo Pines, 2 vols (Chicago: University of Chicago Press, 1963), II, p. 431 (3.8).

62. See Plato, *Cratylus*, 439B–440E.

63. A parallel use of this image, with similar import, occurs in *The Tempest*, when Ferdinand assures Miranda that, under normal circumstances, he had rather have a 'flesh-fly blow my mouth' than serve Prospero in such a debasing manner (3.1.63). Common observation will indicate that flies prefer open cavities on corpses for oviposition, the mouth being one of the first locations colonised. This well-understood phenomenon may have suggested to Shakespeare the general link between generation, decomposition, and language. 'Fly-blowing' returns in the final scene of *The Tempest* (5.1.283–85).

64. Lily's *Grammar* calls *hic, haec,* and *hoc* 'articles'; see, e.g., *A short introduction of Grammar* (London: Assignes of John Battersbie, 1597), sig. A8ʳ. For the 'demonstrative' sense of 'design', see *OED*, 'design', *v.* 1.

65. Edmund Plowden, *The Commentaries or Reports* (London: Catharine Lintot

and Samuel Richardson, 1761), p. 50. Plowden's *Commentaries* were
originally published in 1571; the 1761 edition is the first English translation.

66. Plowden, *Commentaries*, p. 465.

67. Plowden, *Commentaries*, p. 140.

68. See Richard Hooker, *Of the Lawes of Ecclesiasticall Politie Eight Bookes*
(London: John Windet, 1604), p. 47: 'All thinges that are, haue some
operation not violent or casuall . . . That which doth assigne vnto each thing
the kinde, that which doth moderate the force and power, that which doth
appoint the forme and measure of working, the same we tearme a *Lawe*.'
Christopher St German discusses the origins of law in 'synderesis' and reason
in *Doctor and Student*, ed. T. F. T. Plucknett and J. L. Barton (London: Selden
Society, 1974).

69. See G. W. F. Hegel, *Aesthetics*, ed. and transl. T. M. Knox, 2 vols (Oxford:
Clarendon Press, 1975), II. p. 1215: in the 'tragic complication, 'the two sides
that are in conflict with one another preserve the justification which both
have . . .'

70. See Luke Wilson, *Theaters of Intention: Drama and the Law in Early Modern
England* (Stanford: Stanford University Press, 2000), pp. 25–67; and Carolyn
Sale, 'The "Amending Hand": Hales v. Petit, Eyston v. Studd, and Equitable
Action in *Hamlet*', in Constance Jordan and Karen Cunningham, eds, *The
Law in Shakespeare* (Houndmills: Palgrave, 2007), pp. 189–207. The relevant
passage in *Hamlet* is 5.1.1–31.

71. See Plowden, *Commentaries*, pp. 473–76. Of the judges' careful handling of
Archer's fate, Plowden concludes, 'And altho' they were so agreed [i.e. to
release him], yet, rather than make a Precedent of it, they reprieved him from
one Session to another for divers Sessions, to the Intent that he might
purchase his Pardon [i.e. by clemency from the Queen], and by that Means
be set at Liberty' (p. 475).

72. The case can be found in Plowden, *Commentaries*, pp. 253–64.

73. Plowden, *Commentaries*, p. 253.

74. See Plowden, *Commentaries*, pp. 258–59.

75. Plowden, *Commentaries*, p. 262.

76. Plowden, *Commentaries*, p. 263.

77. Plowden, *Commentaries*, p. 264.

78. See Stanley Cavell, *Disowning Knowledge in Seven Plays of Shakespeare*
(Cambridge: Cambridge University Press, 2003), pp. 179–91.

79. See *OED*, 'brother', *n.*, 6. 'Brother' was regularly used by (both real and
fictional) princes in the period to refer to other princes. For Claudius to call
Hamlet 'brother' may seem unlikely to us, but it would have sounded a
common courtliness to a sixteenth-century ear. Polixenes calls Leontes
'brother' at the opening of 1.2. of *The Winter's Tale*, for example (l.4).

7: CODICIL: THE MAXIM AND THE ANALOGY

1. As Lorna Hutson has shown, a merchant's ability to control his daughter, in
the social and literary emblematics of this period, worked as an index of his
probity in governing his financial affairs; and was therefore the key to his

credit and good standing. See *The Usurer's Daughter: Male Friendship and Fictions of Women in Sixteenth-Century England* (London: Routledge, 1994).

2. As I have noted (above, p. 225), the status of maxims in the constellation of principal grounds of the common law was considerable. According to St German, as abstracts of natural law and the rational power, maxims were to be given precedence over any form of custom or statute.

3. Francis Bacon, *The Elements of the Common Lawes of England* (London: Assigns of John More, 1630), p. 11.

4. Bacon, *Elements*, pp. 16–17.

5. Bacon, *Elements*, pp. 18.

BIBLIOGRAPHY

LEGAL, PHILOSOPHICAL, AND LITERARY WORKS

Aristotle, *The Nicomachean Ethics*, ed. H. Rackham (Cambridge: Harvard University Press, 1926).

Aristotle, *Politics*, ed. and transl. H. Rackham (Cambridge: Harvard University Press, 1932).

Ashe, Thomas, *Epieikeia Et Table generall a les Annales del Ley, per facilement troueres touts les cases contenus in yceux; queux concerne le exposition des Statutes per Equitie* (London: Society of Stationers, 1607).

Bacon, Francis, *The Elements of the Common Lawes of England* (London: Assigns of John More, 1630).

Baker, J. H., ed., *The Reports of Sir John Spelman*, 2 vols (London: Selden Society, 1977–78).

Bodin, Jean, *Method for the Easy Comprehension of History*, trans. Beatrice Reynolds (New York: Columbia University Press, 1945).

Baker, J. H. and Milsom, S. F. C., *Sources of English Legal History: Private Law to 1750* (London: Butterworths, 1986).

Bodin, Jean, *The six bookes of a Commonweale*, trans. R. Knolles (London: A. Islip and G. Bishop, 1606).

Bracton, Henry de, *De legibus & consuetudinibus Angliæ libri quinque in varios tractatus distincti*, ed. T. N. (London: Richard Tottel, 1569).

Caesar, Julius, *The Ancient State, Authoritie, and Proceedings of the Court of Requests* (London: Deputies of C. Barker, 1597).

Cicero, *De officiis*, ed. and transl. Walter Miller (Cambridge: Harvard University Press, 1913).

Coke, Edward, *A Booke of Entries* (London: Society of Stationers, 1614).

Coke, Edward, *The First Part of the Institutes of the Lawes of England* (London: Adam Islip for the Societie of Stationers, 1628).

Coke, Edward, *A Little Treatise of Baile and Maineprize* (London: William Cooke, 1635).

Coke, Edward, *The Second Part of the Institutes of the Lawes of England* (London: M. Flesher and R. Young, 1642).

Coke, Edward, *The Third Part of the Institutes of the Laws of England* (London: M. Flesher for W. Lee and D. Pakeman, 1648).

Coke, Edward, *The Reports in Thirteen Parts*, 6 vols (London: John Butterworth and Son, 1826).

Cowell, John, *The Interpreter: or booke containing the signification of words: of all, or the most part of such words and termes, as are mentioned in the lawe writers, or statutes* (Cambridge: J. Legate, 1607).

Dalton, Michael, *The Countrey Justice: Containing the Practice of the Justices of the*

Peace out of their Sessions (London: William Rawlins and Samuel Roycroft, 1697).

D'Ewes, Sir Simonds, *A Compleat Journal of the Votes, Speeches and Debates, Both of the House of Lords and House of Commons Throughout the whole Reign of Queen Elizabeth* (London: Paul Bowes, 1693).

Dyson, Humfrey, ed., *A Booke Containing All Such Proclamations, as were publised during the Raigne of the late Queene Elizabeth* (London: Bonham Norton, 1618).

[Egerton, Thomas, Baron Ellesmere] S. E. Thorne, ed., *A Discourse upon the Exposicion & Understanding of Statutes With Sir Thomas Egerton's Additions* (San Marino: Huntington Library, 1942).

[Egerton, Thomas, Baron Ellesmere] Louis Knafla, ed., *Law and Politics in Jacobean England: The Tracts of Lord Chancellor Ellesmere* (Cambridge: Cambridge University Press, 1977).

Fitzherbert, Anthony, *La Graunde Abbregement de la Ley*, 3 parts (London: John Rastell and W. de Worde, 1516).

Fitzherbert, Anthony, *La Nouuelle Natura Breuium* (London: Richard Tottel, 1553).

Fortescue, John, *De Laudibus Legem Angliae*, ed. S. B. Chrimes (Cambridge: Cambridge University Press, 1942).

Hake, Edward, *Epieikeia: A Dialogue on Equity in Three Parts* (1599), ed. D. E. C. Yale (New Haven: Yale University Press, 1953).

Hatton, Sir Christopher, *A Discourse Concerning Statutes, Or Acts of Parliament: And the Exposition thereof* (London: Richard Tonson, 1677).

Holinshed, Raphael, *The . . . chronicles of England, Scotlande and Irelande . . . .*, ed. John Hooker et al. (London: H. Denham, 1587).

[Homilies] *The seconde Tome of Homelyes*, ed. John Jewel (London: Richard Jugge and John Cawood, 1563).

Hooker, Richard, *Of the Lawes of Ecclesiasticall Politie* (London: John Windet, 1593).

Hudson, William, *The Court of Star Chamber* (1621), in *Collectanea Juridica*, ed. Francis Hargrave (London: E. and R. Brooke, 1792).

Lambarde, William, *The Duties of Constables, Borsholders, Tything-men, and such other lowe Ministers of the Peace* (London: Roger Warde, 1582).

Lambarde, William, *Eirenarcha: or the Offices of the Justices of the Peace* (London, 1582).

Lambarde, William, *Archeion, or, A discourse vpon the high courts of iustice in England* (London: E. Pursloe for Henry Seile, 1635).

Leslie, John, *Treatise towching the right, title, and interest of the most excellent Princess Marie, Queene of Scotland, and of . . . Iames, her Graces sonne, to the succession of the croune of England* (Rouen: G. L'Oyselet, 1584).

Lipsius, Justus, *Sixe Bookes of Politickes or Ciuil Doctrine*, trans. William Jones (London: William Ponsonby, 1594).

Littleton, Thomas, *Les tenures du monsieur Littleton* (London: Richard Tottel, 1579); and *Tenures in Englishe* (London: Richard Tottel, 1576).

[Manningham] *The diary of John Manningham of the Middle Temple, 1602–1603*, ed. R. P. Sorlien (Hanover, NH: University Press of New England, 1976).

Plowden, Edmund, *Les comentaries, ou les reportes . . . de dyuers cases*, 2 parts (London: Richard Tottel, 1578–9).

[Proclamations] Paul L. Hughes and James F. Larkin, eds, *Tudor Royal Proclamations*, 3 vols (New Haven: Yale University Press, 1964–69).

[Proclamations] Paul L. Hughes and James F. Larkin, eds, *Stuart Royal Proclamations*, 2 vols (Oxford: Clarendon Press, 1973).

Quintilian, *Institutio oratoria*, transl. H. E. Butler, 4 vols (Cambridge: Harvard University Press, 1920).

Rastell, John, *An exposition of certaine difficult and obscure words, and termes of the lawes of this Realme, newly set foorth and augmented, both in french and English, for the helpe of such younge students as are desirous to attaine the knowledge of the same. whereunto are also added the olde Tenures* (London: Richard Tottel, 1579).

[Rastell, John] *Les Termes de la Ley: Or, Certain difficult and obscure Words and Terms of the Common Lawes and Statutes of this Realm now in use expounded and explained* (London: J. Streater for the Company of Stationers, 1659).

St German, Christopher, *Doctor and Student* (1528–31), ed. T. F. T. Plucknett and J. L. Barton (London: Selden Society, 1974).

Shakespeare, William, *Complete Works*, ed. Richard Proudfoot, Ann Thompson and David Scott Kastan (London: Arden Shakespeare, 2001).

Smith, Thomas, *De Republica Anglorum: The manner of government or policie of the Realme of England* (written 1562–5, published 1583), ed. Mary Dewar (Cambridge: Cambridge University Press, 1982).

Snagg, Robert, *The antiquity and original of the court of Chancery and authority of the Lord Chancellor of England* [1581] (London: Henry Seile, 1654).

Stanford, William, *An exposicion of the kinges prerogatiue collected out of the great abridgement of justice Fitzherbert and other olde writers of the lawes of Englande* (London: Richard Tottel, 1567).

Starkey, Thomas, *A Dialogue Between Pole and Lupset*, ed. T. F. Mayer (London: Royal Historical Society, 1989); or ed. Kathleen M. Burton (London: Chatto & Windus, 1948).

[State Papers, Domestic] *Calendar of state papers preserved in the Public Record Office, dometic series 1547–1695*, 81 vols (London: HMSO, 1856–1972).

[Statutes, England] *The Statutes at Large*, 2 vols (London: Bonham Norton and John Bill, 1618).

[Statutes, England] Rastell, William, *A colleccion of all the statutes. Whereunto are added the statutes made in the xxxix. yere of Elizabeth* (London: T. White and Bonham Norton, 1598).

Swinburne, Henry, *A Briefe Treatise of Testaments and Last Willes* (London: J. Windet, 1590).

Swinburne, Henry, *A Treatise of Spousals* (London: S. Roycroft for Robert Clavell, 1686).

[Tudor, Elizabeth] *Elizabeth I: Collected Works*, ed. Leah Marcus, Janel Mueller, and Mary Beth Rose (Chicago: University of Chicago Press, 2000).

West, William, *The Second Part of Symboleography* (London: 1601).

Wilson, Thomas, *The Art of Rhetorique* (London: George Robinson, 1585).

[Wilson, Thomas] R. H. Tawney, ed., *Thomas Wilson, A Discourse Upon Usury (1572)* (London: G. Bell, 1925).

Youngs, Jr., Frederic A., *The Proclamations of the Tudor Queens* (Cambridge: Cambridge University Press, 1976).

LITERARY CRITICAL STUDIES

Altman, Joel, *The Tudor Play of Mind* (Berkeley: University of California Press, 1978).

Andrews, Mark Edwin, *Law versus Equity in* The Merchant of Venice (Boulder: University of Colorado Press, 1965).

Axton, Marie, 'The Influence of Edmund Plowden's Succession Treatise', *Huntington Library Quarterly*, 37 (1974), 209–26.

Axton, Marie, *The Queen's Two Bodies: Drama and the Elizabethan Succession* (London: Royal Historical Society, 1977).

Beauregard, David N., 'Sidney, Aristotle, and *The Merchant of Venice*: Shakespeare's Triadic Images of Liberality and Justice', *Shakespeare Studies*, 20 (1988), 33–51.

Benston, Alice, 'Portia, the Law, and the Tripartite Structure of *The Merchant of Venice*', *Shakespeare Quarterly*, 30 (1979), 367–85.

Bernthal, Craig A., 'Treason in the Family: the Trial of Thumpe v. Horner,' *Shakespeare Quarterly*, 42 (1991), 44–54.

Bernthal, Craig A., 'Staging Justice: James I and the Trial Scenes of *Measure for Measure*', *SEL*, 32 (1992), 247–69.

Bolton, W. F., 'Ricardian Law Reports and *Richard II*', *Shakespeare Studies*, 20 (1987), 53–65.

Cacicedo, Alberto, '"She is fast my wife": Sex, Marriage, and Ducal Authority in *Measure for Measure*', *Shakespeare Studies*, 23 (1995), 187–209.

Carlson, Cindy, 'Trials of Marriage in *Measure for Measure*', *Shakespeare Yearbook*, 6 (1996), 355–81.

Chambers, E. K., *William Shakespeare: A Study of Facts and Problems*, 2 vols (Oxford: Clarendon Press, 1930).

Cioni, Maria L., *Women and Law in Elizabethan England, with Particular Reference to the Court of Chancery* (New York: Garland, 1985).

Clarkson, Paul and Warren, Clyde T., *The Law of Property in Shakespeare and the Elizabethan Drama* (New York: Gordian, 1968).

Clarkson, Paul S. and Warren, Clyde T., 'Copyhold Tenure and *Macbeth*', *Modern Language Notes*, 55 (1940), 483–93.

Clegg, Cyndia Susan, *Press Censorship in Elizabethan England* (Cambridge: Cambridge University Press, 2004).

Cooley, Ronald W., 'Kent and Primogeniture in *King Lear*', *Studies in English Literature 1500–1800*, 48 (2008), 327–48.

Coolidge, John S., 'Law and Love in *The Merchant of Venice*', *Shakespeare Quarterly*, 27 (1976), 243–263.

Cormack, Bradin, *A Power to Do Justice: Jurisdiction, English Literature, and the Rise* of *Common Law, 1509–1625* (Chicago: University of Chicago Press, 2007).

Cunningham, Karen. *Imaginary Betrayals: Subjectivity and the Discourses of Treason in Early Modern England* (Philadelphia: University of Pennsylvania Press, 2002).

Denvir, John. 'William Shakespeare and the Jurisprudence of Comedy', *Stanford Law Review*, 39 (1987), 825–49.

Eden, Kathy. *Poetic and Legal Fiction in the Aristotelian Tradition* (Princeton: Princeton University Press, 1986).

Eggert, Katherine. 'Nostalgia and the Not Yet Late Queen: Refusing Female Rule in *Henry V*', *ELH*, 61 (1994), 523–50.

Erickson, Amy Louise. *Women and Property in Early Modern England* (London: Routledge, 1993).

Freeman, Michael and Lewis, Andrew D. E., eds. *Law and Literature* (Oxford: Oxford University Press, 1999).

Gless, Darryl J., *Measure for Measure: The Law and the Convent* (Princeton: Princeton University Press, 1979).

Green, A. Wigfall, *The Inns of Court and Early English Drama* (New Haven: Yale University Press, 1931).

Hadfield, Andrew. *Shakespeare and Republicanism* (Cambridge: Cambridge University Press, 2005).

Halper, Louise, '*Measure for Measure*: Law, Prerogative, Subversion', *Cardozo Studies in Law and Literature*, 13 (2001), 221–64.

Hamill, Monica J., 'Poetry, Law, and the Pursuit of Perfection: Portia's Role in *The Merchant of Venice*', *SEL*, 18 (1978), 229–43.

Hamilton, Donna B., 'The State of Law in *Richard II*', *Shakespeare Quarterly*, 34 (1983), 5–17.

Hawley, William M., *Shakespearean Tragedy and the Common Law: The Art of Punishment* (New York: Peter Lang, 1998).

Herndl, George C., *The High Design: English Renaissance Tragedy and the Natural Law* (Lexington: University of Kentucky, 1970).

Hexter, J. H., 'Property, Monopoly and Shakespeare's *Richard II*', in *Culture and Politics from Puritanism to the Enlightenment*, ed. Perez Zagorin (Berkeley: University of California Press, 1980).

Hinely, Jan Lawson, 'Bond Priories in *The Merchant of Venice*', *SEL*, 20 (1980), 217–39.

Honan, Park, *Shakespeare: A Life* (Oxford: Oxford University Press, 1998).

Hutson, Lorna, '"Our old storehouse": Plowden's *Commentaries* and Political Consciousness in Shakespeare', *Shakespeare Yearbook*, 7 (1996), 249–73.

Hutson, Lorna, *The Usurer's Daughter: Male Friendship and Fictions of Women in Sixteenth-Century England* (London: Routledge & Kegan Paul, 1994).

Hutson, Lorna, 'Not the King's Two Bodies: Reading the 'Body Politic' in Shakespeare's *Henry IV*, Parts 1 and 2', in Victoria Kahn and Lorna Hutson, eds, *Rhetoric and Law in Early Modern Europe* (New Haven: Yale University Press, 2001), pp. 166–98.

Hutson, Lorna, *The Invention of Suspicion: Law and Mimesis in Shakespeare and*

Renaissance Drama (Oxford: Oxford University Press, 2007).

Jardine, Lisa, '"Why should he call her whore?": Defamation and Desdemona's Case', in *Addressing Frank Kermode: Essays in Criticism and Interpretation*, ed. Margaret Tudeau-Clayton and Martin Warner (Urbana: University of Illinois Press, 1991), pp. 124–53.

Jordan, Constance, *Renaissance Feminism: Literary Texts and Political Models* (Ithaca: Cornell University Press, 1990).

Jordan, Constance, 'Contract and Conscience in *Cymbeline*', *Renaissance Drama*, 25 (1994), 33–58.

Jordan, Constance and Cunningham, Karen, eds, *The Law in Shakespeare* (Houndmills: Palgrave Macmillan, 2007).

Jordan, William Chester, 'Approaches to the Court Scene in the Bond Story: Equity and Mercy or Reason and Nature', *Shakespeare Quarterly*, 33 (1982), 49–59.

Kahn, Victoria and Hutson, Lorna, eds, *Rhetoric and Law in Early Modern Europe* (New Haven: Yale University Press, 2001).

Kaplan, Lindsay, 'Slander for Slander in *Measure for Measure*', *Renaissance Drama*, 21 (1990), 23–54.

Kaplan, Lindsay and Eggert, Katherine, '"Good Queen, My Lord, Good Queen": Sexual Slander and the Trials of Female Authority in *The Winter's Tale*', *Renaissance Drama*, 25 (1994), 89–118.

Keeton, George W., *Shakespeare and His Legal Problems* (London: A & C Black, 1930).

Keeton, George W., *Shakespeare's Legal and Political Background* (London: Pitman, 1967).

Knight, W. Nicholas, *Shakespeare's Hidden Life: Shakespeare at the Law, 1585–1595* (New York: Mason and Lipscomb, 1973).

Knight, W. Nicholas, 'Equity, *The Merchant of Venice* and William Lambarde', *Shakespeare Survey*, 27 (1974), 93–104.

Kornstein, Daniel J., *Kill All the Lawyers: Shakespeare's Legal Appeal* (Princeton: Princeton University Press, 1994).

Kreps, Barbara, 'When All Is True: Law, History and Problems of Knowledge in *Henry VIII*', *Shakespeare Survey*, 52 (1999), 166–82.

Lemon, Rebecca, *Treason by Words: Literature, Law and Rebellion in Shakespeare's England* (Ithaca: Cornell University Press, 2006).

Levine, Nina, 'Lawful Symmetry: the Politics of Treason in *2 Henry VI*', *Renaissance Drama*, 25 (1994), 197–218.

Lindley, David, 'The Stubborness of Barnadine: Justice and Mercy in *Measure for Measure*', *Shakespeare Yearbook*, 7 (1996), 333–52.

Lockey, Brian, *Law and Empire in English Renaissance Literature* (Cambridge: Cambridge University Press, 2006).

McCabe, Richard, *Incest, Drama, and Nature's Law 1500–1700* (Cambridge: Cambridge University Press, 1993).

Meron, Theodor, *Henry's Wars and Shakespeare's Laws: Perspectives on the Law of War in the Later Middle Ages* (Oxford: Clarendon Press, 1993).

Mischo, John B., '"That use is not forbidden usury": Shakespeare's Procreation

Sonnets and the Problem of Usury', in *Subjects on the World Stage: Essays on British Literature of the Middle Ages and the Renaissance*, ed. David G. Allen and Robert A. White (Newark: University of Delaware Press, 1995), pp. 262–79.

Mukherji, Subha, '"Lawful deed": Consummation, Custom and Law in *All's Well that Ends Well*', *Shakespeare Survey*, 49 (1996), 181–200.

Mukherji, Subha, *Law and Representation in Early Modern Drama* (Cambridge: Cambridge University Press, 2006).

Nass, Barry, 'The Law and Politics of Treason in Shakespeare's *Lucrece*', *Shakespeare Yearbook*, 7 (1996), 291–311.

Norbrook, David, '"A Liberal Tongue": Language and Rebellion in *Richard II*", in *Shakespeare's Universe: Renaissance Ideas and Conventions*, ed. John M. Mucciolo (London: Scolar Press, 1996), pp. 37–51.

Patterson, Annabel, '"For Words only": from Treason Trial to Liberal Legend in Early Modern England', *Yale Journal of Law and the Humanities*, 5 (1993), 389–416.

Phillips, Owen Hood, 'The Law Relating to Shakespeare 1564–1964', *Law Quarterly Review*, 80 (1967), 172–202, 399–430.

Phillips, Owen Hood, *Shakespeare and the Lawyers* (London: Methuen, 1972).

Powers, Alan, '*Measure for Measure* and law reform in 1604', *The Upstart Crow*, 15 (1996), 35–47.

Raffield, Paul and Watt, Gary, eds, *Shakespeare and the Law* (Oxford: Hart Publishing, 2008).

Raffield, Paul, '*The Comedy of Errors* and the Meaning of Contract', *Law and Humanities*, 3 (2009), 207–29.

Ranald, Margaret Loftus, 'The Betrothals of *All's Well that Ends Well*', *Huntington Library Quarterly*, 26 (1963), 179–92.

Ranald, Margaret Loftus, 'As Marriage Binds and Blood Breaks: English Marriage and Shakespeare', *Shakespeare Quarterly*, 30 (1979), 68–81.

Reynolds, Simon, 'The Lawful Name of Marrying: Contracts and Stratagems in *The Merry Wives of Windsor*', *Shakespeare Yearbook*, 7 (1996), 313–31.

Ross, Charles, 'Shakespeare's Merry Wives and the Law of Fraudulent Conveyance', *Renaissance Drama*, 25 (1994), 145–69.

Schoeck, R. J., "Rhetoric and Law in Sixteenth-Century England", *Studies in Philology*, 50 (1953), 110–27.

Schoenbaum, Samuel, *William Shakespeare: A Compact Documentary life*, rev. edn (Oxford: Oxford University Press, 1987).

Schreiber-McGee, F., '"The view of earthly glory": Visual Strategies and the Issue of Royal Prerogative in *Henry VIII*', *Shakespeare Studies*, 20 (1988), 191–200.

Shupack, Paul, 'Natural Justice and *King Lear*', *Cardozo Studies in Law and Literature*, 9 (1997), 67–105.

Simon, Jocelyn, 'Shakespeare's Legal and Political Background', *Law Quarterly Review*, 84 (1968), 33–47.

Skulsky, Harold, 'Pain, Law, and Conscience in *Measure for Measure*', *Journal of the History of Ideas*, 25 (1964), 147–68.

Sokol, B. J., 'The Merchant of Venice and the Law Merchant', *Renaissance Studies*,

6 (1992), 60–67.

Sokol, B. J., 'Prejudice and Law in the Merchant of Venice', *Shakespeare Survey*, 51 (1998), 159–73.

Sokol, B. J. and Sokol, Mary, 'Shakespeare and the English Equity Jurisdiction: *The Merchant of Venice* and the Two Texts of *King Lear*', *Review of English Studies*, 50 (1999), 417–39.

Sokol, B. J. and Sokol, Mary, *Shakespeare's Legal Language: A Dictionary* (London: Athlone, 2000).

Sokol, B. J. and Sokol, Mary, *Shakespeare, Law, and Marriage* (Cambridge: Cambridge University Press, 2003).

Spinosa, Charles, 'Shylock and Debt and Contract in *The Merchant of Venice*', *Cardozo Studies in Law and Literature*, 5 (1993), 65–85.

Spinosa, Charles, 'The Transformation of Intentionality: Debt and Contract in *The Merchant of Venice*', *English Literary Renaissance*, 24 (1994), 370–409.

Spinosa, Charles, '"The Name and All th'Addition": *King Lear*'s Opening Scene and the Common Law Use', *Shakespeare Studies*, 23 (1995), 146–86.

Srigley, Michael, 'Hamlet, "the Law of Writ", and the Universities', *Studia Neophilologica*, 66 (1994), 35–46.

Tanselle, G. Thomas and Dunbar, Florence W., 'Legal Language in *Coriolanus*', *Shakespeare Quarterly*, 13 (1962), 231–38.

Tucker, E. F. J., 'The Letter of the Law in *The Merchant of Venice*', *Shakespeare Survey*, 29 (1976), 93–101.

Ward, Ian, *Law and Literature: Possibilities and Perspectives* (Cambridge: Cambridge University Press, 1995).

Ward, Ian, 'The Political Context of Shakespeare's Constitutionalism', *Shakespeare Yearbook*, 7 (1996), 275–90.

Ward, Ian, 'Issues of Kingship and Governance in *Richard II*, *Richard III*, and *King John*, *Shakespeare Yearbook*, 8 (1997), 403–29.

Ward, Ian, *Shakespeare and the Legal Imagination* (London: Butterworths, 1999).

Watkin, Thomas Glyn, 'Hamlet and the Law of Homicide', *Law Quarterly Review*, 100 (1984), 282–310.

White, R. S., *Natural Law in English Renaissance Literature* (Cambridge: Cambridge University Press, 1996).

Wilson, Luke, *Theaters of Intention: Drama and the Law in Early Modern England* (Stanford: Stanford University Press, 2000).

Zurcher, Andrew, 'Consideration, Contract, and the End of *The Comedy of Errors*', *Law and Humanities*, 1 (2007), 145–65.

Zurcher, Andrew, *Spenser's Legal Language: Law and Poetry in Early Modern England* (Cambridge: D. S. Brewer, 2007).

HISTORICAL AND LEGAL HISTORICAL STUDIES

Abbot, L. W., *Law Reporting in England 1485–1585* (London: Athlone Press, 1973).

Baker, J. H., ed., *The Reports of Sir John Spelman*, SS 94 (London: Selden Society, 1984).

Baker, J. H., *The Legal Profession and the Common Law* (London: Hambledon, 1986).

Baker, J. H., *The Order of Serjeants at Law* (London: Selden Society, 1984).

Baker, J. H., *An Introduction to English Legal History*, 3rd edn (London: Butterworths, 1990).

Baker, J. H. *Manual of Law French*, 2nd edn (Aldershot: Scolar Press, 1990).

Barton, J. L., 'The Mystery of Bracton', *Journal of Legal History*, 14 (1993), 1–42.

Bell, H. E., *An Introduction to the History and Records of the Court of Wards and Liveries* (Cambridge: Cambridge University Press, 1953).

Bellamy, John, *The Tudor Law of Treason* (London: Routledge & Kegan Paul, 1979).

Blatcher, Marjorie, *The Court of King's Bench: A Study in Self-Help* (London: Athlone, 1978).

Burgess, Glenn, *The Politics of the Ancient Constitution: An Introduction to English Political Thought, 1603–1642* (Basingstoke: Macmillan, 1992).

Burgess, Glenn, *Absolute Monarchy and the Stuart Constitution* (New Haven: Yale University Press, 1996).

Cross, Claire, David Loades, and J. J. Scarisbrick, eds, *Law and Government Under the Tudors* (Cambridge: Cambridge University Press, 1988).

Guy, John, *Christopher St German on Chancery and Statute* (London: Selden Society, 1985).

Hart, H. L. A., *The Concept of Law* (Oxford: Clarendon Press, 1961).

Helmholz, R. H., *Marriage Litigation in Medieval England* (Cambridge: Cambridge University Press, 1974).

Helmholz, R. H., *Select Cases on Defamation to 1600* (London: Selden Society, 1985).

Helmholz, R. H., *Canon Law and the Law of England* (London: Hambledon, 1987).

Helmholz, R. H., *Roman Canon Law in Reformation England* (Cambridge: Cambridge University Press, 1990).

Houlbrooke, Ralph, *Church Courts and the People during the English Reformation* (Oxford: Oxford University Press, 1979).

Hudson, John, *The Formation of the English Common Law* (London: Longman, 1996).

Ibbetson, David, 'Assumpsit and Debt in the Early Sixteenth Century: the Origins of the Indebitatus Count', *Cambridge Law Journal*, 41 (1982), 42–61.

Ingram, Martin, *Church Courts, Sex and Marriage in England, 1570–1640* (Cambridge: Cambridge University Press, 1987).

Ives, E. W. and Manchester, A. H., *Law, Litigants and the Legal Profession* (London: Royal Historical Society, 1983).

Jones, N. G., 'The Bill of Middlesex and the Chancery 1556–1608', *The Journal of Legal History*, 22 (2002), 1–20.

Jones, W. J., *The Elizabethan Court of Chancery* (Oxford: Clarendon Press, 1967).

Kantorowicz, Ernst, *The King's Two Bodies: A Study in Medieval Political Theology* (Princeton: Princeton University Press, 1957).

Laurence, Anne, *Women in England 1500–1760* (London: Weidenfeld and Nicolson, 1994).

Levack, Brian P., *The Civil Lawyers in England 1603–1641* (Oxford: Clarendon Press, 1973).

Levack, Brian P., 'Law and Ideology: the Civil Law and Theories of Absolutism in Elizabethan and Jacobean England', in *The Historical Renaissance: New Essays on Tudor and Stuart Literature and Culture*, ed. Heather Dubrow and Richard Strier (Chicago: University of Chicago Press, 1988), pp. 220–41.

Maclean, Ian, *Interpretation and Meaning in the Renaissance: The Case of Law* (Cambridge: Cambridge University Press, 1992).

Neale, J. E., *The Elizabethan House of Commons* (London: Fontana, 1976).

Outhwaite, R. B., ed., *Marriage and Society: Studies in the Social History of Marriage* (London: Europa, 1981).

Outhwaite, R. B., *Clandestine Marriage in England, 1500–1850* (London: Hambledon, 1995).

Palmiter, Geoffrey de C., *Edmund Plowden: An Elizabethan Recusant Lawyer* (Catholic Record Society, 1987).

Prall, Stuart E., 'The Development of Equity in Tudor England', *American Journal of Legal History*, 8 (1964), 1–19.

Prest, Wilfred R., *The Inns of Court under Elizabeth I and the Early Stuarts 1590–1640* (London: Longmans, 1972).

Prest, Wilfred R., *The Rise of the Barristers: A Social History of the English Bar 1590–1640* (Oxford: Clarendon Press, 1986).

Read, Conyers, *William Lambarde and Local Government* (Ithaca: Folger Shakespeare Library and Cornell University Press, 1962).

Sharpe, J. A., *Defamation and Sexual Slander in Early Modern England: The Church Courts at York*, Borthwick Papers, No. 58 (York: University of York Borthwick Institute of Historical Research, 1980).

Simpson, A. W. B., *A History of the Common Law of Contract: The Rise of Assumpsit* (Oxford: Clarendon Press, 1975).

Simpson, A. W. B., *A History of the Land Law*, 2nd edn (Oxford: Clarendon Press, 1986).

Simpson, A. W. B., *Legal Theory and Legal History* (London: Hambledon, 1987).

Squibb, G. D., *Doctor's Commons: A History of Advocates and Doctors of Law* (Oxford: Clarendon Press, 1977).

INDEX